بسم الله الرحمن الرحيم

Title: The Perfected Beauty & Character of the Prophet Muhammad ﷺ

ISBN: 978-1-952306-57-0

FIRST EDITION | SEPTEMBER 2024

AUTHOR: QĀḌI ʿIYĀḌ B. MŪSĀ AL-YAḤṢUBĪ
TRANSLATOR: WORDSMITHS
PROOFREADING: WORDSMITHS
TYPESETTING: IGP CONSULTING
DISTRIBUTION: INFO@SATTAURPUBLISHING.COM

WWW.IMAMGHAZALI.CO

The Perfected Beauty & Character of the Prophet Muhammad ﷺ

Qāḍi ʿIyāḍ b. Mūsā al-Yaḥṣubī

CONTENTS

PUBLISHER'S MESSAGE

All praise is due to Allah, the First; without a beginning, and the Last; without an end. Peace and prayers be upon the Prophet Muhammad ﷺ, the first Prophet on the Day of Judgement to offer intercession despite being the last Prophet sent, and upon his pure family, his blessed Companions, and all who follow their way upon the path of righteousness, until the day intercession begins with none other than the Prophet Muhammad ﷺ.

Al-Shifā bi Ta'rīf Ḥuqūq al-Muṣṭafā, directly translated as, 'The Remedy (or Cure) Through Recognizing the Rights of the Chosen One', is one of the most celebrated works in the genre of Shamā'il. It stands uniquely amongst the works of Qāḍī 'Iyāḍ as his most celebrated effort–with many surviving manuscripts and commentaries found throughout the Islamic world. Shamā'il is a genre of works that deals with the life, characteristics, and descriptions of the Prophet ﷺ and his station. There are many works in this genre, the most celebrated of which is *al-Shamā'il al-Muḥammadiyyah*, which Imam Ghazali Publishing recently translated and published. Other works include commentaries and summaries of that nature, or hagiographical poems that recount the biography of the Messenger of Allah ﷺ and render praise to the Prophetic station.

However, *al-Shifā*, as it is called for short, stands alone as perhaps the most thorough work in this genre, dealing with both the descriptions of the Prophet ﷺ, his station and his perfections, and with the rulings pertaining to one's belief and treatment of him ﷺ. It is exhaustive in its treatment of the subject, expounding on topics that range from Allah's praise of the Prophet ﷺ and his status and station before Him, to the obligation of loving him and what that entails. In short, the uniqueness of this work can be attributed to its holistic coverage of the Messenger ﷺ. Historically, this work took on a form of sacredness and was revered throughout the Muslim world. With that in mind, the Qāḍī's intention for this blessed work was more so to address, what he understood as, a real and practical need in his society. In today's context, it is our intention to continue the spirit of his desire outlined for us in his introduction:

> You have repeatedly asked me to write something which gathers together all that is necessary to acquaint the reader with the true stature of the Prophet, peace and blessings be upon him, with the esteem and respect which is due to him, and with the verdict regarding anyone who does not fulfill what his stature demands or who attempts to denigrate his supreme status—even by as much as a nail-paring. I have been asked to compile what our forebears and imams have said on this subject, and I will amplify it with *ayāt* from the Qur'an and other examples…Writing about this calls for the evaluation of the primary sources, examination of secondary sources, and investigation of the depths and details of the science of what is necessary for the Prophet, what should be attributed to him, and what is forbidden or permissible in

respect of him; and deep knowledge of Messenger-ship and Prophethood and of the love, intimate friendship and the special qualities of the sublime rank.[1]

Although it has previously been translated into English in its entirety, our intention with this series is to attempt to bring out, for our readers, some of the most relevant smaller, yet critically important, topics related to the Prophet ﷺ, his station, our duty towards him, and the benefit of loving him and fulfilling our duty towards him. Such a task has been made easier for us by the expert arrangement of the text in terms of its sections and subsections. Each larger section is divided into smaller subsections, which facilitates targeted publications that are small but great in benefit. It is our desire, with having isolated smaller and somewhat easier 'quick-reads', as they are called, that readers may be inspired to complete a full reading of the noble Qāḍī's entire work.

TALUT DAWOOD
IMAM GHAZALI PUBLISHING

---

1 Iyad ibn Musa, *Muhammad: Messenger of Allah: Ash-Shifā by Qadi 'Iyad*, translated by Aisha Abdarrahman Bewley, vi.

QĀḌI ʿIYĀḌ B. MŪSĀ AL-YAḤṢUBĪ

The Imām, the unique Ḥāfiẓ, Shaykh al-Islām, ʿAllāmah, Qāḍi Abū al-Faḍl ʿIyāḍ b. Mūsā b. ʿIyāḍ b. ʿUmar b. Mūsā b. ʿIyāḍ al-Yaḥṣubī al-Andalūsi al-Sibti al-Māliki was born in the year 476/1083–84, six months after the Almoravid takeover of the city. His ancestors left Andalus for Fez and then settled in Ceuta. At the age of 22, Qāḍi ʿIyāḍ obtained a license (*ijāzah*) from Ḥāfiẓ Abū ʿAli al-Ghasāni.

He left Ceuta on two occasions, one of which was to travel to Andalus (Spain) seeking out scholars with whom he could take knowledge. Between 507/1113 and 508/1114 the Qāḍi visited Cordoba, Almeria, Murcia, and Granada. During this time, he learned Hadith from the famed scholar, Qāḍi Abū ʿAli b. Sukrah al-Sadafi. Qāḍi ʿIyāḍ stayed with him closely. He also took Ḥadīth from Abū Baḥr b. al-ʿĀs, Muḥammad b. Ḥamdayn, Abū al-Ḥusayn Sirāj al-Saghīr, Abū Muḥammad b. ʿAttab, Hishām b. Aḥmad and many other scholars. He learned jurisprudence (*fiqh*) from Abū ʿAbdullah Muḥammad b. ʿIsa al-Tamīmī and Qāḍi Muḥammad b. ʿAbdullāh al-Masili.

The Qāḍi was first appointed judge of Ceuta in 515/1121 and served in his position until 531/1136. He would later serve again in Cueta from 539–543/1145–48. His tenure as a judge in Cueta was probably his most productive period; his casework created the foundations for his works in jurisprudence (*fiqh*). Khalaf b. Shakwal said of him:

He is among the people of knowledge and polymaths, of great intelligence and understanding. He performed the duties of a judge in Ceuta for a long time, in which he earned a praiseworthy reputation. Then he travelled from there for a judgeship in Granada. However, he did not stay there long. Thereafter, he came to us in Cordoba and we took from him.

The jurist (*faqīh*) Muḥammad b. Ḥammadah al-Sibti said:

The Qāḍi began training at the age of twenty-eight years and assumed judgeship at the age of thirty-five. He was lenient, but not weak, [and] fierce in defence of the truth. He learned jurisprudence (*fiqh*) from Abū ʿAbdullah al-Tamīmī and accompanied Abū Isḥāq b. Jaʿfar. No one in Ceuta wrote more works than him during his time. He wrote the book 'Al-Shifāʾ fi Sharāf al-Mustafaʾ, 'Tartīb al-Madārik wa Taqrīb al-Masālik fī Dhikr Fuqahāʾ Madhab Mālik', a multi-volume work, 'Kitāb al-ʿAqīdah', 'Kitāb Sharḥ Ḥadīth Umm Zar", the book 'Jāmiʾ al-Tārīkh' and others.

Many scholars narrate from Qāḍi ʿIyāḍ. Among them are Imām ʿAbdullah b. Muḥammad al-ʿAshīri, Abū Jaʿfar b. al-Qasir al-Gharnāti, al-Ḥāfiẓ Khalaf b. Bashakwal, Abū Muḥammad b. ʿUbayd Allah al-Hijri, Muḥammad b. al-Ḥasan al-Jābirī and his son, Qāḍi Muḥammad b. ʿIyāḍ, the Qāḍi of Denia (in Spain). Qāḍi b. Khalkhan said, 'The teachers of Qāḍi ʿIyāḍ number around one hundred. He passed away during Ramaḍan 544/December-January 1149–50.' Conversely, it has also been reported that he died in Jumada al-Ākhirah of the same year, in Marrakesh. His son passed away in the year 575 AH.

Ibn Bashakwal said, 'Qāḍi 'Iyāḍ passed away to the west of his hometown, in the middle of the year 544 AH." His son, Qāḍi Muḥammad, said, 'He passed away in the middle of the night, on Friday 9 Jumada al-Ākhirah. He was buried in Marrakesh in the year 544 AH.'

al-Dhahabī said, 'it has reached me that he was killed by an arrow for his denial that Ibn Tumart was infallible'.

Some of the Qāḍi's well-known works are:

1. Al-Shifā' bi Ta'rīf Ḥuqūq al-Mustafā – the Shifa' remains one of the most commentated books of Islām.

2. Tartīb al-Madārik wa Taqrīb al-Masālik li Ma'rifat A'lām Madhab Mālik.

3. Ikmāl al-Mu'lim bi Fawa'id Muslim – Qāḍi 'Iyāḍ's own commentary was expounded upon heavily by Imām al-Nawawi in his commentary of Saḥiḥ Muslim.

4. Al-I'lām bi Ḥudūd Qawā'id al-Islām – a work on the five pillars of Islām.

5. Al-Ilma' ilā Ma'rifa Usūl al-Riwāyah wa Taqyīd al-Sama' – a detailed work on the science of Ḥadīth.

6. Mashāriq al-Anwār 'ala Saḥiḥ al-Athar – a work based on the Muwaṭā of Imām Mālik, Saḥiḥ Al-Bukhāri of Imām Bukhāri, and Saḥiḥ Muslim by Imām Muslim.

7. Al-Tanbihāt al-Mustanbaṭah 'ala al-Kutub al-Mudawwanah wa al-Mukhtalaṭah.

8. Daqā'iq al-Akhbar fi Dhikr al-Jannah wa al-Nār – a work describing the joys of Heaven (*Jannah*) and the horrors of Hell (*Jahannam*).

THE PERFECTED BEAUTY & CHARACTER OF THE PROPHET MUHAMMAD ﷺ

Qāḍi ʿIyāḍ b. Mūsā al-Yaḥṣubī

THE WAY IN WHICH ALLAH EXALTED HAS PERFECTED THE FORM AND CHARACTER OF THE PROPHET ﷺ AND BLESSED HIM WITH BOTH RELIGIOUS AND WORLDLY VIRTUES

Anyone researching the virtue of the noble Prophet ﷺ should know, O beloved readers, that his perfection and magnificence as a human being comprised two types of actions and qualities.

Firstly, those actions and qualities that are necessary to deal with worldly affairs and were a part of his natural disposition, and secondly, those connected to religious affairs.

The person who performs or possesses the second type of actions and qualities is praised, and they draw one closer to Allah Exalted. These characteristics can also be separated between those that fall firmly into one of these two categories and those that display elements of both.

Human beings have no choice or power to acquire the qualities that are part of one's natural disposition. These include a perfected physical form, beautiful appearance, powerful intellect, sound understanding, eloquent tongue, as well as acute senses, balance and poise in one's movements, descending from honourable lineage, an exalted people, and a noble land. This is in addition to those demanded by the necessities of daily life such as food, sleep, clothing, shelter, marriage, wealth, and status. These qualities can be connected to the Hereafter, however, if they are utilized with the intention of being conscious of Allah and keeping one's physical

بَابٌ فِي تَكْمِيلِ اللهِ تَعَالَى لَهُ الْمَحَاسِنَ خَلْقًا وَخُلُقًا وَقِرَانِهِ جَمِيعَ الْفَضَائِلِ الدِّينِيَّةِ وَالدُّنْيَوِيَّةِ فِيهِ نَسَقًا ﷺ

اعْلَمْ أَيُّهَا الْمُحِبُّ لِهَذَا النَّبِيِّ الْكَرِيمِ، الْبَاحِثُ عَنْ تَفَاصِيلِ جُمَلِ قَدْرِهِ الْعَظِيمِ، أَنَّ خِصَالَ الْجَلَالِ وَالْكَمَالِ فِي الْبَشَرِ نَوْعَانِ:

۞ ضَرُورِيٌّ دُنْيَوِيٌّ اقْتَضَتْهُ الْجِبِلَّةُ¹ وَضَرُورَةُ الْحَيَاةِ الدُّنْيَا.

۞ وَمُكْتَسَبٌ دِينِيٌّ: وَهُوَ مَا يُحْمَدُ فَاعِلُهُ، وَيُقَرِّبُ إِلَى اللهِ زُلْفَى².

ثُمَّ هِيَ عَلَى فَنَّيْنِ أَيْضًا:

۞ مِنْهَا مَا يَتَخَلَّصُ لِأَحَدِ الْوَصْفَيْنِ.

۞ وَمِنْهَا مَا يَتَمَازَجُ وَيَتَدَاخَلُ.

فَأَمَّا الضَّرُورِيُّ الْمَحْضُ: فَمَا لَيْسَ لِلْمَرْءِ فِيهِ اخْتِيَارٌ وَلَا اكْتِسَابٌ، مِثْلُ مَا كَانَ فِي جِبِلَّتِهِ مِنْ كَمَالِ خِلْقَتِهِ، وَجَمَالِ صُورَتِهِ، وَقُوَّةِ عَقْلِهِ، وَصِحَّةِ فَهْمِهِ، وَفَصَاحَةِ لِسَانِهِ، وَقُوَّةِ حَوَاسِّهِ وَأَعْضَائِهِ، وَاعْتِدَالِ حَرَكَاتِهِ، وَشَرَفِ نَسَبِهِ، وَعِزَّةِ قَوْمِهِ، وَكَرَمِ أَرْضِهِ. وَيُلْحَقُ بِهِ مَا تَدْعُو ضَرُورَةُ حَيَاتِهِ إِلَيْهِ: مِنْ غِذَائِهِ، وَنَوْمِهِ، وَمَلْبَسِهِ، وَمَسْكَنِهِ، وَمَكْسَبِهِ، وَمَنْكَحِهِ، وَمَالِهِ، وَجَاهِهِ.

وَقَدْ تُلْحَقُ هَذِهِ الْخِصَالُ الْآخِرَةُ بِالْأُخْرَوِيَّةِ إِذَا قُصِدَ بِهَا التَّقَوِّي وَمَعُونَةُ

---

1 الْجِبِلَّةُ: الْخِلْقَةُ.

2 الزُّلْفَى: الْقُرْبَى وَالْمَنْزِلَةُ.

self on the right path, even though they are described as necessities and legislated in the Shariah.

The second category that we mentioned, namely actions and qualities which draw one closer to Allah Exalted, covers a range of exalted characteristics and manners. This includes [displaying] piety, knowledge, forbearance, patience, gratitude, justice, self-restraint, humbleness, a pardoning nature, purity, generosity, courage, modesty, zeal, silent reflection, composure, love, mercy, excellent manners, companionship, and other similar virtues. When combined, these are the features that make up an "excellent character"[1]. Even when these qualities are not accompanied with the intention of seeking the pleasure of Allah and the reward of the Hereafter, they are still considered praiseworthy.

For some people, they may also be innate, but others have to work to acquire them. At the bare minimum, however, a person's natural disposition should bear traces of these features as, Allah willing, we will clarify.

---

1 Translator's note: See, for example, *al-Qalam*, 4.

الْبَدَنِ عَلَى سُلُوكِ طَرِيقِهَا، وَكَانَتْ عَلَى حُدُودِ الضَّرُورَةِ، وَقَوَانِينِ الشَّرِيعَةِ.

وَأَمَّا الْمُكْتَسَبَةُ الْأُخْرَوِيَّةُ: فَسَائِرُ الْأَخْلَاقِ الْعَلِيَّةِ، وَالْآدَابِ الشَّرْعِيَّةِ: مِنَ الدِّينِ، وَالْعِلْمِ، وَالْحِلْمِ، وَالصَّبْرِ، وَالشُّكْرِ، وَالْعَدْلِ، وَالزُّهْدِ، وَالتَّوَاضُعِ، وَالْعَفْوِ، وَالْعِفَّةِ، وَالْجُودِ، وَالشَّجَاعَةِ، وَالْحَيَاءِ، وَالْمُرُوءَةِ، وَالصَّمْتِ، وَالتُّؤَدَةِ³، وَالْوَقَارِ، وَالرَّحْمَةِ، وَحُسْنِ الْأَدَبِ، وَالْمُعَاشَرَةِ وَأَخَوَاتِهَا، وَهِيَ الَّتِي جِمَاعُهَا حُسْنُ الْخُلُقِ.

وَقَدْ يَكُونُ مِنْ هَذِهِ الْأَخْلَاقِ مَا هُوَ فِي الْغَرِيزَةِ⁴ وَأَصْلِ الْجِبِلَّةِ⁵ لِبَعْضِ النَّاسِ، وَبَعْضُهُمْ لَا تَكُونُ فِيهِ فَيَكْتَسِبُهَا، وَلَكِنَّهُ لَا بُدَّ أَنْ يَكُونَ فِيهِ مِنْ أُصُولِهَا فِي أَصْلِ الْجِبِلَّةِ شُعْبَةٌ⁶ كَمَا سَنُبَيِّنُهُ إِنْ شَاءَ اللهُ تَعَالَى.

وَتَكُونُ هَذِهِ الْأَخْلَاقُ دُنْيَوِيَّةً إِذَا لَمْ يُرَدْ بِهَا وَجْهُ اللهِ تَعَالَى وَالدَّارُ الْآخِرَةُ، وَلَكِنَّهَا كُلَّهَا مَحَاسِنُ وَفَضَائِلُ بِاتِّفَاقِ أَصْحَابِ الْعُقُولِ السَّلِيمَةِ، وَإِنِ اخْتَلَفُوا فِي مُوجِبِ حُسْنِهَا وَتَفْضِيلِهَا.

---

٣ «التُّؤَدَةُ»: التَّأَنِّي وَتَرْكُ الْعَجَلَةِ.

٤ الْغَرِيزَةُ: الطَّبِيعَةُ وَالسَّجِيَّةُ.

٥ الْجِبِلَّةُ: الْخِلْقَةُ.

٦ شُعْبَةٌ: قِطْعَةٌ.

THE NOBLE QUALITIES AND PERFECTION OF OUR PROPHET ﷺ

If a person was blessed with just one or two of the noble qualities mentioned above – whether of lineage, beauty, strength, knowledge, forbearance, or bravery – they would be honoured and used as an example for others, even after their bones had turned to dust. So, what can we say about the one who combines all of these qualities in innumerable abundance?

There was no way the Prophet ﷺ could have achieved such perfection except through the Will of the All-Great, the Most Exalted. The virtues bestowed upon him include the positions of Prophet and Messenger, his love of Allah Exalted, closeness to Him, and being specially chosen by Him. The Prophet ﷺ was blessed with the miraculous Night Journey, Burāq, seeing Allah Exalted, proximity to Him, Revelation, intercession, the Highest Station, moral excellence,[2] a lofty rank, and an honoured station. He was sent to the Red and the Black, led the Prophets in prayer, and served as a witness between the Prophets and their nations. He was the leader of the children of Adam, bearing the banner of praise, sent to humanity to deliver good tidings and a warning. The Prophet ﷺ was given a place with the Owner of the Throne and an attachment to his Lord. He was entrusted with guidance and sent as a mercy to all creation. He was blessed with the Pleasure of Allah and the ability to ask of Him. The Prophet ﷺ was given al-Kawthar,[3] and was

---

2 "Al-faḍīlah". See Fatḥ al-Bārī (2/95).

3 A fountain in Paradise. Can also be translated as "abundance".

فَصْل: [فِي اجْتِمَاعِ خِصَالِ الجَلَالِ وَالكَمَالِ فِي نَبِيِّنَا مُحَمَّدٍ ﷺ][7]

إِذَا كَانَتْ خِصَالُ الكَمَالِ وَالجَلَالِ مَا ذَكَرْنَاهُ، وَوَجَدْنَا الوَاحِدَ مِنَّا يَشْرُفُ بِوَاحِدَةٍ مِنْهَا أَوِ اثْنَتَيْنِ – إِنِ اتَّفَقَتْ لَهُ فِي كُلِّ عَصْرٍ – إِمَّا مِنْ نَسَبٍ، أَوْ جَمَالٍ، أَوْ قُوَّةٍ، أَوْ عِلْمٍ، أَوْ حِلْمٍ، أَوْ شَجَاعَةٍ، أَوْ سَمَاحَةٍ، حَتَّى يَعْظُمَ قَدْرُهُ، وَيُضْرَبَ بِاسْمِهِ الأَمْثَالُ، وَيَتَقَرَّرَ لَهُ بِالوَصْفِ بِذَلِكَ فِي القُلُوبِ أَثَرَةٌ وَعَظَمَةٌ، وَهُوَ مُنْذُ عُصُورٍ خَوَالٍ، رَمَمٌ بَوَالٍ، فَمَا ظَنُّكَ بِعَظِيمِ قَدْرِ مَنِ اجْتَمَعَتْ فِيهِ كُلُّ هَذِهِ الخِصَالِ إِلَى مَا لَا يَأْخُذُهُ عَدٌّ، وَلَا يُعَبِّرُ عَنْهُ مَقَالٌ، وَلَا يُنَالُ بِكَسْبٍ وَلَا حِيلَةٍ إِلَّا بِتَخْصِيصِ الكَبِيرِ المُتَعَالِ، مِنْ فَضِيلَةِ النُّبُوَّةِ وَالرِّسَالَةِ، وَالخُلَّةِ وَالمَحَبَّةِ، وَالاصْطِفَاءِ وَالإِسْرَاءِ وَالرُّؤْيَةِ، وَالقُرْبِ، وَالدُّنُوِّ، وَالوَحْيِ، وَالشَّفَاعَةِ، وَالوَسِيلَةِ، وَالفَضِيلَةِ وَالدَّرَجَةِ الرَّفِيعَةِ، وَالمَقَامِ المَحْمُودِ.

وَالبُرَاقِ، وَالمِعْرَاجِ، وَالبَعْثِ إِلَى الأَحْمَرِ وَالأَسْوَدِ، وَالصَّلَاةِ بِالأَنْبِيَاءِ، وَالشَّهَادَةِ بَيْنَ الأَنْبِيَاءِ وَالأُمَمِ، وَسِيَادَةِ وَلَدِ آدَمَ، وَلِوَاءِ الحَمْدِ، وَالبِشَارَةِ، وَالنِّذَارَةِ، وَالمَكَانَةِ عِنْدَ ذِي العَرْشِ، وَالطَّاعَةِ ثَمَّ، وَالأَمَانَةِ (٢/١٦) وَالهِدَايَةِ، وَرَحْمَةٍ لِلْعَالَمِينَ، وَإِعْطَاءِ الرِّضَا وَالسُّؤْلِ، وَالكَوْثَرِ، وَسَمَاعِ القَوْلِ، وَإِتْمَامِ النِّعْمَةِ، وَالعَفْوِ عَمَّا تَقَدَّمَ وَتَأَخَّرَ، وَشَرْحِ الصَّدْرِ، وَوَضْعِ الوِزْرِ[8]، وَرَفْعِ

---

7 This is an addition from the editor of the Arabic edition.

٨ وَوَضْعُ الوِزْرِ: تَخْفِيفٌ وَتَسْهِيلٌ حَمْلِ أَعْبَاءِ النُّبُوَّةِ وَالرِّسَالَةِ. انْظُرْ: كَلِمَاتِ القُرْآنِ لِمَخْلُوفٍ.

forgiven for any past or future mistakes. His speech was listened to and the Blessing of Allah was perfected upon him. His chest was expanded, his task was eased,[4] and his renown was elevated. Allah Exalted guided His Prophet ﷺ to a decisive victory, sending down tranquillity and the Angels to assist him. He gave the Prophet ﷺ The Book, wisdom, the seven oft-repeated,[5] and The Great Qur'an. The Prophet ﷺ was a caller to [the way of] Allah Exalted and a purification for his nation, judging between them according to the laws revealed to him and removing the burden[6] and chains afflicting them. The Almighty blessed him and the Angels supplicated for him. Allah Exalted swears by the name of the Prophet ﷺ and answers his supplications. He also blessed the Prophet ﷺ with many miracles, including the ability to communicate with animals and inanimate objects, to revive the dead, to remove people's pain, and to give hearing to the deaf, as well as the flowing of water from between his fingers, drawing of abundance from scarcity, splitting of the Moon, delaying of the Sun, and transformation of objects. The Prophet ﷺ was assisted by the terror [that Allah Exalted instilled in the hearts of the disbelievers]. He was given knowledge of the Unseen, the clouds shaded him, the stones praised him, and he was protected from the people. There is so much more we could add. The Prophet ﷺ was blessed with the ultimate contentment, and a high station in the Hereafter. Even the most intelligent cannot fully comprehend his noble status with Allah, for true knowledge of the qualities and virtues given to the Prophet ﷺ lies solely with the Almighty, and there is no-one worthy of worship except Him.

---

4 i.e., the responsibilities of Prophethood and Messengership were lightened and eased.

5 This phrase has been variously interpreted as referring to Sūrah al-Fātiḥah, seven lengthy *sūrahs* at the beginning of the Qur'an, or seven features of the Qur'an.

6 *"Al-'iṣr"*, which is also mentioned in the supplication found in al-Baqarah, 286: "Our Lord! Do not place a burden on us like the one You placed on those before us."

الذِّكْرِ، وَعِزَّةِ النَّصْرِ، وَنُزُولِ السَّكِينَةِ، وَالتَّأْيِيدِ بِالمَلَائِكَةِ.

وَإِيتَاءِ الحِكْمَةِ، وَالكِتَابِ، وَالسَّبْعِ المَثَانِي، وَالقُرْآنِ العَظِيمِ، وَتَزْكِيَةِ الأُمَّةِ، وَالدُّعَاءِ إِلَى اللهِ، وَصَلَاةِ اللهِ [تَعَالَى] وَالمَلَائِكَةِ، وَالحُكْمِ بَيْنَ النَّاسِ بِمَا أَرَاهُ اللهُ، وَوَضْعِ الإِصْرِ ⁹ وَالأَغْلَالِ عَنْهُمْ، وَالقَسَمِ بِاسْمِهِ، وَإِجَابَةِ دَعْوَتِهِ، وَتَكْلِيمِ الجَمَادَاتِ، وَالعُجْمِ ¹⁰، وَإِحْيَاءِ المَوْتَى، وَإِسْمَاعِ الصُّمِّ، وَنَبْعِ المَاءِ مِنْ بَيْنِ أَصَابِعِهِ، وَتَكْثِيرِ القَلِيلِ، وَانْشِقَاقِ القَمَرِ، وَرَدِّ الشَّمْسِ.

وَقَلْبِ الأَعْيَانِ، وَالنَّصْرِ بِالرُّعْبِ، وَالاطِّلَاعِ عَلَى الغَيْبِ، وَظِلِّ الغَمَامِ، وَتَسْبِيحِ الحَصَا، وَإِبْرَاءِ الآلَامِ، وَالعِصْمَةِ مِنَ النَّاسِ، إِلَى مَا لَا يَحْوِيهِ مُحْتَفِلٌ ¹¹، وَلَا يُحِيطُ بِعِلْمِهِ إِلَّا مَانِحُهُ ذَلِكَ وَمُفَضِّلُهُ بِهِ، لَا إِلَهَ غَيْرُهُ، إِلَى مَا أَعَدَّ لَهُ فِي الدَّارِ الآخِرَةِ مِنْ مَنَازِلِ الكَرَامَةِ، وَدَرَجَاتِ القُدْسِ، وَمَرَاتِبِ السَّعَادَةِ، وَالحُسْنَى، وَالزِّيَادَةِ الَّتِي تَقِفُ دُونَهَا العُقُولُ وَيَحَارُ دُونَ أَدَانِيهَا الوَهْمُ.

---

⁹ الإِصْرُ: الثِّقَلُ. وَفِي التَّنْزِيلِ: ﴿رَبَّنَا وَلَا تَحْمِلْ عَلَيْنَا إِصْرًا كَمَا حَمَلْتَهُ عَلَى ٱلَّذِينَ مِن قَبْلِنَا﴾.

¹⁰ العُجْمُ: جَمْعُ عَجْمَاءَ، وَهِيَ البَهِيمَةُ.

¹¹ مُحْتَفِلٌ: احْتَفَلَ بِالأَمْرِ: عَنِيَ بِهِ.

THE PHYSICAL CHARACTERISTICS OF THE PROPHET ﷺ

Without question, the Prophet ﷺ is the most honourable human being and the highest in status. His qualities and virtues were perfected and completed, as we will discuss in this chapter. How I have longed to cover his beautiful attributes in detail!

Dear readers, may Allah fill my heart and yours with light, and love for our noble Prophet ﷺ. Understand that if we examine those desirable qualities and characteristics which are not acquired or learnt, but rather are a part of a person's constitution, we will find that the Prophet ﷺ had every single one. Indeed, this has been agreed upon in incontrovertible transmissions.

As for the beauty of his physical appearance and proportions, this is described in many well-known, authentic hadiths. These include narrations from ʿAlī[7], Anas ibn Mālik[8], Abū Hurayrah[9], al-Barāʾ ibn ʿĀzib[10], ʿĀʾishah[11], Ibn Abī Hālah[12], Abū Juḥayfah[13],

---

7   Reported by Tirmidhī in *Al-Sunan* (3637, 3638) and *Al-Shamāʾil* (5, 6, 7), Aḥmad (1/89, 101), Abū Yaʿlā (369, 370) and Baghawī (3707). Tirmidhī said: "This hadith is *ḥasan gharīb*, without a connected chain."

8   Reported by Bukhārī (3547) and Muslim (2347).

9   Reported by Tirmidhī (3648) and Aḥmad (2/350). Authenticated by Ibn Ḥibbān in *Mawārid al-Ẓamʾān* (2118).

10   Reported by Bukhārī (3549, 3551) and Muslim (2337).

11   Reported by Abū Dāwūd (4187), Tirmidhī (1755), and Ibn Mājah (3635). Tirmidhī said: "This hadith is *ḥasan ṣaḥīḥ*, and *gharīb* with this wording."

12   Reported by Tirmidhī in *Al-Shamāʾil* (8, 335, 350) and Baghawī in *Sharḥ al-Sunnah* (3705, 3706).

13   Reported by Bukhārī (3544) and Muslim (2343).

فَصْل

إِنْ قُلْتَ أَكْرَمَكَ اللهُ: لَا خَفَاءَ عَلَى الْقَطْعِ بِالْجُمْلَةِ أَنَّهُ ﷺ أَعْلَى النَّاسِ قَدْرًا وَأَعْظَمُهُمْ مَحَلًّا، وَأَكْمَلُهُمْ مَحَاسِنَ وَفَضْلًا، وَقَدْ ذَهَبْتَ فِي تَفَاصِيلِ خِصَالِ الْكَمَالِ مَذْهَبًا جَمِيلًا، شَوَّقَنِي إِلَى أَنْ أَقِفَ عَلَيْهَا مِنْ أَوْصَافِهِ ﷺ تَفْصِيلًا.

فَاعْلَمْ نَوَّرَ اللهُ قَلْبِي وَقَلْبَكَ، وَضَاعَفَ فِي هَذَا النَّبِيِّ الْكَرِيمِ حُبِّي وَحُبَّكَ، أَنَّكَ إِذَا نَظَرْتَ إِلَى خِصَالِ الْكَمَالِ الَّتِي هِيَ غَيْرُ مُكْتَسَبَةٍ، وَفِي جِبِلَّةِ الْخِلْقَةِ، وَجَدْتَهُ ﷺ حَائِزًا لِجَمِيعِهَا، مُحِيطًا بِشَتَاتِ مَحَاسِنِهَا، دُونَ خِلَافٍ بَيْنَ نَقَلَةِ الْأَخْبَارِ لِذَلِكَ، بَلْ قَدْ بَلَغَ بَعْضُهَا مَبْلَغَ الْقَطْعِ.

أَمَّا الصُّورَةُ وَجَمَالُهَا، وَتَنَاسُبُ أَعْضَائِهِ فِي حُسْنِهَا، فَقَدْ جَاءَتِ الْآثَارُ الصَّحِيحَةُ وَالْمَشْهُورَةُ الْكَثِيرَةُ بِذَلِكَ، مِنْ حَدِيثِ عَلِيٍّ[12]، وَأَنَسِ بْنِ مَالِكٍ[13]، وَأَبِي هُرَيْرَةَ[14]، وَالْبَرَاءِ بْنِ عَازِبٍ[15]، وَعَائِشَةَ أُمِّ الْمُؤْمِنِينَ[16]، وَابْنِ أَبِي هَالَةَ[17]،

---

12 حَدِيثُ عَلِيٍّ أَخْرَجَهُ التِّرْمِذِيُّ فِي السُّنَنِ (٣٦٣٧، ٣٦٣٨)، وَفِي الشَّمَائِلِ (٦)، وَأَحْمَدُ ٨٩/١، ١٠١، وَأَبُو يَعْلَى (٣٦٩، ٣٧٠)، وَالْبَغَوِيُّ (٣٧٠٧). وَقَالَ التِّرْمِذِيُّ: «هَذَا حَدِيثٌ حَسَنٌ غَرِيبٌ لَيْسَ إِسْنَادُهُ بِمُتَّصِلٍ».

13 حَدِيثُ أَنَسِ بْنِ مَالِكٍ رَوَاهُ الْبُخَارِيُّ (٣٥٤٧)، وَمُسْلِمٌ (٢٣٤٧).

14 حَدِيثُ أَبِي هُرَيْرَةَ رَوَاهُ التِّرْمِذِيُّ (٣٦٤٨)، وَأَحْمَدُ ٣٥٠/٢، وَصَحَّحَهُ ابْنُ حِبَّانَ (٢١١٨) مَوَارِدُ، وَهُنَاكَ اسْتَوْفَيْنَا تَخْرِيجَهُ.

15 حَدِيثُ الْبَرَاءِ بْنِ عَازِبٍ رَوَاهُ الْبُخَارِيُّ (٣٥٤٩، ٣٥٥١)، وَمُسْلِمٌ (٢٣٣٧).

16 حَدِيثُ عَائِشَةَ رَوَاهُ أَبُو دَاوُدَ (٤١٨٧)، وَالتِّرْمِذِيُّ (١٧٥٥)، وَابْنُ مَاجَه (٣٦٣٥). وَقَالَ التِّرْمِذِيُّ: هَذَا حَدِيثٌ حَسَنٌ صَحِيحٌ غَرِيبٌ مِنْ هَذَا الْوَجْهِ.

17 حَدِيثُ هِنْدِ بْنِ أَبِي هَالَةَ سَيَذْكُرُهُ الْمُصَنِّفُ وَهُنَاكَ تَخْرِيجُهُ.

Jābir ibn Samurah[14], Umm Maʿbad[15], Ibn ʿAbbās[16], Muʿarriḍ ibn Muʿayqīb[17], Abū al-Ṭufayl[18], al-ʿAddāʾ ibn Khālid[19], Khuraym ibn Fātik, Ḥakīm ibn Ḥizām[20], and others.

As described in the narrations, the Prophet ﷺ had the most beautiful, bright complexion. His eyes had deep, black pupils, with reddish hues perceptible in the whites. They were widely spaced and fringed with luscious eyelashes, and his eyebrows were long and arched.

He had a broad forehead and thick, bushy beard, and there was a gap between his two front teeth. His face was rounded and always illuminated.

The Prophet ﷺ had a broad chest and shoulders, and his abdomen and breast were evenly proportioned. He had solid limbs, strong arms and legs, and wide palms. His fingers were long and

---

14 Reported by Muslim (2339) and Tirmidhī (3647).

15 Reported by Baghawī (3704) in the hadith of Ḥubaysh ibn Khālid. Ḥākim authenticated the hadith in *Al-Mustadrak* (3/9-10) and Dhahabī concurred. Shaykh Shuʿayb al-Arnaʾūṭ said in his commentary of *Sharḥ al-Sunnah*: "This is a strong, *ḥasan* narration." Suyūṭī extended the chain in *Al-Khaṣāʾiṣ* to include Ibn Shāhīn, Ibn al-Sakan, Ibn Mandah, Bayhaqī, and Abū Nuʿaym. Haythamī said in *Majmaʿ al-Zawāʾid* (6/55-58): "It was related by Ṭabarānī and there are a number of narrators in the chain I do not recognize." It was mentioned again by Haythamī (8/278-279) from the hadith of Sulayṭ, and he said: "It was related by Ṭabarānī and the chain contains ʿAbd al-ʿAzīz ibn Yaḥyā al-Madīnī, who Bukhārī and others said lied. Ḥākim said he was truthful. He has some wonderful narrations but also some that are unknown [in origin]." Ibn Kathīr said in *Al-Bidāyah wa al-Nihāyah* (3/166): "The different chains of transmission for this well-known story strengthen each other."

16 Reported by Tirmidhī in *Al-Shamāʾil* (15) and Dārimī (59). Haythamī said in *Majmaʿ al-Zawāʾid* (8/279): "It was related by Ṭabarānī in *Al-Awsaṭ* and the chain contains ʿAbd al-ʿAzīz ibn Abī Thābit, who is a weak narrator."

17 Mentioned by Ibn al-Athīr in *Usd al-Ghābah* (5023) where he attributed the narration to Ibn Mandah and Abū Nuʿaym.

18 Reported by Muslim (2340). See also *Majmaʿ al-Zawāʾid* (8/280).

19 Haythamī said in *Majmaʿ al-Zawāʾid* (8/281): "It was related by Ṭabarānī and the chain contains narrators I do not recognize."

20 Haythamī said in *Majmaʿ al-Zawāʾid* (8/278): "It was related by Ṭabarānī and the chain contains Yaʿqūb ibn Muhammad al-Zuhrī, who the majority said was a weak narrator, although some said he was reliable."

وَأَبِي جُحَيْفَةَ١٨، وَجَابِرِ بْنِ سَمُرَةَ١٩، وَأُمِّ مَعْبَدٍ٢٠، وَابْنِ عَبَّاسٍ٢١، وَمُعَرِّضِ بْنِ مُعَيْقِيبٍ٢٢، وَأَبِي الطُّفَيْلِ٢٣، وَالعَدَّاءِ بْنِ خَالِدٍ٢٤، وَخُرَيْمِ بْنِ فَاتِكٍ، وحَكِيمِ بْنِ حِزَامٍ٢٥، وَغَيْرِهِم رضي الله عنهم مِنْ أَنَّهُ ﷺ:

كَانَ أَزْهَرَ٢٦ اللَّوْنِ، أَدْعَجَ٢٧، أَنْجَلَ٢٨، أَشْكَلَ٢٩، أَهْدَبَ الأَشْفَارِ٣٠، أَبْلَجَ،

---

١٨   حَدِيثُ أَبِي جُحَيْفَةَ رَوَاهُ البُخَارِيُّ (٣٥٤٤)، وَمُسْلِمٌ (٢٣٤٣).

١٩   حَدِيثُ جَابِرِ بْنِ سَمُرَةَ رَوَاهُ مُسْلِمٌ (٢٣٣٩)، وَالتِّرْمِذِيُّ (٣٦٤٧).

٢٠   قِصَّةُ أُمِّ مَعْبَدٍ رَوَاها البَغَوِيُّ (٣٧٠٤)، مِنْ حَدِيثِ حُبَيْشِ بْنِ خَالِدٍ، وَصَحَّحَهُ الحَاكِمُ فِي المُسْتَدْرَكِ ٩-١٠/٣، وَوَافَقَهُ الذَّهَبِيُّ، وَقَالَ الشَّيْخُ شُعَيْبُ الأَرْنَؤُوطُ فِي تَعْلِيقِهِ عَلَى شَرْحِ السُّنَّةِ: «حَدِيثٌ حَسَنٌ قَوِيٌّ». وَزَادَ نِسْبَتَهُ السُّيُوطِيُّ فِي الخَصَائِصِ إِلَى ابْنِ شَاهِينَ وَابْنِ السَّكَنِ وَابْنِ مَنْدَةَ وَالبَيْهَقِي وَأَبِي نُعَيْمٍ. وَذَكَرَهُ الحَافِظُ الهَيْثَمِيُّ فِي مَجْمَع الزَّوَائِدِ ٥٥-٥٨/٦ وَقَالَ: «رَوَاهُ الطَّبَرَانِيُّ وَفِي إِسْنَادِهِ جَمَاعَةٌ لَمْ أَعْرِفْهُم». ثُمَّ ذَكَرَهُ الهَيْثَمِيُّ أَيْضًا ٢٧٨-٢٧٩/٨ مِنْ حَدِيثِ سُلَيْطٍ، وَقَالَ: «رَوَاهُ الطَّبَرَانِيُّ وَفِيهِ عَبْدُ العَزِيزِ بْنُ يَحْيَى المَدِينِي، وَنَسَبَهُ البُخَارِيُّ وَغَيْرُهُ إِلَى الكَذِبِ، وَقَالَ الحَاكِمُ: صَدُوقٌ، فَالعَجَبُ مِنْهُ، وَفِيهِ مَجَاهِيلُ أَيْضًا». وَقَالَ ابْنُ كَثِيرٍ فِي البِدَايَةِ وَالنِّهَايَةِ ١٦٦/٣: «وَقِصَّتُها مَشْهُورَةٌ مَرْوِيَّةٌ مِنْ طُرُقٍ يَشُدُّ بَعْضُها بَعْضًا». وَسَيُورِدُ المُصَنِّفُ طَرَفًا مِنْ قِصَّةِ أُمِّ مَعْبَدٍ.

٢١   حَدِيثُ ابْنِ عَبَّاسٍ أَخْرَجَهُ التِّرْمِذِيُّ فِي الشَّمَائِلِ (١٤)، وَالدَّارِمِي بِرَقْمِ (٥٩)، وَذَكَرَهُ الهَيْثَمِيُّ فِي مَجْمَع الزَّوَائِدِ ٢٧٩/٨ وَقَالَ: «رَوَاهُ الطَّبَرَانِيُّ فِي الأَوْسَطِ، وَفِيهِ عَبْدُ العَزِيزِ بْنُ أَبِي ثَابِتٍ وَهُوَ ضَعِيفٌ».

٢٢   حَدِيثُ مُعَرِّضِ بْنِ مُعَيْقِيبٍ ذَكَرَهُ ابْنُ الأَثِيرِ فِي أُسْدِ الغَابَةِ (٥٠٢٣) وَعَزَاهُ إِلَى ابْنِ مَنْدَةَ وَأَبِي نُعَيْمٍ.

٢٣   حَدِيثُ أَبِي الطُّفَيْلِ أَخْرَجَهُ مُسْلِمٌ (٢٣٤٠)، وَانْظُرْ مَجْمَعَ الزَّوَائِدِ ٢٨٠/٨.

٢٤   حَدِيثُ العَدَّاءِ بْنِ خَالِدٍ ذَكَرَهُ الهَيْثَمِيُّ فِي مَجْمَع الزَّوَائِدِ ٢٨١/٨ وَقَالَ: «رَوَاهُ الطَّبَرَانِيُّ وَفِيهِ مَنْ لَمْ أَعْرِفْهُم».

٢٥   حَدِيثُ حَكِيمِ بْنِ حِزَامٍ ذَكَرَهُ الهَيْثَمِيُّ فِي مَجْمَع الزَّوَائِدِ ٢٧٨/٨ وَقَالَ: «رَوَاهُ الطَّبَرَانِيُّ وَفِيهِ يَعْقُوبُ بْنُ مُحَمَّدٍ الزُّهْرِيُّ، وَضَعَّفَهُ الجُمْهُورُ، وَقَدْ وُثِّقَ».

٢٦   أَزْهَرُ: مُسْتَنِيرٌ، وَهُوَ أَحْسَنُ الأَلْوَانِ، وَالزُّهْرَةُ: البَيَاضُ النَّيِّرُ. (جَامِعُ الأُصُولِ ٢٢٩/١١).

٢٧   أَدْعَجُ: الدَّعَجُ فِي العَيْنِ: شِدَّةُ سَوَادِهَا. (جَامِعُ الأُصُولِ ٢٢٩/١١).

٢٨   أَنْجَلُ: وَاسِعُ العَيْنِ مَعَ حُسْنٍ.

٢٩   أَشْكَلُ: فِي بَيَاضِ عَيْنَيْهِ حُمْرَةٌ، وَهُوَ مَحْمُودٌ مَحْبُوبٌ. (النِّهَايَةُ).

٣٠   أَهْدَبُ الأَشْفَارِ: الَّذِي شَعْرُ أَجْفَانِهِ كَثِيرٌ مُسْتَطِيلٌ. (جَامِعُ الأُصُولِ).

his feet were firm. The Prophet had radiant skin, and a thin line of hair ran from his chest to navel.

He was neither extremely tall nor short, but somewhere between the two. Nevertheless, you would never perceive another person to be taller than him. His hair was neither excessively curly nor completely straight.

When he laughed and his teeth showed, the whiteness resembled a flash of lightning or a burst of hailstones. When he spoke, it was as if a light shone from between his incisors.

He had a perfectly formed neck, and his body and face were healthy and lean. Al-Barā' ibn 'Āzib said: "The most beautiful person I ever saw was the Messenger of Allah with his curly hair, dressed in a red cloak."[21]

Abū Hurayrah commented: "I have not seen anything more beautiful than the Messenger of Allah. The Sun shone from his face and when he laughed, the sparkle would reflect from the walls."[22]

Jābir ibn Samurah was asked: "Was the face of the Messenger of Allah like [the brightness of] a sword?" He replied: "Rather it was like the Sun and the Moon, and he had a rounded face."[23]

---

21 Reported by Bukhārī (5901), Muslim (2337), and Tirmidhī in *Al-Shamā'il* (65).

22 Reported without the last phrase by Tirmidhī in *Al-Sunan* (3648) and in *Al-Shamā'il* (122), Aḥmad (2/350), and Baghawī (3649). Authenticated by Ibn Ḥibbān in *Mawārid al-Ẓam'ān* (2118). The last phrase was related by Ma'mar ibn Rāshid in *Al-Jāmi'* (20490), which was compiled by 'Abd al-Razzāq.

23 Reported by Muslim (2344/109). Suyūṭī attributed the hadith to Bukhārī and Muslim in *Al-Manāhil*, whilst Ibn al-Athīr attributed it only to Muslim in *Jāmi' al-Uṣūl* (11/240), and Allah knows best.

أَزَجّ، أَقْنَى، أَفْلَج، مُدَوَّرَ الوَجْهِ، وَاسِعَ الجَبِينِ، كَثَّ اللِّحْيةِ تَمْلَأُ صَدْرَهُ، سَوَاءَ البَطْنِ وَالصَّدْرِ، وَاسِعَ الصَّدْرِ، عَظِيمَ المَنْكِبَيْنِ، ضَخْمَ العِظَامِ، عَبْلَ العَضُدَيْنِ وَالذِّرَاعَيْنِ وَالأَسَافِلِ، رَحْبَ الكَفَّيْنِ وَالقَدَمَيْنِ، سَائِلَ الأَطْرَافِ[31]، أَنْوَرَ المُتَجَرَّدِ[32]، دَقِيقَ المَسْرَبَةِ[33]، رَبْعَةَ القَدِّ[34]، لَيْسَ بِالطَّوِيلِ البَائِنِ[35]، وَلَا بِالقَصِيرِ المُتَرَدِّدِ، وَمَعَ ذَلِكَ فَلَمْ يَكُنْ يُمَاشِيهِ أَحَدٌ يُنْسَبُ إِلَى الطُّولِ إِلَّا طَالَهُ ﷺ، رَجِلَ الشَّعَرِ[36]، إِذَا افْتَرَّ ضَاحِكًا افْتَرَّ عَنْ مِثْلِ سَنَا البَرْقِ، وَعَنْ مِثْلِ حَبِّ الغَمَامِ[37]، إِذَا تَكَلَّمَ رُئِيَ كَالنُّورِ يَخْرُجُ مِنْ بَيْنِ ثَنَايَاهُ[38]، أَحْسَنَ النَّاسِ عُنُقًا، لَيْسَ بِمُطَهَّمٍ[39]، وَلَا مُكَلْثَمٍ[40]، مُتَمَاسِكَ البَدَنِ، ضَرْبَ اللَّحْمِ[41].

قَالَ البَرَاءُ: مَا رَأَيْتُ مِنْ ذِي لِمَّةٍ فِي حُلَّةٍ حَمْرَاءَ أَحْسَنَ مِنْ رَسُولِ اللهِ

---

٣١ سَائِلُ الأَطْرَافِ: طَوِيلُ الأَصَابِعِ.

٣٢ أَنْوَرَ المُتَجَرَّدِ: أَيْ مَا جُرِّدَ عَنْهُ الثِّيَابُ مِنْ جَسَدِهِ وَكُشِفَ. يُرِيدُ أَنَّهُ كَانَ مُشْرِقَ الجَسَدِ (النِّهَايَةُ).

٣٣ دَقِيقُ المَسْرَبَةِ: المَسْرَبَةُ: الشَّعْرُ النَّابِتُ عَلَى وَسَطِ الصَّدْرِ نَازِلًا إِلَى آخِرِ البَطْنِ (جَامِعُ الأُصُولِ).

٣٤ رَبْعَةُ القَدِّ: مُعْتَدِلُ القَامَةِ بَيْنَ الطَّوِيلِ وَالقَصِيرِ.

٣٥ الطَّوِيلُ البَائِنُ: المُفْرِطُ فِي الطُّولِ.

٣٦ رَجِلُ الشَّعَرِ: أَيْ شَعْرُهُ ﷺ لَمْ يَكُنْ شَدِيدَ الجُعُودَةِ وَلَا شَدِيدَ السُّبُوطَةِ، بَلْ بَيْنَهُمَا. انْظُرِ النِّهَايَةَ.

٣٧ حَبُّ الغَمَامِ: هُوَ البَرَدُ، شَبَّهَ بِهِ بَيَاضَ أَسْنَانِهِ ﷺ.

٣٨ الثَّنَايَا: وَاحِدُهَا ثَنِيَّةٌ. وَهِيَ إِحْدَى الأَسْنَانِ الأَرْبَعِ الَّتِي فِي مُقَدِّمَةِ الفَمِ، ثِنْتَانِ مِنْ فَوْقٍ، وَثِنْتَانِ مِنْ تَحْتِ (المُعْجَمُ الوَسِيطُ).

٣٩ المُطَهَّمُ: المُنْتَفِخُ الوَجْهِ، وَقِيلَ: الفَاحِشُ السِّمَنِ، وَقِيلَ: النَّحِيفُ الجِسْمِ، وَهُوَ مِنَ الأَضْدَادِ (النِّهَايَةُ).

٤٠ المُكَلْثَمُ: المُسْتَدِيرُ الوَجْهِ، وَلَا يَكُونُ إِلَّا مَعَ كَثْرَةِ اللَّحْمِ (جَامِعُ الأُصُولِ ٢٢٦/١١).

٤١ ضَرْبُ اللَّحْمِ: أَيْ خَفِيفُ اللَّحْمِ.

Umm Ma'bad said: "He was the most beautiful person from afar, and the sweetest and most handsome from up close."[24] And Ibn Abī Hālah recalled: "His face shone like a full moon."[25]

Indeed, there are many famous narrations on this topic which we have not covered. But perhaps they can all be best summarized by the words of 'Alī ⚬: "Anyone who saw the Prophet ⚬ was suddenly filled with an overwhelming sense of love, and those who got to know him developed a deep affection.

Everyone who met the Prophet ⚬ would say they had never met anyone like him before or since."[26]

---

24 Reported by Baghawī (3704) in the hadith of Ḥubaysh ibn Khālid. Ḥākim authenticated the hadith in *Al-Mustadrak* (3/9-10) and Dhahabī concurred.

25 Reported by Tirmidhī in *Al-Shamā'il* (8, 335, 350) and Baghawī in *Sharḥ al-Sunnah* (3705, 3706).

26 Reported by Tirmidhī in *Al-Sunan* (3638) and *Al-Shamā'il* (7).

عَلَيْهِ. وَقَالَ أَبُو هُرَيْرَةَ: مَا رَأَيْتُ شَيْئًا أَحْسَنَ مِنْ رَسُولِ اللهِ ﷺ، كَأَنَّ الشَّمْسَ تَجْرِي فِي وَجْهِهِ ﷺ، وَإِذَا ضَحِكَ يَتَلَأْلَأُ فِي الْجُدُرِ. وَقَالَ جَابِرُ بْنُ سَمُرَةَ وَقَالَ لَهُ رَجُلٌ: كَانَ وَجْهُ رَسُولِ اللهِ ﷺ مِثْلَ السَّيْفِ؟ فَقَالَ: لَا، بَلْ مِثْلَ الشَّمْسِ وَالْقَمَرِ. وَكَانَ مُسْتَدِيرًا. وَقَالَتْ أُمُّ مَعْبَدٍ فِي بَعْضِ مَا وَصَفَتْهُ بِهِ: أَجْمَلَ النَّاسِ مِنْ بَعِيدٍ، وَأَحْلَاهُ وَأَحْسَنَهُ مِنْ قَرِيبٍ. صَلَّى اللهُ عَلَيْهِ وَسَلَّمَ تَسْلِيمًا، كُلَّمَا ذَكَرَهُ الذَّاكِرُونَ وَغَفَلَ عَنْ ذِكْرِهِ الْغَافِلُونَ. وَفِي حَدِيثِ ابْنِ أَبِي هَالَةَ: يَتَلَأْلَأُ وَجْهُهُ تَلَأْلُؤَ الْقَمَرِ لَيْلَةَ الْبَدْرِ.

وَقَالَ عَلِيٌّ رَضِيَ اللهُ عَنْهُ فِي آخِرِ وَصْفِهِ لَهُ: مَنْ رَآهُ بَدِيهَةً هَابَهُ، وَمَنْ خَالَطَهُ مَعْرِفَةً أَحَبَّهُ، يَقُولُ نَاعِتُهُ: لَمْ أَرَ قَبْلَهُ وَلَا بَعْدَهُ مِثْلَهُ ﷺ.

وَالْأَحَادِيثُ فِي بَسْطِ صِفَتِهِ مَشْهُورَةٌ كَثِيرَةٌ، فَلَا نُطَوِّلُ بِسَرْدِهَا، وَقَدِ اخْتَصَرْنَا فِي وَصْفِهِ نُكَتَ مَا جَاءَ فِيهَا، وَجُمْلَةً مِمَّا فِيهِ الْكِفَايَةُ فِي الْقَصْدِ إِلَى الْمَطْلُوبِ إِنْ شَاءَ اللهُ تَعَالَى، وَخَتَمْنَا هَذِهِ الْفُصُولَ بِحَدِيثٍ جَامِعٍ لِذَلِكَ، تَقِفُ عَلَيْهِ هُنَالِكَ إِنْ شَاءَ اللهُ تَعَالَى.

---

٤٢ أَخْرَجَهُ الْبُخَارِيُّ (٥٩٠١)، وَمُسْلِمٌ (٢٣٣٧). اللِّمَّةُ: الشَّعْرُ الَّذِي أَلَمَّ بِالْمَنْكِبَيْنِ. أَيْ: قَارَبَهُمَا.

٤٣ أَخْرَجَهُ - بِدُونِ الْفِقْرَةِ الْأَخِيرَةِ - التِّرْمِذِيُّ فِي السُّنَنِ (٣٦٤٨)، وَفِي الشَّمَائِلِ (١١٥)، وَأَحْمَدُ ٣٥٠/٢، وَالْبَغَوِيُّ (٣٦٤٩) وَصَحَّحَهُ ابْنُ حِبَّانَ (٢١١٨) مَوَارِدُ الظَّمْآنِ. وَالْفِقْرَةُ الْأَخِيرَةُ رَوَاهَا مَعْمَرُ بْنُ رَاشِدٍ فِي الْجَامِعِ (٢٠٤٩٠) بِرِوَايَةِ الْإِمَامِ عَبْدِ الرَّزَّاقِ. (يَتَلَأْلَأُ فِي الْجُدُرِ): أَيْ أَنَّ نُورَ وَجْهِهِ الشَّرِيفِ يُشْرِقُ إِشْرَاقًا يَصِلُ إِلَى الْجُدْرَانِ الْمُقَابِلَةِ كَمَا يَكُونُ ذَلِكَ مِنَ الشَّمْسِ.

٤٤ رَوَاهُ مُسْلِمٌ (١٠٩/٢٣٤٤). وَعَزَاهُ فِي الْمَنَاهِلِ إِلَى الشَّيْخَيْنِ. بَيْنَمَا عَزَاهُ ابْنُ الْأَثِيرِ فِي جَامِعِ الْأُصُولِ ٢٤٠/١١ إِلَى مُسْلِمٍ دُونَ الْبُخَارِيِّ. وَاللهُ أَعْلَمُ.

٤٥ (بَدِيهَةً): أَيْ مُفَاجَأَةً وَبَغْتَةً (النِّهَايَةُ). (نَاعِتُهُ): وَاصِفُهُ.

HIS CLEANLINESS AND PURITY

One of the special qualities given exclusively to the Prophet ﷺ was the complete cleanliness of his body, the sweetness of his smell, and the purity of his sweat. These were later emphasized by the acts of purification legislated i n the Shariah and the ten practices of the *fiṭrah* (natural disposition).[27] The Prophet ﷺ said: "This religion is built upon cleanliness."[28]

Sufyān ibn al-ʿĀṣī and others narrated, from Aḥmad ibn ʿUmar, from Abū al-ʿAbbās al-Rāzī, from Abū Aḥmad al-Julūdī, from Ibn Sufyān, from Muslim, who said: "Qutaybah narrated, from Jaʿfar ibn Sulaymān, from Thābit, from Anas, who said: 'I have never smelt ambergris, musk, or anything, sweeter than the scent of the Messenger of Allah ﷺ.'"[29]

---

27 As reported by Muslim (261) from ʿĀ'ishah: "The Messenger of Allah ﷺ said: 'The ten practices of the *fiṭrah* are: trimming the moustache, leaving the beard, using a *miswāk* (toothbrush), rinsing the nose (during *wuḍū'*), cutting the nails, washing the outside of the knuckles, plucking the armpits, shaving pubic hair, and cleaning one's private parts with water.' Zakariyyā (ibn Abī Zā'idah) said that Muṣʿab (ibn Shaybah) said: 'I have forgotten the tenth, but it may have been rinsing the mouth (during *wuḍū'*).'"

28 Suyūṭī commented in *Al-Manāhil*, p. 61: "'Irāqī said in *Takhrīj Aḥādīth al-Iḥyā'*: 'I did not find the narration in this form.' Ibn Ḥibbān reported from ʿĀ'ishah, in *Kitāb al-Majrūḥīn min al-Muḥaddithīn wa al-Ḍuʿafā' wa al-Matrūkīn*, that the Prophet ﷺ said: 'Cleanse yourselves, for Islam is pure.' And Ṭabarānī reported from Ibn Masʿūd, in *Al-Awsaṭ*, that the Prophet ﷺ said: 'Cleanliness calls to īmān.' Both narrations have weak chains of transmission. Tirmidhī reported from Saʿd ibn Abī Waqqāṣ, in a *marfūʿ* narration, that the Prophet ﷺ said: 'Allah is pure ("Naẓīf") and He loves cleanliness, so clean your courtyards.' Al-Rāfiʿī reported in *Tārīkh Qazwīn*, in a *marfūʿ* narration from Abū Hurayrah: 'Clean whatever you can, because Allah built Islam upon cleanliness, and only the virtuous ("naẓīf") will enter Paradise.'" Translator's note: The same word, "*naẓīf*", can be variously interpreted as "clean", "pure", or "virtuous", depending on the context.

29 Reported here from the chain of Muslim (2330). Also reported by Bukhārī (1973) with a similar wording.

فصل

وَأَمَّا نَظَافَةُ جِسْمِهِ وَطِيبُ رِيحِهِ وَعَرَقِهِ، وَنَزَاهَتُهُ عَنِ الْأَقْذَارِ وَعَوْرَاتِ الْجَسَدِ، فَكَانَ قَدْ خَصَّهُ اللهُ تَعَالَى فِي ذَلِكَ بِخَصَائِصَ لَمْ تُوجَدْ فِي غَيْرِهِ، ثُمَّ تَمَّمَهَا بِنَظَافَةِ الشَّرْعِ، وَخِصَالِ الْفِطْرَةِ الْعَشْرِ[46].

وَقَالَ ﷺ: «بُنِيَ الدِّينُ عَلَى النَّظَافَةِ»[47].

حَدَّثَنَا سُفْيَانُ بْنُ الْعَاصِي، وَغَيْرُ وَاحِدٍ، قَالُوا: حَدَّثَنَا أَحْمَدُ بْنُ عُمَرَ، حَدَّثَنَا أَبُو الْعَبَّاسِ الرَّازِيُّ، حَدَّثَنَا أَبُو أَحْمَدَ الْجُلُودِيُّ، حَدَّثَنَا ابْنُ سُفْيَانَ، حَدَّثَنَا مُسْلِمٌ، حَدَّثَنَا قُتَيْبَةُ، حَدَّثَنَا جَعْفَرُ بْنُ سُلَيْمَانَ، عَنْ ثَابِتٍ، عَنْ أَنَسٍ رَضِيَ اللهُ عَنْهُ قَالَ: «مَا شَمِمْتُ عَنْبَرًا قَطُّ وَلَا مِسْكًا وَلَا شَيْئًا أَطْيَبَ مِنْ رِيحِ رَسُولِ اللهِ ﷺ»[48].

وَعَنْ جَابِرِ بْنِ سَمُرَةَ أَنَّهُ ﷺ مَسَحَ خَدَّهُ، قَالَ: فَوَجَدْتُ لِيَدِهِ بَرْدًا وَرِيحًا

---

46 خِصَالُ الْفِطْرَةِ الْعَشْرِ رَوَاهَا مُسْلِمٌ (261) مِنْ حَدِيثِ عَائِشَةَ قَالَتْ: قَالَ رَسُولُ اللهِ ﷺ: عَشْرٌ مِنَ الْفِطْرَةِ: قَصُّ الشَّارِبِ، وَإِعْفَاءُ اللِّحْيَةِ، وَالسِّوَاكُ، وَاسْتِنْشَاقُ الْمَاءِ، وَقَصُّ الْأَظْفَارِ، وَغَسْلُ الْبَرَاجِمِ، وَنَتْفُ الْإِبِطِ، وَحَلْقُ الْعَانَةِ، وَانْتِقَاصُ الْمَاءِ. قَالَ زَكَرِيَّا (ابْنُ أَبِي زَائِدَةَ): قَالَ مُصْعَبٌ (ابْنُ شَيْبَةَ): وَنَسِيتُ الْعَاشِرَةَ، إِلَّا أَنْ تَكُونَ الْمَضْمَضَةَ. زَادَ قُتَيْبَةُ: قَالَ وَكِيعٌ: انْتِقَاصُ الْمَاءِ يَعْنِي: الِاسْتِنْجَاءَ.

47 قَالَ السُّيُوطِيُّ فِي الْمَنَاهِلِ رَقْمَ (61): «قَالَ الْحَافِظُ أَبُو الْفَضْلِ الْعِرَاقِيُّ فِي تَخْرِيجِ الْإِحْيَاءِ (1/125): لَمْ أَجِدْهُ هَكَذَا، وَفِي الضُّعَفَاءِ لِابْنِ حِبَّانَ مِنْ حَدِيثِ عَائِشَةَ: «تَنَظَّفُوا فَإِنَّ الْإِسْلَامَ نَظِيفٌ» وَلِلطَّبَرَانِيِّ فِي الْأَوْسَطِ مِنْ حَدِيثِ ابْنِ مَسْعُودٍ: «وَالنَّظَافَةُ تَدْعُو إِلَى الْإِيمَانِ». وَسَنَدُهُمَا ضَعِيفٌ. قُلْتُ: رَوَى التِّرْمِذِيُّ عَنْ سَعْدِ بْنِ أَبِي وَقَّاصٍ مَرْفُوعًا: «إِنَّ اللهَ نَظِيفٌ يُحِبُّ النَّظَافَةَ فَنَظِّفُوا أَفْنِيَتَكُمْ». وَأَخْرَجَ الرَّافِعِيُّ فِي تَارِيخِ قَزْوِينَ بِسَنَدِهِ عَنْ أَبِي هُرَيْرَةَ مَرْفُوعًا: «تَنَظَّفُوا بِكُلِّ مَا اسْتَطَعْتُمْ فَإِنَّ اللهَ بَنَى الْإِسْلَامَ عَلَى النَّظَافَةِ، وَلَنْ يَدْخُلَ الْجَنَّةَ إِلَّا كُلُّ نَظِيفٍ».

48 أَسْنَدَهُ الْمُصَنِّفُ مِنْ طَرِيقِ مُسْلِمٍ (2330). قُلْتُ: وَأَخْرَجَهُ أَيْضًا الْبُخَارِيُّ (1973) بِلَفْظٍ قَرِيبٍ.

Jābir ibn Samurah said that when the Prophet ﷺ had patted his cheek: "I found that his hand had a coolness and a [beautiful] scent, as if he just took it out from a bag of perfume."[30]

Others mentioned: "Whether the Prophet ﷺ was wearing perfume or not, if he shook a man's hand his scent would be left there for the rest of the day. And if the Prophet ﷺ patted the head of one of the children, you could tell who it was from the fragrance that remained."

The Prophet ﷺ once slept at the home of Anas on a mat and perspired during the night. When Anas' mother[31] came in the morning, she began to pour the sweat from the mat into a bottle. When the Prophet ﷺ asked her about that, she replied: "We collect it in a pot and it is the sweetest of our perfumes."[32]

Jābir said: "Whenever someone walked down a street that the Prophet ﷺ had passed, they would know from his beautiful scent."[33] Isḥāq ibn Rāhawayh[34] commented: "That was his scent without applying perfume."

Al-Muzanī[35] reported, also from Jābir: "The Prophet ﷺ had me ride behind him. I placed my mouth on the Seal of Prophethood and could sense the fragrance of musk."[36] Others mentioned that

---

30 Reported by Muslim (2329).

31 Umm Sulaym, the wife of Abū Ṭalḥah.

32 Reported by Muslim (2331) from Anas, and Bukhārī (6281) in another narration.

33 Reported by Bukhārī in *Al-Tārīkh Al-Kabīr* (1/399-400) and Dārimī (67). Similar was reported by Abū Ya'lā (3125), Bazzār, Ṭabarānī in *Al-Awsaṭ*, and Abū al-Shaykh. Suyūṭī elucidated the chain in *Al-Manāhil*, p. 66. Haythamī said in *Majma' al-Zawā'id* (8/282): "The narrators in the chain of Abū Ya'lā are reliable."

34 Isḥāq ibn Ibrāhīm al-Ḥanẓalī. Dhahabī said: "The scholar of the east and leader of the *huffāẓ* (preservers of knowledge)." He was born in 161 AH and died in 238 AH. See *Siyar A'lām al-Nubalā'* (11/358-383).

35 Ismā'īl ibn Yaḥyā al-Muzanī, a companion of Imam al-Shāfi'ī and prominent scholar. He was born in 175 AH and died in 264 AH. See *Siyar A'lām al-Nubalā'* (12/492-497).

36 Reported by Ibn 'Asākir in his *Tārīkh*, as found in *Al-Manāhil*, p. 67.

كَأَنَّمَا أَخْرَجَهَا مِنْ جُونَةِ عَطَّارٍ⁴⁹.

قَالَ غَيْرُهُ: مَسَّهَا بِطِيبٍ أَوْ لَمْ يَمَسَّهَا، يُصَافِحُ الْمُصَافِحَ فَيَظَلُّ يَوْمَهُ يَجِدُ رِيحَهَا، وَيَضَعُ يَدَهُ عَلَى رَأْسِ الصَّبِيِّ فَيُعْرَفُ مِنْ بَيْنِ الصِّبْيَانِ بِرِيحِهَا.

وَنَامَ رَسُولُ اللهِ ﷺ فِي دَارِ أَنَسٍ فَعَرِقَ، فَجَاءَتْ أُمُّهُ⁵⁰ بِقَارُورَةٍ تَجْمَعُ فِيهَا عَرَقَهُ، فَسَأَلَهَا ﷺ عَنْ ذَلِكَ، فَقَالَتْ: نَجْعَلُهُ فِي طِيبِنَا، وَهُوَ مِنْ أَطْيَبِ الطِّيبِ⁵¹.

وَذَكَرَ الْبُخَارِيُّ فِي تَارِيخِهِ الْكَبِيرِ عَنْ جَابِرٍ ﵁: لَمْ يَكُنِ النَّبِيُّ ﷺ يَمُرُّ فِي طَرِيقٍ فَيَتْبَعُهُ أَحَدٌ إِلَّا عَرَفَ أَنَّهُ سَلَكَهُ مِنْ طِيبِهِ⁵².

ذَكَرَ إِسْحَاقُ بْنُ رَاهَوَيْهِ⁵³ أَنَّ تِلْكَ كَانَتْ رَائِحَتَهُ بِلَا طِيبٍ ﷺ.

وَرَوَى الْحَرْبِيُّ⁵⁴ عَنْ جَابِرٍ: أَرْدَفَنِي رَسُولُ اللهِ ﷺ خَلْفَهُ، فَالْتَقَمْتُ خَاتَمَ

---

٤٩ رَوَاهُ مُسْلِمٌ (٢٣٢٩). (جُونَةُ الْعَطَّارِ): هِيَ الَّتِي يُعَدُّ فِيهَا الطِّيبُ وَيَدَّخِرُهُ (جَامِعُ الْأُصُولِ ٢٥١/١١). وَجُونَةُ: مَهْمُوزَةٌ وَقَدْ يُتْرَكُ هَمْزُهَا.

٥٠ أُمُّهُ: هِيَ أُمُّ سُلَيْمٍ، زَوْجُ أَبِي طَلْحَةَ.

٥١ رَوَاهُ مُسْلِمٌ (٢٣٣١) مِنْ حَدِيثِ أَنَسٍ. وَرَوَاهُ الْبُخَارِيُّ (٦٢٨١) بِسِيَاقَةٍ أُخْرَى.

٥٢ أَخْرَجَهُ الْبُخَارِيُّ فِي التَّارِيخِ الْكَبِيرِ ٣٩٩/١-٤٠٠، وَالدَّارِمِيُّ بِرَقْمِ (٦٧). وَفِي الْبَابِ: عَنْ أَنَسٍ عِنْدَ أَبِي يَعْلَى (٣١٢٥)، وَالْبَزَّارِ، وَالطَّبَرَانِيِّ فِي الْأَوْسَطِ، وَأَبِي الشَّيْخِ. وَجَوَّدَ إِسْنَادَهُ السُّيُوطِيُّ فِي الْمَنَاهِلِ (٦٦). وَقَالَ الْهَيْثَمِيُّ فِي مَجْمَعِ الزَّوَائِدِ ٢٨٢/٨: «وَرِجَالُ أَبِي يَعْلَى وُثِّقُوا».

٥٣ هُوَ إِسْحَاقُ بْنُ إِبْرَاهِيمَ الْحَنْظَلِيُّ. قَالَ الذَّهَبِيُّ: «شَيْخُ الْمَشْرِقِ وَسَيِّدُ الْحُفَّاظِ». وُلِدَ سَنَةَ (١٦١) هـ. وَمَاتَ سَنَةَ (٢٣٨) هـ. انْظُرْ تَرْجَمَتَهُ فِي سِيَرِ أَعْلَامِ النُّبَلَاءِ ٣٥٨/١١-٣٨٣.

٥٤ هُوَ إِسْمَاعِيلُ بْنُ يَحْيَى الْمُزَنِيُّ. صَاحِبُ الْإِمَامِ الشَّافِعِيِّ كَانَ زَاهِدًا عَالِمًا مُجْتَهِدًا قَوِيَّ الْحُجَّةِ. وُلِدَ سَنَةَ (١٧٥) هـ. وَمَاتَ سَنَةَ (٢٦٤) هـ. انْظُرْ تَرْجَمَتَهُ فِي سِيَرِ أَعْلَامِ النُّبَلَاءِ ٤٩٢/١٢-٤٩٧.

when the Prophet wished to relieve himself, the Earth would open up and consume any faeces or urine, and a pleasant fragrance would emanate.[37]

Muhammad ibn Sa'd[38] related from 'Ā'ishah that she said to the Prophet: "When you return from relieving yourself we do not notice any foulness!" He replied: "O 'Ā'ishah! Did you not know that the Earth swallows whatever comes out of Prophets, so that nothing is seen?"[39]

Although this narration is not well-known, people of knowledge did mention the purity of what came out of the Prophet. This was the opinion of some Shāfi'ī scholars[40], as stated by Abū Naṣr al-Ṣabbāgh[41] in his text *Al-Shāmil*. Whichever opinion is followed, the crux of the matter is that nothing from the Prophet was unpleasant or impure.

---

37   Suyūṭī said in *Al-Manāhil*, p. 68: "Bayhaqī reported it from 'Ā'ishah, but he said it was fabricated. Al-Ḥakīm al-Tirmidhī reported in *Nawādir al-Uṣūl*, from 'Abd al-Raḥmān ibn Qays (who is a liar and fabricator of narrations), from 'Abd al-Malik ibn 'Abdullāh ibn al-Rā'id (who is unknown), from Dhakwān, that the Messenger of Allah had no shadow [when he stood under] the Sun or the Moon, and left no traces when he relieved himself."
Dāraquṭnī reported in *Al-Afrād* from 'Ā'ishah, with a solid chain of transmission: "I said: 'O Messenger of Allah! I see you going to relieve yourself and then when you return there are no traces of anything coming out from you?' He said: 'O 'Ā'ishah! Did you not know that the Earth swallows whatever comes out of the Prophets?'" Ibn Diḥyah said in *Al-Khaṣā'iṣ*: "The chain [for this narration] is reliable."
Another narration was reported by Ḥākim (4/72) from Laylā, the servant of 'Ā'ishah, although the chain contained some narrators whose reliability was questioned, that 'Ā'ishah said: "The Messenger of Allah went to relieve himself. When I entered, I could not see anything, and there was a smell of musk. I said: 'O Messenger of Allah! I do not see anything [unpleasant]!' He replied: 'The Earth has been commanded to conceal [what comes from] the Prophets.'"

38   The scribe of Wāqidī and author of *Kitāb al-Ṭabaqāt Al-Kabīr*. He passed away in 230 AH.

39   See *Al-Manāhil*, p. 68, Ḥākim (4/72), and the narration reported by Dāraquṭnī in *Al-Afrād*.

40   Although, as al-Dalajī notes, the prevailing view of the *madhhab* differs on this point. Both sides of the argument are presented by the Mālikī scholar Abū Bakr ibn Sābiq in his text *Al-Badī' fī Furū' al-Mālikiyyah wa Takhrīj mā lam Yaqa' minhā 'alā Madhhabihim min Tafārī' al-Shāfi'iyyah*.

41   'Abd al-Sayyid Muhammad al-Baghdādī, author of *Al-Shāmil*, *Al-Kāmil*, and other works. He was born in 400 AH and died in 477 AH. See *Siyar A'lām al-Nubalā'* (18/464).

النُّبُوَّةِ بِفَمِي، فَكَانَ يَنِمُّ[55] عَلَيَّ مِسْكًا[56].

وَقَدْ حَكَى بَعْضُ المُعْتَنِينَ بِأَخْبَارِهِ وَشَمَائِلِهِ ﷺ أَنَّهُ كَانَ إِذَا أَرَادَ أَنْ يَتَغَوَّطَ انْشَقَّتِ الأَرْضُ فَابْتَلَعَت غَائِطَهُ وَبَوْلَهُ، وَفَاحَتْ لِذَلِكَ رَائِحَةٌ طَيِّبَةٌ ﷺ[57].

وَأَسْنَدَ مُحَمَّدُ بْنُ سَعْدٍ[58] كَاتِبُ الوَاقِدِيِّ فِي هَذَا خَبَرًا عَنْ عَائِشَةَ رَضِيَ اللهُ عَنْهَا أَنَّهَا قَالَتْ لِلنَّبِيِّ ﷺ: إِنَّكَ تَأْتِي الخَلَاءَ فَلَا يُرَى مِنْكَ شَيْءٌ مِنَ الأَذَى، فَقَالَ لَهَا: «يَا عَائِشَةُ، أَوَمَا عَلِمْتِ أَنَّ الأَرْضَ تَبْتَلِعُ مَا يَخْرُجُ مِنَ الأَنْبِيَاءِ، فَلَا يُرَى مِنْهُ شَيْءٌ». وَهَذَا الخَبَرُ وَإِنْ لَمْ يَكُنْ مَشْهُورًا فَقَدْ قَالَ قَوْمٌ مِنْ أَهْلِ العِلْمِ بِطَهَارَةِ الحَدَثَيْنِ مِنْهُ ﷺ، وَهُوَ قَوْلُ بَعْضِ أَصْحَابِ الشَّافِعِيِّ[59]، حَكَاهُ الإِمَامُ أَبُو نَصْرِ بْنُ الصَّبَّاغِ[60] فِي شَامِلِهِ.

---

55 (يَنِمُّ): أَيْ: يَفُوحُ.

56 ابْنُ عَسَاكِرٍ فِي تَارِيخِهِ كَمَا فِي المَنَاهِلِ (٦٧).

57 ذَكَرَهُ السُّيُوطِيُّ فِي مَنَاهِلِ الصَّفَا (٦٨) وَقَالَ: «البَيْهَقِيُّ عَنْ عَائِشَةَ، وَقَالَ: مَوْضُوعٌ. وَأَخْرَجَ الحَكِيمُ التِّرْمِذِيُّ فِي نَوَادِرِ الأُصُولِ، مِنْ طَرِيقِ عَبْدِ الرَّحْمَنِ بْنِ قَيْسٍ - وَهُوَ وَضَّاعٌ كَذَّابٌ - عَنْ عَبْدِ المَلِكِ بْنِ عَبْدِ اللهِ بْنِ الرَّائِدِ - وَهُوَ مَجْهُولٌ - عَنْ ذَكْوَانَ أَنَّ رَسُولَ اللهِ ﷺ لَمْ يَكُنْ لَهُ ظِلٌّ فِي شَمْسٍ، وَلَا قَمَرٍ، وَلَا أَثَرُ قَضَاءِ حَاجَةٍ. وَأَخْرَجَ الدَّارَقُطْنِيُّ فِي «الأَفْرَادِ» بِسَنَدٍ ثَابِتٍ عَنْ عَائِشَةَ قَالَتْ: قُلْتُ: يَا رَسُولَ اللهِ! إِنِّي أَرَاكَ تَدْخُلُ الخَلَاءَ، ثُمَّ يَجِيءُ الَّذِي بَعْدَكَ فَلَا يَرَى لِمَا يَخْرُجُ مِنْكَ أَثَرًا؟ فَقَالَ: يَا عَائِشَةُ! أَمَا عَلِمْتِ أَنَّ اللهَ أَمَرَ الأَرْضَ أَنْ تَبْتَلِعَ مَا خَرَجَ مِنَ الأَنْبِيَاءِ؟». وَقَدْ عَزَا المُصَنِّفُ هَذَا فِي البَابِ، وَقَدْ قَالَ: إِنَّهُ غَيْرُ مَشْهُورٍ. قُلْتُ: هُوَ أَقْوَى مَا فِي البَابِ. وَقَدْ قَالَ ابْنُ دِحْيَةَ فِي «الخَصَائِصِ» بَعْدَ إِيرَادِهِ: هَذَا سَنَدٌ ثَابِتٌ. وَأَخْرَجَ الحَاكِمُ (٧٢/٤) بِسَنَدٍ فِيهِ مُتَّهَمٌ مِنْ حَدِيثِ لَيْلَى مَوْلَاةِ عَائِشَةَ، قَالَتْ: دَخَلَ رَسُولُ اللهِ ﷺ لِقَضَاءِ حَاجَتِهِ، فَدَخَلْتُ، فَلَمْ أَرَ شَيْئًا، وَوَجَدْتُ رِيحَ المِسْكِ، فَقُلْتُ: يَا رَسُولَ اللهِ! إِنِّي لَمْ أَرَ شَيْئًا؟ قَالَ: إِنَّ الأَرْضَ أُمِرَتْ أَنْ تَكْفِنَهُ مِنَّا مَعَاشِرَ الأَنْبِيَاءِ» وَلَهُ طُرُقٌ أُخْرَى أَوْرَدْنَاهَا فِي كِتَابِ المُعْجِزَاتِ، فَهُوَ ثَابِتٌ كَمَا قَالَ ابْنُ دِحْيَةَ.

58 صَاحِبُ كِتَابِ الطَّبَقَاتِ، تُوُفِّيَ سَنَةَ (٢٣٠) هـ.

59 قَالَ القَارِي: لَكِنَّ المُعْتَمَدَ فِي المَذْهَبِ خِلَافُهُ كَمَا ذَكَرَهُ الدَّلَجِيُّ.

60 هُوَ الإِمَامُ العَلَّامَةُ الثَّبَتُ الحُجَّةُ عَبْدُ السَّيِّدِ بْنُ مُحَمَّدٍ البَغْدَادِيُّ مُصَنِّفُ كِتَابِ «الشَّامِلِ»، وَ«الكَامِلِ»

As ʿAlī narrated: "I washed [the body of] the Prophet , and I began to look for the things we usually expected in a dead body, but I could not find anything. I said: 'You are pure in death, as you were in life.'"[42] He added: "And I could sense a sweet fragrance from his body, the likes of which we had never experienced." Abū Bakr said something similar when he mentioned kissing the Prophet of Allah after he passed away.[43]

Mālik ibn Sinān[44] tasted the blood of the Prophet during the Battle of Uḥud. The Prophet did not prevent him from doing so, and said: "The Fire will not afflict you."[45] Ibn Zubayr did the same after the Prophet had *ḥijāmah* (cupping) performed on him.

The Prophet said: "Woe to you from the people, and woe to the people from you!" However, he did not object to the action.[46] There was also a woman who drank his urine, and the Prophet said: "You will never complain of a stomach ache again."[47] None of

---

42   Reported by Ibn Mājah (1467) and Bayhaqī (3/388). Būṣīrī said: "The chain is authentic and the narrators are trustworthy." Also authenticated by Ḥākim (1/362). Dhahabī said: "The chain is disconnected in places." See also *Kitāb al-Marāsīl* (415) by Abū Dāwūd.

43   Reported by Bazzār in *Kashf al-Astār* (852) from Ibn ʿUmar. Suyūṭī authenticated the chain in *Al-Manāhil*, p. 70. Haythamī said in *Majmaʿ al-Zawāʾid* (9/37-38): "Reported by Bazzār. The narrators are all *ṣaḥīḥ* apart from ʿAlī ibn al-Mundhir, who is reliable." The kissing incident was also reported by Bukhārī (4452, 4453) from the hadith of ʿĀʾishah.

44   The father of Abū Saʿīd al-Khudrī.

45   Haythamī reported from the narration of Abū Saʿīd al-Khudrī in *Majmaʿ al-Zawāʾid* (8/270), and said: "It was related by Ṭabarānī in *Al-Awsaṭ*, and I did not find anyone in the chain who was unanimously viewed as a weak narrator." Also reported by Saʿīd ibn Manṣūr and Bayhaqī, with another wording, from ʿUmar ibn al-Sāʾib, who mentioned hearing it via Mālik, the father of Abū Saʿīd al-Khudrī.

46   Reported by Bazzār (2436), Ḥākim (3/554), Bayhaqī (7/67), and others, from ʿAbdullāh ibn al-Zubayr. Suyūṭī elucidated the chain in *Al-Manāhil*, p. 72. Haythamī said in *Majmaʿ al-Zawāʾid* (8/270): "The narrators in the chain of Bazzār are all *ṣaḥīḥ* apart from Hunayd ibn al-Qāsim, who is reliable."

47   Reported with this wording by Abū Yaʿlā in *Al-Musnad Al-Kabīr* and Abū Aḥmad al-ʿAskarī, both from the hadith of Umm Ayman. Also reported by al-Ḥasan ibn Sufyān in his *Musnad*, Ḥākim (4/63-63), Dāraquṭnī, Ṭabarānī, and Abū Nuʿaym, from the narration of Abū Mālik al-Nakhaʿī, from al-Aswad ibn Qays, from Nubayh al-ʿAnazī, from Umm Ayman, who said: "The Prophet woke up during the night and went to urinate in a pot at the side of the house." The narration goes on to say that she drank his urine. "He said: 'I swear by Allah, your

وَقَدْ حَكَى الْقَوْلَيْنِ عَنِ الْعُلَمَاءِ فِي ذَلِكَ أَبُو بَكْرِ بْنُ سَابِقٍ الْمَالِكِيُّ فِي كِتَابِهِ «الْبَدِيعِ فِي فُرُوعِ الْمَالِكِيَّةِ، وَتَخْرِيجِ مَا لَمْ يَقَعْ لَهُمْ مِنْهَا عَلَى مَذْهَبِهِمْ مِنْ تَفَارِيعِ الشَّافِعِيَّةِ».

وَشَاهِدُ هَذَا أَنَّهُ ﷺ لَمْ يَكُنْ مِنْهُ شَيْءٌ يُكْرَهُ، وَلَا غَيْرَ طَيِّبٍ.

وَمِنْهُ حَدِيثُ عَلِيٍّ رضي الله عنه: غَسَّلْتُ النَّبِيَّ ﷺ، فَذَهَبْتُ أَنْظُرُ إِلَى مَا يَكُونُ مِنَ الْمَيِّتِ فَلَمْ أَجِدْ شَيْئًا، فَقُلْتُ: طِبْتَ حَيًّا وَمَيِّتًا.[61] قَالَ: وَسَطَعَتْ مِنْهُ رِيحٌ طَيِّبَةٌ لَمْ نَجِدْ مِثْلَهَا قَطُّ. وَمِثْلُهُ قَالَ أَبُو بَكْرٍ رضي الله عنه حِينَ قَبَّلَ النَّبِيَّ ﷺ بَعْدَ مَوْتِهِ.[62] وَمِنْهُ شُرْبُ مَالِكِ بْنِ سِنَانٍ[63] دَمَهُ يَوْمَ أُحُدٍ، وَمَصُّهُ إِيَّاهُ، وَتَسْوِيغُهُ ﷺ ذَلِكَ لَهُ. وَقَوْلُهُ: «لَنْ تُصِيبَهُ النَّارُ».[64]

وَمِثْلُهُ شُرْبُ عَبْدِ اللهِ بْنِ الزُّبَيْرِ دَمَ حِجَامَتِهِ، فَقَالَ لَهُ ﷺ: «وَيْلٌ لَكَ مِنَ النَّاسِ، وَوَيْلٌ لَهُمْ مِنْكَ»،[65] وَلَمْ يُنْكِرْهُ عَلَيْهِ.

وَغَيْرِهِ. وُلِدَ سَنَةَ (٤٠٠) هـ. وَمَاتَ سَنَةَ (٤٧٧) هـ. انْظُرْ تَرْجَمَتَهُ فِي سِيَرِ أَعْلَامِ النُّبَلَاءِ ٤٦٤/١٨.

٦١   أَخْرَجَهُ ابْنُ مَاجَه (١٤٦٧)، وَالْبَيْهَقِيُّ (٣٨٨/٣)، وَقَالَ الْبُوصِيرِيُّ: «هَذَا إِسْنَادٌ صَحِيحٌ وَرِجَالُهُ ثِقَاتٌ». وَصَحَّحَهُ الْحَاكِمُ (٣٦٢/١) وَقَالَ الذَّهَبِيُّ: «فِيهِ انْقِطَاعٌ»، وَانْظُرِ الْمَرَاسِيلَ لِأَبِي دَاوُدَ رقْم (٤١٥).

٦٢   أَخْرَجَهُ الْبَزَّارُ (٨٥٢) كَشْفُ الْأَسْتَارِ مِنْ حَدِيثِ ابْنِ عُمَرَ، وَصَحَّحَ إِسْنَادَهُ السُّيُوطِيُّ فِي الْمَنَاهِلِ (٧٠)، وَذَكَرَهُ الْحَافِظُ الْهَيْثَمِيُّ فِي مَجْمَعِ الزَّوَائِدِ ٣٨-٣٧/٩ وَقَالَ: «رَوَاهُ الْبَزَّارُ وَرِجَالُهُ رِجَالُ الصَّحِيحِ غَيْرَ عَلِيِّ بْنِ الْمُنْذِرِ وَهُوَ ثِقَةٌ». وَرَوَى التَّقْبِيلَ الْبُخَارِيُّ (٤٤٥٢، ٤٤٥٣) مِنْ حَدِيثِ عَائِشَةَ.

٦٣   مَالِكُ بْنُ سِنَانٍ هُوَ وَالِدُ أَبِي سَعِيدٍ الْخُدْرِيِّ.

٦٤   ذَكَرَهُ الْهَيْثَمِيُّ فِي مَجْمَعِ الزَّوَائِدِ ٢٧٠/٨ مِنْ حَدِيثِ أَبِي سَعِيدٍ الْخُدْرِيِّ، وَقَالَ: «رَوَاهُ الطَّبَرَانِيُّ فِي الْأَوْسَطِ وَلَمْ أَرَ فِي إِسْنَادِهِ مَنْ أُجْمِعَ عَلَى ضَعْفِهِ». وَأَخْرَجَهُ سَعِيدُ بْنُ مَنْصُورٍ وَالْبَيْهَقِيُّ مِنْ وَجْهٍ آخَرَ عَنْ عُمَرَ بْنِ السَّائِبِ أَنَّهُ بَلَغَهُ أَنَّ مَالِكًا وَالِدُ أَبِي سَعِيدٍ الْخُدْرِيِّ.... فَذَكَرَهُ.

٦٥   أَخْرَجَهُ الْبَزَّارُ (٢٤٣٦)، وَالْحَاكِمُ (٥٥٤/٣)، وَالْبَيْهَقِيُّ (٦٧/٧) وَغَيْرُهُ مِنْ حَدِيثِ عَبْدِ اللهِ بْنِ الزُّبَيْرِ. وَجَوَّدَ إِسْنَادَهُ السُّيُوطِيُّ فِي الْمَنَاهِلِ (٧٢)، وَقَالَ الْهَيْثَمِيُّ فِي الْمَجْمَعِ ٢٧٠/٨: «وَرِجَالُ الْبَزَّارِ رِجَالُ الصَّحِيحِ غَيْرَ هُنَيْدٍ

them were ordered to wash their mouths or refrain from repeating what they had done.

The story of the woman drinking his urine is authentic. She was called Barakah (there is some difference of opinion regarding her lineage) and Dāraquṭnī argued that Bukhārī and Muslim should have reported the story in their respective *Ṣaḥīḥ* collections.

Some took the opinion that Barakah was Umm Ayman, a woman who used to serve the Prophet ﷺ. She said: "The Prophet ﷺ used to have a bowl made from strips of date palm that was kept under his bed, which he would use to urinate during the night. One night he did so, but later found the bowl empty.

So, he asked Barakah what had happened. She said: 'I woke up during the night, suffering from thirst, so I drank [from the bowl] without knowing what it was.'" This narration was also reported by Ibn Jurayj[48] and others.

---

stomach will never bother you again!'" The chain of this narration was weak.

Another narration was reported by Bayhaqī (7/67) from Ibn Jurayj, from Ḥakīmah bint Umaymah, from her mother Umaymah, who said that the Prophet ﷺ urinated in a bowl made from strips of date palm, which he then placed under his bed. When he came to use the bowl again, he found that it was empty. He said to Barakah, a lady who used to serve him after arriving with Umm Ḥabībah from Ethiopia: "Where is the urine that was in this bowl?" She replied: "I drank it, O Messenger of Allah!" Haythamī said in *Majmaʿ al-Zawāʾid* (8/281): "It was related by Ṭabarānī. The narrators are *ṣaḥīḥ* apart from ʿAbdullāh ibn Aḥmad ibn Ḥanbal and Ḥakīmah, and they were both reliable."

Ibn Ḥajar said in *Talkhīṣ al-Ḥabīr* (1/31): "The narration has another chain of transmission related by ʿAbd al-Razzāq from Ibn Jurayj, which begins: 'I was informed that the Prophet ﷺ had urinated in a bowl made from strips of date palm.' The hadith follows a similar wording to the narration above, before adding: 'He said: "Here is to your health, Umm Yūsuf!"' Umm Yūsuf was a nickname for Barakah, and she never became sick after that until her final illness." This hadith was authenticated by Dāraquṭnī, as well as the present author.

Ibn Ḥajar commented, again in *Talkhīṣ al-Ḥabīr* (1/32): "Ibn Diḥyah takes the view that these were two separate incidents, and that Umm Ayman and Umm Yūsuf, both known as Barakah, were two different women. And Allah knows best."

Another hadith was reported by Abū Dāwūd (24) and Nasāʾī (1/31) from Ibn Jurayj, from Ḥakīmah, from her mother Umaymah bint Raqīqah, who said: "The Prophet ﷺ had a bowl made from strips of date palm, which he used to urinate in at night." This narration was authenticated by Ibn Ḥibbān in *Mawārid al-Ẓamʾān* (141). Also authenticated by Ḥākim (1/167), and Dhahabī concurred.

48 ʿAbd al-Malik ibn ʿAbd al-ʿAzīz ibn Jurayj al-Umawī, a righteous and trustworthy scholar

وَقَدْ رُوِيَ نَحْوٌ مِنْ هَذَا عَنْهُ ﷺ فِي امْرَأَةٍ شَرِبَتْ بَوْلَهُ، فَقَالَ لَهَا: «لَنْ تَشْتَكِي وَجَعَ بَطْنِكِ أَبَدًا»٦٦. وَلَمْ يَأْمُرْ وَاحِدًا مِنْهُمْ بِغَسْلِ فَمٍ، وَلَا نَهَاهُ عَنْ عَوْدِهِ. وَحَدِيثُ هَذِهِ الْمَرْأَةِ الَّتِي شَرِبَتْ بَوْلَهُ صَحِيحٌ، أَلْزَمَ الدَّارَقُطْنِيُّ مُسْلِمًا وَالْبُخَارِيَّ إِخْرَاجَهُ فِي الصَّحِيحِ. وَاسْمُ هَذِهِ الْمَرْأَةِ بَرَكَةُ، وَقِيلَ: هِيَ أُمُّ أَيْمَنَ، وَاخْتُلِفَ فِي نَسَبِهَا. وَكَانَتْ تَخْدُمُ رَسُولَ اللهِ ﷺ: قَالَتْ: وَكَانَ لِرَسُولِ اللهِ ﷺ قَدَحٌ مِنْ عَيْدَانٍ٦٧ يُوضَعُ تَحْتَ سَرِيرِهِ يَبُولُ فِيهِ مِنَ اللَّيْلِ، فَبَالَ فِيهِ

بْنِ الْقَاسِمِ وَهُوَ ثِقَةٌ».

٦٦ أَخْرَجَهُ - بِهَذَا اللَّفْظِ - أَبُو أَحْمَدَ الْعَسْكَرِيُّ وَأَبُو يَعْلَى فِي الْمُسْنَدِ الْكَبِيرِ مِنْ حَدِيثِ أُمِّ أَيْمَنَ. وَأَخْرَجَهُ الْحَسَنُ بْنُ سُفْيَانَ فِي مُسْنَدِهِ، وَالْحَاكِمُ (٤/٦٣-٦٤)، وَالدَّارَقُطْنِيُّ، وَالطَّبَرَانِيُّ، وَأَبُو نُعَيْمٍ مِنْ حَدِيثِ أَبِي مَالِكٍ النَّخَعِيِّ، عَنِ الْأَسْوَدِ بْنِ قَيْسٍ، عَنْ نُبَيْحٍ الْعَنَزِيِّ، عَنْ أُمِّ أَيْمَنَ قَالَتْ: قَامَ رَسُولُ اللهِ ﷺ مِنَ اللَّيْلِ إِلَى فَخَّارَةٍ فِي جَانِبِ الْبَيْتِ فَبَالَ فِيهَا... وَفِيهِ أَنَّهَا شَرِبَتْ بَوْلَهُ ﷺ، فَقَالَ: «أَمَا وَاللهِ! إِنَّهُ لَا يَجَعُكِ بَطْنُكِ أَبَدًا». وَإِسْنَادُهُ ضَعِيفٌ. وَأَخْرَجَهُ الْبَيْهَقِيُّ ٧/٦٧ مِنْ حَدِيثِ ابْنِ جُرَيْجٍ قَالَ أَخْبَرَتْنِي حَكِيمَةُ بِنْتُ أُمَيْمَةَ، عَنْ أُمَيْمَةَ أُمِّهَا أَنَّ النَّبِيَّ ﷺ كَانَ يَبُولُ فِي قَدَحٍ مِنْ عَيْدَانٍ، ثُمَّ وُضِعَ تَحْتَ سَرِيرِهِ فَجَاءَ فَأَرَادَهُ فَإِذَا الْقَدَحُ لَيْسَ فِيهِ شَيْءٌ، فَقَالَ لِامْرَأَةٍ - يُقَالُ لَهَا بَرَكَةُ كَانَتْ تَخْدُمُهُ لِأُمِّ حَبِيبَةَ، جَاءَتْ مَعَهَا مِنْ أَرْضِ الْحَبَشَةِ -: «أَيْنَ الْبَوْلُ الَّذِي كَانَ فِي هَذَا الْقَدَحِ؟» قَالَتْ: شَرِبْتُهُ يَا رَسُولَ اللهِ. وَقَالَ الْهَيْثَمِيُّ فِي الْمَجْمَعِ ٨/٢٧٠-٢٧١: «رَوَاهُ الطَّبَرَانِيُّ وَرِجَالُهُ رِجَالُ الصَّحِيحِ غَيْرَ عَبْدِ اللهِ بْنِ أَحْمَدَ بْنِ حَنْبَلٍ وَحَكِيمَةَ، وَكِلَاهُمَا ثِقَةٌ».

وَقَالَ الْحَافِظُ فِي تَلْخِيصِ الْحَبِيرِ ١/٣١: «وَلَهُ طَرِيقٌ أُخْرَى رَوَاهَا عَبْدُ الرَّزَّاقِ عَنِ ابْنِ جُرَيْجٍ، أُخْبِرَتْ أَنَّ النَّبِيَّ ﷺ كَانَ يَبُولُ فِي قَدَحٍ مِنْ عَيْدَانٍ، فَذَكَرَ مِثْلَ الرِّوَايَةِ السَّابِقَةِ، وَزَادَ: «قَالَ: صِحَّةً يَا أُمَّ يُوسُفَ! وَكَانَتْ تُكَنَّى أُمَّ يُوسُفَ، فَمَا مَرِضَتْ قَطُّ حَتَّى كَانَ مَرَضُهَا الَّذِي مَاتَتْ فِيهِ». وَصَحَّحَهُ الدَّارَقُطْنِيُّ وَالْقَاضِي عِيَاضٌ كَمَا تَرَى، وَقَالَ الْحَافِظُ فِي تَلْخِيصِ الْحَبِيرِ ١/٣٢: وَصَحَّحَ ابْنُ دِحْيَةَ أَنَّهُمَا قَضِيَّتَانِ وَقَعَتَا لِامْرَأَتَيْنِ، وَهُوَ وَاضِحٌ مِنِ اخْتِلَافِ السِّيَاقِ، وَوَضَّحَ أَنَّ بَرَكَةَ أُمَّ يُوسُفَ غَيْرُ بَرَكَةَ أُمِّ أَيْمَنَ مَوْلَاتِهِ، وَاللهُ أَعْلَمُ».

وَأَخْرَجَ أَبُو دَاوُدَ (٢٤)، وَالنَّسَائِيُّ (١/٣١) مِنْ طَرِيقِ ابْنِ جُرَيْجٍ، حَدَّثَتْنِي حَكِيمَةُ، عَنْ أُمِّهَا أُمَيْمَةَ بِنْتِ رُقَيْقَةَ أَنَّهَا قَالَتْ: كَانَ لِلنَّبِيِّ ﷺ قَدَحٌ مِنْ عَيْدَانٍ تَحْتَ سَرِيرِهِ يَبُولُ فِيهِ بِاللَّيْلِ. وَصَحَّحَهُ ابْنُ حِبَّانَ (١٤١) مَوَارِدُ الظَّمْآنِ، وَالْحَاكِمُ ١٦٧/١ وَوَافَقَهُ الذَّهَبِيُّ.

٦٧ عَيْدَانٌ: النَّخْلُ الطِّوَالُ الْمُنْجَرِدَةُ، الْوَاحِدَةُ: عَيْدَانَةٌ.

The Prophet ﷺ was born circumcised, with his umbilical cord cut.[49] His mother Āminah said: "He was born clean, with no filth on his body."[50]

ʿĀʾishah narrated: "I never saw the private parts of the Messenger of Allah ﷺ."[51] ʿAlī ؓ said: "The Prophet ﷺ asked me to ensure that no-one washed him except me, telling me: 'Any person who saw my *ʿawrah*[52] lost their sight.'"[53]

ʿIkrimah related from Ibn ʿAbbās ؓ that the Prophet ﷺ slept until he was breathing deeply, then woke up and prayed without performing wuḍūʾ (ablutions).[54] ʿIkrimah said: "That is because the Prophet ﷺ was protected."

---

of jurisprudence. He passed away in 150 AH, or possibly later. See *Siyar Aʿlām al-Nubalāʾ* (6/325-336).

49   As found in the narrations of al-ʿAbbās, his son ʿAbdullāh, Abū Hurayrah, Ibn ʿUmar, and Anas ibn Mālik. Authenticated by Ḍiyāʾ in *Al-Mukhtārah*. Ḥākim said in *Al-Mustadrak* (2/602): "There are numerous (*mutawātir*) reports of the Messenger of Allah ﷺ being born circumcised." Dhahabī said: "I do not know of the narration being authentic, let alone *mutawātir*." Ibn Kathīr said in *Al-Sīrah* (1/208-209): "Some of them said the narration was authentic from a number of sources, until it was considered to be *mutawātir*, but this should be re-examined." Ibn Qayyim al-Jawziyyah said in *Zād al-Maʿād* (1/81): "It was mentioned by Abū al-Faraj ibn al-Jawzī in *Al-Mawḍūʿāt*, and it is not a sound narration." Ibn Rajab said in *Majālis fī Sīrah al-Nabī* ﷺ, p. 64: "Imam Aḥmad did not consider this hadith to be authentic." See also the commentary of Ibn al-Qayyim in *Tuḥfah al-Mawdūd* (302-305).

50   Attributed in *Al-Manāhil*, p. 76, to Ibn Saʿd from his *Ṭabaqāt*.

51   Reported by Tirmidhī in *Al-Shamāʾil* (358), Ibn Mājah (1922), and Aḥmad (6/63) with one of the narrators unnamed.

52   The "*ʿawrah*" for a man is everything from the navel to below the knees.

53   Reported by Bazzār in *Kashf al-Astār* (848) and Bayhaqī in *Al-Dalāʾil*. Haythamī said in *Majmaʿ al-Zawāʾid* (9/36): "The chain contains Yazīd ibn Bilāl, whom Bukhārī said there was some discussion about. The rest of the narrators are reliable, but are also subject to differences of opinion." Dhahabī said in *Al-Mīzān*: "The narration of Yazīd ibn Bilāl from ʿAlī is not authentic."

54   Reported by Aḥmad (1/244) from the hadith of ʿIkrimah, and also included in the notes to the hadith describing the overnight stay of Ibn ʿAbbās with his aunt, Maymūnah (who was the wife of the Prophet ﷺ) which was reported, with different wordings, by Bukhārī (117) and Muslim (763/184).

لَيْلَةً، ثُمَّ افْتَقَدَهُ، فَلَمْ يَجِدْ فِيهِ شَيْئًا، فَسَأَلَ عَنْهُ بَرَكَةَ، فَقَالَتْ: قُمْتُ وَأَنَا عَطْشَانَةٌ فَشَرِبْتُهُ، وَأَنَا لَا أَعْلَمُ. رَوَى حَدِيثَهَا ابْنُ جُرَيْجٍ[68] وَغَيْرُهُ. وَكَانَ النَّبِيُّ ﷺ قَدْ وُلِدَ مَخْتُونًا مَقْطُوعَ السُّرَّةِ[69]. وَرُوِيَ فِي بَعْضِ الرِّوَايَاتِ عَنْ أُمِّهِ آمِنَةَ أَنَّهَا قَالَتْ: قَدْ وَلَدْتُهُ نَظِيفًا، مَا بِهِ قَذَرٌ[70]. وَعَنْ عَائِشَةَ رَضِي الله عنها: «مَا رَأَيْتُ فَرْجَ رَسُولِ اللهِ ﷺ قَطُّ»[71]. وَعَنْ عَلِيٍّ رَضِي الله عنه: «أَوْصَانِي النَّبِيُّ ﷺ لَا يُغَسِّلُهُ غَيْرِي، فَإِنَّهُ «لَا يَرَى أَحَدٌ عَوْرَتِي إِلَّا طُمِسَتْ عَيْنَاهُ»[72]. وَفِي حَدِيثِ عِكْرِمَةَ عَنِ ابْنِ عَبَّاسٍ رَضِي الله عنهما أَنَّهُ ﷺ نَامَ حَتَّى سَمِعَ لَهُ غَطِيطٌ[73]، فَقَامَ فَصَلَّى، وَلَمْ يَتَوَضَّأْ[74]. قَالَ عِكْرِمَةُ: لِأَنَّهُ ﷺ كَانَ مَحْفُوظًا.

---

68 هُوَ عَبْدُ الْمَلِكِ بْنُ عَبْدِ الْعَزِيزِ بْنِ جُرَيْجٍ الْأُمَوِيُّ، ثِقَةٌ فَقِيهٌ فَاضِلٌ. مَاتَ سَنَةَ (150) أَوْ بَعْدَهَا. انْظُرْ تَرْجَمَتَهُ فِي سِيَرِ أَعْلَامِ النُّبَلَاءِ 325/6-336.

69 وَرَدَ ذَلِكَ مِنْ حَدِيثِ الْعَبَّاسِ وَابْنِهِ عَبْدِ اللهِ، وَأَبِي هُرَيْرَةَ، وَابْنِ عُمَرَ، وَأَنَسِ بْنِ مَالِكٍ، وَصَحَّحَهُ الضِّيَاءُ فِي «الْمُخْتَارَةِ»، وَقَالَ الْحَاكِمُ فِي الْمُسْتَدْرَكِ 602/2: «وَقَدْ تَوَاتَرَتِ الْأَخْبَارُ أَنَّ رَسُولَ اللهِ ﷺ وُلِدَ مَخْتُونًا مَسْرُورًا» وَتَعَقَّبَهُ الذَّهَبِيُّ فَقَالَ: «مَا أَعْلَمُ صِحَّةَ ذَلِكَ، فَكَيْفَ يَكُونُ مُتَوَاتِرًا...». وَقَالَ الْحَافِظُ ابْنُ كَثِيرٍ فِي السِّيرَةِ 208/1-209: «وَقَدِ ادَّعَى بَعْضُهُمْ صِحَّتَهُ لِمَا وَرَدَ لَهُ مِنَ الطُّرُقِ حَتَّى زَعَمَ بَعْضُهُمْ أَنَّهُ مُتَوَاتِرٌ وَفِي هَذَا كُلِّهِ نَظَرٌ». وَقَالَ الْحَافِظُ ابْنُ الْقَيِّمِ فِي زَادِ الْمَعَادِ 81/1: «ذَكَرَهُ أَبُو الْفَرَجِ ابْنُ الْجَوْزِيِّ فِي الْمَوْضُوعَاتِ وَلَيْسَ فِيهِ حَدِيثٌ ثَابِتٌ». وَقَالَ الْحَافِظُ ابْنُ رَجَبٍ فِي مَجَالِسَ فِي سِيرَةِ النَّبِيِّ ﷺ ص (64) «وَلَمْ يَجْتَرِئْ أَبُو عَبْدِ اللهِ - أَيِ الْإِمَامُ أَحْمَدُ - عَلَى تَصْحِيحِ هَذَا الْحَدِيثِ». وَانْظُرِ الْأَحَادِيثَ 302-305 فِي تُحْفَةِ الْمَوْدُودِ لِابْنِ الْقَيِّمِ بِتَحْقِيقِي.

70 نَسَبَهُ فِي الْمَنَاهِلِ (76) إِلَى ابْنِ سَعْدٍ فِي طَبَقَاتِهِ.

71 رَوَاهُ التِّرْمِذِيُّ فِي الشَّمَائِلِ (352)، وَابْنُ مَاجَه (1922)، وَأَحْمَدُ 63/6 وَفِيهِ رَاوٍ لَمْ يُسَمَّ.

72 رَوَاهُ الْبَزَّارُ (848) كَشْفُ الْأَسْتَارِ، وَالْبَيْهَقِيُّ فِي الدَّلَائِلِ. قَالَ الْهَيْثَمِيُّ فِي الْمَجْمَعِ 36/9: «فِيهِ يَزِيدُ بْنُ بِلَالٍ، قَالَ الْبُخَارِيُّ: فِيهِ نَظَرٌ، وَبَقِيَّةُ رِجَالِهِ وُثِّقُوا، وَفِيهِمْ خِلَافٌ». وَقَالَ الذَّهَبِيُّ فِي الْمِيزَانِ: «يَزِيدُ بْنُ بِلَالٍ، عَنْ عَلِيٍّ، لَمْ يَصِحَّ حَدِيثُهُ».

73 الْغَطِيطُ: الصَّوْتُ الَّذِي يَخْرُجُ مَعَ نَفَسِ النَّائِمِ (النِّهَايَةُ).

74 أَخْرَجَهُ أَحْمَدُ 244/1 مِنْ حَدِيثِ عِكْرِمَةَ بِهِ. وَهُوَ طَرَفٌ مِنْ حَدِيثِ بَيْتُوتَةِ ابْنِ عَبَّاسٍ عِنْدَ خَالَتِهِ مَيْمُونَةَ زَوْجِ

HIS INTELLIGENCE, PERCEPTION, ELOQUENCE, AND GRACE

The Prophet ﷺ was blessed with dazzling intelligence, presence of mind, acute senses, eloquent tongue, graceful movements, and noble characteristics, and there is no doubt that he was the most knowledgeable and perspicacious of humankind. If anyone reflects on how he dealt with the personal and public affairs of the people and the politics of the general public and the elite, as well as the knowledge that poured from him and his explication of the Shariah without prior instruction, experience, or reading, they will have no doubts about his superior intellect and firm understanding.

Wahb ibn Munabbih[55] said: "I read seventy-one books and in every one I found that the Prophet ﷺ was the most intelligent, and the most astute in his opinions." Another wording records: "In every one I found that the intelligence Allah Exalted gave to the rest of humankind compared with the intelligence He gave to the Prophet ﷺ is nothing more than one grain taken from all the sand in the world."

Mujāhid observed: "When he was standing in prayer, the Messenger of Allah ﷺ could see people behind him as if they were in front of him."[56] This point was also articulated in explaining the words of Allah Exalted: "as well as your movements [in prayer]

---

55 Wahb ibn Munabbih ibn Kāmil al-Yamānī, an upstanding Follower. He died some time in the 110s AH.

56 Attributed in *Al-Manāhil*, p. 80, with this wording, to Ibn al-Mundhir and Bayhaqī in a *mursal* narration from Mujāhid.

فصل

وَأَمَّا وُفُورُ عَقْلِهِ، وَذَكَاءُ لُبِّهِ وَقُوَّةُ حَوَاسِّهِ، وَفَصَاحَةُ لِسَانِهِ، وَاعْتِدَالُ حَرَكَاتِهِ، وَحُسْنُ شَمَائِلِهِ، فَلَا مِرْيَةَ[75] أَنَّهُ كَانَ أَعْقَلَ النَّاسِ وَأَذْكَاهُمْ، وَمَنْ تَأَمَّلَ تَدْبِيرَهُ أَمْرَ بَوَاطِنِ الْخَلْقِ وَظَوَاهِرِهِمْ، وَسِيَاسَةَ الْعَامَّةِ وَالْخَاصَّةِ، مَعَ عَجِيبِ شَمَائِلِهِ، وَبَدِيعِ سِيَرِهِ، فَضْلًا عَمَّا أَفَاضَهُ مِنَ الْعِلْمِ، وَقَرَّرَهُ مِنَ الشَّرْعِ، دُونَ تَعَلُّمٍ سَبَقَ، وَلَا مُمَارَسَةٍ تَقَدَّمَتْ، وَلَا مُطَالَعَةٍ لِلْكُتُبِ مِنْهُ، لَمْ يَمْتَرِ[76] فِي رُجْحَانِ عَقْلِهِ وَثُقُوبِ فَهْمِهِ[77] لِأَوَّلِ بَدِيهَةٍ، وَهَذَا مَا لَا يُحْتَاجُ إِلَى تَقْرِيرِهِ لِتَحَقُّقِهِ.

وَقَالَ وَهْبُ بْنُ مُنَبِّهٍ[78]: قَرَأْتُ فِي أَحَدٍ وَسَبْعِينَ كِتَابًا، فَوَجَدْتُ فِي جَمِيعِهَا أَنَّ النَّبِيَّ ﷺ أَرْجَحُ النَّاسِ عَقْلًا، وَأَفْضَلُهُمْ رَأْيًا.

وَفِي رِوَايَةٍ أُخْرَى: فَوَجَدْتُ فِي جَمِيعِهَا أَنَّ اللهَ تَعَالَى لَمْ يُعْطِ جَمِيعَ النَّاسِ مِنْ بَدْءِ الدُّنْيَا إِلَى انْقِضَائِهَا مِنَ الْعَقْلِ فِي جَنْبِ عَقْلِهِ ﷺ إِلَّا كَحَبَّةِ رَمْلٍ مِنْ بَيْنِ رِمَالِ الدُّنْيَا.

النَّبِيَّ ﷺ. رَوَاهُ - بِأَلْفَاظٍ -: الْبُخَارِيُّ (١١٧)، وَمُسْلِمٌ (٧٦٣/١٨٤).

75 لَا مِرْيَةَ: لَا شَكَّ.

76 لَمْ يَمْتَرِ: لَمْ يَشُكَّ.

77 ثُقُوبُ فَهْمِهِ: إِصَابَتُهُ.

78 وَهْبُ بْنُ مُنَبِّهِ بْنِ كَامِلٍ الْيَمَانِيُّ، تَابِعِيٌّ ثِقَةٌ. مَاتَ سَنَةَ مِئَةٍ وَبِضْعَ عَشْرَةَ لِلْهِجْرَةِ (التَّقْرِيبُ).

along with [fellow] worshippers."[57] As the Prophet ﷺ said in a hadith reported in *Al-Muwaṭṭa'*: "Certainly, I can see you behind me."[58] Something similar was narrated by Anas ibn Mālik.[59]

'Ā'ishah said something similar, adding: "[It was] a blessing from Allah and an affirmation [of his Prophethood]."[60] In other reports, the Prophet ﷺ said: "I can look at whoever is behind me as I can look at those in front of me."[61] And in another wording: "I can see whoever is behind my back as I can see those in front of me."[62]

Baqī ibn Makhlad[63] reported from 'Ā'ishah, who said: "The Prophet ﷺ could see in the dark just as he could in the light."[64]

Likewise, there are many authentic narrations describing the ability of the Prophet ﷺ to see Angels[65] and *shayāṭīn*[66]. He was able to see al-Najāshī[67] when he performed his funeral prayer,[68]

---

57   *al-Shuʿarā'*, 219.

58   Reported by Mālik in *Al-Muwaṭṭa'* (1/167) from Abū Hurayrah. Also reported by Bukhārī (418) and Muslim (424). The scholars said: "The meaning is that Allah Exalted gave the Prophet ﷺ a sense in the nape of his neck that he used to 'see' what was happening behind him. And this was not the only time He disrupted [biological] norms in the case of the Prophet ﷺ."

59   Reported by Bukhārī (742) and Muslim (425).

60   Mentioned by Suyūṭī in *Al-Manāhil*, p. 81, without the chain of transmission.

61   Reported by Bazzār in *Kashf al-Astār* (504) and ʿAbd al-Razzāq in *Al-Muṣannaf* (3736) from Abū Hurayrah. Authenticated by Ḥākim (1/236) and Dhahabī concurred. Haythamī said in *Majmaʿ al-Zawā'id* (2/89): "The narrators are reliable."

62   Reported by Muslim (423) from Abū Hurayrah, with the phrase "behind me" instead of "behind my back".

63   An imam, leading example, and noble scholar of Islam. He authored a *Tafsīr* and a *Musnad*, both of which were undisputed in their excellence. He was born at the beginning of 200 AH, or just before, and died in 276 AH. See *Siyar Aʿlām al-Nubalā'* (13/285-296).

64   Reported by Ibn ʿAdiyy, and Bayhaqī in *Al-Dalā'il* who said: "The hadith is not strong." Also reported from Ibn ʿAbbās.

65   Reported by Bukhārī, Muslim, and others. See *Jāmiʿ al-Uṣūl* (2/367-369).

66   Reported by Bukhārī (461) and Muslim (541) from Abū Hurayrah, and by Muslim (542) from Abū al-Dardā'.

67   Al-Najāshī was the name given to all the kings of Ethiopia, but here refers to Aṣḥamah.

68   The prayer of the Prophet ﷺ was reported by Bukhārī (1317) and Muslim (952) from Abū Hurayrah, and by Muslim (953) from ʿImrān ibn Ḥuṣayn, although they do not mention him

وَقَالَ مُجَاهِدٌ: كَانَ رَسُولُ اللهِ ﷺ إِذَا قَامَ فِي الصَّلَاةِ يَرَى مَنْ خَلْفَهُ كَمَا يَرَى مَنْ بَيْنَ يَدَيْهِ[79]. وَبِهِ فُسِّرَ قَوْلُهُ تَعَالَى: ﴿وَتَقَلُّبَكَ فِي السَّاجِدِينَ﴾ [الشعراء: 219].

وَفِي المُوَطَّأِ[80] عَنْهُ ﷺ: «إِنِّي لَأَرَاكُمْ مِنْ وَرَاءِ ظَهْرِي»[81].

وَنَحْوُهُ عَنْ أَنَسٍ فِي الصَّحِيحَيْنِ[82]. وَعَنْ عَائِشَةَ رضي الله عنها مِثْلُهُ. قَالَتْ: زِيَادَةً زَادَهُ اللهُ تَعَالَى إِيَّاهَا فِي حُجَّتِهِ[83]. وَفِي بَعْضِ الرِّوَايَاتِ: «إِنِّي لَأَنْظُرُ مَنْ وَرَائِي كَمَا أَنْظُرُ إِلَى مَنْ بَيْنَ يَدَيَّ»[84]. وَفِي أُخْرَى: «إِنِّي لَأُبْصِرُ مِنْ قَفَايَ كَمَا أُبْصِرُ مِنْ بَيْنَ يَدَيَّ»[85]. وَحَكَى بَقِيُّ بْنُ مَخْلَدٍ[86] عَنْ عَائِشَةَ رضي الله عنها: كَانَ النَّبِيُّ ﷺ

---

79 عَزَاهُ السُّيُوطِيُّ فِي المَنَاهِلِ (80) إِلَى ابْنِ المُنْذِرِ وَالبَيْهَقِيِّ عَنْ مُجَاهِدٍ مُرْسَلًا بِهَذَا اللَّفْظِ.

80 المُوَطَّأُ: كِتَابٌ فِي الحَدِيثِ لِلْإِمَامِ مَالِكِ بْنِ أَنَسٍ. مَطْبُوعٌ بِتَحْقِيقِ مُحَمَّدٍ فُؤَادَ عَبْدِ البَاقِي وَغَيْرِهِ.

81 أَخْرَجَهُ مَالِكٌ فِي المُوَطَّأِ (167/1) مِنْ حَدِيثِ أَبِي هُرَيْرَةَ. قُلْتُ: وَأَخْرَجَهُ أَيْضًا البُخَارِيُّ (418)، وَمُسْلِمٌ (424). قَالَ العُلَمَاءُ: مَعْنَاهُ أَنَّ اللهَ تَعَالَى خَلَقَ لَهُ ﷺ إِدْرَاكًا فِي قَفَاهُ يُبْصِرُ بِهِ مِنْ وَرَائِهِ. وَقَدِ انْخَرَقَتِ العَادَةُ لَهُ ﷺ بِأَكْثَرَ مِنْ هَذَا.

82 أَخْرَجَهُ البُخَارِيُّ (742)، وَمُسْلِمٌ (425).

83 ذَكَرَهُ السُّيُوطِيُّ فِي المَنَاهِلِ (81) وَلَمْ يُخَرِّجْهُ.

84 أَخْرَجَهُ البَزَّارُ (504) كَشْفُ الأَسْتَارِ، وَعَبْدُ الرَّزَّاقِ فِي المُصَنَّفِ (3736) مِنْ حَدِيثِ أَبِي هُرَيْرَةَ، وَصَحَّحَهُ الحَاكِمُ 236/1، وَوَافَقَهُ الذَّهَبِيُّ. وَقَالَ الهَيْثَمِيُّ فِي المَجْمَعِ 89/2: «رِجَالُهُ ثِقَاتٌ».

85 أَخْرَجَهُ مُسْلِمٌ (423) مِنْ حَدِيثِ أَبِي هُرَيْرَةَ. وَفِيهِ «مِنْ وَرَائِي» بَدَلَ «مِنْ قَفَايَ».

86 هُوَ الإِمَامُ، القُدْوَةُ، شَيْخُ الإِسْلَامِ، الحَافِظُ صَاحِبُ التَّفْسِيرِ وَالمُسْنَدِ الَّذِينَ لَا نَظِيرَ لَهُمَا شَهِدَ سَبْعِينَ غَزْوَةً فِي سَبِيلِ اللهِ. وُلِدَ فِي حُدُودِ سَنَةِ (200) هـ أَوْ قَبْلَهَا بِقَلِيلٍ، وَمَاتَ سَنَةَ (276) هـ. انْظُرْ تَرْجَمَتَهُ فِي سِيَرِ أَعْلَامِ النُّبَلَاءِ 13/285-296.

Jerusalem when he described the city to the Quraysh,[69] and the Ka'bah whilst he was building his mosque [in Madinah].[70] It was also related that he saw eleven stars in the Pleiades[71].[72]

As Aḥmad ibn Ḥanbal and others commented, these were all things that would be impossible for anyone else to see. Some took the opinion that these reports refer only to his knowledge rather than actual sightings, but this contradicts the evident meaning of the narrations. This ability was one of the special qualities Allah gifted to His Prophets, so there is no reason they could not have taken place.

Abū Muhammad ('Abdullāh ibn Aḥmad al-'Adl) informed us in writing that Abū al-Ḥasan al-Muqrī al-Faraghānī narrated, from Umm al-Qāsim bint Abī Bakr, from her father, from Abū al-Ḥasan ('Alī ibn Muhammad al-Ḥasanī), from Muhammad ibn Muhammad ibn Sa'īd, from Muhammad ibn Aḥmad ibn Sulay-mān, from Muhammad ibn Muhammad ibn Marzūq, from Ham-mām,[73] who said: "Al-Ḥasan narrated, from Qatādah, from Yaḥyā ibn Waththāb, from Abū Hurayrah, that the Prophet ﷺ said: 'After Allah had revealed His Glory to Mūsā ﷺ, he was able to see an ant

---

seeing al-Najāshī.

69 Reported by Bukhārī (3886) and Muslim (170, 172).

70 Related by al-Zubayr ibn Bakkār in *Tārīkh al-Madīnah* from Ibn Shihāb and Nāfiʿ ibn Jubayr in a *mursal* narration. Al-Dalajī said: "It is *gharīb*."

71 A cluster of stars located in the Taurus constellation.

72 Suyūṭī said in *Al-Manāhil*, p. 88: "I did not come across this narration." Tilmisānī said that it is established in a narration from al-'Abbās ﷺ. Al-Khafājī says in *Nasīm al-Riyāḍ* (1/379), that it was mentioned by Ibn Abī Khaythamah.

73 A more accurate chain, as reported by Ṭabarānī in *Al-Ṣaghīr* (1/32), suggests it was Hānī' ibn Yaḥyā al-Sulamī who took the hadith from al-Ḥasan ibn Abī Ja'far (who was a weak narrator).

يَرَى فِي الظُّلْمَةِ كَمَا يَرَى فِي الضَّوْءِ^٨٧. وَالْأَخْبَارُ كَثِيرَةٌ صَحِيحَةٌ فِي رُؤْيَتِهِ ﷺ لِلْمَلَائِكَةِ وَالشَّيَاطِينِ^٨٨، وَرَفْعِ النَّجَاشِيِّ^٨٩ لَهُ حَتَّى صَلَّى عَلَيْهِ^٩٠، وَبَيْتِ الْمَقْدِسِ حِينَ وَصَفَهُ لِقُرَيْشٍ^٩١، وَالْكَعْبَةِ حِينَ بَنَى مَسْجِدَهُ^٩٢. وَقَدْ حُكِيَ عَنْهُ أَنَّهُ كَانَ يَرَى فِي الثُّرَيَّا^٩٣ أَحَدَ عَشَرَ نَجْمًا^٩٤. وَهَذِهِ كُلُّهَا مَحْمُولَةٌ عَلَى رُؤْيَةِ الْعَيْنِ، وَهُوَ قَوْلُ أَحْمَدَ بْنِ حَنْبَلٍ وَغَيْرِهِ. وَذَهَبَ بَعْضُهُمْ إِلَى رَدِّهَا إِلَى الْعِلْمِ، وَالظَّوَاهِرُ تُخَالِفُهُ، وَلَا إِحَالَةَ فِي ذَلِكَ، وَهِيَ مِنْ خَوَاصِّ الْأَنْبِيَاءِ وَخِصَالِهِمْ.

كَمَا أَخْبَرَنَا أَبُو مُحَمَّدٍ عَبْدُ اللهِ بْنُ أَحْمَدَ الْعَدْلُ مِنْ كِتَابِهِ، حَدَّثَنَا أَبُو الْحَسَنِ الْمُقْرِئُ الْفَرْغَانِيُّ، حَدَّثَتْنَا أُمُّ الْقَاسِمِ بِنْتُ أَبِي بَكْرٍ، عَنْ أَبِيهَا: حَدَّثَنَا الشَّرِيفُ أَبُو الْحَسَنِ عَلِيُّ بْنُ مُحَمَّدٍ الْحُسَيْنِيُّ، حَدَّثَنَا مُحَمَّدُ بْنُ مُحَمَّدِ بْنِ سَعِيدٍ، حَدَّثَنَا مُحَمَّدُ بْنُ أَحْمَدَ بْنِ سُلَيْمَانَ، حَدَّثَنَا مُحَمَّدُ بْنُ مُحَمَّدِ بْنِ مَرْزُوقٍ، حَدَّثَنَا هَانِئٌ^٩٥، حَدَّثَنَا

---

٨٧ أَخْرَجَهُ ابْنُ عَدِيٍّ وَالْبَيْهَقِيُّ فِي الدَّلَائِلِ. وَقَالَ: لَيْسَ بِالْقَوِيِّ. وَأَخْرَجَهُ أَيْضًا عَنِ ابْنِ عَبَّاسٍ.

٨٨ رُؤْيَتُهُ ﷺ الْمَلَائِكَةَ ثَابِتَةٌ فِي الصَّحِيحَيْنِ وَغَيْرِهِمَا. انْظُرْ لِذَلِكَ جَامِعَ الْأُصُولِ ٣٦٧/٢-٣٦٩. وَرُؤْيَتُهُ ﷺ لِلشَّيَاطِينِ ثَابِتَةٌ أَيْضًا فِي الْبُخَارِيِّ (٤٦١)، وَمُسْلِمٍ (٥٤١) مِنْ حَدِيثِ أَبِي هُرَيْرَةَ، وَمُسْلِمٍ (٥٤٢) مِنْ حَدِيثِ أَبِي الدَّرْدَاءِ.

٨٩ النَّجَاشِيُّ: لَقَبٌ لِكُلِّ مَنْ مَلَكَ الْحَبَشَةَ. وَالْمَقْصُودُ هُنَا: أَصْحَمَةُ.

٩٠ صَلَاتُهُ ﷺ عَلَى النَّجَاشِيِّ ثَابِتَةٌ فِي الْبُخَارِيِّ (١٣١٧)، وَمُسْلِمٍ (٩٥٢) مِنْ حَدِيثِ أَبِي هُرَيْرَةَ، وَفِي مُسْلِمٍ (٩٥٣) مِنْ حَدِيثِ عِمْرَانَ بْنِ حُصَيْنٍ. وَلَيْسَ فِيهَا رَفْعُ النَّجَاشِيِّ حِينَ صَلَّى عَلَيْهِ.

٩١ سَيَذْكُرُ فِيهِ الْمُصَنِّفُ حَدِيثًا وَهُوَ مُتَّفَقٌ عَلَيْهِ.

٩٢ رَوَاهُ الزُّبَيْرُ بْنُ بَكَّارٍ فِي تَارِيخِ الْمَدِينَةِ عَنِ ابْنِ شِهَابٍ وَنَافِعِ بْنِ جُبَيْرٍ مُرْسَلًا. قَالَ الدَّلَجِيُّ: وَهُوَ غَرِيبٌ.

٩٣ الثُّرَيَّا: مَجْمُوعَةٌ مِنَ النُّجُومِ فِي صُورَةِ الثَّوْرِ، وَكَلِمَةُ النَّجْمِ عَلَمٌ عَلَيْهَا (الْمُعْجَمُ الْوَسِيطُ).

٩٤ قَالَ السُّيُوطِيُّ فِي الْمَنَاهِلِ (٨٨): «لَمْ أَجِدْهُ». وَقَالَ التِّلِمْسَانِيُّ إِنَّهُ جَاءَ فِي حَدِيثٍ ثَابِتٍ مِنْ طَرِيقِ الْعَبَّاسِ رضى الله عنه، ذَكَرَهُ ابْنُ أَبِي خَيْثَمَةَ، قَالَهُ الْخَفَاجِيُّ فِي نَسِيمِ الرِّيَاضِ ٣٧٩/١.

٩٥ هَانِئُ بْنُ يَحْيَى السُّلَمِيُّ، أَخَذَ عَنِ الْحَسَنِ بْنِ أَبِي جَعْفَرٍ أَحَدِ الضُّعَفَاءِ، كَمَا فِي الطَّبَرَانِيِّ الصَّغِيرِ ٣٢/١.

on the smooth surface of a rock, in the darkness of night and from a distance of ten *farsakhs*[74]."[75]

With this being the case for Mūsā ﷺ, it is not hard to fathom the Prophet ﷺ being given the ability to see the things we have mentioned, especially after having been blessed with the prestige and honour of experiencing the miraculous Night Journey and witnessing from his Lord's greatest signs[76].

Other reports state that he knocked down Rukānah, who was the strongest of his people, and called him to embrace Islam.[77] He also wrestled with Abū Rukānah, who was a fearsome opponent, during the Days of Ignorance (Jāhiliyyah). They had three encounters, and the Messenger of Allah ﷺ defeated him every time.[78]

Abū Hurayrah said: "I never saw who walked more swiftly than the Messenger of Allah ﷺ. It was as if the Earth was rolled up for him. We would be struggling and exhausting ourselves whilst he remained unperturbed."[79]

The Prophet ﷺ only laughed to the extent of a smile; when he turned to face someone, he would face them directly; and when he walked, he did so with purpose and zeal, as if descending a gradient.[80]

---

74 One *farsakh* is equal to approximately three miles, 5544 metres, 12000 footsteps, or one and a half hours of travel. See *Al-Fiqh al-Islāmī wa Adillatuh* (1/175) by Dr. al-Zuḥaylī.

75 Reported by Ṭabarānī in *Al-Ṣaghīr* (1/32) from Muhammad ibn Marzūq with this chain of transmission. Haythamī said in *Majmaʿ al-Zawāʾid* (8/203): "The chain contains al-Ḥasan ibn Abī Jaʿfar al-Jafarī, and he was *matrūk* ("left", i.e., we do not take from him)."

76 Translator's note: A reference to *al-Najm*, 18.

77 Reported by Abū Dāwūd (4078), Tirmidhī (1784), Ḥākim (3/452), and Abū Yaʿlā (1412). Tirmidhī said: "This hadith is *ḥasan gharīb*, and its chain is not established." Ibn Ḥibbān said: "There is some discussion regarding the chain."

78 Al-Dalajī said: "Both this report and the report that he wrestled Abū Jahl are not authentic. In fact, they have no basis whatsoever."

79 Reported by Tirmidhī in *Al-Sunan* (3648) and in *Al-Shamāʾil* (122), Aḥmad (2/350), and Baghawī (3649). Authenticated by Ibn Ḥibbān in *Mawārid al-Ẓamʾān* (2118).

80 It was reported by Tirmidhī (3648) from Jābir ibn Samurah that the Prophet ﷺ would

الْحَسَنُ، عَنْ قَتَادَةَ، عَنْ يَحْيَى بْنِ وَثَّابٍ، عَنْ أَبِي هُرَيْرَةَ ﵁، عَنِ النَّبِيِّ ﷺ قَالَ: «لَمَّا تَجَلَّى اللهُ لِمُوسَى ﵇ كَانَ يُبْصِرُ النَّمْلَةَ عَلَى الصَّفَا فِي اللَّيْلَةِ الظَّلْمَاءِ مَسِيرَةَ عَشَرَةِ فَرَاسِخَ»⁹⁶. وَلَا يَبْعُدُ عَلَى هَذَا أَنْ يُخْتَصَّ نَبِيُّنَا عليه الصلاة والسلام بِمَا ذَكَرْنَاهُ مِنْ هَذَا الْبَابِ بَعْدَ الْإِسْرَاءِ وَالْحُظْوَةِ بِمَا رَأَى مِنْ آيَاتِ رَبِّهِ الْكُبْرَى. وَقَدْ جَاءَتِ الْأَخْبَارُ بِأَنَّهُ صَرَعَ رُكَانَةَ⁹⁷ أَشَدَّ أَهْلِ وَقْتِهِ، وَكَانَ دَعَاهُ إِلَى الْإِسْلَامِ، وَصَارَعَ أَبَا رُكَانَةَ فِي الْجَاهِلِيَّةِ، وَكَانَ شَدِيدًا، وَعَاوَدَهُ ثَلَاثَ مَرَّاتٍ، كُلَّ ذَلِكَ يَصْرَعُهُ رَسُولُ اللهِ ﷺ⁹⁸. وَقَالَ أَبُو هُرَيْرَةَ ﵁: مَا رَأَيْتُ أَحَدًا أَسْرَعَ مِنْ رَسُولِ اللهِ ﷺ فِي مَشْيِهِ، كَأَنَّمَا الْأَرْضُ تُطْوَى لَهُ، إِنَّا لَنُجْهِدُ أَنْفُسَنَا وَهُوَ غَيْرُ مُكْتَرِثٍ⁹⁹. وَفِي صِفَتِهِ ﷺ أَنَّ ضَحِكَهُ كَانَ تَبَسُّمًا، إِذَا الْتَفَتَ الْتَفَتَ مَعًا، وَإِذَا مَشَى مَشَى تَقَلُّعًا، كَأَنَّمَا يَنْحَطُّ مِنْ صَبَبٍ¹⁰⁰.

---

٩٦ أَخْرَجَهُ الطَّبَرَانِيُّ فِي الصَّغِيرِ ٣٢/١ مِنْ طَرِيقِ مُحَمَّدِ بْنِ مَرْزُوقٍ بِهَذَا الْإِسْنَادِ. قَالَ الْهَيْثَمِيُّ فِي الْمَجْمَعِ ٨/٢٠٣: «فِيهِ الْحَسَنُ بْنُ أَبِي جَعْفَرٍ الْجَفَرِيُّ، وَهُوَ مَتْرُوكٌ». (فَرَاسِخَ): جَمْعُ فَرْسَخٍ وَيُسَاوِي ثَلَاثَةَ أَمْيَالٍ أَوْ (٥٥٤٤) مِتْرًا، أَوْ ١٢٠٠٠ خَطْوَةً، حَوَالَيْ ٥٫١ سَاعَةً/ الْفِقْهُ الْإِسْلَامِيُّ وَأَدِلَّتُهُ لِلدُّكْتُورِ الزُّحَيْلِيِّ (١٧٥/١). (الصَّفَا): الْحِجَارَةُ الْمَلْسَاءُ.

٩٧ أَخْرَجَهُ أَبُو دَاوُدَ (٤٠٧٨)، وَالتِّرْمِذِيُّ (١٧٨٤)، وَالْحَاكِمُ (٤٥٢/٣)، وَأَبُو يَعْلَى (١٤١٢). قَالَ التِّرْمِذِيُّ: «هَذَا حَدِيثٌ حَسَنٌ غَرِيبٌ، وَإِسْنَادُهُ لَيْسَ بِالْقَائِمِ...» وَقَالَ ابْنُ حِبَّانَ: «فِي إِسْنَادِ خَبَرِهِ فِي الْمُصَارَعَةِ نَظَرٌ».

٩٨ قَالَ الدَّلَجِيُّ: هَذَا الْخَبَرُ، وَخَبَرُ أَنَّهُ صَارَعَ أَبَا جَهْلٍ وَصَرَعَهُ، لَمْ يَصِحَّا، بَلْ لَا أَصْلَ لَهُمَا.

٩٩ (غَيْرُ مُكْتَرِثٍ): يُقَالُ: مَا أَكْتَرِثُ لَهُ: مَا أُبَالِي بِهِ.

١٠٠ أَخْرَجَ التِّرْمِذِيُّ (٣٦٤٨) عَنْ جَابِرِ بْنِ سَمُرَةَ أَنَّهُ ﷺ كَانَ لَا يَضْحَكُ إِلَّا تَبَسُّمًا. وَفِي الْبَابِ عَنْ هِنْدِ بْنِ أَبِي هَالَةَ، وَعَبْدِ اللهِ بْنِ الْحَارِثِ وَغَيْرِهِمَا. وَالْتِفَاتُهُ ﷺ مَعًا وَمَشْيُهُ تَقَلُّعًا تَقَدَّمَ مِنْ حَدِيثِ عَلِيٍّ. (تَقَلُّعًا): أَرَادَ قُوَّةَ مَشْيِهِ كَأَنَّهُ يَرْفَعُ رِجْلَيْهِ مِنَ الْأَرْضِ رَفْعًا قَوِيًّا، لَا كَمَنْ يَمْشِي اخْتِيَالًا وَيُقَارِبُ خُطَاهُ. (كَأَنَّمَا يَنْحَطُّ مِنْ صَبَبٍ): أَيْ كَأَنَّهُ يَنْحَدِرُ مِنْ مَوْضِعٍ عَالٍ (جَامِعُ الْأُصُولِ ٢٢٧/١١).

THE ELOQUENCE AND BEAUTY OF
HIS LANGUAGE

The Prophet ﷺ was well-known for his eloquent language and powerful rhetoric. He was incredibly fluent and smooth in his speech, skillful in debate, clear, concise, lucid, and without affectation. The Prophet ﷺ was endowed with mastery of the language and was proficient in the full range of Arabic dialects.

He used [unusual] terms with their correct meanings, came up with creative and novel sayings, and spoke to each community in their own dialect and style. On many occasions, his Companions had to ask for an explanation of the words he used.

Anyone who has studied the narrations and biography of the Prophet ﷺ will attest to his linguistic abilities. The way he spoke to the Quraysh, the Anṣār, and the people of Najd and the Ḥijāz, was not the same as his manner with al-Hamdānī[81], Ṭihfah al-Nahadī[82], Qaṭan ibn Ḥārithah al-ʿUlaymī[83], al-Ashʿath ibn Qays[84], Wāʾil ibn

---

not laugh more than a smile. Other narrations describing these characteristics are reported from Hind ibn Abī Hālah, ʿAbdullāh ibn al-Ḥārith, and others.

81 Mālik ibn Namaṭ al-Hamdānī, a Companion who met the Prophet ﷺ when he returned from Tabūk. His biography can be found in *Usd al-Ghābah* (4/274).

82 Ṭihfah ibn Zuhayr al-Nahadī, a Companion who came to the Prophet ﷺ in 9 AH. See *Usd al-Ghābah* (2/478).

83 Qaṭan ibn Ḥārithah al-Kalbī al-ʿUlaymī, from the tribe of Banū ʿUlaym. When he went to the Prophet ﷺ, he asked him to supplicate for rain for himself and his people. See *Usd al-Ghābah* (4/108).

84 Al-Ashʿath ibn Qays al-Kindī. He came to the Prophet ﷺ as a Muslim in 10 AH. He abandoned his religion after the death of the Prophet ﷺ, but returned to Islam during the reign of Abū Bakr. He participated in the Battles of Yarmūk, al-Qādisiyyah, and other than them. He died in 42 AH. See *Usd al-Ghābah* (1/118).

فَصْل

وَأَمَّا فَصَاحَةُ اللِّسَانِ، وَبَلَاغَةُ الْقَوْلِ: فَقَدْ كَانَ رَسُولُ اللهِ ﷺ مِنْ ذَلِكَ بِالْمَحَلِّ الْأَفْضَلِ، وَالْمَوْضِعِ الَّذِي لَا يُجْهَلُ، سَلَاسَةَ طَبْعٍ، وَبَرَاعَةَ مَنْزَعٍ، وَإِيجَازَ مَقْطَعٍ، وَنَصَاعَةَ لَفْظٍ، وَجَزَالَةَ قَوْلٍ، وَصِحَّةَ مَعَانٍ، وَقِلَّةَ تَكَلُّفٍ، أُوتِيَ جَوَامِعَ الْكَلِمِ، وَخُصَّ بِبَدَائِعِ الْحِكَمِ، وَعُلِّمَ أَلْسِنَةَ الْعَرَبِ.

فَكَانَ يُخَاطِبُ كُلَّ أُمَّةٍ مِنْهَا بِلِسَانِهَا، وَيُحَاوِرُهَا بِلُغَاتِهَا، وَبَيَانِهَا فِي مَنْزَعِ بَلَاغَتِهَا، حَتَّى كَانَ كَثِيرٌ مِنْ أَصْحَابِهِ يَسْأَلُونَهُ فِي غَيْرِ مَوْطِنٍ عَنْ شَرْحِ كَلَامِهِ، وَتَفْسِيرِ قَوْلِهِ، مَنْ تَأَمَّلَ حَدِيثَهُ وَسِيرَهُ عَلِمَ ذَلِكَ وَتَحَقَّقَهُ.

وَلَيْسَ كَلَامُهُ مَعَ قُرَيْشٍ وَالْأَنْصَارِ وَأَهْلِ الْحِجَازِ وَنَجْدٍ كَكَلَامِهِ مَعَ ذِي الْمِشْعَارِ الْهَمْدَانِيِّ[101]، وَطِهْفَةَ النَّهْدِيِّ[102]، وَقَطَنِ بْنِ حَارِثَةَ الْعُلَيْمِيِّ[103]، وَالْأَشْعَثِ بْنِ قَيْسٍ[104]، وَوَائِلِ بْنِ حُجْرٍ الْكِنْدِيِّ[105]، وَغَيْرِهِمْ مِنْ أَقْيَالٍ[106] حَضْرَمَوْتَ،

---

101 هُوَ مَالِكُ بْنُ نَمَطِ الْهَمْدَانِيُّ. صَحَابِيٌّ، لَقِيَ النَّبِيَّ ﷺ مَرْجِعَهُ مِنْ تَبُوكَ. انْظُرْ تَرْجَمَتَهُ فِي أُسْدِ الْغَابَةِ ٢٧٤/٤.

102 هُوَ طِهْفَةُ بْنُ زُهَيْرٍ النَّهْدِيُّ، صَحَابِيٌّ وَفَدَ عَلَى النَّبِيِّ ﷺ سَنَةَ تِسْعٍ. انْظُرْ تَرْجَمَتَهُ فِي أُسْدِ الْغَابَةِ ٤٧٨/٢.

103 هُوَ قَطَنُ بْنُ حَارِثَةَ الْكَلْبِيُّ الْعُلَيْمِيُّ، مِنْ بَنِي عُلَيْمٍ، قَدِمَ عَلَى النَّبِيِّ ﷺ فَسَأَلَهُ عَنِ الدُّعَاءِ لَهُ وَلِقَوْمِهِ فِي غَيْثِ السَّمَاءِ/ أُسْدُ الْغَابَةِ ١٠٨/٤.

104 هُوَ الْأَشْعَثُ بْنُ قَيْسٍ الْكِنْدِيُّ. وَفَدَ إِلَى النَّبِيِّ ﷺ مُسْلِمًا سَنَةَ عَشْرٍ مِنَ الْهِجْرَةِ، وَارْتَدَّ بَعْدَ وَفَاتِهِ ﷺ، وَرَجَعَ إِلَى الْإِسْلَامِ فِي عَهْدِ أَبِي بَكْرٍ، وَشَهِدَ الْيَرْمُوكَ وَالْقَادِسِيَّةَ وَغَيْرَهُمَا، تُوُفِّيَ سَنَةَ (٤٢) هـ . انْظُرْ تَرْجَمَتَهُ فِي أُسْدِ الْغَابَةِ ١١٨/١.

105 صَحَابِيٌّ جَلِيلٌ، كَانَ مِنْ مُلُوكِ الْيَمَنِ، مَاتَ فِي وِلَايَةِ مُعَاوِيَةَ (التَّقْرِيب).

106 (أَقْيَالٌ): جَمْعُ قَيْلٍ: وَهُوَ أَحَدُ مُلُوكِ حِمْيَرَ دُونَ الْمَلِكِ الْأَعْظَمِ (النِّهَايَة).

Ḥujr al-Kindī[85], and others from the Himyarite chiefs of Ḥaḍra-mawt and kings of Yemen.[86]

Let us observe the message he wrote to the Hamdān tribe: "You have the highlands, the resting places, and the wild. Your cattle eat the fodder and graze on untouched land. We are entitled to whatever is agreed, either by treaty or [your acceptance of] Islam, from their camels, sheep, and date palms. From the *zakāh*, they are entitled to the *thalb*[87], *nāb*[88], *faḍīl*[89], *fāriḍ*[90], *dājin*[91], and the *ḥawārī*[92] rams, and they are obliged to pay *zakāh* on their *ṣāligh*[93] and *qāriḥ*[94]."[95]

He said to the Nahd tribe: "O Allah! Bless them in their milk, butter, and yoghurt. Make their crops flourish, send their shepherds to abundance, and cause scarcity to flee from them. Bless them in their wealth and their children. Whoever performs the prayer is a Muslim, and whoever gives *zakāh* is a *muḥsin*[96], and whoever bears witness that there is no-one worthy of worship except Allah

---

85   A noble Companion from Yemen. He died during the reign of Muʿāwiyah.

86   Translator's note: Meaning, the Prophet ﷺ spoke to different people in different dialects and styles, of which the examples that follow are included as evidence.

87   An aged male camel whose teeth have cracked.

88   An elderly female camel.

89   An infant camel who has been weaned and then separated from its mother.

90   An elderly camel.

91   Domesticated animals that people feed in their homes and do not go out to graze on the land.

92   Sheep used for their leather.

93   Six-year-old cattle and sheep.

94   Five-year-old horses.

95   Attributed in *Al-Manāhil*, p. 94, to al-Zajjājī in a *muʿḍal* narration from his *Kitāb al-Amānī*. Translator's note: "Muʿḍal" means "problematic" i.e., two or more consecutive narrators have been omitted from the chain.

96   Translator's note: "An excellent one"; the highest position to aim a worshipper to aim for after Muslim (lit., "submitter") and *muʾmin* ("believer"). See the famous hadith of Jibrīl ﷺ, as reported by Bukhārī (50) from Abū Hurayrah and Muslim (8) from ʿUmar ibn al-Khaṭṭāb.

وَمُلُوكِ اليَمَنِ. وَانْظُرْ كِتَابَهُ إِلَى هَمَدَانَ¹⁰⁷: «إِنَّ لَكُمْ فِرَاعَهَا وَوِهَاطَهَا وَعَزَازَهَا، تَأْكُلُونَ عِلَافَهَا وَتَرْعَوْنَ عَفَاءَهَا، لَنَا مِنْ دِفْئِهِمْ وَصِرَامِهِمْ مَا سَلَّمُوا بِالمِيثَاقِ وَالأَمَانَةِ، وَلَهُمْ مِنَ الصَّدَقَةِ الثَّلْبُ، وَالنَّابُ، وَالفَصِيلُ، وَالفَارِضُ الدَّاجِنُ، وَالكَبْشُ الحَوَرِيُّ، وَعَلَيْهِمْ فِيهَا الصَّالِغُ، وَالقَارِحُ»¹⁰⁸.

وَقَوْلُهُ ﷺ لِنَهْدٍ¹⁰⁹: «اللَّهُمَّ بَارِكْ لَهُمْ فِي مَحْضِهَا وَمَخْضِهَا وَمَذْقِهَا، وَابْعَثْ رَاعِيَهَا فِي الدَّثْرِ، وَافْجُرْ لَهُ الثَّمَدَ، وَبَارِكْ لَهُمْ فِي المَالِ وَالوَلَدِ، مَنْ أَقَامَ الصَّلَاةَ كَانَ مُسْلِمًا، وَمَنْ آتَى الزَّكَاةَ كَانَ مُحْسِنًا، وَمَنْ شَهِدَ أَنْ لَا إِلَهَ إِلَّا اللهُ كَانَ مُخْلِصًا، لَكُمْ يَا بَنِي نَهْدٍ وَدَائِعُ الشِّرْكِ، وَوَضَائِعُ المُلْكِ، لَا تُلْطِطْ فِي الزَّكَاةِ، وَلَا تُلْحِدْ فِي الحَيَاةِ، وَلَا تَتَثَاقَلْ عَنِ الصَّلَاةِ».

وَكَتَبَ: «لَهُمْ فِي الوَظِيفَةِ الفَرِيضَةُ، وَلَكُمُ الفَارِضُ¹¹⁰ وَالفَرِيشُ، وَذُو

---

١٠٧ هَمَدَانُ: اسْمُ قَبِيلَةٍ.

١٠٨ عَزَاهُ فِي المَنَاهِلِ (٩٤) إِلَى الزَّجَاجِيِّ فِي أَمَالِيهِ مُعْضَلًا. (فِرَاعَهَا): الفِرَاعُ: مَا عَلَا مِنَ الأَرْضِ وَارْتَفَعَ. (وِهَاطَهَا): الوِهَاطُ: المَوَاضِعُ المُطْمَئِنَّةُ، وَاحِدُهَا: وَهْطٌ. (عَزَازَهَا): العَزَازُ: مَا صَلُبَ مِنَ الأَرْضِ وَاشْتَدَّ وَخَشِنَ، وَإِنَّمَا يَكُونُ فِي أَطْرَافِهَا. (عِلَافَهَا): جَمْعُ عَلَفٍ، وَهُوَ مَا تَأْكُلُهُ المَاشِيَةُ. (عَفَاءَهَا) أَيْ: مَا لَيْسَ فِيهِ لِأَحَدٍ أَثَرٌ، أَوْ مَا لَيْسَ لِأَحَدٍ فِيهِ مِلْكٌ. (مِنْ دِفْئِهِمْ): أَيْ مِنْ إِبِلِهِمْ وَغَنَمِهِمْ. (وَصِرَامِهِمْ): أَيْ مِنْ نَخْلِهِمْ. (المِيثَاقُ) الإِسْلَامُ أَوِ العَهْدُ. (الثَّلْبُ وَالنَّابُ): الثَّلْبُ مِنْ ذُكُورِ الإِبِلِ: الَّذِي هَرِمَ وَتَكَسَّرَتْ أَسْنَانُهُ. وَالنَّابُ: المُسِنَّةُ مِنْ إِنَاثِهَا. (الفَصِيلُ): وَلَدُ الإِبِلِ بَعْدَ فِطَامِهِ وَفَصْلِهِ عَنْ أُمِّهِ. (الفَارِضُ): المُسِنُّ مِنَ الإِبِلِ. (الدَّاجِنُ): مَا يَعْلِفُهُ النَّاسُ فِي مَنَازِلِهِمْ وَلَا يَذْهَبُ إِلَى المَرْعَى. (الحَوَرِيُّ) مَنْسُوبٌ إِلَى الحَوَرِ، وَهِيَ جُلُودٌ تُتَّخَذُ مِنْ جُلُودِ الضَّأْنِ. وَقِيلَ: هُوَ مَا دُبِغَ مِنَ الجُلُودِ بِغَيْرِ القَرَظِ / النِّهَايَةُ. (الصَّالِغُ): هُوَ مِنَ البَقَرِ وَالغَنَمِ الَّذِي كَمُلَ وَانْتَهَى سِنُّهُ، وَذَلِكَ فِي السَّنَةِ السَّادِسَةِ. (القَارِحُ): هُوَ مِنَ الخَيْلِ مَا دَخَلَ فِي السَّنَةِ الخَامِسَةِ، وَجَمْعُهُ: قُرَّحٌ.

١٠٩ نَهْدٌ: اسْمُ القَبِيلَةِ.

١١٠ فِي نُسَخَةٍ: «العَارِضُ»، قَالَ ابْنُ الأَثِيرِ: «العَارِضُ: المَرِيضَةُ. وَقِيلَ: هِيَ الَّتِي أَصَابَهَا كَسْرٌ: أَيْ إِنَّا لَا نَأْخُذُ ذَاتَ عَيْبٍ فَنَضُرُّ بِالصَّدَقَةِ.

is sincere. O Children of Nahd! Your contracts and agreements[97] are valid, and your earnings[98] from before Islam will remain with you. Do not withhold your *zakāh* or abandon the prayer, and do not deviate from the truth for as long as you live."

And he wrote to them: "The elderly animals are for you,[99] as are the *ʿāriḍ*[100], *farīsh*[101], horses tamed for riding, and the boisterous colts. Do not prevent your cattle [from enjoying the pastureland] or cut down the thorny shrubs [that your camels enjoy]. Your milking cows will not be sequestered[102] so long as you do not turn a blind eye[103] or cut your leads[104]. Whoever agrees must fulfil their pledge, and whoever turns away must ascend to higher ground[105]."[106]

His letter to Wāʾil ibn Ḥujr opened with: "To the chiefs of Yemen; the radiant, handsome statesmen." And continued: "The minimum *zakāh* due on lambs [is forty]. Give neither the lean or fat, but those that are in between. One-fifth is due on treasure [ac-

---

97   It is possible that he was referring to wealth that had been deposited with them by those who had not embraced Islam. It was permissible for them, because it had been acquired without any conditions attached.

98   This was said to refer to wealth that was earned from employment and war spoils during Jāhiliyyah.

99   i.e., they are not taken in *zakāh*.

100   A camel who has been sick and recovered.

101   A female camel who was recently given birth.

102   Ibn al-Athīr comments: "The Prophet ﷺ did not want the milking cows crowded together and kept away from the pastureland whilst the other animals were being gathered and counted, because that would be harmful to them."

103   Meaning: "…so long as your hearts do not fall into hypocrisy or deviate from the truth".

104   Meaning: "…or break your covenants". We find an explanation of the metaphor in *Al-Nihāyah*: "The Prophet ﷺ likens the breaking of covenants to an animal cutting the lead from around its neck, because if it did so, it would be released from its responsibilities."

105   Meaning: "…and whoever attempts to shirk their responsibilities in giving *zakāh* will be obligated to give more than is usually required as a form of penalty."

106   Reported by Abū Nuʿaym in *Maʿrifah al-Ṣaḥābah* and Daylamī in *Musnad al-Firdaws*, both from ʿImrān ibn Ḥuṣayn, and by Abū Nuʿaym from Ḥudhayfah ibn al-Yamān in a condensed form. See *Al-Manāhil*, p. 95.

الْعِنَانِ الرَّكُوبِ، وَالْفَلُوَّ الصَّبِيسَ، لَا يُمْنَعُ سَرْحُكُمْ، وَلَا يُعْضَدُ طَلْحُكُمْ، وَلَا يُحْبَسُ دَرُّكُمْ مَا لَمْ تُضْمِرُوا الْإِمَاقَ، وَتَأْكُلُوا الرِّبَاقَ، مَنْ أَقَرَّ فَلَهُ الْوَفَاءُ بِالْعَهْدِ وَالذِّمَّةِ، وَمَنْ أَبَى فَعَلَيْهِ الرِّبْوَةُ».[1]

---

[1] أَخْرَجَهُ كَمَا فِي الْمَنَاهِلِ رَقْمِ (٩٥): أَبُو نُعَيْمٍ فِي مَعْرِفَةِ الصَّحَابَةِ، وَالدَّيْلَمِيُّ فِي مُسْنَدِ الْفِرْدَوْسِ مِنْ حَدِيثِ عِمْرَانَ بْنِ حُصَيْنٍ. وَأَبُو نُعَيْمٍ مِنْ حَدِيثِ حُذَيْفَةَ بْنِ الْيَمَانِ مُخْتَصَرًا. (مَحْضِهَا): اللَّبَنُ الْخَالِصُ. (مَحْضِهَا): اللَّبَنُ الْمَمْحُوضُ الَّذِي أُخِذَ زَبَدُهُ. (مَذْقِهَا): اللَّبَنُ الْمَخْلُوطُ بِالْمَاءِ. (الدَّثْرُ): الْمَالُ الْكَثِيرُ. وَقِيلَ: أَرَادَ بِالدَّثْرِ هَا هُنَا الْخِصْبَ وَالنَّبَاتَ الْكَثِيرَ/ النِّهَايَةِ. (وَأَجْرُهُ لَهُ الثَّمَدَ): الثَّمَدُ: الْمَاءُ الْقَلِيلُ. أَيِ الْأَجْرُهُ لَهُ حَتَّى يَصِيرَ كَثِيرًا/ النِّهَايَةِ. (وَدَائِعُ الشِّرْكِ) أَيِ الْعُهُودَ وَالْمَوَاثِيقَ. وَقِيلَ: يَحْتَمِلُ أَنْ يُرِيدَ بِهَا مَا كَانُوا اسْتَوْدَعُوهُ مِنْ أَمْوَالِ الْكُفَّارِ الَّذِينَ لَمْ يَدْخُلُوا فِي الْإِسْلَامِ: أَرَادَ إِحْلَالَهَا لَهُمْ، لِأَنَّهَا مَالُ كَافِرٍ قُدِرَ عَلَيْهِ مِنْ غَيْرِ عَهْدٍ وَلَا شَرْطٍ/ النِّهَايَةِ بِاخْتِصَارٍ. (وَضَائِعُ الْمُلْكِ): الْوَضَائِعُ: جَمْعُ وَضِيعَةٍ، وَهِيَ الْوَظِيفَةُ الَّتِي تَكُونُ عَلَى الْمِلْكِ، وَهِيَ مَا يَلْزَمُ النَّاسَ فِي أَمْوَالِهِمْ؛ مِنَ الصَّدَقَةِ وَالزَّكَاةِ: أَيْ لَكُمُ الْوَظَائِفُ الَّتِي تَلْزَمُ الْمُسْلِمِينَ، لَا نَتَجَاوَزُهَا مَعَكُمْ، وَلَا نَزِيدُ عَلَيْكُمْ فِيهَا شَيْئًا. وَقِيلَ: مَعْنَاهُ مَا كَانَ مُلُوكُ الْجَاهِلِيَّةِ يُوَظِّفُونَ عَلَى رَعِيَّتِهِمْ، وَيَسْتَأْثِرُونَ بِهِ فِي الْحَرْبِ وَغَيْرِهَا مِنَ الْمَغْنَمِ: أَيْ لَا نَأْخُذُ مِنْكُمْ مَا كَانَ مُلُوكُكُمْ وَظَّفُوهُ عَلَيْكُمْ، بَلْ هُوَ لَكُمْ/ النِّهَايَةِ. (لَا تُلْطَطُ فِي الزَّكَاةِ) أَيْ: لَا تَمْنَعُهَا. (وَلَا تُلْحِدْ فِي الْحَيَاةِ) أَيْ: لَا تَمِيلُ عَنِ الْحَقِّ مَا دُمْتَ حَيًّا. قَالَ فِي النِّهَايَةِ: «قَالَ أَبُو مُوسَى: هَكَذَا رَوَاهُ الْقُتَيْبِيُّ. عَلَى النَّهْيِ لِلْوَاحِدِ. وَالَّذِي رَوَاهُ غَيْرُهُ: «... وَلَا تَثَاقُلْ عَنِ الصَّلَاةِ، وَلَا يُلْطَطُ فِي الزَّكَاةِ، وَلَا يُلْحَدْ فِي الْحَيَاةِ» وَهُوَ الْوَجْهُ لِأَنَّهُ خِطَابٌ لِلْجَمَاعَةِ وَاقِعٌ عَلَى مَا قَبْلَهُ». (وَلَا تَتَثَاقَلْ عَنِ الصَّلَاةِ) أَيْ لَا تَتَبَاطَأْ عَنْ أَدَائِهَا فِي أَوْقَاتِهَا. (فِي الْوَظِيفَةِ الْفَرِيضَةِ) جَاءَتْ هَذِهِ الْعِبَارَةُ فِي النِّهَايَةِ: «لَكُمْ فِي الْوَظِيفَةِ الْفَرِيضَةِ» أَيْ: الْهَرِمَةُ الْمُسِنَّةُ، يَعْنِي هِيَ لَكُمْ وَلَا تُؤْخَذُ مِنْكُمْ فِي الزَّكَاةِ. وَيُرْوَى «عَلَيْكُمْ فِي الْوَظِيفَةِ الْفَرِيضَةِ» أَيْ فِي كُلِّ نِصَابٍ مَا فُرِضَ فِيهِ.

(الْفَرِيشُ): هِيَ النَّاقَةُ الْحَدِيثَةُ الْوَضْعِ (النِّهَايَةِ).

(ذُو الْعِنَانِ الرَّكُوبِ): يُرِيدُ الْفَرَسَ الذَّلُولَ. وَالْعِنَانُ: سَيْرُ اللِّجَامِ. (الْفَلُوُّ): الْمُهْرُ.

(الصَّبِيسُ): الصَّعْبُ الْعَسِرُ. (لَا يُمْنَعُ سَرْحُكُمْ): أَيْ لَا تُمْنَعُ مَاشِيَتُكُمْ عَنْ مَرْعًى تُرِيدُهُ.

(يُعْضَدُ): يُقْطَعُ. (طَلْحُكُمْ): الطَّلْحُ: شَجَرٌ عِظَامٌ مِنْ شَجَرِ الْعِضَاهِ تَرْعَاهُ الْإِبِلُ/ الْمُعْجَمُ الْوَسِيطُ. (لَا يُحْبَسُ دَرُّكُمْ): الدَّرُّ: الْمَاشِيَةُ الَّتِي تُدِرُّ لَبَنًا. قَالَ ابْنُ الْأَثِيرِ فِي النِّهَايَةِ: «أَرَادَ أَنَّهَا لَا تُحْشَرُ إِلَى الْمُصَدِّقِ، وَلَا تُحْبَسُ عَنِ الْمَرْعَى إِلَى أَنْ تَجْتَمِعَ الْمَاشِيَةُ ثُمَّ تُعَدَّ؛ لِمَا فِي ذَلِكَ مِنَ الْإِضْرَارِ بِهَا».

(مَا لَمْ تُضْمِرُوا الْإِمَاقَ): أَيِ النِّفَاقَ، يَعْنِي: مَا لَمْ تَضِقْ قُلُوبُكُمْ عَنِ الْحَقِّ/ النِّهَايَةِ. (مَا لَمْ تَأْكُلُوا الرِّبَاقَ): الرِّبَاقُ جَمْعُ رِبْقٍ: وَهُوَ حَبْلٌ ذُو عُرًى، أَوْ حَلْقَةٌ لِرَبْطِ الدَّوَابِّ. قَالَ فِي النِّهَايَةِ: «شَبَّهَ مَا يَلْزَمُ الْأَعْنَاقَ مِنَ الْعَهْدِ بِالرِّبَاقِ، وَاسْتَعَارَ الْأَكْلَ لِنَقْضِ الْعَهْدِ، فَإِنَّ الْبَهِيمَةَ إِذَا أَكَلَتِ الرِّبْقَ خَلَصَتْ مِنَ الشَّدِّ». (مَنْ أَبَى فَعَلَيْهِ الرِّبْوَةُ): أَيْ مَنْ تَقَاعَدَ عَنْ أَدَاءِ الزَّكَاةِ فَعَلَيْهِ الزِّيَادَةُ فِي الْفَرِيضَةِ الْوَاجِبَةِ، كَالْعُقُوبَةِ لَهُ (النِّهَايَةِ).

quired before Islam]. If an unmarried person commits fornication, give them one hundred lashes and banish them for one year. If a married person commits fornication, they should be stoned. Do not be lax or hesitant in establishing the religion, and do not conceal the obligations due to Allah. Every intoxicant is forbidden. Wā'il ibn Ḥujr is appointed leader of the chiefs of Yemen."[107]

Compare these letters with the message he wrote to Anas about charity.[108] When speaking to different tribes, the Prophet ﷺ employed the style and language particular to their dialects. This was in order to effectively communicate what had been revealed to them in a way they would understand. In the same way, when he said to 'Atiyyah al-Sa'dī, "The upper hand is the giver and the lower hand is the receiver", 'Atiyyah confirmed: "The Messenger of Allah ﷺ spoke to us in our dialect."[109]

In another narration, when al-'Āmirī asked him for something, the Prophet replied with "*Sal 'ank*", which meant "Ask for whatever you wish" in the dialect of the Banū 'Āmir tribe.[110]

The linguistic mastery of the Prophet ﷺ is well-known, and many volumes have been compiled examining the eloquence, wisdom, and comprehensive nature of his everyday speech, and analysing the meaning of his words and turns of phrase. The Prophet of Allah ﷺ was unparalleled in his fluency and expression.

---

107 Attributed in *Al-Manāhil*, p. 96, to Ṭabarānī from *Al-Ṣaghīr* and Khaṭṭābī from *Al-Gharā'ib*.

108 Reported by Isḥāq ibn Rāhawayh in his *Musnad*, as found in *Fatḥ al-Bārī* (3/318). Also reported by Dāraquṭnī (2/114-115), who said: "The chain is ṣaḥīḥ and all the narrators are trustworthy." Reported by Bukhārī (1454) from the chain of Thumāmah ibn 'Abdullāh ibn Anas, from Anas, who said that Abū Bakr ﷺ wrote for him when he was sent to Bahrain: "In the Name of Allah, the Most Compassionate, the Most Merciful, this is the obligatory amount of charity…"

109 Reported by Bayhaqī (4/198). Authenticated by Ḥākim (4/327) and Dhahabī concurred.

110 Reported by Abū Nu'aym in *Al-Dalā'il* from Shaddād ibn Aws. See also *Al-Manāhil*, p. 98.

وَفِي كِتَابِهِ ﷺ لِوَائِلِ بْنِ حُجْرٍ: «إِلَى الأَقْيَالِ العَبَاهِلَةِ، وَالأَرْوَاعِ المَشَابِيبِ». وَفِيهِ: «فِي التِّيعَةِ شَاةٌ، لَا مُقَوَّرَةُ الأَلْيَاطِ، وَلَا ضِنَاكٌ، وَأَنْطُوا الثَّبَجَةَ، وَفِي السُّيُوبِ الخُمُسُ، وَمَنْ زَنَى مِمْ بِكْرٍ فَاصْقَعُوهُ مِائَةً، وَاسْتَوْفِضُوهُ عَامًا، وَمَنْ زَنَى مِمْ ثَيِّبٍ فَضَرِّجُوهُ بِالأَضَامِيمِ، وَلَا تَوْصِيمَ فِي الدِّينِ، وَلَا غُمَّةَ فِي فَرَائِضِ اللهِ، وَكُلُّ مُسْكِرٍ حَرَامٌ، وَوَائِلُ ابْنُ حُجْرٍ يَتَرَفَّلُ عَلَى الأَقْيَالِ».[112]

أَيْنَ هَذَا مِنْ كِتَابِهِ ﷺ لِأَنَسٍ فِي الصَّدَقَةِ المَشْهُورِ؟!.[113]

لَمَّا كَانَ كَلَامُ هَؤُلَاءِ عَلَى هَذَا الحَدِّ، وَبَلَاغَتُهُمْ عَلَى هَذَا النَّمَطِ، وَأَكْثَرُ اسْتِعْمَالِهِمْ هَذِهِ الأَلْفَاظِ، اسْتَعْمَلَهَا مَعَهُمْ لِيُبَيِّنَ لِلنَّاسِ مَا نُزِّلَ إِلَيْهِمْ، وَلِيُحَدِّثَ النَّاسَ بِمَا يَعْلَمُونَ.

وَكَقَوْلِهِ ﷺ فِي حَدِيثِ عَطِيَّةَ السَّعْدِيِّ: «فَإِنَّ اليَدَ العُلْيَا هِيَ المُنْطِيَةُ

---

١١٢ نَسَبَهُ السُّيُوطِيُّ فِي المَنَاهِلِ (٩٦) إِلَى الطَّبَرَانِيِّ فِي الصَّغِيرِ، وَالخَطَّابِيُّ فِي الغَرَائِبِ. (الأَقْيَالُ العَبَاهِلَةِ) الأَقْيَالُ: تَقَدَّمَ شَرْحُهَا. (العَبَاهِلَةِ): قَالَ فِي النِّهَايَةِ: هُمُ الَّذِينَ أُقِرُّوا عَلَى مُلْكِهِمْ لَا يُزَالُونَ عَنْهُ. (الأَرْوَاعُ): جَمْعُ رَائِعٍ، وَهُمُ الحِسَانُ الوُجُوهِ. وَقِيلَ غَيْرُ ذَلِكَ. (المَشَابِيبُ): أَيِ السَّادَةُ الرُّؤُوسُ. وَاحِدُهُمْ مَشْبُوبٌ، كَأَنَّمَا أُوقِدَتْ أَلْوَانُهُمْ بِالنَّارِ / النِّهَايَةِ. (التِّيعَةُ): اسْمٌ لِأَدْنَى مَا تَجِبُ فِيهِ الزَّكَاةُ مِنَ الحَيَوَانِ. وَهِيَ - هُنَا - أَرْبَعُونَ شَاةً. (لَا مُقَوَّرَةُ شَاةٍ): الإِقْوِرَارُ: الاسْتِرْخَاءُ فِي الجُلُودِ. وَالأَلْيَاطُ: جَمْعُ لِيَطٍ، وَهُوَ قِشْرُ العُودِ. شَبَّهَ بِهِ الجِلْدَ لِالْتِزَاقِهِ بِاللَّحْمِ. أَرَادَ: غَيْرَ مُسْتَرْخِيَةِ الجُلُودِ لِهُزَالِهَا/ النِّهَايَةِ. (ضِنَاكٌ): الضِّنَاكُ: المُكْتَنِزُ اللَّحْمِ. (أَنْطُوا): أَعْطُوا، وَهِيَ لُغَةٌ يَمَانِيَّةٌ. (الثَّبَجَةُ): المُتَوَسِّطُ بَيْنَ الخِيَارِ وَالرُّذَالِ. (السُّيُوبُ): الرِّكَازُ، وَهُوَ المَالُ المَدْفُونُ قَبْلَ الإِسْلَامِ. (مِمْ بِكْرٍ) مِنْ بِكْرٍ، وَالمِيمُ السَّاكِنَةُ بَدَلٌ مِنْ لَامِ التَّعْرِيفِ أَوِ النُّونِ. (فَاصْقَعُوهُ): أَيِ اضْرِبُوهُ. (وَاسْتَوْفِضُوهُ): أَيِ اطْرُدُوهُ وَانْفُوهُ. (ضَرِّجُوهُ بِالأَضَامِيمِ): يُرِيدُ الرَّجْمَ بِالحِجَارَةِ، وَالأَضَامِيمُ: الحِجَارَةُ، وَاحِدَتُهَا: إِضْمَامَةٌ. وَ (لَا تَوْصِيمَ فِي الدِّينِ): أَيْ لَا تَفْتُرُوا فِي إِقَامَةِ الحُدُودِ، وَلَا تُحَابُوا فِيهَا/ النِّهَايَةِ. (وَلَا غُمَّةَ فِي فَرَائِضِ اللهِ) أَيْ لَا تُسْتَرَ وَتُخْفَى فَرَائِضُهُ، وَإِنَّمَا تُظْهَرُ وَتُعْلَنُ وَيُجْهَرُ بِهَا. (يَتَرَفَّلُ) أَيْ يَنْسَوَّدُ وَيَتَرَأَّسُ/ النِّهَايَةِ.

١١٣ كِتَابُهُ ﷺ لِأَنَسٍ أَخْرَجَهُ إِسْحَاقُ بْنُ رَاهَوَيْهِ فِي مُسْنَدِهِ - كَمَا فِي الفَتْحِ ٣١٨/٣ - وَالدَّارَقُطْنِيُّ ١١٤-١١٥/٢. وَقَالَ: «إِسْنَادٌ صَحِيحٌ وَكُلُّهُمْ ثِقَاتٌ». وَأَخْرَجَ البُخَارِيُّ (١٤٥٤) مِنْ طَرِيقِ ثُمَامَةَ بْنِ عَبْدِ اللهِ بْنِ أَنَسٍ أَنَّ أَنَسًا حَدَّثَهُ أَنَّ أَبَا بَكْرٍ ﵁ كَتَبَ لَهُ هَذَا الكِتَابَ لَمَّا وَجَّهَهُ إِلَى البَحْرَيْنِ: بِسْمِ اللهِ الرَّحْمَنِ الرَّحِيمِ، هَذِهِ فَرِيضَةُ الصَّدَقَةِ....

Amongst his beautiful sayings, the Prophet ﷺ said: "The lives of all Muslims are equal, and they are one hand against others."[111] And: "The people are like the teeth of a comb."[112] And: "A person will be with whoever they love."[113]

He said: "There is no good in the friendship of one who does not see for you what you see for them."[114] And: "People are like treasure chests [i.e., they are of different natures]."[115] And: "The person who knows his own abilities will not be destroyed."[116]

The Prophet ﷺ said: "The person being asked for counsel is in a position of trust, and he has the choice whilst he has not yet spoken."[117] And: "Allah shows mercy to the slave of His who either speaks well and benefits, or remains silent and safeguards."[118]

---

111   Reported by Abū Dāwūd (4531) from 'Amr ibn Shu'ayb, from his father and then his grandfather, and the chain is *ḥasan*. Also reported by Abū Dāwūd (4530), Nasā'ī (8/19-20), and others, from 'Alī, and this narration is *ṣaḥīḥ* on account of supporting evidences.

112   Reported by al-Quḍā'ī in *Musnad al-Shihāb* (195) and Ibn 'Adī in *Al-Kāmil*, both from Anas ibn Mālik. Also mentioned by Ibn al-Jawzī in *Al-Mawḍū'āt*. Ibn 'Adī said: "Sulaymān ibn 'Amr had the narration with another chain from Sahl ibn Sa'd, as recorded by Ibn Ḥibbān in *Al-Majrūḥīn* (1/198), Dūlābī in *Al-Kunā*, and al-Ḥasan ibn Sufyān in *Al-Musnad*. This chain contains Bakkār ibn Shu'ayb, who was a weak narrator, although he was accepted by Ibn Lāl in *Makārim al-Akhlāq*. See *Al-Lā'ālī' al-Maṣnū'ah fī al-Aḥādīth al-Mawḍū'ah* (2/290) by Suyūṭī and *Musnad al-Shihāb* (907).

113   Reported by Bukhārī (6168) and Muslim (2640) from Ibn Mas'ūd, and by Bukhārī (6170) and Muslim (2641) from Abū Mūsā al-Ash'arī.

114   Reported by Ibn 'Adī in *Al-Kāmil* from Anas, with a weak chain, as recorded in *Al-Manāhil*, p. 102.

115   Reported by Bukhārī (3496) and Muslim (2638/160) from Abū Hurayrah.

116   Reported by al-Sam'ānī in his *Tārīkh* from 'Alī, with a chain containing unknown narrators, as recorded in *Al-Manāhil*, p. 104.

117   Attributed by Sakhāwī in *Maqāṣid al-Ḥasanah* (1019) and Suyūṭī in *Al-Manāhil*, p. 105, to Aḥmad, from the narration of Abū Mas'ūd al-Badrī. I could not find the whole narration in the *Musnad* of Aḥmad. The first part of the hadith is *ṣaḥīḥ* and was also related from Abū Hurayrah, Ibn 'Umar, Umm Salamah, Ibn 'Abbās, and others.

118   This narration is *ḥasan* from all its chains. Reported by Ṭabarānī in *Al-Kabīr* (7706) from Abū Umāmah, al-Quḍā'ī (582) and others from Anas, al-Quḍā'ī (581) in a *mursal* narration from al-Ḥasan, and Ibn al-Mubārak in *Al-Zuhd* in a *mu'ḍal* narration from the chain of Khālid ibn Abī 'Imrān. See *Siyar A'lām al-Nubalā'* (4/571).

وَالْيَدَ السُّفْلَى هِيَ الْمُنْطَاةُ». قَالَ: فَكَلَّمَنَا رَسُولُ اللهِ ﷺ بِلُغَتِنَا[114].

وَقَوْلِهِ فِي حَدِيثِ الْعَامِرِيِّ حِينَ سَأَلَهُ فَقَالَ لَهُ النَّبِيُّ ﷺ: «سَلْ عَنْكَ»[115]، أَيْ: سَلْ عَمَّ شِئْتَ، وَهِيَ لُغَةُ بَنِي عَامِرٍ.

وَأَمَّا كَلَامُهُ الْمُعْتَادُ ﷺ، وَفَصَاحَتُهُ الْمَعْلُومَةُ، وَجَوَامِعُ كَلِمِهِ، وَحِكَمُهُ الْمَأْثُورَةُ، فَقَدْ أَلَّفَ النَّاسُ فِيهَا الدَّوَاوِينَ، وَجُمِعَتْ فِي أَلْفَاظِهَا وَمَعَانِيهَا الْكُتُبُ، وَمِنْهَا[116] مَا لَا يُوَازَى فَصَاحَةً، وَلَا يُبَارَى بَلَاغَةً:

كَقَوْلِهِ عليه الصلاة والسلام: «الْمُسْلِمُونَ تَتَكَافَأُ دِمَاؤُهُمْ، وَيَسْعَى بِذِمَّتِهِمْ أَدْنَاهُمْ، وَهُمْ يَدٌ عَلَى مَنْ سِوَاهُمْ»[117].

وَقَوْلِهِ: «النَّاسُ كَأَسْنَانِ الْمُشْطِ»[118]. وَ«الْمَرْءُ مَعَ مَنْ أَحَبَّ»[119].

---

114 أَخْرَجَهُ الْبَيْهَقِيُّ ١٩٨/٤، وَصَحَّحَهُ الْحَاكِمُ ٣٢٧/٤، وَوَافَقَهُ الذَّهَبِيُّ.

115 أَخْرَجَهُ أَبُو نُعَيْمٍ فِي الدَّلَائِلِ عَنْ شَدَّادِ بْنِ أَوْسٍ/ الْمَنَاهِلِ (٩٨).

116 أَيْ: مِنْ جَوَامِعِ كَلِمِهِ ﷺ.

117 أَخْرَجَهُ أَبُو دَاوُدَ (٤٥٣١) مِنْ حَدِيثِ عَمْرِو بْنِ شُعَيْبٍ، عَنْ أَبِيهِ، عَنْ جَدِّهِ، وَإِسْنَادُهُ حَسَنٌ. وَأَخْرَجَهُ أَيْضًا أَبُو دَاوُدَ (٤٥٣٠)، وَالنَّسَائِيُّ ١٩/٨-٢٠ وَغَيْرُهُ مِنْ حَدِيثِ عَلِيٍّ. وَهُوَ حَدِيثٌ صَحِيحٌ بِشَوَاهِدِهِ. (تَتَكَافَأُ دِمَاؤُهُمْ): أَيْ أَنَّهُمْ يَتَسَاوَوْنَ فِي الْقِصَاصِ وَالدِّيَاتِ. (يَسْعَى بِذِمَّتِهِمْ أَدْنَاهُمْ): أَيْ أَدْنَى الْمُسْلِمِينَ إِذَا أَعْطَى أَمَانًا وَعَهْدًا كَانَ عَلَى الْبَاقِينَ مُوَافَقَتُهُ، وَأَنْ لَا يَنْقُضُوا عَهْدَهُ وَلَا ذِمَّتَهُ. (وَهُمْ يَدٌ عَلَى مَنْ سِوَاهُمْ): أَيْ أَنَّهُمْ مُجْتَمِعُونَ يَدًا وَاحِدَةً عَلَى غَيْرِهِمْ مِنْ أَرْبَابِ الْمِلَلِ وَالْأَدْيَانِ (جَامِعُ الْأُصُولِ ٢٥٤/١٠).

118 أَخْرَجَهُ الْقُضَاعِيُّ فِي مُسْنَدِ الشِّهَابِ (١٩٥)، وَابْنُ عَدِيٍّ فِي الْكَامِلِ، مِنْ حَدِيثِ أَنَسِ بْنِ مَالِكٍ. وَأَوْرَدَهُ ابْنُ الْجَوْزِيِّ فِي الْمَوْضُوعَاتِ. وَقَالَ ابْنُ عَدِيٍّ: وَضَعَهُ سُلَيْمَانُ (بْنُ عَمْرو). وَلَهُ طَرِيقٌ آخَرُ عَنْ سَهْلِ بْنِ سَعْدٍ عِنْدَ ابْنِ حِبَّانَ فِي الْمَجْرُوحِينَ ١٩٨/١، وَالدُّولَابِيُّ فِي الْكُنَى، وَالْحَسَنُ بْنُ سُفْيَانَ فِي مُسْنَدِهِ، وَفِي إِسْنَادِهِ بَكَّارُ بْنُ شُعَيْبٍ وَهُوَ ضَعِيفٌ. لَكِنَّهُ تُوبِعَ عِنْدَ ابْنِ لَالٍ فِي مَكَارِمِ الْأَخْلَاقِ. انْظُرِ اللَّآلِئَ الْمَصْنُوعَةَ فِي الْأَحَادِيثِ الْمَوْضُوعَةِ لِلسُّيُوطِيِّ ٢٩٠/٢، وَمُسْنَدَ الشِّهَابِ (٩٠٧).

119 أَخْرَجَهُ الْبُخَارِيُّ (٦١٦٨)، وَمُسْلِمٌ (٢٦٤٠) مِنْ حَدِيثِ ابْنِ مَسْعُودٍ، وَالْبُخَارِيُّ (٦١٧٠)، وَمُسْلِمٌ (٢٦٤١) مِنْ حَدِيثِ أَبِي مُوسَى الْأَشْعَرِيِّ.

When calling to the religion, the Prophet ﷺ once advised: "Embrace Islam and you will be safe. Embrace Islam, and Allah will double your reward."[119]

He said: "The most beloved of you to me and the ones who will sit closest to me on the Day of Judgement are those with the best character, who are facilitating and accommodating to their neighbours, and who bring people together (*ya'lafūn*) and whose company is enjoyed (*yu'lafūn*)."[120]

The Prophet ﷺ once said [as a warning not to presume a dying man was guaranteed Paradise]: "Perhaps he spoke of that which did not concern him (*lā ya'nīh*), or was greedy with that which did not enrich him (*lā yughnīh*)."[121] On another occasion, he said: "The one who is two-faced (*dhū al-wajhayn*) will not be distinguished (*wajīh*) with Allah."[122]

The Prophet ﷺ prohibited: "…rumours and hearsay, persistent questioning, wasting money, withholding the rights of others, dis-

---

119 Taken from the letter the Prophet ﷺ wrote to the great Roman leader Heraclius. Reported by Bukhārī (2941) and Muslim (1773) from Ibn ʿAbbās from Abū Sufyān ibn Ḥarb.

120 Reported by Ṭabarānī in *Al-Ṣaghīr* and *Al-Awsaṭ* from Abū Hurayrah, without the phrase "and the ones who will sit closest to me on the Day of Judgement". Haythamī said in *Majmaʿ al-Zawāʾid* (8/21): "The chain contains Ṣāliḥ ibn Bashīr al-Murī, who is a weak narrator." A similar hadith was reported by Tirmidhī (2018) from Jābir, which Tirmidhī graded as *ḥasan gharīb*. Another narration reported from Abū Thaʿlabah al-Khushanī al-Dārānī (hailing from the town of Dārayā) was reported and authenticated by Ibn Ḥibbān in *Mawārid al-Ẓamʾān* (1918).

121 Reported by Tirmidhī (2316) and Abū Yaʿlā (4017) from Anas ibn Mālik. Tirmidhī said: "This narration is *gharīb*." Also reported by Abū Yaʿlā (6646) from Abū Hurayrah, with a weak chain.

122 I have not found the narration with this particular wording. An alternative wording was reported by Abū Dāwūd (4873), Abū Yaʿlā (1620), and others, from ʿAmmār ibn Yāsir: "Whoever has two faces in this world will have two tongues of fire in the Hereafter." Authenticated by Ibn Ḥibbān in *Mawārid al-Ẓamʾān* (1979). Another narration was reported by Bukhārī (7179) and Muslim (2526), from Abū Hurayrah: "The worst of humankind is the two-faced one, who comes to some people with one face and to others with another." The wording here is from Bukhārī. See also *Majmaʿ al-Zawāʾid* (8/95).

وَ«لَا خَيْرَ فِي صُحْبَةِ مَنْ لَا يَرَى لَكَ مَا تَرَى لَهُ»[120].

وَ«النَّاسُ مَعَادِنُ»[121]. وَ«مَا هَلَكَ امْرُؤٌ عَرَفَ قَدْرَهُ»[122].

وَ«الْمُسْتَشَارُ مُؤْتَمَنٌ، وَهُوَ بِالْخِيَارِ مَا لَمْ يَتَكَلَّمْ»[123].

وَ«رَحِمَ اللهُ عَبْدًا قَالَ خَيْرًا فَغَنِمَ، أَوْ سَكَتَ فَسَلِمَ»[124].

وَقَوْلِهِ عليه الصلاة والسلام: «أَسْلِمْ تَسْلَمْ، وَأَسْلِمْ يُؤْتِكَ اللهُ أَجْرَكَ مَرَّتَيْنِ»[125].

وَ«إِنَّ أَحَبَّكُمْ إِلَيَّ، وَأَقْرَبَكُمْ مِنِّي مَجْلِسًا يَوْمَ الْقِيَامَةِ: أَحَاسِنُكُمْ أَخْلَاقًا، الْمُوَطَّئُونَ أَكْنَافًا، الَّذِينَ يَأْلَفُونَ وَيُؤْلَفُونَ»[126].

---

120 أَخْرَجَهُ ابْنُ عَدِيٍّ فِي الْكَامِلِ عَنْ أَنَسٍ بِسَنَدٍ ضَعِيفٍ/ الْمَنَاهِلُ (١٠٢).

121 أَخْرَجَهُ الْبُخَارِيُّ (٣٤٩٦)، وَمُسْلِمٌ (١٦٠/٢٦٣٨) مِنْ حَدِيثِ أَبِي هُرَيْرَةَ.

122 أَخْرَجَهُ ابْنُ السَّمْعَانِي فِي تَارِيخِهِ مِنْ حَدِيثِ عَلِيٍّ بِسَنَدٍ فِيهِ مَنْ لَا يُعْرَفُ حَالُهُ/ الْمَنَاهِلُ (١٠٤).

123 هَذِهِ الرِّوَايَةُ نَسَبَهَا السَّخَاوِيُّ فِي الْمَقَاصِدِ الْحَسَنَةِ (١٠١٩)، وَالسُّيُوطِيُّ فِي الْمَنَاهِلِ(١٠٥) إِلَى أَحْمَدَ مِنْ حَدِيثِ أَبِي مَسْعُودٍ الْبَدْرِيِّ. وَلَمْ أَجِدْهَا تَامَّةً فِي مُسْنَدِهِ. وَصَدْرُ الْحَدِيثِ صَحِيحٌ رُوِيَ أَيْضًا عَنْ أَبِي هُرَيْرَةَ، وَابْنِ عُمَرَ، وَأُمِّ سَلَمَةَ، وَابْنِ عَبَّاسٍ، وَغَيْرِهِ.

124 حَدِيثٌ حَسَنٌ بِمَجْمُوعِ طُرُقِهِ. رَوَاهُ الطَّبَرَانِيُّ فِي الْكَبِيرِ (٧٧٠٦) مِنْ حَدِيثِ أَبِي أُمَامَةَ، وَالْقُضَاعِيُّ (٥٨٢) وَغَيْرُهُ مِنْ حَدِيثِ أَنَسٍ، وَ(٥٨١) مِنْ حَدِيثِ الْحَسَنِ مُرْسَلًا، وَابْنُ الْمُبَارَكِ فِي الزُّهْدِ مِنْ طَرِيقِ خَالِدِ بْنِ أَبِي عِمْرَانَ مُعْضَلًا. وَانْظُرْ سِيَرَ أَعْلَامِ النُّبَلَاءِ ٥٧١/٤.

125 أَخْرَجَهُ الْبُخَارِيُّ (٢٩٤١)، وَمُسْلِمٌ (١٧٧٣) مِنْ حَدِيثِ ابْنِ عَبَّاسٍ عَنْ أَبِي سُفْيَانَ بْنِ حَرْبٍ. وَالْحَدِيثُ فِقْرَةٌ مِنْ رِسَالَةِ النَّبِيِّ ﷺ إِلَى هِرَقْلَ عَظِيمِ الرُّومِ.

126 أَخْرَجَهُ الطَّبَرَانِيُّ فِي الصَّغِيرِ وَالْأَوْسَطِ مِنْ حَدِيثِ أَبِي هُرَيْرَةَ. وَلَيْسَ فِيهِ: «وَأَقْرَبَكُمْ مِنِّي مَجْلِسًا يَوْمَ الْقِيَامَةِ». قَالَ الْهَيْثَمِيُّ فِي الْمَجْمَعِ ٢١/٨: «فِيهِ صَالِحُ بْنُ بَشِيرٍ الْمُرِّيُّ، وَهُوَ ضَعِيفٌ». وَفِي الْبَابِ عَنْ جَابِرٍ عِنْدَ التِّرْمِذِي (٢٠١٨) وَقَالَ: «هَذَا حَدِيثٌ حَسَنٌ غَرِيبٌ». وَعَنْ أَبِي ثَعْلَبَةَ الْخُشَنِي الدَّارَانِي - نِسْبَةً إِلَى مَدِينَتِنَا دَارَيَّا - صَحَّحَهُ ابْنُ حِبَّانَ (١٩١٧) مَوَارِدُ الظَّمْآنِ، وَهُنَاكَ اسْتَوْفَيْنَا تَخْرِيجَهُ. (الْمُوَطَّئُونَ أَكْنَافًا): قَالَ فِي النِّهَايَةِ: «هَذَا مَثَلٌ وَحَقِيقَتُهُ مِنَ التَّوْطِئَةِ، وَهِيَ التَّمْهِيدُ وَالتَّذْلِيلُ. وَالْأَكْنَافُ: الْجَوَانِبُ. أَرَادَ الَّذِينَ جَوَانِبُهُمْ وَطِيئَةٌ، يَتَمَكَّنُ فِيهَا مَنْ يُصَاحِبُهُمْ

obeying one's mother, and burying daughters alive."[123] And he advised: "Be conscious of Allah wherever you are, follow sinful actions with good deeds to wipe them out, and treat people with good manners."[124]

He said: "The best of affairs is the middle way."[125] And "Love your beloved moderately, for perhaps one day they will be your enemy."[126] And he observed: "Oppression (*al-ẓulm*) will be darkness (*ẓulumāt*) on the Day of Judgement."[127]

The Prophet ﷺ once supplicated: "O Allah, I ask You from Your Mercy to guide my heart, straighten my affairs, bring together that which has been scattered of my affairs, correct my inner state, elevate my outer presence, purify my actions, inspire me to guidance, return my closeness, and protect me from every evil. O Allah, I ask You for a successful outcome in the Judgment, the provision of the martyrs,[128] a life of contentment, and victory against our enemies."[129]

Much more was related from the addresses, conversations, and supplications of the Prophet ﷺ, and his linguistic ability was be-

---

123   Reported by Bukhārī (5975), and Muslim (593/12) in his chapter on judicial decisions, both from al-Mughīrah ibn Shuʻbah.

124   Reported by Tirmidhī (1987) and others, from Abū Dharr. Authenticated by Ḥākim (1/54) and Dhahabī concurred. Tirmidhī said: "This narration is *ḥasan ṣaḥīḥ*."

125   Reported by Ibn al-Athīr in *Jāmiʻ al-Uṣūl* (101) from Abū Hurayrah, without any attribution. Sakhāwī attributed the narration in *Al-Maqāṣid al-Ḥasanah* to Ibn al-Samʻānī in his "*dhayl*" (continuation) of *Tārīkh Baghdād* with a *marfūʻ* hadith, with a *majhūl* chain leading back to ʻAlī. See also Abū Yaʻlā (6115).

126   Reported by Tirmidhī (1997) from Muhammad ibn Sīrīn, from Abū Hurayrah. Suyūṭī graded the hadith as *ḥasan* in *Al-Jāmiʻ al-Ṣaghīr* (223) in *marfūʻ* narrations reported from several Companions, and in a *mawqūf* narration from ʻAlī ﷺ. Tirmidhī graded the narration as weak and said: "This hadith is *gharīb*." See also *Majmaʻ al-Zawā'id* (8/88).

127   Reported by Bukhārī (2447) with this wording, and Muslim (2579) from Ibn ʻUmar.

128   i.e., their reward and status with Allah Exalted.

129   Reported by Tirmidhī (3419) from Ibn ʻAbbās. He said: "This hadith is *gharīb*." Shaykh Shuʻayb al-Arna'ūṭ graded the narration as weak in his commentary of *Siyar Aʻlām al-Nubalā'* (5/444). Suyūṭī graded the hadith as *ḥasan* in *Al-Jāmiʻ al-Ṣaghīr* (1477).

وَقَوْلِهِ: «لَعَلَّهُ كَانَ يَتَكَلَّمُ بِمَا لَا يَعْنِيهِ، وَيَبْخَلُ بِمَا لَا يُغْنِيهِ»[127].

وَقَوْلِهِ ﷺ: «ذُو الوَجْهَيْنِ لَا يَكُونُ عِنْدَ اللهِ وَجِيهًا»[128].

وَنَهْيِهِ عَنْ «قِيلَ وَقَالَ، وَكَثْرَةِ السُّؤَالِ، وَإِضَاعَةِ المَالِ، وَمَنْعٍ وَهَاتِ، وَعُقُوقِ الأُمَّهَاتِ، وَوَأْدِ البَنَاتِ»[129].

وَقَوْلِهِ عليه الصلاة والسلام: «اتَّقِ اللهَ حَيْثُ كُنْتَ، وَأَتْبِعِ السَّيِّئَةَ الحَسَنَةَ تَمْحُهَا، وَخَالِقِ النَّاسَ بِخُلُقٍ حَسَنٍ»[130]. وَقَوْلِهِ: «خَيْرُ الأُمُورِ أَوْسَاطُهَا»[131]. وَقَوْلِهِ: «أَحْبِبْ حَبِيبَكَ هَوْنًا مَا؛ عَسَى أَنْ يَكُونَ بَغِيضَكَ يَوْمًا مَا»[132].

وَلَا يَتَأَذَّى».

127 أَخْرَجَهُ التِّرْمِذِيُّ (٢٣١٦)، وَأَبُو يَعْلَى (٤٠١٧) وَغَيْرُهُ مِنْ حَدِيثِ أَنَسِ بْنِ مَالِكٍ. قَالَ التِّرْمِذِيُّ: «هَذَا حَدِيثٌ غَرِيبٌ»: وَأَخْرَجَهُ أَبُو يَعْلَى (٦٦٤٦) مِنْ حَدِيثِ أَبِي هُرَيْرَةَ، وَإِسْنَادُهُ ضَعِيفٌ.

128 لَمْ أَجِدْهُ بِهَذَا اللَّفْظِ. وَأَخْرَجَ أَبُو دَاوُدَ (٤٨٧٣)، وَأَبُو يَعْلَى (١٦٢٠)، وَغَيْرُهُ عَنْ عَمَّارِ بْنِ يَاسِرٍ رَفَعَهُ: «مَنْ كَانَ لَهُ وَجْهَانِ فِي الدُّنْيَا كَانَ لَهُ يَوْمَ القِيَامَةِ لِسَانَانِ مِنْ نَارٍ» وَصَحَّحَهُ ابْنُ حِبَّانَ (١٩٧٩) مَوَارِدُ الظَّمْآنِ. وَأَخْرَجَ البُخَارِيُّ (٧١٧٩) وَاللَّفْظُ لَهُ، وَمُسْلِمٌ (٢٥٢٦) عَنْ أَبِي هُرَيْرَةَ رَفَعَهُ: «إِنَّ شَرَّ النَّاسِ ذُو الوَجْهَيْنِ، الَّذِي يَأْتِي هَؤُلَاءِ بِوَجْهٍ، وَهَؤُلَاءِ بِوَجْهٍ». وَانْظُرْ مَجْمَعَ الزَّوَائِدِ (٩٥/٨).

129 أَخْرَجَهُ البُخَارِيُّ (٥٩٧٥)، وَمُسْلِمٌ فِي الأَقْضِيَةِ (١٢/٥٩٣) مِنْ حَدِيثِ المُغِيرَةِ بْنِ شُعْبَةَ.

130 أَخْرَجَهُ التِّرْمِذِيُّ (١٩٨٧) وَغَيْرُهُ، مِنْ حَدِيثِ أَبِي ذَرٍّ، وَصَحَّحَهُ الحَاكِمُ (٥٤/١) وَوَافَقَهُ الذَّهَبِيُّ. وَقَالَ التِّرْمِذِيُّ: «هَذَا حَدِيثٌ حَسَنٌ صَحِيحٌ».

131 أَوْرَدَهُ ابْنُ الأَثِيرِ فِي جَامِعِ الأُصُولِ بِرَقْمِ (١٠١) مِنْ حَدِيثِ أَبِي هُرَيْرَةَ، وَلَمْ يَنْسُبْهُ إِلَى أَحَدٍ. وَعَزَاهُ السَّخَاوِيُّ فِي المَقَاصِدِ الحَسَنَةِ ص(٢٠٥) إِلَى ابْنِ السَّمْعَانِيِّ فِي ذَيْلِ تَارِيخِ بَغْدَادَ بِسَنَدٍ مَجْهُولٍ عَنْ عَلِيٍّ مَرْفُوعًا. وَانْظُرْ مُسْنَدَ أَبِي يَعْلَى (٦١١٥).

132 أَخْرَجَهُ التِّرْمِذِيُّ (١٩٩٧) مِنْ حَدِيثِ مُحَمَّدِ بْنِ سِيرِينَ عَنْ أَبِي هُرَيْرَةَ أَرَاهُ رَفَعَهُ. وَذَكَرَهُ السُّيُوطِيُّ فِي الجَامِعِ الصَّغِيرِ (٢٢٣) عَنْ عَدَدٍ مِنَ الصَّحَابَةِ مَرْفُوعًا، وَمَوْقُوفًا عَلَى عَلِيٍّ رَضِيَ اللهُ عَنْهُ وَرَمَزَ لِحُسْنِهِ. وَضَعَّفَهُ التِّرْمِذِيُّ وَقَالَ: «هَذَا حَدِيثٌ غَرِيبٌ». وَقَدِ اسْتَدْرَكَ الحَافِظُ العِرَاقِيُّ عَلَى التِّرْمِذِيِّ دَعْوَاهُ غَرَابَتَهُ وَضَعَّفَهُ فَقَالَ: رِجَالُهُ رِجَالُ مُسْلِمٍ لَكِنَّ الرَّاوِيَ تَرَدَّدَ فِي رَفْعِهِ. وَانْظُرْ مَجْمَعَ الزَّوَائِدِ ٨٨/٨. (أَحْبِبْ حَبِيبَكَ هَوْنًا مَا): أَيْ حُبًّا مُقْتَصِدًا لَا إِفْرَاطَ فِيهِ.

yond compare. He employed expressions never uttered before him, which were both deep in meaning and profound in implication.

For example, the Prophet ﷺ said: "…the oven is raging."[130] And: "He took his final breath."[131]

The Prophet ﷺ said: "A believer is not stung twice from the same hole."[132] And: "The successful person is the one who learns from others."[133] So much can be derived from these pearls of wisdom.

His Companions said to him: "There is no-one more eloquent than you!" The Prophet ﷺ replied: "How could it be otherwise? The Qur'an was revealed in my language[134]; clear, lucid Arabic."[135]

On another occasion, he said: "[I am the most eloquent of the Arabs] because I am from the Quraysh and I was brought up by the Banū Saʿd."[136]

This gave him the strength and purity of the Bedouins, the clear expression of the city dwellers, and the beauty of both. Furthermore, he was assisted with Divine Inspiration in the form of the

---

130   Meaning: "The battle (or 'event') is heating up." Part of a narration reported by Muslim (1775) from al-ʿAbbās ibn ʿAbd al-Muṭṭalib.

131   lit., "His nose was destroyed." Meaning: "He passed away on his bed, without a sound or a struggle." Reported by Bayhaqī in *Shuʿab al-Īmān* in a *marfūʿ* narration from ʿAbdullāh ibn ʿAtīk; see *Al-Manāhil*, p. 121.

132   Reported by Bukhārī (6133) and Muslim (2998) from Abū Hurayrah.

133   Reported by Ibn Mājah (46), Ibn Abī ʿĀṣim in *Al-Sunnah* (178), and al-Quḍāʿī in *Musnad al-Shihāb* (76, 1325) in a *marfūʿ* narration from Ibn Masʿūd. Ibn Taymiyyah said in *Iqāmah al-Dalīl*, p. 59: "It was reported by Ibn Mājah and Ibn Abī ʿĀṣim with a good chain, but it is better known as a *mawqūf* narration from Ibn Masʿūd." Also reported by Muslim (2645) from Ibn Masʿūd. See also *Al-Durr al-Manthūr* (253) by Suyūṭī.

134   Or, "on my tongue".

135   Reported by Bayhaqī in *Shuʿab al-Īmān*; see *Al-Manāhil*, p. 121. ʿIrāqī graded the chain as weak in *Takhrīj Aḥādīth al-Iḥyā'* (2/367).

136   Related by those known for *gharīb* narrations, and I do not know of a chain of transmission for it. Suyūṭī cited another narration in *Al-Manāhil*, p. 122, reported by Ṭabarānī from Abū Saʿīd al-Khudrī, where the Prophet ﷺ said: "I am the most articulate [*aʿrab*] of the Arabs [*ʿarab*]. I was born from the Quraysh and brought up amongst the Banū Saʿd, so how could I falter in my language?" See also *Majmaʿ al-Zawā'id* (8/218) and *Al-Maqāṣid al-Ḥasanah* (45).

وَقَوْلِهِ: «الظُّلْمُ ظُلُمَاتٌ يَوْمَ القِيَامَةِ»^{١٣٣}.

وَقَوْلِهِ عليه الصلاة والسلام فِي بَعْضِ دُعَائِهِ: «اللَّهُمَّ إِنِّي أَسْأَلُكَ رَحْمَةً تَهْدِي بِهَا قَلْبِي، وَتَجْمَعُ بِهَا أَمْرِي، وَتَلُمُّ بِهَا شَعَثِي، وَتُصْلِحُ بِهَا غَائِبِي، وَتَرْفَعُ بِهَا شَاهِدِي، وَتُزَكِّي بِهَا عَمَلِي، وَتُلْهِمُنِي بِهَا رُشْدِي، وَتَرُدُّ بِهَا أُلْفَتِي، وَتَعْصِمُنِي بِهَا مِنْ كُلِّ سُوءٍ، اللَّهُمَّ إِنِّي أَسْأَلُكَ الفَوْزَ فِي القَضَاءِ، وَنُزُلَ الشُّهَدَاءِ، وَعَيْشَ السُّعَدَاءِ، وَالنَّصْرَ عَلَى الأَعْدَاءِ»^{١٣٤}.

إِلَى مَا رَوَتْهُ الكَافَّةُ عَنِ الكَافَّةِ مِنْ مَقَامَاتِهِ، وَمُحَاضَرَاتِهِ، وَخُطَبِهِ، وَأَدْعِيَتِهِ، وَمُخَاطَبَاتِهِ، وَعُهُودِهِ، مِمَّا لَا خِلَافَ أَنَّهُ ﷺ نَزَلَ مِنْ ذَلِكَ مَرْتَبَةً لَا يُقَاسُ بِهَا غَيْرُهُ، وَحَازَ فِيهَا سَبْقًا لَا يُقَدَّرُ قَدْرُهُ، وَقَدْ جُمِعَتْ مِنْ كَلِمَاتِهِ الَّتِي لَمْ يُسْبَقْ إِلَيْهَا، وَلَا قَدَرَ أَحَدٌ أَنْ يُفْرِغَ فِي قَالَبِهِ عَلَيْهَا:

كَقَوْلِهِ ﷺ: «حَمِيَ الوَطِيسُ»^{١٣٥}. وَ «مَاتَ حَتْفَ أَنْفِهِ»^{١٣٦}. وَ «لَا يُلْدَغُ

---

^{١٣٣} أَخْرَجَهُ البُخَارِيُّ (٢٤٤٧) وَاللَّفْظُ لَهُ، وَمُسْلِمٌ (٢٥٧٩) مِنْ حَدِيثِ ابْنِ عُمَرَ.

^{١٣٤} أَخْرَجَهُ التِّرْمِذِيُّ (٣٤١٩) مِنْ حَدِيثِ ابْنِ عَبَّاسٍ، وَقَالَ: «هَذَا حَدِيثٌ غَرِيبٌ» وَضَعَّفَهُ الشَّيْخُ شُعَيْبُ الأَرْنَاؤُوطُ فِي تَعْلِيقِهِ عَلَى سِيَرِ أَعْلَامِ النُّبَلَاءِ ٥/٤٤٤، وَرَمَزَ لِحُسْنِهِ السُّيُوطِيُّ فِي الجَامِعِ الصَّغِيرِ (١٤٧٧). (تَلُمُّ بِهَا شَعَثِي): أَيْ تَجْمَعُ بِهَا مَا تَفَرَّقَ مِنْ أَمْرِي. (وَتُصْلِحُ بِهَا غَائِبِي): أَيْ بَاطِنِي بِكَمَالِ الإِيمَانِ وَالأَخْلَاقِ الحِسَانِ، وَالمَلَكَاتِ الفَاضِلَةِ. (وَتَرْفَعُ بِهَا شَاهِدِي): أَيْ ظَاهِرِي، بِالأَعْمَالِ الصَّالِحَةِ وَالخِلَالِ الجَمِيلَةِ. (وَتُزَكِّي بِهَا عَمَلِي): أَيْ تَزِيدُهُ وَتُنَمِّيهِ وَتُطَهِّرُهُ مِنْ أَدْنَاسِ الرِّيَاءِ وَالسُّمْعَةِ. (وَتُلْهِمُنِي بِهَا رُشْدِي) أَيْ: تَهْدِينِي بِهَا إِلَى مَا يُرْضِيكَ. (أُلْفَتِي) أَيْ مَا كُنْتُ آلَفُهُ. (تَعْصِمُنِي) تَمْنَعُنِي وَتَحْفَظُنِي. (الفَوْزَ فِي القَضَاءِ): أَيِ الفَوْزَ بِاللُّطْفِ فِيهِ. (نُزُلَ الشُّهَدَاءِ) النُّزُلُ فِي الأَصْلِ: قِرَى الضَّيْفِ. وَتُضَمُّ زَايُهُ. يُرِيدُ: مَا لِلشُّهَدَاءِ عِنْدَ اللهِ مِنَ الأَجْرِ وَالثَّوَابِ (النِّهَايَةُ).

^{١٣٥} فِقْرَةٌ مِنْ حَدِيثٍ رَوَاهُ مُسْلِمٌ (١٧٧٥) عَنِ العَبَّاسِ بْنِ عَبْدِ المُطَّلِبِ. (حَمِيَ الوَطِيسُ): أَيِ اشْتَدَّتِ الحَرْبُ وَالأَمْرُ. وَالوَطِيسُ فِي اللُّغَةِ: التَّنُّورُ.

^{١٣٦} رَوَاهُ البَيْهَقِيُّ فِي الشُّعَبِ عَنْ عَبْدِ اللهِ بْنِ عَتِيكٍ مَرْفُوعًا/ المَنَاهِلُ رَقْمُ (١٢١). (مَاتَ حَتْفَ أَنْفِهِ): أَيْ مَاتَ عَلَى فِرَاشِهِ بِلَا ضَرْبٍ وَلَا قَتْلٍ، وَالحَتْفُ: الهَلَاكُ (المُعْجَمُ الوَسِيطُ).

Qur'an, a Revelation which no human being will ever fully comprehend.

Umm Ma'bad said in her description of the Prophet ﷺ: "His speech was sweet and precise; he was neither verbose nor taciturn. His words were beautifully composed, like a string of pearls, and he had a deep, melodious voice."[137]

---

137 Reported by Baghawī (3704) in the hadith of Ḥubaysh ibn Khālid. Ḥākim authenticated the hadith in *Al-Mustadrak* (3/9-10) and Dhahabī concurred.

الْمُؤْمِنُ مِنْ جُحْرٍ مَرَّتَيْنِ»[137]. وَ«السَّعِيدُ مَنْ وُعِظَ بِغَيْرِهِ»[138].

في أَخَوَاتِهَا مَا يُدْرِكُ النَّاظِرَ الْعَجَبُ في مُضَمَّنِهَا، وَيَذْهَبُ بِهِ الْفِكْرُ في أَدَانِي حِكَمِهَا. وَقَدْ قَالَ لَهُ أَصْحَابُهُ ﷺ وَرَضِيَ عَنْهُمْ: مَا رَأَيْنَا الَّذِي هُوَ أَفْصَحُ مِنكَ.

فَقَالَ: «وَمَا يَمْنَعُنِي؟! وَإِنَّمَا أُنْزِلَ الْقُرْآنُ بِلِسَانِي، لِسَانٍ عَرَبِيٍّ مُبِينٍ»[139].

وَقَالَ مَرَّةً أُخْرَى: «بَيْدَ أَنِّي مِنْ قُرَيْشٍ، وَنَشَأْتُ في بَنِي سَعْدٍ»[140].

فَجُمِعَ لَهُ بِذَلِكَ ﷺ قُوَّةُ عَارِضَةِ الْبَادِيَةِ وَجَزَالَتِهَا، وَنَصَاعَةُ أَلْفَاظِ الْحَاضِرَةِ وَرَوْنَقُ كَلَامِهَا[141]، إِلَى التَّأْيِيدِ الْإِلَهِيِّ الَّذِي مَدَدُهُ الْوَحْيُ الَّذِي لَا يُحِيطُ بِعِلْمِهِ بَشَرِيٌّ[142].

وَقَالَتْ أُمُّ مَعْبَدٍ في وَصْفِهَا لَهُ ﷺ: حُلْوُ الْمَنْطِقِ، فَصْلٌ، لَا نَزْرٌ، وَلَا هَذَرٌ، كَأَنَّ مَنْطِقَهُ خَرَزَاتُ نُظِمْنَ[143]. وَكَانَ جَهِيرَ الصَّوْتِ، حَسَنَ النَّغْمَةِ ﷺ.

---

١٣٧ أَخْرَجَهُ الْبُخَارِيُّ (٦١٣٣)، وَمُسْلِمٌ (٢٩٩٨) عَنْ أَبِي هُرَيْرَةَ.

١٣٨ أَخْرَجَهُ ابْنُ مَاجه (٤٦)، وَابْنُ أَبِي عَاصِمٍ في السُّنَّةِ (١٧٨)، وَالْقُضَاعِيُّ في مُسْنَدِ الشِّهَابِ (٧٦) وَ(١٣٢٥) مِنْ حَدِيثِ ابْنِ مَسْعُودٍ مَرْفُوعًا. وَقَالَ شَيْخُ الْإِسْلَامِ ابْنُ تَيْمِيَةَ في إِقَامَةِ الدَّلِيلِ ص (٥٩): «رَوَاهُ ابْنُ مَاجه وَابْنُ أَبِي عَاصِمٍ بِأَسَانِيدَ جَيِّدَةٍ... لَكِنَّ الْمَشْهُورَ أَنَّهُ مَوْقُوفٌ عَلَى ابْنِ مَسْعُودٍ». قُلْتُ: أَخْرَجَهُ مُسْلِمٌ (٢٦٤٥) عَنِ ابْنِ مَسْعُودٍ مِنْ قَوْلِهِ. وَانْظُرِ الدُّرَرَ الْمُنْتَثِرَةَ لِلسُّيُوطِيِّ رَقْمَ (٢٥٣).

١٣٩ أَخْرَجَهُ الْبَيْهَقِيُّ في الشُّعَبِ/ الْمَنَاهِلِ رَقْمَ (١٢١). وَضَعَّفَ إِسْنَادَهُ الْعِرَاقِيُّ في تَخْرِيجِهِ لِأَحَادِيثِ الْإِحْيَاءِ (٢/٣٦٧).

١٤٠ أَوْرَدَهُ أَصْحَابُ الْغَرِيبِ، وَلَا يُعْرَفُ لَهُ إِسْنَادٌ، وَلِلطَّبَرَانِيِّ مِنْ حَدِيثِ أَبِي سَعِيدٍ الْخُدْرِيِّ: «أَنَا أَعْرَبُ الْعَرَبِ، وُلِدْتُ في قُرَيْشٍ، وَنَشَأْتُ في بَنِي سَعْدٍ، فَأَنَّى يَأْتِينِي اللَّحْنُ؟!» قَالَهُ السُّيُوطِيُّ في الْمَنَاهِلِ (١٢٢). وَانْظُرْ مَجْمَعَ الزَّوَائِدِ ٨/٢١٨، وَالْمَقَاصِدَ الْحَسَنَةَ رَقْمَ (٤٥).

١٤١ رَوْنَقُ كَلَامِهَا: حُسْنُهُ.

١٤٢ بَشَرِيٌّ: مَنْسُوبٌ إِلَى الْبَشَرِ.

١٤٣ (فَصْلٌ): أَيْ بَيِّنٌ. (لَا نَزْرٌ، وَلَا هَذَرٌ) تُرِيدُ: وَسَطٌ لَيْسَ بِقَلِيلٍ وَلَا كَثِيرٍ.

THE NOBILITY OF HIS LINEAGE AND THE HONOUR OF HIS HOMELAND

The noble lineage of the Prophet ﷺ and the honour of his homeland are well-known and do not require proof or clarification. He was from the Banū Hāshim clan, the core of the Quraysh and the best of the Arabs. He descended from the most distinguished amongst them, both from his mother's and father's side, and hailed from the people of Makkah, the most honourable land in the sight of Allah and in the sight of His servants.

The great *qāḍī* Ḥusayn ibn Muhammad al-Ṣadafī ﷺ narrated, from Abū al-Walīd (Sulaymān ibn Khalaf), from Abū Dharr ('Abd ibn Aḥmad), from Abū Muhammad al-Sarkhasī, Abū Isḥāq[138], and Abū al-Haytham, from Muhammad ibn Yūsuf, from Muhammad ibn Ismā'īl[139], from Qutaybah ibn Sa'īd, from Ya'qūb ibn 'Abd al-Raḥmān, from 'Amr, from Sa'īd al-Maqburī, from Abū Hurayrah, that the Messenger of Allah ﷺ said: "I was sent from the very best generation of the Children of Adam (i.e., of all humankind)."[140]

Al-'Abbās related that the Prophet ﷺ said: "Allah Exalted created the creation and made me from the best of them and from the best generation.[141] Then, He chose between the tribes and made

---

138 Ibrāhīm ibn Aḥmad al-Balkhī al-Mustamlī. Bukhārī related, on the authority of al-Farabrī, that he died in 376 AH. See *Siyar A'lām al-Nubalā'* (16/492).

139 Translator's note: This is Imam Bukhārī.

140 Reported here from the chain of Bukhārī (3557).

141 In the wording reported by Tirmidhī (3607), and in *Jāmi' al-Uṣūl* (8/535): "...and made me from the best of them, from the best of their groups, and from the best of the two groups (i.e., Arabs and non-Arabs)."

فَصْل

وَأَمَّا شَرَفُ نَسَبِهِ، وَكَرَمُ بَلَدِهِ وَمَنْشَئِهِ: فَمَا لَا يُحْتَاجُ إِلَى إِقَامَةِ دَلِيلٍ عَلَيْهِ، وَلَا بَيَانٍ مُشْكِلٍ وَلَا خَفِيٍّ مِنْهُ، فَإِنَّهُ نُخْبَةُ بَنِي هَاشِمٍ، سُلَالَةُ قُرَيْشٍ وَصَمِيمُهَا، وَأَفْضَلُ[144] الْعَرَبِ، وَأَعَزُّهُمْ نَفَرًا مِنْ قِبَلِ أَبِيهِ وَأُمِّهِ، وَمِنْ أَهْلِ مَكَّةَ مِنْ أَكْرَمِ بِلَادِ اللهِ عَلَى اللهِ وَعَلَى عِبَادِهِ.

حَدَّثَنَا الْقَاضِي حُسَيْنُ بْنُ مُحَمَّدٍ الصَّدَفِيُّ رَحِمَهُ اللهُ، حَدَّثَنَا الْقَاضِي أَبُو الْوَلِيدِ سُلَيْمَانُ بْنُ خَلَفٍ، حَدَّثَنَا أَبُو ذَرٍّ عَبْدُ بْنُ أَحْمَدَ، حَدَّثَنَا أَبُو مُحَمَّدٍ السَّرَخْسِيُّ، وَأَبُو إِسْحَاقَ، وَأَبُو الْهَيْثَمِ، قَالُوا: حَدَّثَنَا مُحَمَّدُ بْنُ يُوسُفَ، حَدَّثَنَا مُحَمَّدُ بْنُ إِسْمَاعِيلَ، حَدَّثَنَا قُتَيْبَةُ بْنُ سَعِيدٍ، حَدَّثَنَا يَعْقُوبُ بْنُ عَبْدِ الرَّحْمَنِ، عَنْ عَمْرٍو، عَنْ سَعِيدٍ الْمَقْبُرِيِّ، عَنْ أَبِي هُرَيْرَةَ رَضِيَ اللهُ عَنْهُ أَنَّ رَسُولَ اللهِ ﷺ قَالَ: «بُعِثْتُ مِنْ خَيْرِ قُرُونِ بَنِي آدَمَ قَرْنًا فَقَرْنًا، حَتَّى كُنْتُ مِنَ الْقَرْنِ الَّذِي كُنْتُ مِنْهُ»[145].

وَعَنِ الْعَبَّاسِ رَضِيَ اللهُ عَنْهُ: قَالَ النَّبِيُّ ﷺ: «إِنَّ اللهَ خَلَقَ الْخَلْقَ فَجَعَلَنِي مِنْ خَيْرِهِمْ، مِنْ خَيْرِ قَرْنِهِمْ[146]، ثُمَّ تَخَيَّرَ الْقَبَائِلَ فَجَعَلَنِي مِنْ خَيْرِ قَبِيلَةٍ، ثُمَّ تَخَيَّرَ

---

١٤٤ (وَأَفْضَلُ): أَثْبَتَ النَّاسِخُ فَوْقَهَا كَلِمَةَ «وَأَشْرَفُ» وَرَمَزَ لَهَا بِالصِّحَّةِ.

١٤٥ أَسْنَدَهُ الْمُصَنِّفُ مِنْ طَرِيقِ مُحَمَّدِ بْنِ إِسْمَاعِيلَ الْبُخَارِيِّ (٣٥٥٧). (قَرْنًا فَقَرْنًا) الْقَرْنُ: الطَّبَقَةُ مِنَ النَّاسِ الْمُجْتَمِعِينَ فِي عَصْرٍ وَاحِدٍ، وَمِنْهُمْ مَنْ حَدَّهُ بِمِئَةِ سَنَةٍ. وَقِيلَ غَيْرُ ذَلِكَ.

١٤٦ فِي التِّرْمِذِيِّ وَجَامِعِ الْأُصُولِ ٨/٥٣٥: «فَجَعَلَنِي مِنْ خَيْرِ فِرْقِهِمْ، وَخَيْرِ الْفَرِيقَيْنِ».

me from the best tribe. Then, He chose between the families[142] and made me from the best family. Accordingly, I am the best of them, from the best family."[143]

As Wāthilah ibn al-Asqaʿ narrated, the Prophet ﷺ said: "Allah chose Ismāʿīl from the children of Ibrāhīm, from the children of Ismāʿīl. He chose Banū Kinānah, from Banū Kinānah He chose the Quraysh, from the Quraysh He chose Banū Hāshim, and from Banū Hāshim He chose me."[144]

Ṭabarānī[145] reported from Ibn ʿUmar that the Prophet ﷺ said: "Allah chose the Children of Adam from amongst His creation, then He chose the Arabs from the Children of Adam, then He chose the Quraysh from amongst the Arabs, then He chose the Banū Hāshim from amongst the Quraysh, then He chose me from amongst the Banū Hāshim."[146]

Ibn ʿAbbās related that the soul of the Prophet ﷺ was a light in front of Allah Exalted, which He created two thousand years before He created Adam. The light glorified Allah, and the Angels followed its example. Then, when Allah created Adam, He cast that light into his loins. The Messenger of Allah ﷺ said: "Allah sent me to the Earth in the loins of Adam, then He cast me into the loins of Nūḥ, and then the loins of Ibrāhīm. Allah Exalted continued to move me between noble loins and pure wombs until He brought

---

142 lit., "houses".

143 Reported by Tirmidhī (3607). He said: "This hadith is *hasan*."

144 Reported by Tirmidhī (3605) with this wording, and Muslim (2276). Tirmidhī said: "This hadith is *hasan ṣaḥīḥ*."

145 Muhammad ibn Jarīr al-Ṭabarī, a diligent and renowned scholar. He was the author of *Al-Tafsīr, Al-Tārīkh, Tahdhīb al-Āthār*, and other works. He was born in 224 AH and died in 310 AH. See *Siyar Aʿlām al-Nubalāʾ* (14/267-282).

146 Haythamī attributed the hadith in *Majmaʿ al-Zawāʾid* (6/55-58) to Ṭabarānī from *Al-Kabīr* and *Al-Awsaṭ*, and said: "The chain includes Ḥammād ibn Wāqid, who was considered to be a weak narrator, but the rest are reliable." Suyūṭī graded the chain as *hasan* in *Al-Manāhil*, p. 127. Ibn Kathīr said in *Al-Bidāyah wa al-Nihāyah* (2/232): "This hadith is *gharīb*."

الْبُيُوتَ فَجَعَلَنِي مِنْ خَيْرِ بُيُوتِهِمْ، فَأَنَا خَيْرُهُمْ نَفْسًا، وَخَيْرُهُمْ بَيْتًا»[147]. ﷺ تَسْلِيمًا.

وَعَنْ وَاثِلَةَ بْنِ الْأَسْقَعِ ﵁ قَالَ: قَالَ رَسُولُ اللهِ ﷺ: «إِنَّ اللهَ اصْطَفَى مِنْ وَلَدِ إِبْرَاهِيمَ إِسْمَاعِيلَ، وَاصْطَفَى مِنْ وَلَدِ إِسْمَاعِيلَ بَنِي كِنَانَةَ، وَاصْطَفَى مِنْ بَنِي كِنَانَةَ قُرَيْشًا، وَاصْطَفَى مِنْ قُرَيْشٍ بَنِي هَاشِمٍ، وَاصْطَفَانِي مِنْ بَنِي هَاشِمٍ»[148]. قَالَ التِّرْمِذِيُّ: وَهَذَا حَدِيثٌ صَحِيحٌ.

وَفِي حَدِيثٍ عَنِ ابْنِ عُمَرَ ﵄ رَوَاهُ الطَّبَرِيُّ[149] أَنَّهُ ﷺ قَالَ: «إِنَّ اللهَ اخْتَارَ خَلْقَهُ، فَاخْتَارَ مِنْهُمْ بَنِي آدَمَ، ثُمَّ اخْتَارَ بَنِي آدَمَ فَاخْتَارَ مِنْهُمُ الْعَرَبَ، ثُمَّ اخْتَارَ الْعَرَبَ فَاخْتَارَ مِنْهُمْ قُرَيْشًا، ثُمَّ اخْتَارَ قُرَيْشًا فَاخْتَارَ بَنِي هَاشِمٍ، ثُمَّ اخْتَارَ بَنِي هَاشِمٍ فَاخْتَارَنِي، فَلَمْ أَزَلْ خِيَارًا مِنْ خِيَارٍ، أَلَا مَنْ أَحَبَّ الْعَرَبَ فَبِحُبِّي أَحَبَّهُمْ، وَمَنْ أَبْغَضَ الْعَرَبَ فَبِبُغْضِي أَبْغَضَهُمْ»[150].

وَعَنِ ابْنِ عَبَّاسٍ ﵄ أَنَّ قُرَيْشًا كَانَتْ نُورًا بَيْنَ يَدَيِ اللهِ تَعَالَى قَبْلَ أَنْ يَخْلُقَ آدَمَ بِأَلْفَيْ عَامٍ، يُسَبِّحُ ذَلِكَ النُّورُ، وَتُسَبِّحُ الْمَلَائِكَةُ بِتَسْبِيحِهِ، فَلَمَّا خَلَقَ اللهُ آدَمَ أَلْقَى ذَلِكَ النُّورَ فِي صُلْبِهِ، فَقَالَ رَسُولُ اللهِ ﷺ: «فَأَهْبَطَنِي اللهُ إِلَى

---

147 أَخْرَجَهُ التِّرْمِذِيُّ (٣٦٠٧) وَقَالَ: «هَذَا حَدِيثٌ حَسَنٌ».

148 أَخْرَجَهُ مُسْلِمٌ (٢٢٧٦)، وَالتِّرْمِذِيُّ (٣٦٠٥) وَاللَّفْظُ لَهُ.

149 هُوَ مُحَمَّدُ بْنُ جَرِيرٍ الطَّبَرِيُّ، إِمَامُ عِلْمٍ مُجْتَهِدٌ، صَاحِبُ التَّارِيخِ وَالتَّفْسِيرِ وَتَهْذِيبِ الآثَارِ وَغَيْرِهِ. وُلِدَ سَنَةَ (٢٢٤) هـ وَتُوُفِّيَ سَنَةَ (٣١٠). انْظُرْ تَرْجَمَتَهُ فِي سِيَرِ أَعْلَامِ النُّبَلَاءِ ٢٦٧/١٤-٢٨٢.

150 نَسَبَهُ الْهَيْثَمِيُّ فِي مَجْمَعِ الزَّوَائِدِ ٢١٥/٨ إِلَى الطَّبَرَانِيِّ فِي الْكَبِيرِ وَالْأَوْسَطِ وَقَالَ: «فِيهِ حَمَّادُ بْنُ وَاقِدٍ، وَهُوَ ضَعِيفٌ يُعْتَبَرُ بِهِ، وَبَقِيَّةُ رِجَالِهِ وُثِّقُوا»، وَحَسَّنَ السُّيُوطِيُّ إِسْنَادَهُ فِي الْمَنَاهِلِ (١٢٧). وَقَالَ ابْنُ كَثِيرٍ فِي الْبِدَايَةِ وَالنِّهَايَةِ ٢٣٢/٢: «حَدِيثٌ غَرِيبٌ».

me out from my parents. None of my ancestors ever engaged in immoral behaviour[147]."[148] The famous poetry of al-ʿAbbās in praise of the Prophet ﷺ[149] also supports the authenticity of this narration.

---

147   i.e., relations outside of marriage.

148   Reported by Ibn Abī ʿUmar al-ʿAdanī in his *Musnad*. See *Al-Manāhil*, p. 128.

149   The *qaṣīdah* of al-ʿAbbās (to be quoted later in the text) was reported by Ḥākim in *Al-Mustadrak* (3/327), Dhahabī in *Siyar Aʿlām al-Nubalāʾ* (2/102-103), Ibn al-Athīr in *Usd al-Ghābah* (1438), Ibn ʿAbd al-Barr in *Al-Istīʿāb*, and others, in the narration of Khuraym ibn Aws, who said that he heard al-ʿAbbās reciting it to the Messenger of Allah ﷺ. Haythamī said in *Majmaʿ al-Zawāʾid* (8/217-218): "It was related by Ṭabarānī and the chain contains narrators I do not recognize." Suyūṭī said in *Al-Laʾālī al-Maṣnūʿah* (1/265): "There being no difference of opinion regarding the verses of poetry belonging to al-ʿAbbās."

الأَرْضِ فِي صُلْبِ آدَمَ، وَجَعَلَنِي فِي صُلْبِ نُوحٍ، وَقَذَفَ بِي فِي صُلْبِ إِبْرَاهِيمَ، ثُمَّ لَمْ يَزَلِ اللهُ تَعَالَى يَنْقُلُنِي مِنَ الأَصْلَابِ الكَرِيمَةِ إِلَى الأَرْحَامِ الطَّاهِرَةِ، حَتَّى أَخْرَجَنِي بَيْنَ أَبَوَيَّ لَمْ يَلْتَقِيَا عَلَى سِفَاحٍ قَطُّ»[151].

وَيَشْهَدُ بِصِحَّةِ هَذَا الخَبَرِ شِعْرُ العَبَّاسِ المَشْهُورُ فِي مَدْحِ النَّبِيِّ ﷺ[152].

---

١٥١ أَخْرَجَهُ ابْنُ أَبِي عُمَرَ العَدَنِيُّ فِي مُسْنَدِهِ/ المَنَاهِلُ رَقْمُ (١٢٨٠).

١٥٢ سَيَذْكُرُ المُصَنِّفُ شِعْرَ العَبَّاسِ وَهُنَاكَ تَخْرِيجُهُ.

ACTIONS OF THE PROPHET ﷺ THAT WERE PERFORMED IN MODERATION

Those actions we described at the beginning of this chapter as being connected to the necessities of daily life can be split into three types: those actions that are praiseworthy when they are reduced or performed in moderation, those that are praiseworthy when they are performed in abundance, and those whose praiseworthiness differs according to the context.

Things that are agreed to be praiseworthy when they are performed in moderation, both according to the Shariah and local custom, include eating and sleeping. For these two actions, the Arabs and the people of wisdom would always commend those who made do with little and censure those who went to excess, because overindulging in food and drink is an indication of gluttony and rapacious greed. It signals a person's succumbing to their desires and it is harmful both in this life and the Hereafter. It damages the body, clouds the soul, and deluges the intellect. In contrast, eating in moderation is a sign of contentment and self-control, and develops a healthy body, a clear mind, and a sharp and perceptive intellect.

Likewise, sleeping excessively indicates weak-mindedness and a lack of intelligence. It leads to laziness, incompetence, and wasting away one's life without benefit. As a result, the heart becomes hardened, heedless, and moribund.

The evidence of these facts can be gleaned from numerous sources and has been related from many chains of transmission. It was attested to by the nations of the past, wise men who preceded

فصل

وَأَمَّا مَا تَدْعُو ضَرُورَةُ الْحَيَاةِ إِلَيْهِ مِمَّا فَصَّلْنَاهُ: فَعَلَى ثَلَاثَةِ ضُرُوبٍ[153]: ضَرْبُ الْفَضْلِ فِي قِلَّتِهِ، وَضَرْبُ الْفَضْلِ فِي كَثْرَتِهِ، وَضَرْبٌ تَخْتَلِفُ الْأَحْوَالُ فِيهِ.

فَأَمَّا مَا التَّمَدُّحُ وَالْكَمَالُ بِقِلَّتِهِ اتِّفَاقًا وَعَلَى كُلِّ حَالٍ عَادَةً وَشَرِيعَةً: كَالْغِذَاءِ، وَالنَّوْمِ، وَلَمْ تَزَلِ الْعُلَمَاءُ وَالْعَرَبُ وَالْحُكَمَاءُ تَتَمَادَحُ بِقِلَّتِهِمَا، وَتَذُمُّ بِكَثْرَتِهِمَا؛ لِأَنَّ كَثْرَةَ الْأَكْلِ وَالشُّرْبِ دَلِيلٌ عَلَى النَّهَمِ[154] وَالْحِرْصِ[155] وَالشَّرَهِ[156] وَغَلَبَةِ الشَّهْوَةِ، مُسَبِّبٌ لِمَضَارِّ الدُّنْيَا وَالْآخِرَةِ، جَالِبٌ لِأَدْوَاءِ الْجَسَدِ، وَخَثَارَةِ النَّفْسِ[157]، وَامْتِلَاءِ الدِّمَاغِ، وَقِلَّتُهُ دَلِيلٌ عَلَى الْقَنَاعَةِ، وَمِلْكِ النَّفْسِ، وَقَمْعِ الشَّهْوَةِ، مُسَبِّبٌ لِلصِّحَّةِ، وَصَفَاءِ الْخَاطِرِ، وَحِدَّةِ الذِّهْنِ، كَمَا أَنَّ كَثْرَةَ النَّوْمِ دَلِيلٌ عَلَى الْفُسُولَةِ[158]، وَالضَّعْفِ، وَعَدَمِ الذَّكَاءِ وَالْفِطْنَةِ، مُسَبِّبٌ لِلْكَسَلِ، وَعَادَةِ الْعَجْزِ، وَتَضْيِيعِ الْعُمْرِ فِي غَيْرِ نَفْعٍ، وَقَسَاوَةِ الْقَلْبِ وَغَفْلَتِهِ وَمَوْتِهِ.

وَالشَّاهِدُ عَلَى هَذَا مَا يُعْلَمُ ضَرُورَةً وَيُوجَدُ مُشَاهَدَةً وَيُنْقَلُ مُتَوَاتِرًا مِنْ كَلَامِ

---

153   ضُرُوبٌ: جَمْعُ ضَرْبٍ، وَهُوَ الصِّنْفُ وَالنَّوْعُ.

154   النَّهَمُ: نَهِمَ فِي الشَّيْءِ: أَفْرَطَ الشَّهْوَةَ أَوِ الرَّغْبَةَ فِيهِ.

155   الْحِرْصُ: الْجَشَعُ.

156   الشَّرَهُ: شَرِهَ إِلَى الطَّعَامِ وَغَيْرِهِ: اشْتَدَّ حِرْصُهُ عَلَيْهِ وَاشْتِهَاؤُهُ لَهُ.

157   خَثَارَةُ النَّفْسِ: اخْتِلَاطُهَا وَعَدَمُ نَشَاطِهَا.

158   الْفُسُولَةُ: قِلَّةُ الْمُرُوءَةِ وَضُعْفُ الرَّأْيِ (الْمُعْجَمُ الْوَسِيطُ).

us, the poetry and narrations of the Arabs, authentic hadiths, and the sayings of the Predecessors and those who came after them. The Prophet ﷺ was the most abstemious when it came to food and sleep and he encouraged others to follow his example.

I read the following hadith to Abū ʿAlī al-Ṣadafī, who narrated from Abū al-Faḍl al-Aṣbahānī, from Abū Nuʿaym al-Ḥāfiẓ, from Sulaymān ibn Aḥmad, from Bakr ibn Sahl[150], from ʿAbdullāh ibn Ṣāliḥ, from Muʿāwiyah ibn Ṣāliḥ, from Yaḥyā ibn Jābir, from al-Miqdām ibn Maʿdī Karib, that the Messenger of Allah ﷺ said: "The son of Adam does not fill any container worse than his stomach. Enough to support his backbone is sufficient for him. If that is not possible, then [he should leave] a third for food, a third for drink, and a third to breathe."[151] He also said that excessive sleeping was a result of eating and drinking too much.

Sufyān al-Thawrī commented: "The one who decreases his food will manage to stay up at night[152]." Some of the Predecessors used to say: "Do not eat too much, because then you will drink too much, sleep too much, and lose too much."

The Prophet ﷺ said that his favourite food was "that with many hands in it" (i.e., that which was shared).[153] ʿĀʾishah ﷺ observed: "Not once did I see the stomach of the Prophet ﷺ full. He never asked his family for food, neither would he crave it, but he would accept any food or drink they offered. Whatever his family served,

---

150 Bakr ibn Sahl al-Dimyāṭī, also known as Abū Muḥammad al-Hāshimī. He passed away in Dimyāṭ in 289 AH. See *Siyar Aʿlām al-Nubalāʾ* (13/425).

151 Reported here from the chain of Ṭabarānī in *Al-Kabīr* (20/283 no. 645). Also reported by Tirmidhī (2380), Ibn Mājah (3349), and others. Tirmidhī said: "This narration is *ḥasan ṣaḥīḥ*." Authenticated by Ḥākim (4/121, 331) and Dhahabī concurred. Also authenticated by Ibn Ḥibbān in *Mawārid al-Ẓamʾān* (1348, 1349) with the complete chain of transmission.

152 i.e., so that he can offer *qiyām al-layl*, the voluntary night prayer.

153 Reported by Abū Yaʿlā (3108) and others, from Anas ibn Mālik. Authenticated by Ibn Ḥibbān in *Mawārid al-Ẓamʾān* (2533). Also reported by Abū Yaʿlā (2045) from Jābir, and the chain was approved by Suyūṭī in *Al-Manāhil*, p. 130.

الأُمَمِ المُتَقَدِّمَةِ، وَالْحُكَمَاءِ السَّالِفِينَ، وَأَشْعَارِ العَرَبِ وَأَخْبَارِهَا، وَصَحِيحِ الحَدِيثِ وَآثَارِ مَنْ سَلَفَ وَخَلَفَ، مِمَّا لَا يُحْتَاجُ إِلَى الاسْتِشْهَادِ عَلَيْهِ اخْتِصَارًا وَاقْتِصَارًا عَلَى اشْتِهَارِ العِلْمِ بِهِ.

وَكَانَ النَّبِيُّ ﷺ قَدْ أَخَذَ مِنْ هَذَيْنِ الفَنَّيْنِ بِالأَقَلِّ، هَذَا مَا لَا يُدْفَعُ مِنْ سِيرَتِهِ، وَهُوَ الَّذِي أَمَرَ بِهِ وَحَضَّ عَلَيْهِ، لَا سِيَّمَا بِارْتِبَاطِ أَحَدِهِمَا بِالآخَرِ.

حَدَّثَنَا أَبُو عَلِيٍّ الصَّدَفِيُّ الحَافِظُ بِقِرَاءَتِي عَلَيْهِ، حَدَّثَنَا أَبُو الفَضْلِ الأَصْبَهَانِيُّ، حَدَّثَنَا أَبُو نُعَيْمٍ الحَافِظُ، حَدَّثَنَا سُلَيْمَانُ بْنُ أَحْمَدَ، حَدَّثَنَا بَكْرُ بْنُ سَهْلٍ[159]، حَدَّثَنَا عَبْدُ اللهِ بْنُ صَالِحٍ، حَدَّثَنِي مُعَاوِيَةُ بْنُ صَالِحٍ أَنَّ يَحْيَى بْنَ جَابِرٍ حَدَّثَهُ عَنِ المِقْدَامِ ابْنِ مَعْدِي كَرِبَ أَنَّ رَسُولَ اللهِ ﷺ قَالَ: «مَا مَلَأَ ابْنُ آدَمَ وِعَاءً شَرًّا مِنْ بَطْنِهِ، حَسْبُ ابْنِ آدَمَ أُكُلَاتٌ يُقِمْنَ صُلْبَهُ، فَإِنْ كَانَ لَا مَحَالَةَ فَثُلُثٌ لِطَعَامِهِ، وَثُلُثٌ لِشَرَابِهِ، وَثُلُثٌ لِنَفَسِهِ»[160].

وَلِأَنَّ كَثْرَةَ النَّوْمِ مِنْ كَثْرَةِ الأَكْلِ وَالشُّرْبِ.

قَالَ سُفْيَانُ الثَّوْرِيُّ: بِقِلَّةِ الطَّعَامِ يُمْلَكُ سَهَرُ اللَّيْلِ.

وَقَالَ بَعْضُ السَّلَفِ: لَا تَأْكُلُوا كَثِيرًا، فَتَشْرَبُوا كَثِيرًا، فَتَرْقُدُوا كَثِيرًا، فَتَخْسَرُوا كَثِيرًا.

---

159   وَهُوَ بَكْرُ بْنُ سَهْلٍ الدِّمْيَاطِيُّ، أَبُو مُحَمَّدٍ الهَاشِمِيُّ. مَاتَ بِدِمْيَاطَ سَنَةَ (٢٨٩) هـ انْظُرْ تَرْجَمَتَهُ فِي سِيَرِ أَعْلَامِ النُّبَلَاءِ ١٣/٤٢٥.

160   أَسْنَدَهُ المُصَنِّفُ مِنْ طَرِيقِ سُلَيْمَانَ بْنِ أَحْمَدَ الطَّبَرَانِيِّ فِي الكَبِيرِ ٢٠/٢٧٣ رَقْمُ (٦٤٥) وَأَخْرَجَهُ التِّرْمِذِيُّ (٢٣٨٠)، وَابْنُ مَاجَهْ (٣٣٤٩) وَغَيْرُهُ، وَقَالَ التِّرْمِذِيُّ: «هَذَا حَدِيثٌ حَسَنٌ صَحِيحٌ»، وَصَحَّحَهُ الحَاكِمُ (٤/١٢١ وَ ٣٣١)، وَوَافَقَهُ الذَّهَبِيُّ، وَصَحَّحَهُ أَيْضًا ابْنُ حِبَّانَ (١٣٤٨ وَ ١٣٤٩) مَوَارِدُ، وَهُنَاكَ اسْتَوْفَيْنَا تَخْرِيجَهُ.

he ate, and whatever they poured, he drank."[154] This is not contradicted by the narration of Barīrah[155], when the Prophet ﷺ said: "Do I see a pot with meat inside?"[156] He may have been asking because he thought that they imagined the meat was not permissible for him, and he wanted to clarify the issue. He had noticed that they had not offered him any, even though he knew that they would not give themselves preference over him, so he told them: "It is charity for her, and a gift[157] for us."

Luqmān advised his son: "O son! When the stomach is full, thought is stifled[158], wisdom is muted, and the limbs become lazy to worship." Saḥnūn[159] said: "Knowledge will not benefit the one who eats until he is satiated." The Prophet ﷺ also said: "I do not eat whilst reclining."[160]

"Reclining" implies a person in a relaxed position and completely at ease; sitting cross-legged, for example. It does not refer to someone merely leaning on their side, according to the scholars who have investigated the matter.

Someone who has prepared themselves in such a manner is ready to eat copious amounts. The Prophet ﷺ, on the other hand,

---

154 See *Jāmiʿ al-Uṣūl* (4/682-689). Part of a longer narration that will appear later in the text.

155 She was a servant of ʿĀʾishah and a famous Companion. She lived until the time of Yazīd ibn Muʿāwiyah. ʿĀʾishah said: "Three aspects of the Sunnah were established on account of Barīrah. When she was freed, she was given the option (to remain with her husband or not). She had been given some meat as charity (ṣadaqah). The Messenger of Allah entered whilst the pot was on the fire. He said: 'Can I see a pot on the fire with meat inside?' They replied: 'O Messenger of Allah! It is meat that was given to Barīrah as charity, so we did not like to serve it to you.' He said: 'It is charity for her, and a gift for us.' The Prophet ﷺ had also said: 'The right to inherit is for the one who emancipates.'"

156 Reported by Bukhārī (5097) and Muslim (1504/14) from ʿĀʾishah.

157 And therefore permissible.

158 lit., "goes to sleep".

159 ʿAbd al-Salām ibn Saʿīd ibn Ḥabīb, a knowledgeable scholar and jurist. He was given the nickname "al-Saḥnūn", which was a type of bird, and was the author of *Al-Mudawwanah*. He died in 240 AH at the age of eighty. See *Siyar Aʿlām al-Nubalāʾ* (12/63-69).

160 Reported by Tirmidhī (1830) with this wording and Bukhārī (5398), from Abū Juḥayfah.

وَقَدْ رُوِيَ عَنْهُ ﷺ أَنَّهُ كَانَ أَحَبُّ الطَّعَامِ إِلَيْهِ مَا كَانَ عَلَى ضَفَفٍ[161]. أَيْ كَثْرَةِ الْأَيْدِي.

وَعَنْ عَائِشَةَ رضي الله عنها: لَمْ يَمْتَلِئْ جَوْفُ النَّبِيِّ ﷺ شِبَعًا قَطُّ، وَأَنَّهُ كَانَ فِي أَهْلِهِ لَا يَسْأَلُهُمْ طَعَامًا، وَلَا يَتَشَهَّاهُ، إِنْ أَطْعَمُوهُ أَكَلَ، وَمَا أَطْعَمُوهُ قَبِلَ، وَمَا سَقَوْهُ شَرِبَ[162].

وَلَا يُعْتَرَضُ عَلَى هَذَا بِحَدِيثِ بَرِيرَةَ[163]، وَقَوْلِهِ: «أَلَمْ أَرَ الْبُرْمَةَ فِيهَا لَحْمٌ»[164]؛ إِذْ لَعَلَّ سَبَبَ سُؤَالِهِ ﷺ ظَنُّهُ اعْتِقَادَهُمْ أَنَّهُ لَا يَحِلُّ لَهُ، فَأَرَادَ بَيَانَ سُنَّتِهِ، إِذْ رَآهُمْ لَمْ يُقَدِّمُوهُ إِلَيْهِ، مَعَ عِلْمِهِ أَنَّهُمْ لَا يَسْتَأْثِرُونَ عَلَيْهِ بِهِ، فَصَدَقَ عَلَيْهِمْ ظَنُّهُ، وَبَيَّنَ لَهُمْ مَا جَهِلُوهُ مِنْ أَمْرِهِ بِقَوْلِهِ: «هُوَ لَهَا صَدَقَةٌ، وَلَنَا هَدِيَّةٌ».

وَفِي حِكْمَةِ لُقْمَانَ: «يَا بُنَيَّ، إِذَا امْتَلَأَتِ الْمَعِدَةُ نَامَتِ الْفِكْرَةُ، وَخَرِسَتِ الْحِكْمَةُ، وَقَعَدَتِ الْأَعْضَاءُ عَنِ الْعِبَادَةِ».

وَقَالَ سَحْنُونُ[165]: «لَا يَصْلُحُ الْعِلْمُ لِمَنْ يَأْكُلُ حَتَّى يَشْبَعَ».

---

161 أَخْرَجَهُ التِّرْمِذِيُّ فِي الشَّمَائِلِ (١٣٨)، وَأَبُو يَعْلَى (٣١٠٨) وَغَيْرُهُ مِنْ حَدِيثِ أَنَسِ بْنِ مَالِكٍ، وَصَحَّحَهُ ابْنُ حِبَّانَ (٢٥٣٣) مَوَارِد، وَأَخْرَجَهُ أَبُو يَعْلَى (٢٠٤٥) مِنْ حَدِيثِ جَابِرٍ، وَجَوَّدَ إِسْنَادَهُ السُّيُوطِيُّ فِي الْمَنَاهِلِ (١٣٠).

162 انْظُرْ جَامِعَ الْأُصُولِ ٦٨٢/٤ ٦٨٩-.

163 هِيَ مَوْلَاةُ عَائِشَةَ، صَحَابِيَّةٌ مَشْهُورَةٌ. عَاشَتْ إِلَى زَمَنِ يَزِيدَ بْنِ مُعَاوِيَةَ. قَالَتْ عَائِشَةُ: كَانَ فِي بَرِيرَةَ ثَلَاثُ سُنَنٍ: خُيِّرَتْ عَلَى زَوْجِهَا حِينَ عُتِقَتْ. وَأُهْدِيَ لَهَا لَحْمٌ، فَدَخَلَ عَلَيَّ رَسُولُ اللهِ ﷺ وَالْبُرْمَةُ عَلَى النَّارِ، فَدَعَا بِطَعَامٍ، فَأُتِيَ بِخُبْزٍ وَأُدُمٍ مِنْ أُدُمِ الْبَيْتِ. فَقَالَ: «أَلَمْ أَرَ بُرْمَةً عَلَى النَّارِ فِيهَا لَحْمٌ؟» فَقَالُوا: بَلَى، يَا رَسُولَ اللهِ! ذَلِكَ لَحْمٌ تُصُدِّقَ بِهِ عَلَى بَرِيرَةَ. فَكَرِهْنَا أَنْ نُطْعِمَكَ مِنْهُ. فَقَالَ: هُوَ عَلَيْهَا صَدَقَةٌ وَهُوَ مِنْهَا لَنَا هَدِيَّةٌ. وَقَالَ النَّبِيُّ ﷺ فِيهَا: «إِنَّمَا الْوَلَاءُ لِمَنْ أَعْتَقَ».

164 أَخْرَجَهُ الْبُخَارِيُّ (٥٠٩٧)، وَمُسْلِمٌ (١٤/١٥٠٤) مِنْ حَدِيثِ عَائِشَةَ. (الْبُرْمَةُ): الْقِدْرُ.

165 هُوَ عَبْدُ السَّلَامِ بْنُ سَعِيدِ بْنِ حَبِيبٍ، إِمَامٌ عَلَّامَةٌ فَقِيهٌ، يُلَقَّبُ بِسَحْنُونَ: اسْمُ طَائِرٍ بِالْمَغْرِبِ. لَهُ «الْمُدَوَّنَةُ» فِي فِقْهِ الْإِمَامِ مَالِكٍ. مَاتَ سَنَةَ (٢٤٠) هـ، وَلَهُ ثَمَانُونَ سَنَةً. انْظُرْ تَرْجَمَتَهُ فِي سِيَرِ أَعْلَامِ النُّبَلَاءِ ٦٣/١٢ - ٦٩.

sat in a squatting position, as if he was ready to leave.[161] He once said: "I am a slave. I eat as a slave eats, and I sit as a slave sits."[162]

The Prophet ﷺ also slept little, as confirmed in authentic narrations, and he once said: "My eyes sleep but my heart does not."[163] He would rest on his right side[164] in order to shorten his sleep, because sleeping on the left side is easier on the heart and surrounding organs which lean to the left, and leads to a long, deep sleep. When someone sleeps on the right side, however, the heart remains in a state of suspense, they are not completely submerged in a deep sleep, and they tend to wake up sooner.

---

161   Reported by Muslim (2044) from Anas.

162   Reported by Abū Yaʿlā (4920) and others from ʿĀ'ishah. The chain was graded as *ḥasan* by Haythamī in *Majmaʿ al-Zawā'id* (9/19), and Suyūṭī in *Al-Manāhil*, p. 135, where he records chains from a number of Companions.

163   Reported by Bukhārī (1147) and Muslim (738) from ʿĀ'ishah.

164   Reported by Tirmidhī in *Al-Sunan* (3399) and *Al-Shamā'il* (253, 254), and Nasā'ī in ʿAmal al-Yawm wa al-Laylah (785), from al-Barā' ibn ʿĀzib. Tirmidhī said: "This narration is *ḥasan gharīb.*"

وَفِي صَحِيحِ الحَدِيثِ قَوْلُهُ: «أَمَّا أَنَا فَلَا آكُلُ مُتَّكِئًا».[166]

وَالاتِّكَاءُ: هُوَ التَّمَكُّنُ لِلْأَكْلِ، وَالتَّقَعُّدُ فِي الجُلُوسِ لَهُ، كَالمُتَرَبِّعِ وَشِبْهِهِ مِنْ تَمَكُّنِ الجَلَسَاتِ الَّتِي يَعْتَمِدُ فِيهَا الجَالِسُ عَلَى مَا تَحْتَهُ، وَالجَالِسُ عَلَى هَذِهِ الهَيْئَةِ يَسْتَدْعِي الأَكْلَ وَيَسْتَكْثِرُ مِنْهُ، وَالنَّبِيُّ ﷺ إِنَّمَا كَانَ جُلُوسُهُ لِلْأَكْلِ جُلُوسَ المُسْتَوْفِزِ مُقْعِيًا،[167] وَيَقُولُ: «إِنَّمَا أَنَا عَبْدٌ، آكُلُ كَمَا يَأْكُلُ العَبْدُ، وَأَجْلِسُ كَمَا يَجْلِسُ العَبْدُ».[168]

وَلَيْسَ مَعْنَى الحَدِيثِ فِي الاتِّكَاءِ المَيْلَ عَلَى شِقٍّ عِنْدَ المُحَقِّقِينَ.

وَكَذَلِكَ نَوْمُهُ ﷺ كَانَ قَلِيلًا، شَهِدَتْ بِذَلِكَ الآثَارُ الصَّحِيحَةُ، وَمَعَ ذَلِكَ فَقَدْ قَالَ: «إِنَّ عَيْنَيَّ تَنَامَانِ، وَلَا يَنَامُ قَلْبِي».[169]

وَكَانَ نَوْمُهُ عَلَى جَانِبِهِ الأَيْمَنِ[170] اسْتِظْهَارًا عَلَى قِلَّةِ النَّوْمِ؛ لِأَنَّهُ عَلَى الجَانِبِ الأَيْسَرِ أَهْدَأُ لِهُدُوِّ القَلْبِ وَمَا يَتَعَلَّقُ بِهِ مِنَ الأَعْضَاءِ البَاطِنَةِ حِينَئِذٍ لِمَيْلِهَا إِلَى الجَانِبِ الأَيْسَرِ، فَيَسْتَدْعِي ذَلِكَ الاسْتِثْقَالَ فِيهِ وَالطُّولَ، وَإِذَا نَامَ النَّائِمُ عَلَى الأَيْمَنِ تَعَلَّقَ القَلْبُ وَقَلِقَ، فَأَسْرَعَ الإِفَاقَةَ، وَلَمْ يَغْمُرْهُ الاسْتِغْرَاقُ.

---

166 أَخْرَجَهُ البُخَارِيُّ (٥٣٩٨)، وَالتِّرْمِذِيُّ (١٨٣٠) وَاللَّفْظُ لَهُ، مِنْ حَدِيثِ أَبِي جُحَيْفَةَ.

167 أَخْرَجَهُ مُسْلِمٌ (٢٠٤٤) مِنْ حَدِيثِ أَنَسٍ. (المُسْتَوْفِزُ): المُسْتَعْجِلُ، غَيْرُ المُتَمَكِّنِ فِي جُلُوسِهِ. (مُقْعِيًا): أَيْ جَالِسًا عَلَى أَلْيَتَيْهِ، نَاصِبًا سَاقَيْهِ.

168 أَخْرَجَهُ أَبُو يَعْلَى (٤٩٢٠) وَغَيْرُهُ مِنْ حَدِيثِ عَائِشَةَ. وَحَسَّنَ إِسْنَادَهُ الهَيْثَمِيُّ فِي مَجْمَعِ الزَّوَائِدِ ١٩/٩، وَالسُّيُوطِيُّ فِي مَنَاهِلِ الصَّفَا (١٣٥)، وَلَهُ طُرُقٌ عَنْ عَدَدٍ مِنَ الصَّحَابَةِ انْظُرْهَا فِي مَنَاهِلِ الصَّفَا (١٣٥).

169 أَخْرَجَهُ البُخَارِيُّ (١١٤٧)، وَمُسْلِمٌ (٧٣٨) مِنْ حَدِيثِ عَائِشَةَ.

170 أَخْرَجَهُ التِّرْمِذِيُّ فِي السُّنَنِ (٣٣٩٩)، وَفِي الشَّمَائِلِ (٢٥٢)، وَالنَّسَائِيُّ فِي «عَمَلِ اليَوْمِ وَاللَّيْلَةِ» بِرَقْمِ (٧٨٥) مِنْ حَدِيثِ البَرَاءِ بْنِ عَازِبٍ. قَالَ التِّرْمِذِيُّ: «هَذَا حَدِيثٌ حَسَنٌ غَرِيبٌ».

ACTIONS OF THE PROPHET ﷺ THAT WERE PERFORMED IN ABUNDANCE

The second type of action or quality were those whose virtue lay in being performed in great quantities and whose abundance was celebrated, like marriage and prestige.

As for marriage, it is unanimously agreed upon, both as a custom and as a legislated practice in the Shariah. It is a sign of wholeness and healthy masculinity, and people are known to celebrate and congratulate those who marry abundantly. And according to the Shariah, marriage is an established Sunnah. Ibn ʿAbbās said: "The best of this nation (i.e., the Prophet ﷺ) had the most wives."[165]

The Prophet ﷺ said: "Get married and have children, for I will show off my nation on the Day of Judgement."[166] He forbade celibacy,[167] because marriage is an effective means of cooling the desires and lowering the sight. As the Prophet ﷺ said: "Whoever is able to do so should marry, because it lowers the sight and protects the private parts."[168] Because of this, the scholars did not consider marriage to be something that detracts from the principles of as-

---

165   Reported by Bukhārī (5069).

166   Reported by Ibn Mardawayh in his *Tafsīr* from Ibn ʿUmar. Graded as *daʿīf* by ʿIrāqī, and Suyūṭī followed his opinion. Sakhāwī said in *Al-Maqāṣid al-Ḥasanah* (350): "The [same] meaning has been related from a number of Companions." Reported in *Mawārid al-Ẓamʾān* (1228) from Anas and again (1229) from Maʿqil ibn Yasār.

167   Reported by Bukhārī (5073) and Muslim (1402) from Saʿd ibn Abī Waqqāṣ.

168   Reported by Bazzār (1399) and Ṭabarānī from Anas, without the phrase: "because it lowers the sight and protects the private parts." Haythamī said in *Majmaʿ al-Zawāʾid* (4/252): "The narrators in the chain of Ṭabarānī are reliable." Also reported by Bukhārī (5066) and Muslim (1400) from Ibn Masʿūd, with the wording: "Those among you who can support a wife should marry, because it lowers the sight and protects the private parts."

فصل

وَالضَّرْبُ الثَّانِي: مَا يَتَّفِقُ التَّمَدُّحُ بِكَثْرَتِهِ وَالفَخْرُ بِوُفُورِهِ كَالنِّكَاحِ وَالجَاهِ.

❊ أَمَّا النِّكَاحُ فَمُتَّفَقٌ فِيهِ شَرْعًا وَعَادَةً، فَإِنَّهُ دَلِيلُ الكَمَالِ، وَصِحَّةِ الذُّكُورِيَّةِ، وَلَمْ يَزَلِ التَّفَاخُرُ بِكَثْرَتِهِ عَادَةً مَعْرُوفَةً، وَالتَّمَادُحُ بِهِ سِيرَةً مَاضِيَةً. وَأَمَّا فِي الشَّرْعِ فَسُنَّةٌ مَأْثُورَةٌ.

وَقَدْ قَالَ ابْنُ عَبَّاسٍ: «أَفْضَلُ هَذِهِ الأُمَّةِ أَكْثَرُهَا نِسَاءً»[١٧١]، مُشِيرًا إِلَيْهِ ﷺ.

وَقَدْ قَالَ ﷺ: «تَنَاكَحُوا؛ فَإِنِّي مُبَاهٍ بِكُمُ الأُمَمَ»[١٧٢].

وَنَهَى عَنِ التَّبَتُّلِ[١٧٣] مَعَ مَا فِيهِ مِنْ قَمْعِ الشَّهْوَةِ، وَغَضِّ البَصَرِ اللَّذَيْنِ نَبَّهَ عَلَيْهِمَا ﷺ بِقَوْلِهِ: «مَنْ كَانَ ذَا طَوْلٍ فَلْيَتَزَوَّجْ، فَإِنَّهُ أَغَضُّ لِلْبَصَرِ، وَأَحْصَنُ لِلْفَرْجِ»[١٧٤]، حَتَّى لَمْ يَرَهُ العُلَمَاءُ مِمَّا يَقْدَحُ فِي الزُّهْدِ.

---

١٧١   أَخْرَجَهُ البُخَارِيُّ (٥٠٦٩).

١٧٢   أَخْرَجَهُ ابْنُ مَرْدَوَيْهِ فِي تَفْسِيرِهِ مِنْ حَدِيثِ ابْنِ عُمَرَ، وَضَعَّفَ إِسْنَادَهُ العِرَاقِيُّ، وَتَبِعَهُ السُّيُوطِيُّ. وَقَالَ السَّخَاوِيُّ فِي المَقَاصِدِ الحَسَنَةِ (٣٥٠): «جَاءَ مَعْنَاهُ عَنْ عَدَدٍ مِنَ الصَّحَابَةِ». وَقَدْ خَرَّجْنَاهُ فِي مَوَارِدِ الظَّمْآنِ عَنْ أَنَسٍ بِرَقْمِ (١٢٢٨)، وَعَن مَعْقِلِ بْنِ يَسَارٍ (١٢٢٩).

١٧٣   أَخْرَجَهُ البُخَارِيُّ (٥٠٧٣)، وَمُسْلِمٌ (١٤٠٢) مِنْ حَدِيثِ سَعْدِ بْنِ أَبِي وَقَّاصٍ. (التَّبَتُّلُ): الانْقِطَاعُ عَنِ النِّسَاءِ وَتَرْكُ النِّكَاحِ (النِّهَايَة).

١٧٤   أَخْرَجَهُ الطَّبَرَانِيُّ وَالبَزَّارُ (١٣٩٩) مِنْ حَدِيثِ أَنَسٍ، بِدُونِ قَوْلِهِ: فَإِنَّهُ أَغَضُّ...، قَالَ الهَيْثَمِيُّ فِي مَجْمَعِ الزَّوَائِدِ ٤/٢٥٢: «وَرِجَالُ الطَّبَرَانِيِّ ثِقَاتٌ». وَأَخْرَجَهُ البُخَارِيُّ (٥٠٦٦)، وَمُسْلِمٌ (١٤٠٠) مِنْ حَدِيثِ ابْنِ مَسْعُودٍ بِلَفْظِ: «مَنِ اسْتَطَاعَ مِنْكُمُ البَاءَةَ فَلْيَتَزَوَّجْ فَإِنَّهُ أَغَضُّ لِلْبَصَرِ...». (ذَا طَوْلٍ): صَاحِبُ يُسْرٍ وَغِنًى وَمَقْدِرَةٍ.

ceticism and self-restraint.

Sahl ibn ʿAbdullāh said: "The Leader of the Messengers ﷺ loved women, so how could we abstain from them?" Ibn ʿUtaybah[169] said something similar. In fact, the most devoted and ascetic of the Companions had many wives and female servants, and would regularly engage in sexual relations with them. This was related in the case of ʿAlī, al-Ḥasan, Ibn ʿUmar, and many others. In addition, several of the Companions were reported to have disliked the idea of meeting their Creator whilst still unmarried.

One might ask how marriage can be such a virtuous action, when Allah Exalted has praised Yaḥyā, the son of Zakariyyā, as "chaste"[170]. Why would Allah Exalted praise turning away from a righteous action and a blessing? ʿĪsā ibn Maryam also remained celibate. If things were as we have claimed, would he not have married?

Understand that the praise of Allah Exalted upon Yaḥyā ﷺ for being "chaste" is not, as some have claimed, a result of his fear of marriage or lack of masculinity. The most accomplished scholars have rejected this assertion, noting that it would imply an imperfection unbefitting of a Prophet. The correct meaning is that he abstained, or was "chaste" from, committing sinful actions. There were others who interpreted the word to imply that he restrained himself from physical desires, or that he had no desire for women in the first place.

What is clear is that a person lacking the competence to get married has a fault and is missing out on a virtuous action. However, avoiding marriage in order to strive in the cause of Allah

---

169   Sufyān ibn ʿUyaynah, a *ḥāfiẓ*, jurist, and authority in the religion. He died in 198 AH at the age of ninety-one. See *Siyar Aʿlām al-Nubalāʾ* (8/454-475).

170   Āl ʿImrān, 39. "Chaste", meaning, he does not marry even though he has the ability to do so.

قَالَ سَهْلُ بْنُ عَبْدِ اللهِ: «قَدْ حُبِّبْنَ إِلَى سَيِّدِ الْمُرْسَلِينَ، فَكَيْفَ يُزْهَدُ فِيهِنَّ؟!».

وَنَحْوُهُ لِابْنِ عُيَيْنَةَ[175].

وَقَدْ كَانَ زُهَّادُ الصَّحَابَةِ كَثِيرِي الزَّوْجَاتِ وَالسَّرَارِيِّ[176]، كَثِيرِي النِّكَاحِ.

وَحُكِيَ فِي ذَلِكَ عَنْ عَلِيٍّ، وَالْحَسَنِ، وَابْنِ عُمَرَ وَغَيْرِهِمْ غَيْرُ شَيْءٍ، وَقَدْ كَرِهَ غَيْرُ وَاحِدٍ أَنْ يَلْقَى اللهَ عَزَبًا.

فَإِنْ قُلْتَ: كَيْفَ يَكُونُ النِّكَاحُ وَكَثْرَتُهُ مِنَ الْفَضَائِلِ وَهَذَا يَحْيَى بْنُ زَكَرِيَّا قَدْ أَثْنَى اللهُ تَعَالَى عَلَيْهِ أَنَّهُ كَانَ حَصُورًا[177]، فَكَيْفَ يُثْنِي اللهُ عَلَيْهِ بِالْعَجْزِ عَمَّا تَعُدُّهُ فَضِيلَةً؟ وَهَذَا عِيسَى عَلَيْهِ السَّلَامُ قَدْ تَبَتَّلَ مِنَ النِّسَاءِ، وَلَوْ كَانَ كَمَا قَرَّرْتَهُ لَنَكَحَ.

فَاعْلَمْ أَنَّ ثَنَاءَ اللهِ تَعَالَى عَلَى يَحْيَى بِأَنَّهُ حَصُورٌ لَيْسَ كَمَا قَالَ بَعْضُهُمْ: إِنَّهُ كَانَ هَيُوبًا[178]، أَوْ لَا ذَكَرَ لَهُ، بَلْ قَدْ أَنْكَرَ هَذَا حُذَّاقُ[179] الْمُفَسِّرِينَ وَنُقَّادُ الْعُلَمَاءِ، وَقَالُوا: هَذِهِ نَقِيصَةٌ وَعَيْبٌ وَلَا تَلِيقُ بِالْأَنْبِيَاءِ عَلَيْهِمُ الصَّلَاةُ وَالسَّلَامُ، وَإِنَّمَا مَعْنَاهُ أَنَّهُ مَعْصُومٌ مِنَ الذُّنُوبِ: أَيْ لَا يَأْتِيهَا، كَأَنَّهُ حُصِرَ عَنْهَا. وَقِيلَ: مَانِعًا نَفْسَهُ

---

175 هُوَ سُفْيَانُ بْنُ عُيَيْنَةَ، ثِقَةٌ حَافِظٌ، فَقِيهٌ، حُجَّةٌ. مَاتَ سَنَةَ (198) وَلَهُ (91) سَنَةً. انْظُرْ تَرْجَمَتَهُ فِي سِيَرِ أَعْلَامِ النُّبَلَاءِ 8/454-475.

176 السَّرَارِي: الْإِمَاءُ.

177 حَصُورًا: لَا يَأْتِي النِّسَاءَ، مَعَ الْقُدْرَةِ عَلَى إِتْيَانِهِنَّ، تَعَفُّفًا وَزُهْدًا (كَلِمَاتُ الْقُرْآنِ لِمَخْلُوفٍ).

178 هَيُوبًا: الْمُرَادُ - هُنَا - جَبَانًا عَنِ النِّكَاحِ.

179 حُذَّاقٌ: جَمْعُ حَاذِقٍ، وَهُوَ الْمَاهِرُ.

Exalted, as was the case of ʿĪsā ﷺ, or to suffice oneself with the blessings of Allah Exalted, as was the case of Yaḥyā ﷺ, can also be virtuous, because marriage has a habit of occupying one's time and causing an attachment to worldly life.

People who are capable of fulfilling the responsibilities of marriage without being distracted from their Lord are promised a lofty rank. This is the rank of the Prophet ﷺ. Having many wives did not distract him from worshipping Allah Exalted. In fact, he increased in worship by protecting his wives, fulfilling their rights, providing for them, and guiding them.

When the Prophet ﷺ said, "In this worldly life of yours, I was made to love…",[171] he indicated that his love for women and perfume was for the purpose of benefitting his Hereafter, rather than his worldly life. We have mentioned the spiritual benefits of marriage, and he loved to meet the presence of Angels[172] whilst wearing perfume. A sweet scent carries the additional benefit of encouraging and stimulating sexual relations with one's spouse. His love for women and perfume were for a higher cause, and as a means of restraining desire. The true love of the Prophet ﷺ was to witness the Grandeur of his Protector and engage in intimate conversation with Him. For this reason, he differentiated between the two types of love, adding: "…and the coolness of my eyes[173] has been provided in the prayer."[174]

The Prophet ﷺ was like Yaḥyā and ʿĪsā in his self-restraint, but

---

171 Reported by Nasāʾī (7/61), Aḥmad (3/128), Abū Yaʿlā (3482), Bayhaqī (7/87), and others, from the
narration of Anas ibn Mālik. Authenticated by Ḥākim (2/160) and Dhahabī agreed. ʿIrāqī approved of the
chain. Ibn Ḥajar graded the hadith as *ḥasan*, and Suyūṭī shared the same view.

172 i.e., the Angels that visit us in this world.

173 i.e., my source of comfort.

174 See above.

مِنَ الشَّهَوَاتِ. وَقِيلَ: لَيْسَتْ لَهُ شَهْوَةٌ فِي النِّسَاءِ.

فَقَدْ بَانَ لَكَ مِنْ هَذَا أَنَّ عَدَمَ الْقُدْرَةِ عَلَى النِّكَاحِ نَقْصٌ، وَإِنَّمَا الْفَضْلُ فِي كَوْنِهَا مَوْجُودَةً، ثُمَّ قَمْعِهَا، إِمَّا بِمُجَاهَدَةٍ، كَعِيسَى ﵇، أَوْ بِكِفَايَةٍ مِنَ اللهِ تَعَالَى كَيَحْيَى ﵇، فَضِيلَةً زَائِدَةً؛ لِكَوْنِهَا مَشْغَلَةً فِي كَثِيرٍ مِنَ الأَوْقَاتِ، حَاطَّةً إِلَى الدُّنْيَا.

ثُمَّ هِيَ فِي حَقِّ مَنْ أُقْدِرَ عَلَيْهَا وَمَلَكَهَا، وَقَامَ بِالْوَاجِبِ فِيهَا، وَلَمْ تَشْغَلْهُ عَنْ رَبِّهِ: دَرَجَةٌ عُلْيَا، وَهِيَ دَرَجَةُ نَبِيِّنَا ﷺ الَّذِي لَمْ تَشْغَلْهُ كَثْرَتُهُنَّ عَنْ عِبَادَةِ رَبِّهِ عز وجل، بَلْ زَادَهُ ذَلِكَ عِبَادَةً لِتَحْصِينِهِنَّ، وَقِيَامِهِ بِحُقُوقِهِنَّ، وَاكْتِسَابِهِ لَهُنَّ، وَهِدَايَتِهِ إِيَّاهُنَّ.

بَلْ صَرَّحَ أَنَّهَا لَيْسَتْ مِنْ حُظُوظِ دُنْيَاهُ هُوَ، وَإِنْ كَانَتْ مِنْ حُظُوظِ دُنْيَا غَيْرِهِ، فَقَالَ: «حُبِّبَ إِلَيَّ مِنْ دُنْيَاكُمْ»[180]، فَدَلَّ أَنَّ حُبَّهُ لِمَا ذَكَرَ مِنَ النِّسَاءِ وَالطِّيبِ - اللَّذَيْنِ مِنْ أُمُورِ دُنْيَا غَيْرِهِ - وَاسْتِعْمَالَهُ لِذَلِكَ لَيْسَ لِدُنْيَاهُ، بَلْ لِآخِرَتِهِ، لِلْفَوَائِدِ الَّتِي ذَكَرْنَاهَا فِي التَّزْوِيجِ، وَلِلِقَاءِ الْمَلَائِكَةِ فِي الطِّيبِ، وَلِأَنَّهُ أَيْضًا مِمَّا يَحُضُّ عَلَى الْجِمَاعِ، وَيُعِينُ عَلَيْهِ، وَيُحَرِّكُ أَسْبَابَهُ.

وَكَانَ حُبُّهُ ﷺ لِهَاتَيْنِ الْخَصْلَتَيْنِ لِأَجْلِ غَيْرِهِ، وَقَمْعِ شَهْوَتِهِ، وَكَانَ حُبُّهُ الْحَقِيقِيُّ الْمُخْتَصُّ بِذَاتِهِ فِي مُشَاهَدَةِ جَبَرُوتِ مَوْلَاهُ، وَمُنَاجَاتِهِ، وَلِذَلِكَ مَيَّزَ بَيْنَ الْحُبَّيْنِ، وَفَصَلَ بَيْنَ الْحَالَيْنِ، فَقَالَ: «وَجُعِلَتْ قُرَّةُ عَيْنِي فِي الصَّلَاةِ»، فَقَدْ سَاوَى يَحْيَى وَعِيسَى ﵉ فِي كِفَايَةِ فِتْنَتِهِنَّ، وَزَادَ فَضِيلَةً بِالْقِيَامِ بِهِنَّ.

---

[180] تَتِمَّتُهُ: «النِّسَاءُ وَالطِّيبُ، وَجُعِلَتْ قُرَّةُ عَيْنِي فِي الصَّلَاةِ».

taking care of women and fulfilling their rights is an extra virtue. The Prophet ﷺ was given abundant strength and ability in this regard, and for that reason was allowed a greater number of wives than any other man.[175]

Anas related that the Prophet ﷺ would visit his eleven wives within a single hour of the day or night, adding: "We used to say that the Prophet ﷺ was given the strength of thirty men."[176] A similar narration was reported from Abū Rāfiʿ.[177] Ṭāwūs[178] commented: "In sexual intercourse, he was given the strength of forty men." Ṣafwān ibn Sulaym[179] said the same. Salmā said: "The Prophet ﷺ visited his nine wives in one night, and he purified himself each time before leaving for the next. He said: 'This is purer and more attractive.'"[180]

Prophet Sulaymān ﷺ once said: "Tonight, I will have sexual intercourse with one hundred (or ninety-nine) women."[181] And he did as he promised. Ibn ʿAbbās commented: "Sulaymān had the sexual capabilities of one hundred (or ninety-nine) men. He had three hundred wives, and three hundred female servants."[182] Al-

---

175 Part of the wisdom in having many wives is that they would witness certain actions of the Sunnah that take place in private and pass them on to others. ʿĀ'ishah, for example, was a source of many beneficial narrations to such effect. See *Fatḥ al-Bārī* (1/379).

176 Reported by Bukhārī (268) and Nasā'ī (6/53-54). Reported again by Bukhārī (284) with the wording: "The Prophet ﷺ visited all his wives in a single night, and he had nine wives at the time." Reported by Muslim (309) with the wording: "He would visit all his wives, and perform *ghusl* (major ablution) only once."

177 It was reported by Abū Dāwūd (219), Ibn Mājah (590), and others, from Salmā, from Abū Rāfiʿ, that one night, the Prophet ﷺ visited all of his wives, performing *ghusl* between each one. Abū Rāfiʿ narrates: "I said to the Prophet ﷺ: 'O Messenger of Allah! Why not perform *ghusl* only once?' He replied: 'This is purer, more attractive, and cleaner.'"

178 Ṭāwūs ibn Kaysān al-Yamānī. Others said his real name was Dhakwān and Ṭāwūs was a nickname. A virtuous and knowledgeable Follower. He died in 106 AH, or slightly later.

179 Devout and wise Follower. He passed away in 132 AH at the age of seventy-two.

180 Reported by Ibn Saʿd in *Al-Ṭabaqāt*. See *Al-Manāhil*, p. 145.

181 Reported by Bukhārī (2819) from Abū Hurayrah. See also Muslim (1654).

182 Reported by Ibn Jarīr in his *Tafsīr* in a *mawqūf* narration. See *Al-Manāhil*, p. 147.

وَكَانَ ﷺ مِمَّنْ أُقْدِرَ عَلَى القُوَّةِ فِي هَذَا وَأُعْطِيَ الكَثِيرَ مِنْهُ، وَلِهَذَا أُبِيحَ لَهُ مِنْ عَدَدِ الحَرَائِرِ مَا لَمْ يُبَحْ لِغَيْرِهِ[181]. وَقَدْ رَوَيْنَا عَنْ أَنَسٍ رَضِيَ اللهُ عَنْهُ أَنَّهُ ﷺ كَانَ يَدُورُ عَلَى نِسَائِهِ فِي السَّاعَةِ مِنَ اللَّيْلِ وَالنَّهَارِ وَهُنَّ إِحْدَى عَشْرَةَ. قَالَ أَنَسٌ: «وَكُنَّا نَتَحَدَّثُ أَنَّهُ أُعْطِيَ قُوَّةَ ثَلَاثِينَ رَجُلًا»[182]. خَرَّجَهُ النَّسَائِيُّ. وَرُوِيَ نَحْوُهُ عَنْ أَبِي رَافِعٍ[183]. وَعَنْ طَاوُسٍ[184]: أُعْطِيَ النَّبِيُّ ﷺ قُوَّةَ أَرْبَعِينَ رَجُلًا فِي الجِمَاعِ. وَمِثْلُهُ عَنْ صَفْوَانَ بْنِ سُلَيْمٍ[185]. وَقَالَتْ سَلْمَى مَوْلَاتُهُ: طَافَ النَّبِيُّ ﷺ لَيْلَةً عَلَى نِسَائِهِ التِّسْعِ، وَتَطَهَّرَ مِنْ كُلِّ وَاحِدَةٍ قَبْلَ أَنْ يَأْتِيَ الأُخْرَى. وَقَالَ: «هَذَا أَطْهَرُ وَأَطْيَبُ»[186].

وَقَدْ قَالَ سُلَيْمَانُ عَلَيْهِ السَّلَام: لَأَطُوفَنَّ اللَّيْلَةَ عَلَى مِائَةِ امْرَأَةٍ أَوْ تِسْعٍ وَتِسْعِينَ[187]،

---

١٨١   وَالحِكْمَةُ فِي كَثْرَةِ أَزْوَاجِهِ ﷺ أَنَّ الأَحْكَامَ الَّتِي لَيْسَتْ ظَاهِرَةً، يُطْلَعْنَ عَلَيْهَا، فَيَنْقُلْنَهَا. وَقَدْ جَاءَ عَنْ عَائِشَةَ مِنْ ذَلِكَ الكَثِيرُ الطَّيِّبُ (الفَتْحُ ٣٧٩/١).

١٨٢   أَخْرَجَهُ البُخَارِيُّ (٢٦٨). وَأَخْرَجَهُ النَّسَائِيُّ ٥٣/٦-٥٤، وَالبُخَارِيُّ (٢٨٤) بِلَفْظِ: أَنَّ النَّبِيَّ ﷺ كَانَ يَطُوفُ عَلَى نِسَائِهِ فِي اللَّيْلَةِ الوَاحِدَةِ وَلَهُ يَوْمَئِذٍ تِسْعُ نِسْوَةٍ. وَأَخْرَجَهُ مُسْلِمٌ (٣٠٩) بِلَفْظِ: أَنَّ النَّبِيَّ ﷺ كَانَ يَطُوفُ عَلَى نِسَائِهِ بِغُسْلٍ وَاحِدٍ.

١٨٣   أَخْرَجَهُ أَبُو دَاوُدَ (٢١٩)، وَابْنُ مَاجَه (٥٩٠) وَغَيْرُهُ مِنْ حَدِيثِ سَلْمَى، عَنْ أَبِي رَافِعٍ أَنَّ النَّبِيَّ ﷺ طَافَ ذَاتَ يَوْمٍ عَلَى نِسَائِهِ يَغْتَسِلُ عِنْدَ هَذِهِ وَعِنْدَ هَذِهِ. قَالَ: فَقُلْتُ لَهُ: يَا رَسُولَ اللهِ! أَلَا تَجْعَلُهُ غُسْلًا وَاحِدًا؟ قَالَ: «هَذَا أَزْكَى وَأَطْيَبُ وَأَطْهَرُ». قَالَ أَبُو دَاوُدَ: وَحَدِيثُ أَنَسٍ - أَيِ الحَدِيثُ السَّابِقُ - أَصَحُّ مِنْ هَذَا». قَالَ النَّوَوِيُّ: هُوَ مَحْمُولٌ عَلَى أَنَّهُ فَعَلَ الأَمْرَيْنِ فِي وَقْتَيْنِ مُخْتَلِفَيْنِ.

١٨٤   هُوَ طَاوُسُ بْنُ كَيْسَانَ اليَمَانِيُّ: يُقَالُ: اسْمُهُ ذَكْوَانُ، وَطَاوُوسُ لَقَبٌ. تَابِعِيٌّ ثِقَةٌ فَقِيهٌ فَاضِلٌ. مَاتَ سَنَةَ (١٠٦) هـ. وَقِيلَ بَعْدَ ذَلِكَ/ التَّقْرِيبُ.

١٨٥   تَابِعِيٌّ، مُفْتٍ، عَابِدٌ، ثِقَةٌ. مَاتَ سَنَةَ (١٣٢) هـ وَلَهُ (٧٢) سَنَةً/ التَّقْرِيبُ.

١٨٦   أَخْرَجَهُ ابْنُ سَعْدٍ فِي الطَّبَقَاتِ/ المَنَاهِلُ (١٤٥). وَانْظُرِ الحَدِيثَ السَّابِقَ.

١٨٧   أَخْرَجَهُ البُخَارِيُّ (٢٨١٩) مِنْ حَدِيثِ أَبِي هُرَيْرَةَ. وَانْظُرْ رِوَايَاتٍ أُخْرَى عِنْدَ مُسْلِمٍ (١٦٥٤).

Naqqāsh and others said it was: "Seven hundred wives, and three hundred female servants."[183]

Prophet Dāwūd ﷺ, who was a devout worshipper and worked to earn his living, had ninety-nine wives, which he made one hundred by marrying the wife of Ūriyā.[184] This was indicated in the words of Allah Exalted: "This is my brother. He has ninety-nine sheep".[185]

Anas narrated that the Prophet ﷺ said: "I have been preferred above the people in four aspects: generosity, courage, [the ability to engage in] much sexual intercourse, and great physical strength."[186]

As for being a person of prestige and distinction, it is a quality generally praised by intelligent observers, and the honourable one finds his way into the hearts of the people. Allah Exalted describes ʿĪsā ﷺ as "honoured in this world and the Hereafter".[187] For many, however, a high rank in this world can lead to suffering and misery, and harm their Hereafter. For that reason, some warned against pursuing such a position, and praised the complete opposite. The Shariah also commends those who seek obscurity, and censures

---

183   This is the original wording. Also reported in *Al-Manāhil*, p. 148, with the wording: "Sulaymān had three hundred wives, and seven hundred female servants." The narration from *Al-Manāhil* was reported by Ḥākim (2/589) from Muhammad ibn Kaʿb al-Quraẓī, and again by Ḥākim (2/596) from Ibn ʿAbbās, with the wording: "Sulaymān had nine hundred female servants, and three hundred wives (lit., 'receivers of the *mahr*')."

184   Reported by Ḥākim (2/586) from the words of al-Suddī. Ūriyā was a military general for Dāwūd ﷺ. As cited by al-Khāzin in his *Tafsīr* (4/35), the present author says: "This story is not reliable, and it goes against the prohibition against killing a Muslim without a right or lusting for his wife. These are both serious crimes, so how could an intelligent person attribute them to Dāwūd ﷺ?"

185   *Ṣād*, 23.

186   Haythamī said in *Majmaʿ al-Zawāʾid* (8/269): "It was related by Ṭabarānī in *Al-Awsaṭ* with a chain of reliable narrators." ʿIrāqī said in *Takhrīj Aḥādīth al-Iḥyāʾ* (2/360): "The narrators are trustworthy." Suyūṭī approved the chain in *Al-Manāhil*, p. 149, although he graded it as *ḍaʿīf* in *Al-Jāmiʿ al-Ṣaghīr* (5884). Dhahabī said in *Al-Mīzān*: "It is a *munkar* narration." And Ibn al-Jawzī commented: "It is not authentic."

187   *Āl ʿImrān*, 45.

وَأَنَّهُ فَعَلَ ذَلِكَ. قَالَ ابْنُ عَبَّاسٍ: كَانَ فِي ظَهْرِ سُلَيْمَانَ عَلَيْهِ السَّلام مَاءُ مِائَةِ رَجُلٍ، وَكَانَتْ لَهُ ثَلاثُمِائَةِ امْرَأَةٍ وَثَلاثُمِائَةِ سُرِّيَّةٍ[188]. وَحَكَى النَّقَّاشُ: سَبْعُمِائَةِ امْرَأَةٍ وَثَلاثُمِائَةِ سُرِّيَّةٍ[189]. وَقَدْ كَانَ لِدَاوُدَ عَلَيْهِ السَّلام عَلَى زُهْدِهِ وَأَكْلِهِ مِنْ عَمَلِ يَدَيْهِ تِسْعٌ وَتِسْعُونَ امْرَأَةً، وَتَمَّتْ بِزَوْجِ أُورِيَا مِائَةً[190]، وَقَدْ نَبَّهَ عَلَى ذَلِكَ فِي الْكِتَابِ الْعَزِيزِ بِقَوْلِهِ تَعَالَى: ﴿إِنَّ هَذَا أَخِي لَهُ تِسْعٌ وَتِسْعُونَ نَعْجَةً﴾ [ص: ٢٣].

وَفِي حَدِيثِ أَنَسٍ عَنْهُ عَلَيْهِ الصَّلاة والسلام: «فُضِّلْتُ عَلَى النَّاسِ بِأَرْبَعٍ: بِالسَّخَاءِ، وَالشَّجَاعَةِ، وَكَثْرَةِ الْجِمَاعِ، وَقُوَّةِ الْبَطْشِ»[191].

وَأَمَّا الْجَاهُ فَمَحْمُودٌ عِنْدَ الْعُقَلاءِ عَادَةً، وَبِقَدْرِ جَاهِهِ عِظَمُهُ فِي الْقُلُوبِ، وَقَدْ قَالَ تَعَالَى فِي صِفَةِ عِيسَى عَلَيْهِ السَّلام: ﴿وَجِيهًا فِي ٱلدُّنْيَا وَٱلْآخِرَةِ﴾ [آل عمران: ٤٥]، لَكِنْ آفَاتُهُ كَثِيرَةٌ، فَهُوَ مُضِرٌّ لِبَعْضِ النَّاسِ لِعُقْبَى الْآخِرَةِ، فَلِذَلِكَ ذَمَّهُ مَنْ ذَمَّهُ وَمَدَحَ ضِدَّهُ، وَوَرَدَ فِي الشَّرْعِ مَدْحُ الْخُمُولِ[192] وَذَمُّ الْعُلُوِّ فِي

---

١٨٨ رَوَاهُ ابْنُ جَرِيرٍ فِي تَفْسِيرِهِ مَوْقُوفًا/ الْمَنَاهِلُ (١٤٧). (سُرِّيَّةٌ): الْأَمَةُ يُتَسَرَّى بِهَا.

١٨٩ وَجَاءَتِ الرِّوَايَةُ فِي الْمَنَاهِلِ (١٤٨): «أَنَّهُ كَانَ لِسُلَيْمَانَ ثَلاثُ مِئَةِ امْرَأَةٍ، وَسَبْعُ مِئَةِ سُرِّيَّةٍ». وَرِوَايَةُ الْمَنَاهِلِ هَذِهِ أَخْرَجَهَا الْحَاكِمُ ٥٨٩/٢ عَنْ مُحَمَّدِ بْنِ كَعْبٍ الْقُرَظِيِّ مِنْ قَوْلِهِ. وَأَخْرَجَ الْحَاكِمُ أَيْضًا ٥٩٦/٢ عَنِ ابْنِ عَبَّاسٍ مِنْ قَوْلِهِ: «وَكَانَتْ لَهُ - أَيْ لِسُلَيْمَانَ - تِسْعُ مِئَةِ سُرِّيَّةٍ، وَثَلاثُ مِئَةِ مَهْرِيَّةٍ».

١٩٠ رَوَاهُ الْحَاكِمُ ٥٨٦/٢ عَنِ السُّدِّيِّ مِنْ قَوْلِهِ. (أُورِيَا): قَائِدٌ مِنْ قُوَّادِ دَاوُدَ عَلَيْهِ السَّلام. قَالَ الْمُصَنِّفُ - فِيمَا نَقَلَهُ عَنِ الْخَازِنِ فِي التَّفْسِيرِ ٣٥/٤ -: «لَيْسَ فِي قِصَّةِ دَاوُدَ وَأُورِيَا خَبَرٌ ثَابِتٌ» وَحَاصِلُ الْقِصَّةِ يَرْجِعُ إِلَى السَّعْيِ فِي قَتْلِ رَجُلٍ مُسْلِمٍ بِغَيْرِ حَقٍّ، وَإِلَى الطَّمَعِ فِي زَوْجَتِهِ، وَكِلاهُمَا مُنْكَرٌ عَظِيمٌ، فَلا يَلِيقُ بِعَاقِلٍ أَنْ يَظُنَّ بِدَاوُدَ عَلَيْهِ السَّلام هَذَا».

١٩١ ذَكَرَهُ الْهَيْثَمِيُّ فِي مَجْمَعِ الزَّوَائِدِ ٢٦٩/٨ وَقَالَ: «رَوَاهُ الطَّبَرَانِيُّ فِي الْأَوْسَطِ، وَإِسْنَادُهُ رِجَالُهُ مُوَثَّقُونَ» وَقَالَ الْعِرَاقِيُّ فِي تَخْرِيجِ أَحَادِيثِ الْإِحْيَاءِ (٣٦٠/٢): «وَرِجَالُهُ ثِقَاتٌ». وَجَوَّدَ إِسْنَادَهُ السُّيُوطِيُّ فِي الْمَنَاهِلِ (١٤٩)، بَيْنَمَا رَمَزَهُ بِالضَّعْفِ فِي الْجَامِعِ الصَّغِيرِ (٥٨٨٤)، وَفِي مِيزَانِ الذَّهَبِيِّ: إِنَّهُ خَبَرٌ مُنْكَرٌ. وَقَالَ ابْنُ الْجَوْزِيِّ: حَدِيثٌ لا يَصِحُّ.

١٩٢ تَرْكُ الظُّهُورِ.

those who are arrogant on Earth. The Prophet ﷺ was blessed with modesty, a place in the hearts of the people, and their respect and honour both before and after he became a Messenger. Some may have rejected him, harassed his Companions, and secretly wished to hurt him, but whenever they came face to face with the Prophet ﷺ, they would treat him with good manners and assist with whatever he needed, as many narrations reflect.

When someone saw the Prophet ﷺ for the first time, they would be overcome with fear and amazement. For example, it was related that when Qaylah first saw him, she shuddered with fear. The Prophet ﷺ said: "O, poor girl [*miskīnah*]! Have calm and tranquillity [*sakīnah*]."[188]

Abū Mas‘ūd[189] mentioned a man who trembled when he stood in front of the Prophet ﷺ. The Prophet ﷺ said to the man: "Be calm, for I am not a king."[190]

He was blessed in this world with the great status of a Prophet, the honourable station of a Messenger, and the lofty rank of the Chosen One. And in the Hereafter, he will be the leader of the Children of Adam[191]. Indeed, the essence of the entire chapter can be drawn from the content of this section.

---

188   Taken from a lengthy hadith which was reported in its entirety by Ṭabarānī in *Al-Kabīr*, Ibn Mandah, and others. The first part of the hadith was reported by Abū Dāwūd (4847), Tirmidhī in *Al-Shamā'il* (126), and Bukhārī in *Al-Adab al-Mufrad* (1178).

189   ‘Uqbah ibn ‘Amr al-Badrī.

190   Reported by Ibn Mājah (3312). Authenticated by Ḥākim (3/47-48) and Dhahabī concurred. Būṣīrī said in *Al-Zawā'id*: "This chain is *ṣaḥīḥ*, and the narrators are trustworthy." Attributed by Suyūṭī an *Al-Manāhil*, p. 151, to Bayhaqī, in a *mawṣūl* narration from the chain of Qays and a *mursal* narration, also from Qays.
A similar narration from Jarīr ibn ‘Abdullāh was also authenticated by Ḥākim (2/466) and Dhahabī concurred. Haythamī said in *Majma‘ al-Zawā'id* (9/20): "Reported by Ṭabarānī in *Al-Awsaṭ*, and the chain contains narrators I do not recognize."

191   i.e., of all humanity.

الأَرْضِ. وَكَانَ ﷺ قَدْ رُزِقَ مِنَ الحِشْمَةِ¹⁹³ وَالمَكَانَةِ في القُلُوبِ وَالعَظَمَةِ قَبْلَ النُّبُوَّةِ عِنْدَ الجَاهِلِيَّةِ وَبَعْدَهَا، وَهُمْ يُكَذِّبُونَهُ وَيُؤْذُونَ أَصْحَابَهُ، وَيَقْصِدُونَ أَذَاهُ في نَفْسِهِ خُفْيَةً، حَتَّى إِذَا وَاجَهَهُمْ أَعْظَمُوا أَمْرَهُ، وَقَضَوْا حَاجَتَهُ، وَأَخْبَارُهُ في ذَلِكَ مَعْرُوفَةٌ سَيَأْتِي بَعْضُهَا. وَقَدْ كَانَ يُبْهَتُ وَيَفْرَقُ¹⁹⁴ مِنْ رُؤْيَتِهِ مَنْ لَمْ يَرَهُ، كَمَا رُوِيَ عَنْ قَيْلَةَ أَنَّهَا لَمَّا رَأَتْهُ أُرْعِدَتْ مِنَ الفَرَقِ، فَقَالَ: «يَا مِسْكِينَةُ، عَلَيْكِ السَّكِينَةَ»¹⁹⁵. وَفي حَدِيثِ أَبِي مَسْعُودٍ أَنَّ رَجُلًا قَامَ بَيْنَ يَدَيْهِ فَأُرْعِدَ، فَقَالَ لَهُ النَّبِيُّ ﷺ: «هَوِّنْ عَلَيْكَ فَإِنِّي لَسْتُ بِمَلِكٍ»¹⁹⁶. الحَدِيثَ.

فَأَمَّا عَظِيمُ قَدْرِهِ بِالنُّبُوَّةِ، وَشَرِيفُ مَنْزِلَتِهِ بِالرِّسَالَةِ، وَإِنَافَةُ رُتْبَتِهِ¹⁹⁷ بِالاصْطِفَاءِ وَالكَرَامَةِ في الدُّنْيَا فَأَمْرٌ هُوَ مَبْلَغُ النِّهَايَةِ، ثُمَّ هُوَ في الآخِرَةِ سَيِّدُ وَلَدِ آدَمَ، وَعَلَى مَعْنَى هَذَا الفَصْلِ نَظَمْنَا هَذَا القِسْمَ بِأَسْرِهِ.

---

١٩٣ الحِشْمَةُ: الحَيَاءُ، وَالمَسْلَكُ الوَسَطُ المَحْمُودُ/ المُعْجَمُ الوَسِيطُ.

١٩٤ أَيْ يَدْهَشُ وَيَفْزَعُ.

١٩٥ طَرَفٌ مِنْ حَدِيثٍ طَوِيلٍ حَسَنٍ. أَخْرَجَهُ بِطُولِهِ ابْنُ مَنْدَةَ وَالطَّبَرَانِيُّ في الكَبِيرِ وَغَيْرُهُ. وَأَخْرَجَ الفِقْرَةَ الأُولَى مِنْهُ: أَبُو دَاوُدَ (٤٨٤٧)، وَالتِّرْمِذِيُّ في الشَّمَائِلِ (١١٩)، وَالبُخَارِيُّ في الأَدَبِ المُفْرَدِ (١١٨٣). (أُرْعِدَتْ مِنَ الفَرَقِ): رَجَفَتْ وَاضْطَرَبَتْ مِنَ الخَوْفِ.

١٩٦ أَخْرَجَهُ ابْنُ مَاجَه (٣٣١٢)، وَصَحَّحَهُ الحَاكِمُ (٣/ ٤٧-٤٨)، وَوَافَقَهُ الذَّهَبِيُّ وَقَالَ البُوصِيرِيُّ في الزَّوَائِدِ: «هَذَا إِسْنَادٌ صَحِيحٌ، وَرِجَالُهُ ثِقَاتٌ» وَعَزَاهُ السُّيُوطِيُّ في المَنَاهِلِ (١٥١) إِلَى البَيْهَقِيِّ مِنْ طَرِيقِ قَيْسٍ عَنْهُ مَوْصُولًا، وَعَنْ قَيْسٍ مُرْسَلًا وَقَالَ: «هُوَ المَحْفُوظُ». وَفي البَابِ عَنْ جَرِيرِ بْنِ عَبْدِ اللهِ صَحَّحَهُ الحَاكِمُ ٢/ ٤٦٦ وَأَقَرَّهُ الذَّهَبِيُّ. وَذَكَرَهُ الهَيْثَمِيُّ في المَجْمَعِ ٢٠/٩ وَقَالَ: «رَوَاهُ الطَّبَرَانِيُّ في الأَوْسَطِ وَفِيهِ مَنْ لَمْ أَعْرِفْهُمْ». (أَبُو مَسْعُودٍ): هُوَ عُقْبَةُ بْنُ عَمْرٍو البَدْرِيُّ. (هَوِّنْ): خَفِّفْ. (أُرْعِدَ): رَجَفَ وَاضْطَرَبَ مِنَ الخَوْفِ.

١٩٧ إِنَافَةُ رُتْبَتِهِ: رِفْعَتُهَا.

ACTIONS OR QUALITIES WHOSE PRAISE-WORTHINESS DIFFERS ACCORDING TO THE CONTEXT

The third type of action or quality are those who may be praise-worthy or not, depending on the situation. An example of this is possessing great wealth. In general, a wealthy person is admired and considered to be in a position to satisfy his needs, but the money itself is not a virtue.

If a wealthy person spends to satisfy his needs and the needs of those who request his assistance, then he is loved by others and virtuous in the eyes of the people of this world. If he spends on noble and righteous causes, seeking the Pleasure of Allah and the reward of the Hereafter, then he is virtuous to all.

However, if he withholds and hoards his wealth, then possessing an abundance becomes like having nothing at all. The person who manages his fortune in this way is lacking, and his money will not take him to safe ground. Instead, it throws him into a pit of stinginess and he tastes humiliation.

Therefore, virtue does not lie in wealth for its own sake, but in how it is utilized. If a person does not use their wealth in the correct manner, they will not be rich or self-sufficient in the true sense of the words, and no intelligent person would praise them. They will always be poor, unable to achieve their goals despite the money at their disposal. They are like a treasurer overseeing the wealth of others, but without a penny to their name.

The one who spends is truly rich and has benefited from his

فصل

وَأَمَّا الضَّرْبُ الثَّالِثُ: فَهُوَ مَا تَخْتَلِفُ الحَالَاتُ فِي التَّمَدُّحِ بِهِ، وَالتَّفَاخُرِ بِسَبَبِهِ، وَالتَّفْضِيلِ لِأَجْلِهِ، كَكَثْرَةِ المَالِ، فَصَاحِبُهُ عَلَى الجُمْلَةِ مُعَظَّمٌ عِنْدَ العَامَّةِ، لِاعْتِقَادِهَا تَوَصُّلَهُ بِهِ إِلَى حَاجَاتِهِ، وَتَمَكُّنِ أَغْرَاضِهِ بِسَبَبِهِ، وَإِلَّا فَلَيْسَ فَضِيلَةً فِي نَفْسِهِ. فَمَتَى كَانَ المَالُ بِهَذِهِ الصُّورَةِ، وَصَاحِبُهُ مُنْفِقًا لَهُ فِي مُهِمَّاتِهِ وَمُهِمَّاتِ مَنِ اعْتَرَاهُ[198] وَأَمَّلَهُ، وَتَصْرِيفِهِ فِي مَوَاضِعِهِ، مُشْتَرِيًا بِهِ المَعَالِي وَالثَّنَاءَ الحَسَنَ، وَالمَنْزِلَةَ مِنَ القُلُوبِ، كَانَ فَضِيلَةً فِي صَاحِبِهِ عِنْدَ أَهْلِ الدُّنْيَا. وَإِذَا صَرَفَهُ فِي وُجُوهِ البِرِّ، وَأَنْفَقَهُ فِي سَبِيلِ الخَيْرِ، وَقَصَدَ بِذَلِكَ اللهَ تَعَالَى وَالدَّارَ الآخِرَةَ، كَانَ فَضِيلَةً عِنْدَ الكُلِّ بِكُلِّ حَالٍ. وَمَتَى كَانَ صَاحِبُهُ مُمْسِكًا لَهُ، غَيْرَ مُوَجِّهِ وُجُوهَهُ، حَرِيصًا عَلَى جَمْعِهِ، عَادَ كَثْرُهُ كَالعَدَمِ، وَكَانَ مَنْقَصَةً فِي صَاحِبِهِ، وَلَمْ يَقِفْ بِهِ عَلَى جَدَدٍ[199] السَّلَامَةِ، بَلْ أَوْقَعَهُ فِي هُوَّةٍ[200] رَذِيلَةِ البُخْلِ وَمَذَمَّةِ النَّذَالَةِ[201].

فَإِذَا المُتَمَدِّحُ بِالمَالِ وَفَضِيلَتِهِ عِنْدَ مُفَضِّلِيهِ لَيْسَتْ لِنَفْسِهِ، وَإِنَّمَا هُوَ لِلتَّوَصُّلِ بِهِ إِلَى غَيْرِهِ، وَتَصْرِيفِهِ فِي مُتَصَرَّفَاتِهِ، فَجَامِعُهُ إِذَا لَمْ يَضَعْهُ مَوَاضِعَهُ، وَلَا وَجَّهَهُ وُجُوهَهُ، غَيْرَ

---

198 اعْتَرَاهُ: جَاءَهُ طَالِبًا مَعْرُوفَهُ.

199 جَدَدٌ: الجَدَدُ: الأَرْضُ المُسْتَوِيَةُ. وَفِي المَثَلِ: «مَنْ سَلَكَ الجَدَدَ أَمِنَ العِثَارَ».

200 الهُوَّةُ: الحُفْرَةُ البَعِيدَةُ القَعْرِ / المُعْجَمُ الوَسِيطُ.

201 النَّذَالَةُ: الخِسَّةُ وَالحَقَارَةُ وَالسَّفَالَةُ.

wealth, even if none of it remains in his possession. Let us study the example of the Prophet ﷺ, and the way he dealt with wealth.

He was given the treasures of the Earth and the keys to the land. War spoils, which were not permissible for any Prophet before him, were made permissible for him. The Ḥijāz, Yemen, the entire Arabian Peninsula[192], as well as Syria and Iraq, were all conquered and liberated during his lifetime.

From all of these lands, the Prophet ﷺ received one-fifth of any war spoils, as well as all charity and *jizyah* payments, of which previous rulers only received a portion. He also received gifts from a number of foreign kings.

The Prophet ﷺ did not keep a single dirham for himself. Rather, he used the wealth to enrich others and strengthen the Muslim community. He said: "If I had an Uḥud[193] worth of gold, I would not like a single dinar to stay with me overnight, except a dinar I use to repay my debts."[194]

On one occasion, the Prophet ﷺ was brought some dinars which he apportioned out [for other people] until he had six left, which he sent to some of his wives. He could not sleep until the money had been divided. He said: "Now, I can rest."[195] When the Prophet ﷺ died, his body armour had been pawned in order to provide for his family.[196]

As for his own clothing and living arrangements, the Messen-

---

192   From Aden in the south to rural parts of Iraq in the north, and from Jeddah and surrounding areas in the west to the borders of Syria in the east, as described by al-Aṣmaʿī. See *Fatḥ al-Bārī* (6/171).

193   Mount Uḥud.

194   Reported by Bukhārī (6444) and Muslim (94/32) from Abū Dharr, and again by Bukhārī (6445) and Muslim (991) from Abū Hurayrah.

195   Reported with this wording by Ibn Saʿd from ʿĀʾishah. See *Al-Manāhil*, p. 153.

196   Reported by Bukhārī (4467) from ʿĀʾishah. Also reported, in another context, by Muslim (1603).

مَلِيٌّ[202] بِالحَقِيقَةِ، وَلَا غَنِيٌّ بِالمَعْنَى، وَلَا مُتَمَدَّحٌ بِهِ عِنْدَ أَحَدٍ مِنَ العُقَلَاءِ، بَلْ هُوَ فَقِيرٌ أَبَدًا، غَيْرُ وَاصِلٍ إِلَى غَرَضٍ مِنْ أَغْرَاضِهِ، إِذْ مَا بِيَدِهِ مِنَ المَالِ المُوَصِّلِ إِلَيْهَا لَمْ يُسَلَّطْ عَلَيْهِ، فَأَشْبَهَ خَازِنَ مَالِ غَيْرِهِ وَلَا مَالَ لَهُ، فَكَأَنَّهُ لَيْسَ فِي يَدِهِ مِنْهُ شَيْءٌ، وَالمُنْفِقُ مَلِيٌّ غَنِيٌّ بِتَحْصِيلِهِ فَوَائِدَ المَالِ، وَإِنْ لَمْ يَبْقَ فِي يَدِهِ مِنَ المَالِ شَيْءٌ. فَانْظُرْ سِيرَةَ نَبِيِّنَا ﷺ وَخُلُقَهُ فِي المَالِ، تَجِدْهُ قَدْ أُوتِيَ خَزَائِنَ الأَرْضِ، وَمَفَاتِيحَ البِلَادِ، وَأُحِلَّتْ لَهُ الغَنَائِمُ وَلَمْ تُحَلَّ لِنَبِيٍّ قَبْلَهُ، وَفُتِحَ عَلَيْهِ فِي حَيَاتِهِ ﷺ بِلَادُ الحِجَازِ وَاليَمَنِ وَجَمِيعُ جَزِيرَةِ العَرَبِ[203]، وَمَا دَانَى ذَلِكَ مِنَ الشَّامِ وَالعِرَاقِ، وَجُلِبَ إِلَيْهِ مِنْ أَخْمَاسِهَا وَجِزْيَتِهَا وَصَدَقَاتِهَا مَا لَا يُجْبَى لِلمُلُوكِ إِلَّا بَعْضُهُ، وَهَادَتْهُ[204] جَمَاعَةٌ مِنْ مُلُوكِ الأَقَالِيمِ، فَمَا اسْتَأْثَرَ بِشَيْءٍ مِنْهُ، وَلَا أَمْسَكَ مِنْهُ دِرْهَمًا، بَلْ صَرَفَهُ مَصَارِفَهُ، وَأَغْنَى بِهِ غَيْرَهُ، وَقَوَّى بِهِ المُسْلِمِينَ، وَقَالَ عليه الصلاة والسلام: «مَا يَسُرُّنِي أَنَّ لِي أُحُدًا ذَهَبًا يَبِيتُ عِنْدِي مِنْهُ دِينَارٌ، إِلَّا دِينَارًا أُرْصِدُهُ لِدَيْنٍ»[205]. وَأَتَتْهُ دَنَانِيرُ مَرَّةً فَقَسَمَهَا، وَبَقِيَتْ مِنْهَا بَقِيَّةٌ، فَدَفَعَهَا لِبَعْضِ نِسَائِهِ، فَلَمْ يَأْخُذْهُ نَوْمٌ حَتَّى قَامَ وَقَسَمَهَا، وَقَالَ ﷺ: «الآنَ اسْتَرَحْتُ»[206]. وَمَاتَ ﷺ وَدِرْعُهُ

---

202 اَلمَلِيُّ: الغَنِيُّ الثِّقَةُ، وَالقَادِرُ عَلَى دَفْعِ المَالِ المَطْلُوبِ/ المُعْجَمُ الاقْتِصَادِيُّ الإِسْلَامِيُّ.

203 جَزِيرَةُ العَرَبِ: مَا بَيْنَ أَقْصَى عَدَنِ اليَمَنِ إِلَى رِيفِ العِرَاقِ فِي الطُّولِ. وَأَمَّا فِي العَرْضِ فَمِنْ أَطْرَافِ الشَّامِ. قَالَهُ الأَصْمَعِيُّ. وَانْظُرِ الفَتْحَ ١٧١/٦.

204 هَادَتْهُ: أَرْسَلَتْ لَهُ بِهَدَايَا.

205 أَخْرَجَهُ البُخَارِيُّ (٦٤٤٤)، وَمُسْلِمٌ فِي الزَّكَاةِ (٣٢/٩٤) مِنْ حَدِيثِ أَبِي ذَرٍّ. وَالبُخَارِيُّ (٦٤٤٥)، وَمُسْلِمٌ (٩٩١) مِنْ حَدِيثِ أَبِي هُرَيْرَةَ. (أُرْصِدُهُ): أُعِدُّهُ وَأَحْفَظُهُ.

206 أَخْرَجَهُ ابْنُ سَعْدٍ عَنْ عَائِشَةَ بِهَذَا اللَّفْظِ/ المَنَاهِلُ (١٥٣).

ger of Allah ﷺ sought only the most basic necessities. He would wear whatever he had available. He would usually wear a loose outer cloak or a heavy, patterned cloak, and coarse clothing.

Any garments made from silk or embroidered with gold would be distributed to others. Taking great care in one's dress and beautification is not an attribute of noble men, but of women. Commendable clothes are those which are clean and of average quality.

Wearing such clothes does not take away from a man's prowess, but neither does it lead to self-aggrandizement on his part, or from the people around him, which the Shariah prohibits. Most showing off stems from abundance and wealth. But whoever owns some land and harvests it, then gives away the produce as a means of asceticism and self-restraint, he has truly achieved the benefit of his wealth.

If showing off can ever be considered virtuous, then he would be most deserving. There is generosity and honour in his turning away from his wealth, spending it in the best way, and remaining steadfast if it disappears.

مَرْهُونَةٌ فِي نَفَقَةِ عِيَالِهِ٢٠٧، وَاقْتَصَرَ مِنْ نَفَقَتِهِ وَمَلْبَسِهِ وَمَسْكَنِهِ عَلَى مَا تَدْعُوهُ ضَرُورَتُهُ إِلَيْهِ، وَزَهِدَ فِيمَا سِوَاهُ، فَكَانَ يَلْبَسُ مَا وَجَدَهُ، فَيَلْبَسُ فِي الْغَالِبِ الشَّمْلَةَ٢٠٨، وَالْكِسَاءَ الْخَشِنَ، وَالْبُرْدَ٢٠٩ الْغَلِيظَ، وَيَقْسِمُ عَلَى مَنْ حَضَرَهُ أَقْبِيَةَ الدِّيبَاجِ٢١٠ الْمُخَوَّصَةَ٢١١ بِالذَّهَبِ، وَيَرْفَعُ لِمَنْ لَمْ يَحْضُرْ، إِذِ الْمُبَاهَاةُ فِي الْمَلَابِسِ وَالتَّزَيُّنُ بِهَا لَيْسَتْ مِنْ خِصَالِ الشَّرَفِ وَالْجَلَالَةِ، وَهِيَ مِنْ سِمَاتِ النِّسَاءِ، وَالْمَحْمُودُ مِنْهَا نَقَاوَةُ الثَّوْبِ، وَالتَّوَسُّطُ فِي جِنْسِهِ، وَكَوْنُهُ لُبْسَ مِثْلِهِ، غَيْرَ مُسْقِطٍ لِمُرُوءَةِ حَسَبِهِ، مِمَّا لَا يُؤَدِّي إِلَى الشُّهْرَةِ فِي الطَّرَفَيْنِ، وَقَدْ ذَمَّ الشَّرْعُ ذَلِكَ. وَغَايَةُ الْفَخْرِ فِيهِ عِنْدَ النَّاسِ إِنَّمَا يَعُودُ إِلَى الْفَخْرِ بِكَثْرَةِ الْمَوْجُودِ وَوُفُورِ الْحَالِ، وَكَذَلِكَ التَّبَاهِي بِجَوْدَةِ الْمَسْكَنِ وَسَعَةِ الْمَنْزِلِ، وَتَكْثِيرِ آلَاتِهِ وَخَدَمِهِ وَمَرْكُوبَاتِهِ.

وَمَنْ مَلَكَ الْأَرْضَ وَجُبِيَ إِلَيْهِ مَا فِيهَا فَتَرَكَ ذَلِكَ زُهْدًا وَتَنَزُّهًا فَهُوَ حَائِزٌ لِفَضِيلَةِ الْمَالِيَّةِ، وَمَالِكٌ لِلْفَخْرِ بِهَذِهِ الْخَصْلَةِ إِنْ كَانَتْ فَضِيلَةً، زَائِدٌ عَلَيْهَا فِي الْفَخْرِ، وَمُعْرِقٌ٢١٢ فِي الْمَدْحِ بِإِضْرَابِهِ٢١٣ عَنْهَا، وَزُهْدِهِ فِي فَانِيهَا، وَبَذْلِهَا فِي مَظَانِّهَا.

---

٢٠٧ أَخْرَجَهُ الْبُخَارِيُّ (٤٤٦٧) مِنْ حَدِيثِ عَائِشَةَ. وَانْظُرْ سِيَاقَةً أُخْرَى عِنْدَ مُسْلِمٍ (١٦٠٣).

٢٠٨ الشَّمْلَةُ: شُقَّةٌ مِنَ الثِّيَابِ ذَاتُ خَمْلٍ يُتَوَشَّحُ بِهَا وَيُتَلَفَّعُ/ الْمُعْجَمُ الْوَسِيطُ.

٢٠٩ الْبُرْدُ: كِسَاءٌ مُخَطَّطٌ يُلْتَحَفُ بِهِ/ الْمُعْجَمُ الْوَسِيطُ.

٢١٠ أَقْبِيَةُ الدِّيبَاجِ: ثِيَابُ الْحَرِيرِ.

٢١١ الْمُخَوَّصَةُ: الْمَنْسُوجَةُ.

٢١٢ مُعْرِقٌ: مَعْنَاهُ أَنَّهُ عَلَى أَصْلٍ فِي الْكَرَمِ وَالْحَسَبِ.

٢١٣ بِإِضْرَابِهِ: بِإِعْرَاضِهِ.

HIS EXCELLENT CHARACTER

There are certain noble characteristics and praiseworthy manners which are acquired. All intelligent people agree that displaying just one of these qualities is a great virtue, and anything beyond that is exceptional. They are characteristics that are commended and enjoined in the Shariah, and eternal happiness is promised to those who adopt them. Some are described as a feature of Prophethood. In practice, they consist of moderation in one's actions, and staying away from extremes. When taken in conjunction, these qualities are known as "excellent character".

The Prophet ﷺ perfected every one of these attributes, until Allah Exalted praised him for that, saying: "And you are truly [a man] of outstanding character."[197]

'Ā'ishah ؓ narrated: "His character was the Qur'an; he was pleased by that which pleases it and angered by that which goes against it."[198] The Prophet ﷺ said: "I was sent to perfect good character."[199] Anas reported that the Prophet ﷺ had the best character,[200] and 'Alī ibn Abī Ṭālib ؓ said the same.[201]

---

197   *al-Qalam*, 4.

198   The first part of the narration was reported by Muslim (746). This wording was attributed by Suyūṭī in *Al-Manāhil*, p. 155, to Bayhaqī.

199   Reported by Aḥmad (2/381), Bazzār (2470), Bukhārī in *Al-Adab al-Mufrad* (273), and al-Quḍāʿī in *Musnad al-Shihāb* (1165), from Abū Hurayrah. Authenticated by Ḥākim (2/613). Ibn ʿAbd al-Barr said: "It is an authentic Madinan hadith, reported with reliable, connected chains from Abū Hurayrah and others." Some versions of the hadith are recorded with a different wording, with the phrase "*ṣāliḥ al-akhlāq*" used instead of "*makārim al-akhlāq*", both of which can be translated as "good", "noble", or "righteous character".

200   Reported by Bukhārī (6203) and Muslim (2150). This is the beginning of the hadith in which the Prophet ﷺ said: "O Abū ʿUmayr, what happened to the *nughayr* (baby bird)?"

201   Attributed in *Al-Manāhil*, p. 158, to Abū ʿUbayd in *Al-Gharīb*.

فَصْل

وَأَمَّا الْخِصَالُ الْمُكْتَسَبَةُ مِنَ الْأَخْلَاقِ الْحَمِيدَةِ، وَالْآدَابِ الشَّرِيفَةِ الَّتِي اتَّفَقَ جَمِيعُ الْعُقَلَاءِ عَلَى تَفْضِيلِ صَاحِبِهَا، وَتَعْظِيمِ الْمُتَّصِفِ بِالْخُلُقِ الْوَاحِدِ مِنْهَا، فَضْلًا عَمَّا فَوْقَهُ، وَأَثْنَى الشَّرْعُ عَلَى جَمِيعِهَا، وَأَمَرَ بِهَا، وَوَعَدَ السَّعَادَةَ الدَّائِمَةَ لِلْمُتَخَلِّقِ بِهَا، وَوَصَفَ بَعْضَهَا بِأَنَّهُ مِنْ أَجْزَاءِ النُّبُوَّةِ، وَهِيَ الْمُسَمَّاةُ بِحُسْنِ الْخُلُقِ، وَهُوَ الِاعْتِدَالُ فِي قُوَى النَّفْسِ وَأَوْصَافِهَا وَالتَّوَسُّطُ فِيهَا، دُونَ الْمَيْلِ إِلَى مُنْحَرِفِ أَطْرَافِهَا، فَجَمِيعُهَا قَدْ كَانَتْ خُلُقَ نَبِيِّنَا ﷺ عَلَى الِانْتِهَاءِ فِي كَمَالِهَا، وَالِاعْتِدَالِ فِي غَايَتِهَا، حَتَّى أَثْنَى اللهُ تَعَالَى عَلَيْهِ بِذَلِكَ، فَقَالَ: ﴿وَإِنَّكَ لَعَلَىٰ خُلُقٍ عَظِيمٍ﴾ [القلم: ٤].

قَالَتْ عَائِشَةُ رضي الله عنها: «كَانَ خُلُقُهُ الْقُرْآنَ، يَرْضَى بِرِضَاهُ، وَيَسْخَطُ بِسَخَطِهِ»[٢١٤].

وَقَالَ ﷺ: «بُعِثْتُ لِأُتَمِّمَ مَكَارِمَ الْأَخْلَاقِ»[٢١٥].

قَالَ أَنَسٌ: كَانَ رَسُولُ اللهِ ﷺ أَحْسَنَ النَّاسِ خُلُقًا»[٢١٦].

---

٢١٤ عَزَاهُ السُّيُوطِيُّ فِي الْمَنَاهِلِ (١٥٥) إِلَى الْبَيْهَقِيِّ بِهَذَا اللَّفْظِ. وَصَدْرُهُ رَوَاهُ مُسْلِمٌ (٧٤٦).

٢١٥ أَخْرَجَهُ أَحْمَدُ ٣٨١/٢، وَالْبَزَّارُ (٢٤٧٠)، وَالْبُخَارِيُّ فِي الْأَدَبِ الْمُفْرَدِ (٢٧٤)، وَالْقُضَاعِيُّ فِي مُسْنَدِ الشِّهَابِ (١١٦٥) مِنْ حَدِيثِ أَبِي هُرَيْرَةَ، وَصَحَّحَهُ الْحَاكِمُ ٦١٣/٢، وَقَالَ ابْنُ عَبْدِ الْبَرِّ: «هُوَ حَدِيثٌ مَدَنِيٌّ صَحِيحٌ مُتَّصِلٌ مِنْ وُجُوهٍ صِحَاحٍ عَنْ أَبِي هُرَيْرَةَ وَغَيْرِهِ». قُلْتُ: فِي بَعْضِ رِوَايَاتِهِ: «بُعِثْتُ لِأُتَمِّمَ صَالِحَ الْأَخْلَاقِ».

٢١٦ أَخْرَجَهُ الْبُخَارِيُّ (٦٢٠٣)، وَمُسْلِمٌ (٢١٥٠). وَهُوَ صَدْرُ حَدِيثٍ: «مَا فَعَلَ النُّغَيْرُ؟ يَا أَبَا عُمَيْرٍ!».

In the case of the Prophet ﷺ, these qualities were neither acquired nor learnt. Rather, they were a part of his natural disposition since birth, specially gifted from the Generosity of his Lord. Indeed, the same was true for all Prophets, as can be glimpsed from the life stories of ʿĪsā, Mūsā, Yaḥyā, Sulaymān, and others ﷺ. They were imbued with these characteristics and given knowledge and wisdom as part of their natural disposition.

Allah Exalted said, in the case of Yaḥyā: "And We granted him wisdom while [he was still] a child."[202] Some scholars commented that this "wisdom" was knowledge of the Book of Allah. Maʿmar[203] said: "Yaḥyā was two or three years old and the other children asked: 'Why do you not play?' He replied: 'Was I created to play?'"[204]

In another verse, Allah Exalted says that Yaḥyā "will confirm the Word of Allah"[205]. This was said to refer to his confirmation, at the age of three, of ʿĪsā as the "Word of Allah" and "His Spirit". Others said that he made the confirmation whilst still in his mother's womb. His mother would say to Maryam: "The child in my womb is bowing to greet the child in your womb!"

Allah Exalted says, concerning the birth of ʿĪsā: "So a voice reassured her from below her [*min taḥtihā*], 'Do not grieve!'" Some recitations include "*man taḥtahā*",[206] which gives the meaning of

---

202 *Maryam*, 12.

203 Maʿmar ibn Rāshid, from the most prominent Followers of the Followers. Ibn Ḥajar said: "He was virtuous and trustworthy." He died in 154 AH at the age of fifty-eight. See *Siyar Aʿlām al-Nubalāʾ* (7/5-18).

204 Suyūṭī said in *Al-Manāhil*, p. 159: "Reported by Daylamī from Maʿād ibn Ḥabl without the chain of narration, and by Ḥākim in *Al-Tārīkh* from Ibn ʿAbbās in a *marfūʿ* narration. Also reported by Aḥmad in *Al-Zuhd*, Ibn Abī Ḥātim in his *Tafsīr* from Maʿmar, and al-Zaylaʿī."

205 Āl ʿImrān, 39.

206 "*Min taḥtihā*", with a *kasrah* on the *mīm* and on the *tā*, meaning "from below her", was the recitation of Abū Jaʿfar, Nāfiʿ, Ḥafṣ ʿan ʿĀṣim, Ḥamzah, al-Kisāʾī, and Khalaf al-ʿĀshir. And "*Man taḥtahā*", with a *fatḥah* on the *mīm* and on the *tā*, meaning "whoever is below her", was the recitation of Ibn Kathīr, Abū ʿAmr, Ibn ʿĀmir, Abū Bakr ibn ʿĀṣim, and Yaʿqūb. See *Al-Mabsūṭ fī al-Qirāʾāt al-ʿAshar*, p. 288.

وَعَنْ عَلِيِّ بْنِ أَبِي طَالِبٍ رَضِيَ اللهُ عَنْهُ مِثْلُهُ²¹⁷.

وَكَانَ فِيمَا ذَكَرَهُ الْمُحَقِّقُونَ مَجْبُولًا عَلَيْهَا فِي أَصْلِ خِلْقَتِهِ وَأَوَّلِ فِطْرَتِهِ، لَمْ تَحْصُلْ لَهُ بِاكْتِسَابٍ وَلَا رِيَاضَةٍ، إِلَّا بِجُودٍ إِلَهِيٍّ، وَخُصُوصِيَّةٍ رَبَّانِيَّةٍ.

وَهَكَذَا سَائِرُ الْأَنْبِيَاءِ صَلَوَاتُ اللهِ وَسَلَامُهُ عَلَيْهِ وَعَلَيْهِمْ، وَمَنْ طَالَعَ سِيَرَهُمْ مُنْذُ صِبَاهُمْ إِلَى مَبْعَثِهِمْ حَقَّقَ ذَلِكَ، كَمَا عُرِفَ مِنْ حَالِ مُوسَى وَعِيسَى وَيَحْيَى وَسُلَيْمَانَ وَغَيْرِهِمْ عَلَيْهِمُ السَّلَامُ. بَلْ غُرِزَتْ فِيهِمْ هَذِهِ الْأَخْلَاقُ فِي الْجِبِلَّةِ، وَأُودِعُوا الْعِلْمَ وَالْحِكْمَةَ فِي الْفِطْرَةِ.

قَالَ اللهُ تَعَالَى: ﴿وَءَاتَيْنَهُ الْحُكْمَ صَبِيًّا﴾ [مريم: ١٢].

قَالَ الْمُفَسِّرُونَ: أُعْطِيَ يَحْيَى الْعِلْمَ بِكِتَابِ اللهِ فِي حَالِ صِبَاهُ.

وَقَالَ مَعْمَرٌ²¹⁸: كَانَ ابْنَ سَنَتَيْنِ أَوْ ثَلَاثٍ، فَقَالَ لَهُ الصِّبْيَانُ: لِمَ لَا تَلْعَبُ؟ فَقَالَ: أَلِلَّعِبِ خُلِقْتُ؟!²¹⁹.

وَقِيلَ فِي قَوْلِهِ تَعَالَى: ﴿مُصَدِّقًا بِكَلِمَةٍ مِّنَ اللَّهِ﴾ [آل عمران: ٣٩]: صَدَّقَ يَحْيَى بِعِيسَى وَهُوَ ابْنُ ثَلَاثِ سِنِينَ، فَشَهِدَ لَهُ أَنَّهُ كَلِمَةُ اللهِ وَرُوحُهُ.

وَقِيلَ: صَدَّقَهُ وَهُوَ فِي بَطْنِ أُمِّهِ، وَكَانَتْ أُمُّ يَحْيَى تَقُولُ لِمَرْيَمَ: إِنِّي أَجِدُ مَا فِي بَطْنِي يَسْجُدُ لِمَا فِي بَطْنِكِ تَحِيَّةً لَهُ.

وَقَدْ نَصَّ اللهُ تَعَالَى عَلَى كَلَامِ عِيسَى عِنْدَ أُمِّهِ عِنْدَ وِلَادَتِهَا إِيَّاهُ بِقَوْلِهِ: ﴿لَا

---

٢١٧   عَزَاهُ فِي الْمَنَاهِلِ (١٥٨) إِلَى أَبِي عُبَيْدٍ فِي الْغَرِيبِ.

٢١٨   هُوَ مَعْمَرُ بْنُ رَاشِدٍ، مِنْ كِبَارِ أَتْبَاعِ التَّابِعِينَ. قَالَ عَنْهُ ابْنُ حَجَرٍ: ثِقَةٌ ثَبْتٌ فَاضِلٌ. مَاتَ سَنَةَ (١٥٤ هـ) وَهُوَ ابْنُ (٥٨) سَنَةً. انْظُرْ تَرْجَمَتَهُ فِي سِيَرِ أَعْلَامِ النُّبَلَاءِ ٧/٥-١٨.

٢١٩   قَالَ السُّيُوطِيُّ فِي الْمَنَاهِلِ (١٥٩): «الدَّيْلَمِيُّ عَنْ مُعَاذِ بْنِ جَبَلٍ وَلَمْ يُسْنِدْهُ، وَالْحَاكِمُ فِي التَّارِيخِ عَنِ ابْنِ عَبَّاسٍ مَرْفُوعًا، وَسَنَدُهُ وَاهٍ، وَأَخْرَجَهُ أَحْمَدُ فِي الزُّهْدِ، وَابْنُ أَبِي حَاتِمٍ فِي تَفْسِيرِهِ عَنْ مَعْمَرٍ، وَالزَّيْلَعِيُّ، فَذَكَرَهُ».

the verse as "She was reassured by the one below her", and it is said that ʿĪsā was the one calling his mother. Allah Exalted also quotes the speech of ʿĪsā in the cradle, when he said: "I am truly a servant of Allah. He has destined me to be given the Scripture and to be a Prophet."[207]

Allah Exalted said: "We guided [young] Sulaymān to a fairer settlement, and granted each of them[208] wisdom and knowledge."[209]

The judgement of an infant Sulaymān is mentioned in the case of a woman who was due to be stoned,[210] as well as regarding the boy [that was snatched by the wolf], when his father Dāwūd followed his advice.[211] Ṭabarī stated that Sulaymān was made king at the age of twelve.

Mūsā grabbed onto the beard of Pharoah as an infant. And the words of Allah Exalted, "And indeed, We had granted Ibrāhīm sound judgment early on"[212], were interpreted by Mujāhid and others to mean: "We guided him at a young age." Ibn ʿAṭāʾ said: "Allah Exalted chose him before He created him." Others commented: "When Ibrāhīm ﷺ was born, Allah sent an Angel who commanded him to know Allah with his heart and to remember Him with

---

207 *Maryam*, 30.

208 i.e., Prophets Sulaymān and Dāwūd.

209 *al-Anbiyāʾ*, 79.

210 Reported by Ibn ʿAsākir in *Al-Tārīkh* from Ibn ʿAbbās. See *Al-Manāhil*, p. 160. And Allah knows best about the authenticity of this narration.

211 In a narration reported by Bukhārī (6769) and Muslim (1720) from Abū Hurayrah, the Prophet ﷺ said: "There were two women with their sons, and a wolf came and snatched one of the sons. One of the women said to the other: 'It was your son that the wolf took!' But the other woman replied: 'Rather, it was your son!' They came to Dāwūd to judge between them, and he ruled in favour of the elder of the two women. Then, they went to Sulaymān ibn Dāwūd ﷺ and informed him [of what had taken place]. Sulaymān said: 'Bring me a knife so I can split the boy [who survived] between the two of you.' The younger woman cried out: 'No! May Allah have mercy on you! It is her son.' So, he judged in favour of the younger woman." The wording here is from Muslim.

212 *al-Anbiyāʾ*, 51.

تَحْزَنِي﴾ [مريم: ٢٤] عَلَى قِرَاءَةِ مَنْ قَرَأَ: «مَنْ تَحْتَها»²²⁰ وَعَلَى قَوْلِ مَنْ قَالَ: إِنَّ الْمُنَادِيَ عِيسَى.

وَنَصَّ عَلَى كَلَامِهِ فِي مَهْدِهِ فَقَالَ: ﴿إِنِّي عَبْدُ ٱللَّهِ ءَاتَنِيَ ٱلْكِتَبَ وَجَعَلَنِي نَبِيًّا﴾ [مريم: ٣٠].

وَقَالَ تَعَالَى: ﴿فَفَهَّمْنَهَا سُلَيْمَنَ وَكُلًّا ءَاتَيْنَا حُكْمًا وَعِلْمًا﴾ [الأنبياء: ٧٩].

وَقَدْ ذُكِرَ مِنْ حُكْمِ سُلَيْمَانَ وَهُوَ صَبِيٌّ يَلْعَبُ فِي قَضِيَّةِ الْمَرْجُومَةِ²²¹، وَفِي قِصَّةِ الصَّبِيِّ²²² مَا اقْتَدَى بِهِ دَاوُدُ أَبُوهُ، وَحَكَى الطَّبَرِيُّ أَنَّ عُمُرَهُ كَانَ حِينَ أُوتِيَ الْمُلْكَ اثْنَيْ عَشَرَ عَامًا.

وَكَذَلِكَ قِصَّةُ مُوسَى مَعَ فِرْعَوْنَ وَأَخْذُهُ بِلِحْيَتِهِ وَهُوَ طِفْل.

---

٢٢٠ قَرَأَ أَبُو جَعْفَرٍ وَنَافِعٌ، وَحَفْصٌ عَنْ عَاصِمٍ، وَحَمْزَةُ وَالْكِسَائِيُّ وَخَلَفٌ. «مِنْ تَحْتِها» بِكَسْرِ الْمِيمِ وَالتَّاءِ. وَقَرَأَ ابْنُ كَثِيرٍ، وَأَبُو عَمْرٍو، وَابْنُ عَامِرٍ، وَأَبُو بَكْرِ بْنُ عَاصِمٍ، وَيَعْقُوبُ: «مَنْ تَحْتَها» بِفَتْحِ الْمِيمِ وَالتَّاءِ. انْظُرِ الْمَبْسُوطَ فِي الْقِرَاءَاتِ الْعَشْرِ ص (٢٨٨).

٢٢١ رَوَاهُ ابْنُ عَسَاكِرٍ فِي تَارِيخِهِ بِسَنَدِهِ إِلَى ابْنِ عَبَّاسٍ أَنَّ امْرَأَةً حَسْنَاءَ فِي بَنِي إِسْرَائِيلَ رَاوَدَهَا عَنْ نَفْسِهَا أَرْبَعَةٌ مِنْ رُؤَسَائِهِمْ، فَامْتَنَعَتْ عَلَى كُلٍّ مِنْهُمْ، فَاتَّفَقُوا فِيمَا بَيْنَهُمْ عَلَيْهَا عِنْدَ دَاوُدَ، أَنَّهَا مَكَّنَتْ مِنْ نَفْسِهَا كَلْبًا لَهَا، قَدْ عَوَّدَتْهُ ذَلِكَ مِنْهَا، فَأَمَرَ بِرَجْمِهَا، فَلَمَّا كَانَ عَشِيَّةَ ذَلِكَ الْيَوْمِ، جَلَسَ سُلَيْمَانُ، وَاجْتَمَعَ مَعَهُ وَلَدَانِ، مِثْلُهُ، فَانْتَصَبَ حَاكِمًا، وَتَزَيَّا أَرْبَعَةٌ مِنْهُمْ بِزِيِّ أُولَئِكَ، وَآخَرُ بِزِيِّ الْمَرْأَةِ، وَشَهِدُوا عَلَيْهَا بِأَنَّهَا مَكَّنَتْ مِنْ نَفْسِهَا كَلْبًا. فَقَالَ سُلَيْمَانُ: فَرِّقُوا بَيْنَهُمْ. فَسَأَلَ الْأَوَّلَ: مَا كَانَ لَوْنُ الْكَلْبِ؟ فَقَالَ: أَسْوَدُ. فَعَزَلَهُ. وَاسْتَدْعَى الْآخَرَ، فَسَأَلَهُ عَنْ لَوْنِهِ، فَقَالَ: أَحْمَرُ. وَقَالَ الْآخَرُ: أَغْبَشُ، وَقَالَ الْآخَرُ: أَبْيَضُ. فَأَمَرَ عِنْدَ ذَلِكَ بِقَتْلِهِمْ، فَحَكَى ذَلِكَ لِدَاوُدَ، فَاسْتَدْعَى مِنْ فَوْرِهِ أُولَئِكَ الْأَرْبَعَةَ فَسَأَلَهُمْ مُنْفَرِدِينَ عَنْ لَوْنِ ذَلِكَ الْكَلْبِ، فَاخْتَلَفُوا عَلَيْهِ، فَأَمَرَ بِقَتْلِهِمْ/ الْمَنَاهِل (١٦٠). وَاللهُ أَعْلَمُ بِصِحَّةِ هَذَا الْخَبَرِ.

٢٢٢ رَوَاهَا الْبُخَارِيُّ (٦٧٦٩)، وَمُسْلِمٌ (١٧٢٠) مِنْ حَدِيثِ أَبِي هُرَيْرَةَ عَنِ النَّبِيِّ ﷺ. قَالَ: «بَيْنَمَا امْرَأَتَانِ مَعَهُمَا ابْنَاهُمَا. جَاءَ الذِّئْبُ فَذَهَبَ بِابْنِ إِحْدَاهُمَا، فَقَالَتْ هَذِهِ لِصَاحِبَتِهَا: إِنَّمَا ذَهَبَ بِابْنِكِ أَنْتِ. وَقَالَتِ الْأُخْرَى: إِنَّمَا ذَهَبَ بِابْنِكِ. فَتَحَاكَمَتَا إِلَى دَاوُدَ. فَقَضَى بِهِ لِلْكُبْرَى. فَخَرَجَتَا عَلَى سُلَيْمَانَ بْنِ دَاوُدَ ﷺ فَأَخْبَرَتَاهُ. فَقَالَ: ائْتُونِي بِالسِّكِّينِ أَشُقُّهُ بَيْنَكُمَا. فَقَالَتِ الصُّغْرَى: لَا. يَرْحَمُكَ اللهُ! هُوَ ابْنُهَا. فَقَضَى بِهِ لِلصُّغْرَى» وَاللَّفْظُ لِمُسْلِمٍ.

his tongue. Ibrāhīm replied: 'I have done it.' He did not say, 'I will do it', and that was the 'sound judgement'[213] [he was granted]."

It was said that Ibrāhīm ﷺ was sixteen years old when he was thrown into the fire and tested,[214] and just fifteen months when he used the planets, the Sun, and the Moon to deduce [the existence of his Lord].[215] Isḥāq was seven years old when he was tested with the sacrifice.[216] Yūsuf received Revelation as a child when his brothers were plotting to throw him in the well. Allah Exalted said: "We inspired him: '[One day] you will remind them of this deed of theirs while they are unaware [of who you are].'"[217] These are just some of the stories related about the Prophets as children.

Āminah bint Wahb recounted that when Prophet ﷺ was born, he spread his hands on the ground and raised his head towards the sky.[218] The Prophet ﷺ said: "When I was born, idols were made abhorrent to me, as was poetry[219]."[220] He continued: "I was never tempted to practice the customs of Jāhiliyyah except on two occasions. Allah protected me both times, and I never went back [to those practices]."[221]

---

213 ibid.

214 Translator's note: See *al-Anbiyā'*, 51-70.

215 Translator's note: See *al-An'ām*, 75-79.

216 The well-known and correct opinion is that it was Ismāʿīl, in fact, who was tested with the sacrifice.

217 *Yūsuf*, 15.

218 This is a portion of the hadith from Ḥalīmah al-Saʿdiyah about breastfeeding the Prophet ﷺ. Reported by Ṭabarānī (24/545), Abū Yaʿlā (7163), and others. Haythamī said in *Majmaʿ al-Zawā'id* (8/221): "The narrators are reliable." Authenticated by Ibn Ḥibbān in *Mawārid al-Ẓamʾān* (2094). Suyūṭī graded the chain as *ḥasan* in *Al-Manāhil*, p. 680. Dhahabī was quoted in *Al-Manāhil*, p. 875, as approving the chain. Ibn Kathīr said in *Al-Sīrah* (1/228): "It is a well-known hadith amongst the scholars of the *sīrah*." The chain is disconnected in places.

219 Translator's note: The poetry of Jāhiliyyah.

220 Reported by Abū Nuʿaym in *Al-Dalāʾil* from Shaddād ibn Aws. See *Al-Manāhil*, p. 162.

221 Reported by Bazzār (2403) and others from ʿAlī. Haythamī said in *Majmaʿ al-Zawā'id* (8/226): "The narrators are reliable." Authenticated by Ibn Ḥibbān in *Mawārid al-Ẓamʾān* (2100). Also authenticated by Ḥākim (4/245) and Dhahabī concurred. Suyūṭī graded the

وَقَالَ الْمُفَسِّرُونَ فِي قَوْلِهِ تَعَالَى: ﴿وَلَقَدْ ءَاتَيْنَآ إِبْرَاهِيمَ رُشْدَهُۥ مِن قَبْلُ﴾ [الأنبياء: ٥١] ، أَيْ: هَدَيْنَاهُ صَغِيرًا، قَالَهُ مُجَاهِدٌ وَغَيْرُهُ.

وَقَالَ ابْنُ عَطَاءٍ: اصْطَفَاهُ قَبْلَ إِبْدَاءِ خَلْقِهِ.

وَقَالَ بَعْضُهُمْ: لَمَّا وُلِدَ إِبْرَاهِيمُ ﷺ بَعَثَ اللهُ تَعَالَى إِلَيْهِ مَلَكًا يَأْمُرُهُ عَنِ اللهِ أَنْ يَعْرِفَهُ بِقَلْبِهِ، وَيَذْكُرَهُ بِلِسَانِهِ، فَقَالَ: قَدْ فَعَلْتُ، وَلَمْ يَقُلْ أَفْعَلُ، فَذَلِكَ رُشْدُهُ.

وَقِيلَ: إِنَّ إِلْقَاءَ إِبْرَاهِيمَ فِي النَّارِ وَمِحْنَتَهُ كَانَتْ وَهُوَ ابْنُ سِتَّ عَشْرَةَ سَنَةً، وَإِنَّ ابْتِلَاءَ إِسْحَاقَ بِالذَّبْحِ٢٢٣ وَهُوَ ابْنُ سَبْعِ سِنِينَ، وَإِنَّ اسْتِدْلَالَ إِبْرَاهِيمَ بِالْكَوْكَبِ وَالْقَمَرِ وَالشَّمْسِ كَانَ وَهُوَ ابْنُ خَمْسَةَ عَشَرَ شَهْرًا.

وَقِيلَ: أُوحِيَ إِلَى يُوسُفَ وَهُوَ صَبِيٌّ عِنْدَمَا هَمَّ إِخْوَتُهُ بِإِلْقَائِهِ فِي الْجُبِّ، يَقُولُ اللهُ تَعَالَى: ﴿وَأَوْحَيْنَآ إِلَيْهِ لَتُنَبِّئَنَّهُم بِأَمْرِهِمْ هَذَا وَهُمْ لَا يَشْعُرُونَ﴾ [يوسف: ١٥] الْآيَةَ، إِلَى غَيْرِ ذَلِكَ مِنْ أَخْبَارِهِمْ.

وَقَدْ حَكَى أَهْلُ السِّيَرِ أَنَّ آمِنَةَ بِنْتَ وَهْبٍ أَخْبَرَتْ أَنَّ نَبِيَّنَا مُحَمَّدًا ﷺ وُلِدَ حِينَ وُلِدَ بَاسِطًا يَدَيْهِ إِلَى الْأَرْضِ، رَافِعًا رَأْسَهُ إِلَى السَّمَاءِ٢٢٤.

وَقَالَ فِي حَدِيثِهِ ﷺ: «لَمَّا نَشَأْتُ بُغِّضَتْ إِلَيَّ الْأَوْثَانُ، وَبُغِّضَ إِلَيَّ

---

٢٢٣ الْمَشْهُورُ الصَّحِيحُ أَنَّ إِسْمَاعِيلَ هُوَ الذَّبِيحُ.

٢٢٤ هُوَ طَرَفٌ مِنْ حَدِيثِ حَلِيمَةَ السَّعْدِيَّةِ فِي رَضَاعِهِ ﷺ. أَخْرَجَهُ الطَّبَرَانِيُّ فِي الْمُجَلَّدِ (٢٤) بِرَقْمِ (٥٤٥)، وَأَبُو يَعْلَى (٧١٦٣) وَغَيْرُهُ، قَالَ الْهَيْثَمِيُّ فِي الْمَجْمَعِ ٢٢١/٨: «رِجَالُهُمَا ثِقَاتٌ». وَصَحَّحَهُ ابْنُ حِبَّانَ (٢٠٩٤) مَوَارِدُ الظَّمْآنِ، وَحَسَّنَ إِسْنَادَهُ السُّيُوطِيُّ فِي مَنَاهِلِ الصَّفَا (٦٨٠). وَنُقِلَ فِي الْمَنَاهِلِ (٨٧٥) قَوْلُ الذَّهَبِيِّ: جَيِّدُ الْإِسْنَادِ. وَقَالَ الْحَافِظُ ابْنُ كَثِيرٍ فِي السِّيرَةِ ٢٢٨/١: «وَهُوَ مِنَ الْأَحَادِيثِ الْمَشْهُورَةِ الْمُتَدَاوَلَةِ بَيْنَ أَهْلِ السِّيَرِ وَالْمَغَازِي». قُلْتُ: وَفِي إِسْنَادِهِ انْقِطَاعٌ.

[As they grew up], the Prophets were given capability in their affairs, a gentle breeze from [the Mercy of] Allah washed over them, and the light of true knowledge shone in their hearts until they reached their goal. They met this objective by the decision of Allah to choose them as Prophets and to bless them with the honourable qualities we have mentioned. Allah Exalted said [in the case of Mūsā]: "And when he reached full strength and maturity, We gave him wisdom and knowledge."[222]

We may find other people who possess some, but not all, of these virtuous characteristics. A person may be born with these traits embedded within their natural disposition, and they are able to complete them with the guidance and support of Allah Exalted. In this way, we see that some children already display a sound understanding, healthy sense of self-esteem, truthful manner, and generous and forgiving nature, whereas others display the opposite. Nevertheless, people are able to pick up those virtues that are lacking through acquisition, by striving with discipline and diligence. The Prophet ﷺ said: "Every person will find whatever [actions] they were created for easy [to perform]."[223] For this reason, the Predecessors differed about whether such virtues were typically innate or acquired. Ṭabarī cited a number of the Predecessors, including ʿAbdullāh ibn Masʿūd and al-Ḥasan, as taking the view that good character is innate and a natural instinct in the servant of Allah, and we have found this opinion to be the most accurate.

Saʿd related that the Prophet ﷺ said: "The believer may naturally possess every character trait, except for treachery and ly-

---

chain as *ṣaḥīḥ* in *Al-Manāhil*, p. 163, and Ibn Ḥajar graded it as *ḥasan*.

222 *al-Qaṣaṣ*, 14.

223 Reported by Bukhārī (4945) and Muslim (2646/7) in a *marfūʿ* narration from ʿAlī.

الشِّعْرُ»٢٢٥. وَ«لَمْ أَهُمَّ بِشَيْءٍ مِمَّا كَانَتِ الجَاهِلِيَّةُ تَفْعَلُهُ إِلَّا مَرَّتَيْنِ، فَعَصَمَنِي اللهُ مِنْهَا، ثُمَّ لَمْ أَعُدْ»٢٢٦.

ثُمَّ يَتَمَكَّنُ الأَمْرُ لَهُمْ، وَتَتَرَادَفُ نَفَحَاتُ اللهِ عَلَيْهِمْ، وَتُشْرِقُ أَنْوَارُ المَعَارِفِ فِي قُلُوبِهِمْ، حَتَّى يَصِلُوا الغَايَةَ، وَيَبْلُغُوا بِاصْطِفَاءِ اللهِ تَعَالَى لَهُمْ بِالنُّبُوَّةِ فِي تَحْصِيلِ هَذِهِ الخِصَالِ الشَّرِيفَةِ النِّهَايَةَ، دُونَ مُمَارَسَةٍ وَلَا رِيَاضَةٍ، قَالَ اللهُ تَعَالَى: ﴿وَلَمَّا بَلَغَ٢٢٧ أَشُدَّهُ وَاسْتَوَىٰ ءَاتَيْنَاهُ حُكْمًا وَعِلْمًا﴾ [القصص: ١٤].

وَقَدْ نَجِدُ غَيْرَهُمْ يُطْبَعُ عَلَى بَعْضِ هَذِهِ الأَخْلَاقِ دُونَ جَمِيعِهَا وَيُولَدُ عَلَيْهَا، فَيَسْهُلُ عَلَيْهِ اكْتِسَابُ تَمَامِهَا عِنَايَةً مِنَ اللهِ تَعَالَى، كَمَا نُشَاهِدُ مِنْ خِلْقَةِ بَعْضِ الصِّبْيَانِ عَلَى حُسْنِ السَّمْتِ٢٢٨ أَوِ الشَّهَامَةِ٢٢٩ أَوْ صِدْقِ اللِّسَانِ أَوِ السَّمَاحَةِ، وَكَمَا نَجِدُ بَعْضَهُمْ عَلَى ضِدِّهَا، فَبِالاكْتِسَابِ يَكْمُلُ نَاقِصُهَا، وَبِالرِّيَاضَةِ وَالمُجَاهَدَةِ يُسْتَجْلَبُ مَعْدُومُهَا وَيَعْتَدِلُ مُنْحَرِفُهَا، وَبِاخْتِلَافِ هَذَيْنِ الحَالَيْنِ يَتَفَاوَتُ٢٣٠ النَّاسُ فِيهَا، وَ«كُلٌّ مُيَسَّرٌ لِمَا خُلِقَ لَهُ»٢٣١.

وَلِهَذَا اخْتَلَفَ السَّلَفُ فِيهَا هَلْ هَذَا الخُلُقُ جِبِلَّةٌ أَوْ مُكْتَسَبَةٌ؟ فَحَكَى

---

٢٢٥ رَوَاهُ أَبُو نُعَيْمٍ فِي الدَّلَائِلِ عَنْ شَدَّادِ بْنِ أَوْسٍ / المَنَاهِلِ (١٦٢).

٢٢٦ أَخْرَجَهُ البَزَّارُ (٢٤٠٣) وَغَيْرُهُ مِنْ حَدِيثِ عَلِيٍّ. قَالَ الهَيْثَمِيُّ فِي المَجْمَعِ ٨/٢٢٦: «رِجَالُهُ ثِقَاتٌ» وَصَحَّحَهُ ابْنُ حِبَّانَ (٢١٠٠) مَوَارِدُ، وَالحَاكِمُ (٢٤٥/٤)، وَأَقَرَّهُ الذَّهَبِيُّ، وَصَحَّحَ إِسْنَادَهُ السُّيُوطِيُّ فِي المَنَاهِلِ (١٦٣)، وَحَسَّنَهُ الحَافِظُ ابْنُ حَجَرٍ.

٢٢٧ فَاعِلُ «بَلَغَ» هُوَ مُوسَى عليه السلام.

٢٢٨ السَّمْتُ: الطَّرِيقُ الوَاضِحُ، وَالمَذْهَبُ، وَالسَّكِينَةُ وَالوَقَارُ، وَالهَيْئَةُ (المُعْجَمُ الوَسِيطُ).

٢٢٩ الشَّهَامَةُ: عِزَّةُ النَّفْسِ وَحِرْصُهَا عَلَى مُبَاشَرَةِ أُمُورٍ عَظِيمَةٍ تَسْتَتْبِعُ الذِّكْرَ الجَمِيلَ (المُعْجَمُ الوَسِيطُ).

٢٣٠ يَتَفَاوَتُ: يَتَفَاضَلُ.

٢٣١ رَوَاهُ البُخَارِيُّ (٤٩٤٥)، وَمُسْلِمٌ (٢٦٤٦/٧) مِنْ حَدِيثِ عَلِيٍّ مَرْفُوعًا.

ing."[224] And 'Umar ibn al-Khaṭṭāb ﷺ said: "Courage and cowardice are both natural instincts that Allah places wherever He wills."[225]

The praiseworthy characteristics and virtues a person may aspire to are many, but we will suffice with mentioning the most fundamental of them. And we will clarify, Allah willing, that the Prophet ﷺ possessed every one.

---

224   Reported by Bazzār in *Kashf al-Astār* (102), Abū Yaʻlā (711), Bayhaqī (10/197), and others. Haythamī said in *Majmaʻ al-Zawāʼid* (330): "The narrators are sound." Also reported by Bayhaqī (10/197) from Saʻd, and he said: "He is sound."

225   Reported by Mālik in *Al-Muwaṭṭa'* (2/463), Bayhaqī in *Al-Sunan* (9/170), and others, in a *mawqūf* narration from ʻUmar. Also reported by Abū Yaʻlā (6451), al-Quḍāʻī (297), and Ibn Ḥibbān in *Al-Majrūḥīn* (3/41) in a *marfūʻ* narration from Abū Hurayrah. The chain of the latter narration contains Maʻdī ibn Sulaymān. Ibn Ḥajar said in *Taqrīb al-Tahdhīb*: "He was a devout worshipper. [However,] he was weak in narrating."

الطَّبَرِيُّ عَنْ بَعْضِ السَّلَفِ أَنَّ الْخُلُقَ الْحَسَنَ جِبِلَّةٌ وَغَرِيزَةٌ فِي الْعَبْدِ، وَحَكَاهُ عَنْ عَبْدِ اللهِ بْنِ مَسْعُودٍ وَالْحَسَنِ، وَبِهِ قَالَ هُوَ.

وَالصَّوَابُ مَا أَصَّلْنَاهُ.

وَقَدْ رَوَى سَعْدٌ عَنِ النَّبِيِّ ﷺ، قَالَ: «كُلُّ الْخِلَالِ يُطْبَعُ عَلَيْهَا الْمُؤْمِنُ، إِلَّا الْخِيَانَةَ وَالْكَذِبَ»٢٣٢.

وَقَالَ عُمَرُ بْنُ الْخَطَّابِ رضي الله عنه فِي حَدِيثِهِ: «وَالْجُرْأَةُ وَالْجُبْنُ غَرَائِزُ يَضَعُهَا اللهُ حَيْثُ يَشَاءُ»٢٣٣.

وَهَذِهِ الْأَخْلَاقُ الْمَحْمُودَةُ وَالْخِصَالُ الْجَمِيلَةُ كَثِيرَةٌ، وَلَكِنَّا نَذْكُرُ أُصُولَهَا، وَنُشِيرُ إِلَى جَمِيعِهَا، وَنُحَقِّقُ وَصْفَهُ ﷺ بِهَا إِنْ شَاءَ اللهُ تَعَالَى.

---

٢٣٢ أَخْرَجَهُ الْبَزَّارُ (١٠٢) كَشْفُ الْأَسْتَارِ، وَأَبُو يَعْلَى (٧١١)، وَالْبَيْهَقِيُّ (١٩٧/١٠) وَغَيْرُهُ. وَقَالَ الْهَيْثَمِيُّ فِي الْمَجْمَعِ رَقْم (٣٣٠): «رِجَالُهُ رِجَالُ الصَّحِيحِ». وَأَخْرَجَهُ الْبَيْهَقِيُّ ١٩٧/١٠ عَنْ سَعْدٍ مِنْ قَوْلِهِ: وَقَالَ: «وَهُوَ الصَّحِيحُ»، وَقَالَ الدَّارَقُطْنِيُّ: الْمَوْقُوفُ أَشْبَهُ بِالصَّوَابِ. (الْخِلَالُ): جَمْعُ خُلَّةٍ وَهِيَ الْخَصْلَةُ.

٢٣٣ أَخْرَجَهُ مَالِكٌ فِي الْمُوَطَّأِ ٤٦٣/٢، وَالْبَيْهَقِيُّ فِي السُّنَنِ ١٧٠/٩ وَغَيْرُهُ مَوْقُوفًا عَلَى عُمَرَ. وَأَخْرَجَهُ مِنْ حَدِيثِ أَبِي هُرَيْرَةَ مَرْفُوعًا: أَبُو يَعْلَى (٦٤٥١)، وَالْقُضَاعِيُّ (٢٩٧) وَابْنُ حِبَّانَ فِي الْمَجْرُوحِينَ ٤١/٣، وَفِي إِسْنَادِهِ مَعْدِيُّ بْنُ سُلَيْمَانَ. قَالَ فِي التَّقْرِيبِ: «ضَعِيفٌ وَكَانَ عَابِدًا».

HIS SHARP INTELLECT

The intellect is the root of all branches of knowledge, and the wellspring from which deep understanding flows. Clear understanding, sharp perception, keen observation, foresight, self-restraint, sincere principles, organization of one's affairs, and the ability to acquire virtuous qualities whilst avoiding harmful habits all stem from the intellect.

We have already indicated the intellectual accomplishments of the Prophet ﷺ and his position in this regard, in which he was unmatched by any human. This was part of the honour of his status and can be verified by studying the course of his life and how he developed, his virtuous qualities and characteristics, and the wisdom of his words. Further evidence is his knowledge of the Torah, the Injīl, other Books sent down by Allah Exalted, the parables of wise men, the stories of past nations, and the blessings they enjoyed and trials they endured[226]. He was adept at [teaching others through] metaphors and examples, organizing society, establishing the Shariah, and setting the example of a praiseworthy character. This is clear from the scholars who take his words as a model and his examples as evidence, including in the sciences of dream interpretation, medicine, mathematics, laws of inheritance, and genealogy. He achieved all of this without prior education or instruction, neither did he read from books or sit with scholars. Rather, he was the unlettered Prophet who did not know any of these things until Allah expanded his chest, clarified his affair, taught him, and

---

226   Translator's note: lit., "and their days". See, for example, *Ibrāhīm*, 14.

فصل

أَمَّا أَصْلُ فُرُوعِهَا، وَعُنْصُرُ يَنَابِيعِهَا، وَنُقْطَةُ دَائِرَتِهَا، فَالعَقْلُ الَّذِي مِنْهُ يَنْبَعِثُ العِلْمُ وَالمَعْرِفَةُ، وَيَتَفَرَّعُ عَنْ هَذَا ثُقُوبُ الرَّأْيِ، وَجَوْدَةُ الفِطْنَةِ، وَالإِصَابَةُ، وَصِدْقُ الظَّنِّ، وَالنَّظَرُ لِلْعَوَاقِبِ وَمَصَالِحِ النَّفْسِ، وَمُجَاهَدَةُ الشَّهْوَةِ، وَحُسْنُ السِّيَاسَةِ وَالتَّدْبِيرِ، وَاقْتِنَاءُ الفَضَائِلِ، وَتَجَنُّبُ الرَّذَائِلِ.

وَقَدْ أَشَرْنَا إِلَى مَكَانِهِ مِنْهُ ﷺ، وَبُلُوغِهِ مِنْهُ وَمِنَ العِلْمِ الغَايَةَ الَّتِي لَمْ يَبْلُغْهَا بَشَرٌ سِوَاهُ، وَإِذْ جَلَالَةُ مَحَلِّهِ مِنْ ذَلِكَ وَمَا يَتَفَرَّعُ مِنْهُ مُتَحَقَّقٌ عِنْدَ مَنْ تَتَبَّعَ مَجَارِيَ أَحْوَالِهِ وَاطِّرَادَ سِيَرِهِ، وَطَالَعَ جَوَامِعَ كَلَامِهِ، وَحُسْنَ شَمَائِلِهِ، وَبَدَائِعَ سِيَرِهِ، وَحِكَمَ حَدِيثِهِ، وَعِلْمَهُ بِمَا فِي التَّوْرَاةِ وَالإِنْجِيلِ وَالكُتُبِ المُنْزَلَةِ، وَحِكَمَ الحُكَمَاءِ، وَسِيَرَ الأُمَمِ الخَالِيَةِ وَأَيَّامِهَا، وَضَرْبَ الأَمْثَالِ، وَسِيَاسَاتِ الأَنَامِ، وَتَقْرِيرَ الشَّرَائِعِ، وَتَأْصِيلَ الآدَابِ النَّفْسِيَّةِ، وَالشِّيَمِ الحَمِيدَةِ، إِلَى فُنُونِ العُلُومِ الَّتِي اتَّخَذَ أَهْلُهَا كَلَامَهُ ﷺ فِيهَا قُدْوَةً، وَإِشَارَاتِهِ حُجَّةً، كَالعِبَارَةِ[234]، وَالطِّبِّ، وَالحِسَابِ، وَالفَرَائِضِ، وَالنَّسَبِ، وَغَيْرِ ذَلِكَ كَمَا سَنُبَيِّنُهُ فِي مُعْجِزَاتِهِ ﷺ إِنْ شَاءَ اللهُ تَعَالَى، دُونَ تَعْلِيمٍ، وَلَا مُدَارَسَةٍ، وَلَا مُطَالَعَةِ كُتُبِ مَنْ تَقَدَّمَ، وَلَا الجُلُوسِ إِلَى عُلَمَائِهِمْ، بَلْ نَبِيٌّ أُمِّيٌّ لَمْ يَعْرِفْ بِشَيْءٍ مِنْ ذَلِكَ، حَتَّى شَرَحَ اللهُ صَدْرَهُ، وَأَبَانَ أَمْرَهُ، وَعَلَّمَهُ وَأَقْرَأَهُ، يُعْلَمُ ذَلِكَ بِالمُطَالَعَةِ وَالبَحْثِ عَنْ حَالِهِ ضَرُورَةً، وَبِالبُرْهَانِ القَاطِعِ عَلَى نُبُوَّتِهِ نَظَرًا، فَلَا نُطَوِّلُ بِسَرْدِ الأَقَاصِيصِ وَآحَادِ

---

٢٣٤ العِبَارَةُ: تَعْبِيرُ الرُّؤْيَا وَتَأْوِيلُهَا.

enabled him to recite the Qur'an. In accordance with his intellect, he was given knowledge of what has passed and what will be, the wonders of His Power, and the supremacy of His Sovereignty.

Allah Exalted said: "[He] taught you what you never knew. Great [indeed] is Allah's favour upon you!"[227] Minds have been confounded trying to assess the extent of this favour, and tongues are rendered speechless in giving any description.

---

227 *al-Nisā'*, 113.

الْقَضَايَا؛ إِذْ مَجْمُوعُهَا مَا لَا يَأْخُذُهُ حَصْرٌ، وَلَا يُحِيطُ بِهِ حِفْظٌ جَامِعٌ. وَبِحَسَبِ عَقْلِهِ كَانَتْ مَعَارِفُهُ ﷺ، إِلَى سَائِرِ مَا عَلَّمَهُ اللهُ تَعَالَى، وَأَطْلَعَهُ عَلَيْهِ مِنْ عِلْمِ مَا كَانَ وَمَا يَكُونُ، وَعَجَائِبِ قُدْرَتِهِ، وَعَظِيمِ مَلَكُوتِهِ، قَالَ جَلَّ وَعَزَّ: ﴿وَعَلَّمَكَ مَا لَمْ تَكُن تَعْلَمُ وَكَانَ فَضْلُ ٱللَّهِ عَلَيْكَ عَظِيمًا﴾ [النساء: ١١٣] حَارَتِ الْعُقُولُ فِي تَقْدِيرِ فَضْلِهِ عَلَيْهِ، وَخَرِسَتِ الْأَلْسُنُ دُونَ وَصْفٍ يُحِيطُ بِذَلِكَ أَوْ يَنْتَهِي إِلَيْهِ.

HIS PARDONING, ENDURANCE, FORBEAR-ANCE, AND PATIENCE

Scholars have separated the meanings of different types of patience: "forbearance" (*ḥilm*) refers to standing firm in the face of provocations; "endurance" (*iḥtimāl*) refers to displaying self-restraint despite suffering pain or harm; "patience" (*ṣabr*) has a similar meaning; and "pardoning" (*ʿafw*) refers to letting go. Allah Exalted educated His Prophet ﷺ in each of these virtues.

Allah Exalted said: "Be gracious (*khudh al-ʿafw*), enjoin what is right, and turn away from those who act ignorantly."[228] When this verse was revealed, the Prophet ﷺ asked Jibrīl ﷺ about its interpretation. Jibrīl ﷺ replied: "Wait until I ask the Knower (i.e., Allah Exalted)." When he returned, he said: "O Muhammad! Allah Exalted commands you to maintain ties with the one who cuts you off, to give to those who withhold from you, and to pardon those who wrong you."[229]

Allah Exalted said: "…and endure patiently whatever befalls you. Surely this is a resolve to aspire to."[230] And: "So endure patiently, as did the Messengers of Firm Resolve[231]."[232] And: "Let them pardon and forgive. Do you not love to be forgiven by Allah? And Allah is All-Forgiving, Most Merciful."[233]

---

228 *al-Aʿrāf*, 199.

229 Reported by Ibn Jarīr, Ibn Abī Ḥātim, and others.

230 *Luqmān*, 17.

231 This refers to Nūḥ, Ibrāhīm, Mūsā, ʿĪsā, and Muhammad ﷺ.

232 *al-Aḥqāf*, 35.

233 *al-Nūr*, 22.

فَصْل

وَأَمَّا الْحِلْمُ وَالِاحْتِمَالُ، وَالْعَفْوُ مَعَ الْقُدْرَةِ، وَالصَّبْرُ عَلَى مَا يُكْرَهُ، وَبَيْنَ هَذِهِ الْأَلْقَابِ فَرْقٌ، فَإِنَّ الْحِلْمَ: حَالَةُ تَوَقُّرٍ وَثَبَاتٍ عِنْدَ الْأَسْبَابِ الْمُحَرِّكَاتِ، وَالِاحْتِمَالُ حَبْسُ النَّفْسِ عِنْدَ الْآلَامِ وَالْمُؤْذِيَاتِ، وَمِثْلُهَا الصَّبْرُ، وَمَعَانِيهَا مُتَقَارِبَةٌ. وَأَمَّا الْعَفْوُ فَهُوَ تَرْكُ الْمُؤَاخَذَةِ.

وَهَذَا كُلُّهُ مِمَّا أَدَّبَ اللهُ بِهِ نَبِيَّهُ ﷺ، فَقَالَ: ﴿خُذِ ٱلْعَفْوَ وَأْمُرْ بِٱلْعُرْفِ﴾ [الأعراف: ١٩٩] الْآيَةَ.

رُوِيَ أَنَّ النَّبِيَّ ﷺ لَمَّا نَزَلَتْ عَلَيْهِ هَذِهِ الْآيَةُ سَأَلَ جِبْرِيلَ عَلَيْهِ السَّلَام عَنْ تَأْوِيلِهَا فَقَالَ لَهُ: حَتَّى أَسْأَلَ الْعَالِمَ، ثُمَّ ذَهَبَ ثُمَّ أَتَاهُ فَقَالَ: يَا مُحَمَّدُ! إِنَّ اللهَ يَأْمُرُكَ أَنْ تَصِلَ مَنْ قَطَعَكَ، وَتُعْطِيَ مَنْ حَرَمَكَ، وَتَعْفُوَ عَن مَنْ ظَلَمَكَ[235].

وَقَالَ لَهُ: ﴿وَٱصْبِرْ عَلَىٰ مَآ أَصَابَكَ﴾ [لقمان: ١٧] الْآيَةَ.

وَقَالَ: ﴿فَٱصْبِرْ كَمَا صَبَرَ أُوْلُواْ ٱلْعَزْمِ مِنَ ٱلرُّسُلِ﴾ [الأحقاف: ٣٥].

وَقَالَ: ﴿وَلْيَعْفُواْ وَلْيَصْفَحُواْ﴾ [النور: ٢٢] الْآيَةَ.

وَقَالَ: ﴿وَلَمَن صَبَرَ وَغَفَرَ إِنَّ ذَٰلِكَ لَمِنْ عَزْمِ ٱلْأُمُورِ﴾ [الشورى: ٤٣]. وَلَا خَفَاءَ بِمَا يُؤْثَرُ مِنْ حِلْمِهِ وَاحْتِمَالِهِ ﷺ، وَأَنَّ كُلَّ حَلِيمٍ قَدْ عُرِفَتْ مِنْهُ

---

[235] أَخْرَجَهُ ابْنُ جَرِيرٍ وَابْنُ أَبِي حَاتِمٍ وَغَيْرُهُ مِنْ طُرُقٍ مُرْسَلَةٍ. وَوَصَلَهُ ابْنُ مَرْدَوَيْهِ مِنْ حَدِيثِ جَابِرٍ وَقَيْسِ بْنِ سَعْدِ بْنِ عُبَادَةَ.

He also said: "And whoever endures patiently and forgives – surely this is a resolve to aspire to."[234]

The effects of the forbearance and endurance of the Prophet ﷺ are evident. Whereas any other tolerant person would be prone to lapses, harm and insult only made the Prophet ﷺ more patient, and a deluge of ignorant people only increased his forbearance.

Abū ʿAbdullāh and others narrated, from Muhammad ibn ʿAttāb, from Abū Bakr ibn Wāfid[235] and others, from Abū ʿĪsā, from ʿUbaydullāh, from Yahyā ibn Yahyā, from Mālik, from Ibn Shihāb, from ʿUrwah, from ʿĀʾishah ﷺ, who said: "Whenever the Messenger of Allah ﷺ had to choose between two things he would choose the easier of the two, as long as it was not a sin. If it was a sin, he was the furthest away from it. And the Messenger of Allah ﷺ would never avenge for his own sake. But if the sanctities of Allah Exalted were violated, then he would avenge for the sake of Allah."[236]

When the face of the Prophet ﷺ was wounded during the Battle of Uhud and his front teeth were smashed, the Companions were profoundly affected and seething with anger. They said: "If only you would supplicate against them!" But the Prophet ﷺ replied: "I was not sent to curse. Rather, I was sent as a caller and a mercy. O Allah! Guide my people, for they do not know."[237]

---

234 *al-Shūrā*, 43.

235 Yahyā ibn ʿAbd al-Rahmān ibn Wāfid al-Lakhmī, a *qādī* of Cordoba. He died in 404 AH. See *Tabsīr al-Muntabih*, p. 1466.

236 Reported here from the chain of Mālik (2/903). Also reported by Bukhārī (3560) and Muslim (2327).

237 Reported by Bayhaqī with this wording in *Al-Shuʿab* from ʿAbdullāh ibn ʿUbayd, in a narration he declared as *mursal*. See *Al-Manāhil*, p. 168. Reported by Bukhārī (2903) and Muslim (1790) from the hadith of Sahl ibn Saʿd. This portion of the hadith was also reported in the commentary of Bukhārī (2903) and by Muslim (1791) from Anas ibn Mālik. Also reported by Bukhārī (3477) and Muslim (1792) from Ibn Masʿūd, who said: "It was as if I was watching the Prophet ﷺ speak about another Prophet who had been beaten and bloodied by his people.

زَلَّةٌ^{٢٣٦}، وَحُفِظَتْ عَنْهُ هَفْوَةٌ^{٢٣٧}، وَهُوَ ﷺ لَا يَزِيدُ مَعَ كَثْرَةِ الْأَذَى إِلَّا صَبْرًا، وَعَلَى إِسْرَافِ الْجَاهِلِ إِلَّا حِلْمًا.

حَدَّثَنَا الْقَاضِي أَبُو عَبْدِ اللهِ مُحَمَّدُ بْنُ عَلِيٍّ التَّغْلِبِيُّ وَغَيْرُهُ، قَالُوا: حَدَّثَنَا مُحَمَّدُ ابْنُ عَتَّابٍ، حَدَّثَنَا أَبُو بَكْرِ بْنِ وَاقِدٍ^{٢٣٨} الْقَاضِي وَغَيْرُهُ، حَدَّثَنَا أَبُو عِيسَى، حَدَّثَنَا عُبَيْدُ اللهِ، حَدَّثَنَا يَحْيَى بْنُ يَحْيَى، حَدَّثَنَا مَالِكٌ، عَنِ ابْنِ شِهَابٍ، عَنْ عُرْوَةَ، عَنْ عَائِشَةَ رَضِيَ اللهُ عَنْهَا، قَالَتْ: «مَا خُيِّرَ رَسُولُ اللهِ ﷺ فِي أَمْرَيْنِ قَطُّ إِلَّا اخْتَارَ أَيْسَرَهُمَا مَا لَمْ يَكُنْ إِثْمًا، فَإِنْ كَانَ إِثْمًا كَانَ أَبْعَدَ النَّاسِ مِنْهُ، وَمَا انْتَقَمَ رَسُولُ اللهِ ﷺ لِنَفْسِهِ، إِلَّا أَنْ تُنْتَهَكَ حُرْمَةُ اللهِ تَعَالَى، فَيَنْتَقِمُ لِلهِ بِهَا»^{٢٣٩}.

وَرُوِيَ أَنَّ النَّبِيَّ ﷺ لَمَّا كُسِرَتْ رَبَاعِيَتُهُ وَشُجَّ وَجْهُهُ يَوْمَ أُحُدٍ شَقَّ ذَلِكَ عَلَى أَصْحَابِهِ شَدِيدًا، وَقَالُوا: لَوْ دَعَوْتَ عَلَيْهِمْ، فَقَالَ: «إِنِّي لَمْ أُبْعَثْ لَعَّانًا، وَلَكِنِّي بُعِثْتُ دَاعِيًا وَرَحْمَةً، اللَّهُمَّ اهْدِ قَوْمِي فَإِنَّهُمْ لَا يَعْلَمُونَ»^{٢٤٠}.

وَرُوِيَ عَنْ عُمَرَ رَضِيَ اللهُ عَنْهُ أَنَّهُ قَالَ فِي بَعْضِ كَلَامِهِ: بِأَبِي أَنْتَ وَأُمِّي يَا رَسُولَ

---

٢٣٦ زَلَّةٌ: سَقْطَةٌ وَخَطِيئَةٌ.

٢٣٧ هَفْوَةٌ: غَلْطَةٌ.

٢٣٨ هُوَ يَحْيَى بْنُ عَبْدِ الرَّحْمَنِ بْنِ وَافِدٍ اللَّخْمِيِّ، قَاضِي قُرْطُبَةَ، مَاتَ سَنَةَ (٤٠٤) هـ / تَبْصِيرُ الْمُنْتَبِهِ ص: (١٤٦٦).

٢٣٩ أَسْنَدَهُ الْمُصَنِّفُ مِنْ طَرِيقِ مَالِكٍ ٩٠٣/٢، وَأَخْرَجَهُ أَيْضًا الْبُخَارِيُّ (٣٥٦٠)، وَمُسْلِمٌ (٢٣٢٧).

٢٤٠ أَخْرَجَهُ الْبَيْهَقِيُّ فِي الشُّعَبِ بِهَذَا اللَّفْظِ عَنْ عَبْدِ اللهِ بْنِ عُبَيْدٍ، وَقَالَ: مُرْسَلٌ/ الْمَنَاهِلِ (١٦٨). وَأَخْرَجَ الْبُخَارِيُّ (٢٩٠٣)، وَمُسْلِمٌ (١٧٩٠) مِنْ حَدِيثِ سَهْلِ بْنِ سَعْدٍ مَا يَتَعَلَّقُ بِجُرْحِ وَجْهِهِ الشَّرِيفِ ﷺ وَكَسْرِ رَبَاعِيَتِهِ. وَهَذِهِ الْفِقْرَةُ أَيْضًا فِي الْبُخَارِيِّ تَعْلِيقًا، وَمُسْلِمٌ (١٧٩١) مِنْ حَدِيثِ أَنَسِ بْنِ مَالِكٍ. وَأَخْرَجَ الْبُخَارِيُّ (٣٤٧٧)، وَمُسْلِمٌ (١٧٩٢) عَنِ ابْنِ مَسْعُودٍ قَالَ: كَأَنِّي أَنْظُرُ إِلَى النَّبِيِّ ﷺ يَحْكِي نَبِيًّا مِنَ الْأَنْبِيَاءِ ضَرَبَهُ قَوْمُهُ، فَأَدْمَوْهُ، وَهُوَ يَمْسَحُ الدَّمَ عَنْ وَجْهِهِ، وَيَقُولُ: اللَّهُمَّ! اغْفِرْ لِقَوْمِي فَإِنَّهُمْ لَا يَعْلَمُونَ». (رَبَاعِيَتُهُ): هِيَ السِّنُّ الَّتِي تَلِي الثَّنِيَّةَ مِنْ كُلِّ جَانِبٍ. وَلِلْإِنْسَانِ أَرْبَعُ رَبَاعِيَاتٍ. (شُجَّ): جُرِحَ.

'Umar ⁕ once said to the Prophet ⁕: "May my father and mother be your ransom, O Messenger of Allah! Nūḥ supplicated against his people: 'My Lord! Do not leave a single disbeliever on earth.'[238] If you had made a supplication like that, every one of us would have been destroyed. Your people trod on your back, bloodied your face, smashed your front teeth, and yet you refused to say anything but kind words, and you supplicated: 'O Allah! Forgive my people, for they do not know.'"[239]

Look at the virtue in the words of the Prophet ⁕, the degrees of excellence, perfect manners, selfless generosity, patience, and forbearance. He did not simply remain silent about them. Rather, he pardoned them, showed mercy and compassion towards them, and supplicated on their behalf. He prayed for Allah to "forgive" or "guide" them. The reason for his mercy and compassion was made clear when he described them as "my people". Finally, he petitioned Allah to excuse their ignorance, "for they do not know".

A man once said to the Prophet ⁕: "Be just. For this division [of the spoils] does not reflect seeking the Face of Allah." In his response, the Prophet ⁕ clarified the ignorance of the man's words, admonished him, and reminded him, but went no further than that, and restrained those Companions who wished to see him executed. Instead, he said to the man: "Woe to you! If I do not act with justice, then who would? Indeed, you would be disappointed and at a loss if I did not act with justice."[240]

Ghawrath ibn al-Ḥārith went to the Messenger of Allah ⁕,

Meanwhile, he was wiping the blood from his face and saying: 'O Allah! Forgive my people, for they do not know.'"

238 *Nūḥ*, 26.

239 Suyūṭī said in *Al-Manāhil*, p. 169: "[This narration is] unknown."

240 Reported by Bukhārī (3138) and Muslim (1063) from Jābir, Bukhārī (3610) and Muslim (1064/148) from al-Khudrī, and Bukhārī (3150) and Muslim (1062) from Ibn Mas'ūd.

اللهِ، لَقَدْ دَعَا نُوحٌ عَلَى قَوْمِهِ، فَقَالَ: ﴿رَبِّ لَا تَذَرْ عَلَى ٱلْأَرْضِ مِنَ ٱلْكَٰفِرِينَ دَيَّارًا﴾ [نُوحُ: ٢٦]، وَلَوْ دَعَوْتَ عَلَيْنَا مِثْلَهَا لَهَلَكْنَا مِنْ عِنْدِ آخِرِنَا، فَلَقَدْ وُطِيءَ ظَهْرُكَ، وَأُدْمِيَ وَجْهُكَ، وَكُسِرَتْ رَبَاعِيَتُكَ، فَأَبَيْتَ أَنْ تَقُولَ إِلَّا خَيْرًا، فَقُلْتَ: «اللَّهُمَّ اغْفِرْ لِقَوْمِي فَإِنَّهُمْ لَا يَعْلَمُونَ»[٢٤١].

قَالَ القَاضِي أَبُو الفَضْلِ رَضِيَاللهُعَنْهُ: انْظُرْ مَا فِي هَذَا القَوْلِ مِنْ جِمَاعِ الفَضْلِ، وَدَرَجَاتِ الإِحْسَانِ، وَحُسْنِ الخُلُقِ، وَكَرَمِ النَّفْسِ، وَغَايَةِ الصَّبْرِ وَالحِلْمِ؛ إِذْ لَمْ يَقْتَصِرْ ﷺ عَلَى السُّكُوتِ عَنْهُمْ حَتَّى عَفَا، ثُمَّ أَشْفَقَ عَلَيْهِمْ وَرَحِمَهُمْ، وَدَعَا وَشَفَعَ لَهُمْ، فَقَالَ: «اللَّهُمَّ اغْفِرْ» أَوِ «اهْدِ»، ثُمَّ أَظْهَرَ سَبَبَ الشَّفَقَةِ وَالرَّحْمَةِ بِقَوْلِهِ: «لِقَوْمِي»، ثُمَّ اعْتَذَرَ عَنْهُمْ بِجَهْلِهِمْ، فَقَالَ: «فَإِنَّهُمْ لَا يَعْلَمُونَ».

وَلَمَّا قَالَ لَهُ الرَّجُلُ: «اعْدِلْ فَإِنَّ هَذِهِ قِسْمَةٌ مَا أُرِيدَ بِهَا وَجْهُ اللهِ» لَمْ يَرُدَّهُ فِي جَوَابِهِ أَنْ بَيَّنَ لَهُ مَا جَهِلَهُ، وَوَعَظَ نَفْسَهُ وَذَكَّرَهَا بِمَا قَالَ لَهُ، فَقَالَ: «وَيْحَكَ! فَمَنْ يَعْدِلُ إِنْ لَمْ أَعْدِلْ؟! خِبْتَ وَخَسِرْتَ إِنْ لَمْ أَعْدِلْ»[٢٤٢]، وَنَهَى مَنْ أَرَادَ مِنْ أَصْحَابِهِ قَتْلَهُ.

وَلَمَّا تَصَدَّى لَهُ غَوْرَثُ بْنُ الحَارِثِ لِيَفْتِكَ بِهِ، وَرَسُولُ اللهِ ﷺ مُنْتَبِذٌ تَحْتَ شَجَرَةٍ وَحْدَهُ قَائِلًا، وَالنَّاسُ قَائِلُونَ، فِي غَزَاةٍ، فَلَمْ يَنْتَبِهْ رَسُولُ اللهِ ﷺ إِلَّا وَهُوَ قَائِمٌ وَالسَّيْفُ صَلْتًا فِي يَدِهِ، فَقَالَ: مَنْ يَمْنَعُكَ مِنِّي؟ فَقَالَ: «اللهُ»، فَسَقَطَ السَّيْفُ مِنْ يَدِهِ، فَأَخَذَهُ النَّبِيُّ ﷺ، وَقَالَ: «مَنْ يَمْنَعُكَ مِنِّي؟» قَالَ:

---

٢٤١ قَالَ السُّيُوطِيُّ فِي المَنَاهِلِ (١٦٩): «لَا يُعْرَفُ».

٢٤٢ أَخْرَجَهُ البُخَارِيُّ (٣١٣٨)، وَمُسْلِمٌ (١٠٦٣) مِنْ حَدِيثِ جَابِرٍ، وَالبُخَارِيُّ (٣٦١٠)، وَمُسْلِمٌ (١٠٦٤/١٤٨) مِنْ حَدِيثِ الخُذْرِيِّ، وَالبُخَارِيُّ (٣١٥٠)، وَمُسْلِمٌ (١٠٦٢) مِنْ حَدِيثِ ابْنِ مَسْعُودٍ.

who was out on a military expedition, with the intention of killing him. He found him alone, resting under a tree. The people with the Messenger of Allah ﷺ were also taking a nap, so he did not notice the presence of Ghawrath until he was standing over him with his sword in his hand. "Who will protect you from me?" Ghawrath threatened. "Allah", the Messenger of Allah ﷺ replied. Suddenly, the sword dropped from Ghawrath's hand and the Messenger of Allah ﷺ picked it up. "Who will protect you from me?" he asked. Ghawrath replied: "Be lenient in your punishment." So, the Messenger of Allah ﷺ left him and pardoned him, and he returned to the group saying: "I have come to you from the best of people."[241]

One of the greatest actions of forgiving from the Prophet ﷺ was his pardoning of the Jewish woman who brought him a poisoned sheep to eat, even after she had confessed.[242] When he was informed [in a dream] that Labīd ibn al-Aʿsam was the man that had performed black magic on him, and the details of what he had done were revealed to him, the Prophet ﷺ did not even admonish him, let alone punish him.[243] Neither did he punish ʿAbdullāh ibn Ubayy or the other Hypocrites, despite the severity of their words and actions. Instead, he said to those who wished to have them killed: "Do not let the people say that Muhammad kills his Companions."[244]

Anas ﷺ narrated: "I was with the Prophet ﷺ and he was wearing a thick cloak. A Bedouin man came and pulled the cloak so violently it left an impression on his shoulder. Then, he said: 'O Muhammad! Let me load these two camels of mine with the

---

241 Reported by Bayhaqī with this wording from Jābir ibn ʿAbdullāh. See *Al-Manāhil*, p. 171. Reported in another context by Bukhārī (2910) and Muslim (843).

242 Reported by Bukhārī (2617) and Muslim (2190) from Anas ibn Mālik.

243 Reported by Bukhārī (3268) and Muslim (2189) from ʿĀ'ishah.

244 Reported by Bukhārī (4905) and Muslim (2584/63) from Jābir.

كُنْ خَيْرَ آخِذٍ، فَتَرَكَهُ وَعَفَا عَنْهُ، فَجَاءَ إِلَى قَوْمِهِ فَقَالَ: جِئْتُكُمْ مِنْ عِنْدِ خَيْرِ النَّاسِ[٢٤٣].

وَمِنْ عَظِيمِ خَبَرِهِ فِي العَفْوِ عَفْوُهُ عَنِ اليَهُودِيَّةِ الَّتِي سَمَّتْهُ فِي الشَّاةِ بَعْدَ اعْتِرَافِهَا[٢٤٤]، عَلَى الصَّحِيحِ مِنَ الرِّوَايَةِ، وَأَنَّهُ لَمْ يُؤَاخِذْ لَبِيدَ بْنَ الأَعْصَمِ إِذْ سَحَرَهُ، وَقَدْ أُعْلِمَ بِهِ، وَأُوحِيَ إِلَيْهِ بِشَرْحِ أَمْرِهِ، وَلَا عَتَبَ عَلَيْهِ فَضْلًا عَنْ مُعَاقَبَتِهِ[٢٤٥].

وَكَذَلِكَ لَمْ يُؤَاخِذْ عَبْدَ اللهِ بْنَ أُبَيٍّ وَأَشْبَاهَهُ مِنَ المُنَافِقِينَ بِعَظِيمِ مَا نُقِلَ عَنْهُمْ فِي جِهَتِهِ قَوْلًا وَفِعْلًا، بَلْ قَالَ لِمَنْ أَشَارَ بِقَتْلِ بَعْضِهِمْ: «لَا يُتَحَدَّثُ أَنَّ مُحَمَّدًا يَقْتُلُ أَصْحَابَهُ»[٢٤٦].

وَعَنْ أَنَسٍ رَضِيَاللهُعَنْهُ: كُنْتُ مَعَ النَّبِيِّ ﷺ وَعَلَيْهِ بُرْدٌ غَلِيظُ الحَاشِيَةِ، فَجَبَذَهُ أَعْرَابِيٌّ بِرِدَائِهِ جَبْذَةً شَدِيدَةً، حَتَّى أَثَّرَتْ حَاشِيَةُ البُرْدِ فِي صَفْحَةِ عَاتِقِهِ، ثُمَّ قَالَ: يَا مُحَمَّدُ، احْمِلْ لِي عَلَى بَعِيرَيَّ هَذَيْنِ مِنْ مَالِ اللهِ الَّذِي عِنْدَكَ، فَإِنَّكَ لَا تَحْمِلُ لِي مِنْ مَالِكَ وَلَا مَالِ أَبِيكَ. فَسَكَتَ النَّبِيُّ ﷺ، ثُمَّ قَالَ: «المَالُ مَالُ اللهِ، وَأَنَا عَبْدُهُ». ثُمَّ قَالَ: «وَيُقَادُ مِنْكَ يَا أَعْرَابِيُّ مَا فَعَلْتَ بِي». قَالَ: لَا. قَالَ: «لِمَ؟» قَالَ: لِأَنَّكَ لَا تُكَافِئُ بِالسَّيِّئَةِ السَّيِّئَةَ[٢٤٧]. فَضَحِكَ النَّبِيُّ ﷺ، ثُمَّ

---

٢٤٣ أَخْرَجَهُ البَيْهَقِيُّ بِهَذَا اللَّفْظِ مِنْ حَدِيثِ جَابِرِ بْنِ عَبْدِ اللهِ/ المَنَاهِل (١٧١). قُلْتُ: رَوَاهُ بِسِيَاقَةٍ أُخْرَى البُخَارِيُّ (٢٩١٠)، وَمُسْلِمٌ (٨٤٣). (لِيَفْتِكَ بِهِ): لِيَقْتُلَهُ. (مُنْتَبَذٌ): مُنْفَرِدٌ بَعِيدٌ عَنْ أَصْحَابِهِ. (قَائِلًا): نَائِمًا وَقْتَ القَيْلُولَةِ. (قَائِلُونَ): نَائِمُونَ وَقْتَ القَيْلُولَةِ. (صَلْتًا): مَشْهُورًا، مُجَرَّدًا مِنْ غِمْدِهِ.

٢٤٤ أَخْرَجَهُ البُخَارِيُّ (٢٦١٧)، وَمُسْلِمٌ (٢١٩٠) مِنْ حَدِيثِ أَنَسِ بْنِ مَالِكٍ.

٢٤٥ حَدِيثُ السِّحْرِ أَخْرَجَهُ البُخَارِيُّ (٣٢٦٨). وَمُسْلِمٌ (٢١٨٩) مِنْ حَدِيثِ عَائِشَةَ.

٢٤٦ أَخْرَجَهُ البُخَارِيُّ (٤٩٠٥)، وَمُسْلِمٌ (٦٣/٢٥٨٤) مِنْ حَدِيثِ جَابِرٍ.

٢٤٧ أَخْرَجَهُ - بِلَفْظِ المُصَنِّفِ - البَيْهَقِيُّ فِي الأَدَبِ مِنْ حَدِيثِ أَبِي هُرَيْرَةَ / المَنَاهِل (١٧٨). قُلْتُ: وَأَخْرَجَهُ مُخْتَصَرًا: البُخَارِيُّ (٣١٤٩)، وَمُسْلِمٌ (١٠٥٧). (يُقَادُ مِنْكَ) يُقْتَصُّ مِنْكَ.

wealth of Allah, for it is not your wealth or your father's wealth you will be supplying me with.' The Prophet ﷺ was silent. Then, he replied: '[All] wealth is the wealth of Allah, and I am His slave.' And he asked the man: 'O Bedouin! Should I retaliate for the way you treated me?' He said: 'No.' The Prophet ﷺ asked: 'Why not?' And the Bedouin replied: 'Because you do not repay evil with evil.' So, the Prophet ﷺ laughed, and he ordered for one of the camels to be loaded with barley and the other with dates."245

'Ā'ishah ﵐ related: "Not once did I see the Messenger ﷺ taking revenge against a person who had wronged him, so long as the sanctities of Allah had not been affected. He never struck anything with his hand unless he was fighting in the path of Allah, and he never hit a servant or a woman."246

A man was brought to the Prophet ﷺ and he was told: "This person intended to kill you." The Prophet ﷺ said to him: "Do not fear! Do not fear! Even if you wished to do so, you would not have been given the ability to overcome me."247

Before embracing Islam, Zayd ibn Sa'nah248 once came to the Prophet ﷺ asking for a debt to be repaid. He grabbed the cloak of the Prophet ﷺ by the shoulders, roughly bunching the *thawb* in his hands, and said to him: "O [son of] Banū 'Abd al-Muṭṭalib, you

---

245   Reported with this wording by Bayhaqī in *Al-Adab* from Abū Hurayrah. See *Al-Manāhil*, p. 178. A condensed form of the narration was reported by Bukhārī (3149) and Muslim (1057).

246   The first part of the hadith was reported by Tirmidhī in *Al-Shamā'il* (348), al-Ḥumaydī (260), and Abū Ya'lā (4452). Reported by Bukhārī (3560) and Muslim (2327) with the wording: "The Messenger of Allah ﷺ never avenged for his own sake, but he would if the sanctities of Allah ﷻ had been violated." The rest of the hadith was also reported by Muslim (2328) and Tirmidhī in *Al-Shamā'il* (347).

247   Reported by Aḥmad (3/471) and Ṭabarānī from Ja'dah. Haythamī said in *Majma' al-Zawā'id* (8/226): "The narrators are *ṣaḥīḥ*, apart from Abū Isrā'īl al-Jashmī, who was reliable." Suyūṭī graded the chain as *ṣaḥīḥ* in *Al-Manāhil*, p. 177.

248   He was a Jewish rabbi who embraced Islam and went on to participate in many battles alongside the Prophet ﷺ. He died at the Battle of Tabūk whilst on his way back to Madinah. See *Usd al-Ghābah* (2/136).

أَمَرَ أَنْ يُحْمَلَ لَهُ عَلَى بَعِيرٍ شَعِيرٌ، وَعَلَى الْآخَرِ تَمْرٌ.

قَالَتْ عَائِشَةُ رَضِيَ اللهُ عَنْهَا: مَا رَأَيْتُ رَسُولَ اللهِ ﷺ مُنْتَصِرًا مِنْ مَظْلَمَةٍ ظُلِمَهَا قَطُّ، مَا لَمْ تَكُنْ حُرْمَةً مِنْ مَحَارِمِ اللهِ تَعَالَى، وَمَا ضَرَبَ بِيَدِهِ شَيْئًا قَطُّ، إِلَّا أَنْ يُجَاهِدَ فِي سَبِيلِ اللهِ، وَمَا ضَرَبَ خَادِمًا وَلَا امْرَأَةً[248].

وَجِيءَ إِلَيْهِ بِرَجُلٍ، فَقِيلَ: هَذَا أَرَادَ أَنْ يَقْتُلَكَ. فَقَالَ لَهُ ﷺ: «لَنْ تُرَاعَ، لَنْ تُرَاعَ، وَلَوْ أَرَدْتَ ذَلِكَ لَمْ تُسَلَّطْ عَلَيَّ»[249].

وَجَاءَهُ زَيْدُ بْنُ سَعْنَةَ[250] قَبْلَ إِسْلَامِهِ يَتَقَاضَاهُ دَيْنًا عَلَيْهِ، فَجَبَذَ ثَوْبَهُ عَنْ مَنْكِبِهِ، وَأَخَذَ بِمَجَامِعِ ثِيَابِهِ وَأَغْلَظَ لَهُ، ثُمَّ قَالَ: إِنَّكُمْ يَا بَنِي عَبْدِ الْمُطَّلِبِ مُطُلٌ. فَانْتَهَرَهُ عُمَرُ، وَشَدَّدَ لَهُ فِي الْقَوْلِ، وَالنَّبِيُّ ﷺ يَتَبَسَّمُ، فَقَالَ رَسُولُ اللهِ ﷺ: «أَنَا وَهُوَ كُنَّا إِلَى غَيْرِ هَذَا مِنْكَ أَحْوَجُ يَا عُمَرُ! تَأْمُرُنِي بِحُسْنِ الْقَضَاءِ، وَتَأْمُرُهُ بِحُسْنِ التَّقَاضِي»، ثُمَّ قَالَ ﷺ: «لَقَدْ بَقِيَ مِنْ أَجَلِهِ ثَلَاثٌ»، وَأَمَرَ عُمَرَ يَقْضِيهِ مَالَهُ، وَيَزِيدُهُ عِشْرِينَ صَاعًا لِمَا رَوَّعَهُ، فَكَانَ سَبَبَ إِسْلَامِهِ؛ وَذَلِكَ أَنَّهُ كَانَ يَقُولُ: مَا بَقِيَ مِنْ عَلَامَاتِ النُّبُوَّةِ شَيْءٌ إِلَّا وَقَدْ عَرَفْتُهَا فِي مُحَمَّدٍ، إِلَّا اثْنَتَيْنِ لَمْ أَخْبُرْهُمَا: يَسْبِقُ حِلْمُهُ جَهْلَهُ، وَلَا تَزِيدُهُ شِدَّةُ الْجَهْلِ عَلَيْهِ إِلَّا حِلْمًا. فَاخْتَبَرْتُهُ

---

248 أَخْرَجَ الْفِقْرَةَ الْأُولَى مِنْهُ: التِّرْمِذِيُّ فِي الشَّمَائِلِ (٣٤٢)، وَالْحُمَيْدِيُّ (٢٦٠)، وَأَبُو يَعْلَى (٤٤٥٢)، وَهِيَ فِي الْبُخَارِيِّ (٣٥٦٠)، وَمُسْلِمٌ (٢٣٢٧) بِلَفْظِ: «وَمَا انْتَقَمَ رَسُولُ اللهِ ﷺ لِنَفْسِهِ، إِلَّا أَنْ تُنْتَهَكَ حُرْمَةٌ مِنْ حُرُمَاتِ اللهِ عَزَّ وَجَلَّ» وَبَاقِي الْحَدِيثِ أَخْرَجَهُ مُسْلِمٌ (٢٣٢٨).

249 أَخْرَجَهُ أَحْمَدُ ٤٧١/٣ وَالطَّبَرَانِيُّ مِنْ حَدِيثِ جَعْدَةَ. قَالَ فِي الْمَجْمَعِ ٢٢٦-٢٢٧/٨: «رِجَالُهُ رِجَالُ الصَّحِيحِ، غَيْرُ أَبِي إِسْرَائِيلَ الْجَشَمِيِّ، وَهُوَ ثِقَةٌ». وَصَحَّحَ إِسْنَادَهُ السُّيُوطِيُّ فِي الْمَنَاهِلِ (١٧٧). (لَنْ تُرَاعَ): أَيْ لَا فَزَعَ وَلَا خَوْفَ.

250 وَهُوَ حَبْرٌ مِنْ أَحْبَارِ الْيَهُودِ، أَسْلَمَ وَحَسُنَ إِسْلَامُهُ، وَشَهِدَ مَعَ النَّبِيِّ ﷺ مَشَاهِدَ كَثِيرَةً. تُوُفِّيَ فِي غَزْوَةِ تَبُوكَ مُقْبِلًا إِلَى الْمَدِينَةِ/ أُسْدُ الْغَابَةِ ١٣٦/٢.

have delayed!" 'Umar unleashed a barrage of rebuke against the man, and the Prophet ﷺ was smiling.

The Messenger of Allah ﷺ said: "O 'Umar! We need something else from you. Instruct me to repay the debt in an excellent manner, and instruct him to ask for the debt in an excellent manner." Then, he said: "I still owe him three." He told 'Umar to repay the man and to add twenty extra *ṣā*'s for scaring him. The event prompted Zayd ibn Sa'nah to embrace Islam. He said: "I had already recognized all the signs of Prophethood in Muhammad except for two: forbearance overcoming anger[249], and extreme ignorance only increasing his forbearance. I tested him for these two features, and found him as described[250]."[251]

There are many more hadiths describing the forbearance, patience, and pardoning of the Prophet ﷺ, but we will suffice with the authentic, established narrations we have recorded here, many of which were transmitted from multiple chains. They detail his patience in spite of the oppression of the Quraysh and the suffering meted out to him during Jāhiliyyah. He endured until Allah Exalted gave him victory. The Quraysh were certain that they would be wiped out and their leaders executed, but the Prophet ﷺ continued to pardon and forgive.

He said to them: "How would you say I have treated you?" They replied: "Excellently, O generous brother, son of a generous brother." The Prophet ﷺ said: "I will say the same as the brother of Yūsuf: 'There is no blame on you today. May Allah forgive you! He is

---

249   lit., "ignorance".

250   i.e., as the Final Prophet had been described in their texts.

251   Reported by Ṭabarānī in *Al-Kabīr* (5147), and others, from 'Abdullāh ibn Salām. Haythamī said in *Majma' al-Zawā'id* (8/239-240): "The narrators are trustworthy." Authenticated by Ibn Ḥibbān in *Mawārid al-Ẓam'ān* (2105). Also authenticated by Ḥākim (3/604-605) and Dhahabī concurred. Suyūṭī graded the chain as *ṣaḥīḥ* in *Al-Manāhil*, p. 178. Al-Mizzī said in *Tahdhīb al-Kāmil*: "This well-known hadith is *ḥasan*."

بِهَذَا فَوَجَدْتُهُ كَمَا وُصِفَ٢٥١. وَالْحَدِيثُ عَنْ حِلْمِهِ ﷺ وَصَبْرِهِ وَعَفْوِهِ عِنْدَ الْمَقْدَرَةِ أَكْثَرُ مِنْ أَنْ نَأْتِيَ عَلَيْهِ، وَحَسْبُكَ مَا ذَكَرْنَاهُ مِمَّا فِي الصَّحِيحِ وَالْمُصَنَّفَاتِ الثَّابِتَةِ، إِلَى مَا بَلَغَ مُتَوَاتِرًا مَبْلَغَ الْيَقِينِ: مِنْ صَبْرِهِ عَلَى مُقَاسَاةِ قُرَيْشٍ، وَأَذَى الْجَاهِلِيَّةِ، وَمُصَابَرَتِهِ الشَّدَائِدَ الصَّعْبَةَ مِنْهُمْ إِلَى أَنْ أَظْهَرَهُ اللهُ عَلَيْهِمْ، وَحَكَّمَهُ فِيهِمْ، وَهُمْ لَا يَشُكُّونَ فِي اسْتِئْصَالِ شَأْفَتِهِمْ٢٥٢، وَإِبَادَةِ خَضْرَائِهِمْ٢٥٣، فَمَا زَادَ عَلَى أَنْ عَفَا وَصَفَحَ، وَقَالَ: «مَا تَقُولُونَ إِنِّي فَاعِلٌ بِكُمْ؟»، قَالُوا: خَيْرًا، أَخٌ كَرِيمٌ، وَابْنُ أَخٍ كَرِيمٍ، فَقَالَ: «أَقُولُ كَمَا قَالَ أَخِي يُوسُفُ: ﴿لَا تَثْرِيبَ عَلَيْكُمُ ٱلْيَوْمَ يَغْفِرُ ٱللَّهُ لَكُمْ وَهُوَ أَرْحَمُ ٱلرَّاحِمِينَ﴾ [يوسف: ٩٢]، اذْهَبُوا فَأَنْتُمُ الطُّلَقَاءُ»٢٥٤. وَقَالَ أَنَسٌ: هَبَطَ ثَمَانُونَ رَجُلًا مِنَ التَّنْعِيمِ صَلَاةَ الصُّبْحِ لِيَقْتُلُوا رَسُولَ اللهِ ﷺ، فَأُخِذُوا، فَأَعْتَقَهُمْ رَسُولُ اللهِ ﷺ، فَأَنْزَلَ اللهُ عَزَّ وَجَلَّ: ﴿وَهُوَ ٱلَّذِى كَفَّ أَيْدِيَهُمْ عَنكُمْ وَأَيْدِيَكُمْ

---

٢٥١ أَخْرَجَهُ الطَّبَرَانِيُّ فِي الْكَبِيرِ (٥١٤٧) وَغَيْرُهُ مِنْ حَدِيثِ عَبْدِ اللهِ بْنِ سَلَامٍ. قَالَ الْحَافِظُ الْهَيْثَمِيُّ فِي مَجْمَعِ الزَّوَائِدِ ٢٣٩/٨-٢٤٠: «رِجَالُهُ ثِقَاتٌ». وَصَحَّحَهُ ابْنُ حِبَّانَ (٢١٠٥) وَمَوَارِدُ الظَّمْآنِ، وَالْحَاكِمُ ٦٠٤/٣-٦٠٥ وَتَعَقَّبَهُ الذَّهَبِيُّ فَقَالَ: «مَا أَنْكِرُهُ وَمَا أَرِكُّهُ!». وَصَحَّحَ إِسْنَادَهُ السُّيُوطِيُّ فِي الْمَنَاهِلِ (١٧٨). وَقَالَ الْحَافِظُ الْمِزِّيُّ فِي تَهْذِيبِ الْكَمَالِ: هَذَا حَدِيثٌ حَسَنٌ مَشْهُورٌ. (رَوَّعَهُ): أَفْزَعَهُ. (صَاعًا): الصَّاعُ: أَرْبَعَةُ أَمْدَادٍ. وَالْمُدُّ: مِلْءُ الْكَفَّيْنِ مُجْتَمِعَيْنِ لَا مَبْسُوطَيْنِ وَلَا مَقْبُوضَيْنِ. وَيُقَدَّرُ بِ (٦٠٠) غِرَامٍ. (الْجَهْلُ): السَّفَهُ وَالْجَفَاءُ.

٢٥٢ اسْتِئْصَالِ شَأْفَتِهِمْ: أَيْ إِزَالَتِهِمْ مِنْ أَصْلِهِمْ. وَالشَّأْفَةُ: قُرْحَةٌ تَخْشُنُ فَتُسْتَأْصَلُ بِالْكَيِّ/ الْمُعْجَمُ الْوَسِيطُ.

٢٥٣ خَضْرَائِهِمْ: جَمْعِهِمْ وَسَوَادِهِمْ.

٢٥٤ أَخْرَجَهُ النَّسَائِيُّ فِي الْكُبْرَى (تُحْفَةُ الْأَشْرَافِ ١٣٤/١٠) مِنْ حَدِيثِ أَبِي هُرَيْرَةَ. وَقَالَ الْحَافِظُ الْعِرَاقِيُّ فِي تَخْرِيجِ الْإِحْيَاءِ ١٨٢/٣-١٨٣ «رَوَاهُ ابْنُ الْجَوْزِيِّ فِي الْوَفَا مِنْ طَرِيقِ ابْنِ أَبِي الدُّنْيَا وَفِيهِ ضَعْفٌ». وَذَكَرَهُ الْعَلَّامَةُ ابْنُ قَيِّمِ الْجَوْزِيَّةِ فِي زَادِ الْمَعَادِ ٤٠٧/٣-٤٠٨ وَسَكَتَ عَنْهُ. وَذَكَرَهُ الْغَزَالِيُّ فِي الْإِحْيَاءِ ١٨٣/٣ مِنْ حَدِيثِ سُهَيْلِ بْنِ عَمْرٍو، وَنَسَبَهُ فِي الْمَنَاهِلِ (١٧٩) إِلَى حُمَيْدِ بْنِ زَنْجَوَيْهِ فِي كِتَابِ الْأَمْوَالِ. (لَا تَثْرِيبَ) لَا تَأْنِيبَ وَلَا لَوْمَ عَلَيْكُمْ/ كَلِمَاتُ الْقُرْآنِ لِمَخْلُوفٍ.

the Most Merciful of the merciful!'[252] You are free to go!"[253]

Anas recalled: "Eighty men came swarming down from al-Tanʿīm at the time of the dawn prayer, intent on killing the Messenger of Allah ﷺ. They were caught, but the Messenger of Allah ﷺ let them go free. So, Allah Exalted revealed: 'He is the One Who held back their hands from you and your hands from them in the valley [of Ḥudaybiyyah, near Makkah], after giving you the upper hand over [a group of] them. And Allah is All-Seeing of what you do.'[254]"[255]

When Abū Sufyān was brought to the Prophet ﷺ, after he had gathered the Allies[256] against him, killed his uncle and Companions, and made an example of them, he forgave him and spoke considerately. He said: "Woe to you, Abū Sufyān! Is it not time for you to know that there is no-one worthy of worship except Allah?" Abū Sufyān replied: "May my father and mother be your ransom. There is nobody more forbearing, more generous, and better at maintaining ties than you."[257]

As we can see, the Messenger of Allah ﷺ was the last person to be angered, and the first to be pleased.

---

252 *Yūsuf*, 92.

253 Reported by Nasā'ī in *Al-Kubrā* (see *Tuḥfah al-Ashrāf*, 10/134) from Abū Hurayrah. ʿIrāqī said in *Takhrīj Aḥādīth al-Iḥyā'* (3/182-183): "It was related by Ibn al-Jawzī in *Al-Wafā'* from the chain of Ibn Abī al-Dunyā, and the chain contains some weakness." Mentioned by Ibn Qayyim al-Jawziyyah in *Zād al-Maʿād* (3/407-408), but he did not comment on the narration. Reported by Ghazālī in *Al-Iḥyā'* (3/183) from Sahl ibn ʿAmr. The narration was attributed in *Al-Manāhil*, p. 179, to Ḥumayd ibn Zanjawayh from *Kitāb al-Amwāl*.

254 *al-Fatḥ*, 24.

255 Reported by Muslim (1808).

256 "*al-aḥzāb*".

257 Reported by Ṭabarānī in *Al-Kabīr* (5147), and others. Haythamī said in *Majmaʿ al-Zawā'id* (6/164-167): "The narrators are *ṣaḥīḥ*." Suyūṭī graded the chain as *ṣaḥīḥ* in *Al-Manāhil*, p. 181.

عَنْهُمْ ۞ ²⁵⁵ [الفتح: ٢٤] الآيَةَ. وَقَالَ لِأَبِي سُفْيَانَ وَقَدْ سِيقَ إِلَيْهِ بَعْدَ أَنْ جَلَبَ إِلَيْهِ الأَحْزَابَ، وَقَتَلَ عَمَّهُ وَأَصْحَابَهُ وَمَثَّلَ بِهِمْ، فَعَفَا عَنْهُ وَلَاطَفَهُ فِي القَوْلِ: «وَيْحَكَ! يَا أَبَا سُفْيَانَ! أَلَمْ يَأْنِ لَكَ أَنْ تَعْلَمَ أَنْ لَا إِلَهَ إِلَّا اللهُ؟» فَقَالَ: بِأَبِي أَنْتَ وَأُمِّي، مَا أَحْلَمَكَ وَأَوْصَلَكَ وَأَكْرَمَكَ! ²⁵⁶ وَكَانَ رَسُولُ اللهِ ﷺ أَبْعَدَ النَّاسِ غَضَبًا، وَأَسْرَعَهُمْ رِضًى.

صَلَّى اللهُ عَلَيْهِ وَسَلَّمَ تَسْلِيمًا، كُلَّمَا ذَكَرَهُ الذَّاكِرُونَ، وَغَفَلَ عَنْ ذِكْرِهِ الغَافِلُونَ.

---

²⁵⁵ أَخْرَجَهُ مُسْلِمٌ (١٨٠٨). (التَّنْعِيمُ): مَوْضِعٌ عَلَى ثَلَاثَةِ أَمْيَالٍ مِنْ مَكَّةَ. وَهُوَ اليَوْمَ مِنْ أَحْيَائِهَا. وَلَيْسَ فِي الحِلِّ أَقْرَبُ إِلَى الحَرَمِ مِنْهُ.

²⁵٦ رَوَاهُ الطَّبَرَانِيُّ فِي الكَبِيرِ وَغَيْرُهُ، قَالَ الهَيْثَمِيُّ فِي مَجْمَعِ الزَّوَائِدِ ١٦٤/٦-١٦٧: «رِجَالُهُ رِجَالُ الصَّحِيحِ». وَصَحَّحَ إِسْنَادَهُ السُّيُوطِيُّ فِي المَنَاهِلِ (١٨١).

HIS IMMENSE GENEROSITY

Again, scholars have distinguished between different types of giving. "Generosity" (*karam*) means to give cheerfully to causes that are urgent and will benefit others, and is also referred to as "freedom" (*ḥurriyyah*)[258], which is the opposite of "pettiness" (*nadhālah*); "magnanimity" (*samāḥah*) is to forgo what others owe you with kindness, and is the opposite of "fractiousness" (*shakāsah*)[259]; and "open-handedness" (*sakhā'*) is to give with ease, and is also known as "munificence" (*jūd*), which is the opposite of "stinginess" (*taqtīr*). In each of these categories, the Prophet ﷺ was neither matched nor surpassed, and everyone who knew him confirmed this to be the case.

Abū ʿAlī al-Ṣadafī narrated, from Abū al-Walīd al-Bājī, from Abū Dharr al-Harawī, from Abū al-Haytham al-Kushmīhanī, Abū Muḥammad al-Sarkhasī, and Abū Isḥāq al-Balkhī, from Abū ʿAbdullāh al-Farabrī, from Bukhārī, from Muḥammad ibn Kathīr, from Sufyān, from Ibn al-Munkadir, who said: "I heard Jābir ibn ʿAbdullāh saying: 'The Prophet ﷺ never said "No" when I asked him for something.'"[260] Similar narrations were reported from Anas and Sahl ibn Saʿd.[261]

Ibn ʿAbbās related: "The Messenger of Allah ﷺ was the most

---

258   "Ḥurriyyah" here means "freedom from contemptible behaviour".

259   Meaning: "to be ill-tempered and unreasonably impatient".

260   Reported here from the chain of Bukhārī (6034). Also reported by Muslim (2311).

261   The hadith of Anas was reported by Muslim (2312), with the wording: "Any time the Messenger of Allah ﷺ was asked for something for the cause of Islam, he would give it." The hadith of Sahl was reported by Dārimī (72) and others, with the wording: "For as long as he lived, the Messenger of Allah ﷺ gave anything he was asked for."

فصل

وَأَمَّا الجُودُ وَالكَرَمُ وَالسَّخَاءُ وَالسَّمَاحَةُ وَمَعَانِيها مُتَقَارِبَةٌ، وَقَدْ فَرَّقَ بَعْضُهُمْ بَيْنَهَا بِفُرُوقٍ: فَجَعَلُوا الكَرَمَ: الإِنْفَاقَ بِطِيبِ النَّفْسِ فِيمَا يَعْظُمُ خَطَرُهُ وَنَفْعُهُ، وَسَمَّوْهُ أَيْضًا حُرِّيَّةً[257]، وَهُوَ ضِدُّ النَّذَالَةِ[258]. وَالسَّمَاحَةُ: التَّجَافِي عَمَّا يَسْتَحِقُّهُ المَرْءُ عِنْدَ غَيْرِهِ بِطِيبِ نَفْسٍ، وَهُوَ ضِدُّ التَّشَاكُسِ. وَالسَّخَاءُ: سُهُولَةُ الإِنْفَاقِ، وَتَجَنُّبُ اكْتِسَابِ مَا لَا يُحْمَدُ، وَهُوَ الجُودُ، وَهُوَ ضِدُّ التَّقْتِيرِ. وَكَانَ ﷺ لَا يُوَازَى فِي هَذِهِ الأَخْلَاقِ الكَرِيمَةِ وَلَا يُبَارَى، بِهَذَا وَصَفَهُ كُلُّ مَنْ عَرَفَهُ. حَدَّثَنَا القَاضِي الشَّهِيدُ أَبُو عَلِيٍّ الصَّدَفِيُّ رحمه الله، حَدَّثَنَا القَاضِي أَبُو الوَلِيدِ البَاجِيُّ، حَدَّثَنَا أَبُو ذَرٍّ الهَرَوِيُّ، حَدَّثَنَا أَبُو الهَيْثَمِ الكُشْمِيهَنِيُّ، وَأَبُو مُحَمَّدٍ السَّرَخْسِيُّ، وَأَبُو إِسْحَاقَ البَلْخِيُّ، قَالُوا: حَدَّثَنَا أَبُو عَبْدِ اللهِ الفِرَبْرِيُّ، حَدَّثَنَا البُخَارِيُّ، حَدَّثَنَا مُحَمَّدُ ابْنُ كَثِيرٍ، أَخْبَرَنَا سُفْيَانُ، عَنِ ابْنِ المُنْكَدِرِ، سَمِعْتُ جَابِرَ بْنَ عَبْدِ اللهِ يَقُولُ: مَا سُئِلَ النَّبِيُّ ﷺ شَيْئًا قَطُّ فَقَالَ: لَا[259]. وَعَنْ أَنَسٍ وَسَهْلِ بْنِ سَعْدٍ مِثْلُهُ[260]. وَقَالَ ابْنُ عَبَّاسٍ: كَانَ النَّبِيُّ ﷺ أَجْوَدَ النَّاسِ بِالخَيْرِ، وَأَجْوَدَ

---

[257] الحُرِّيَّةُ - هُنَا -: الخُلُوصُ مِنَ اللُّؤْمِ. انْظُرِ المُعْجَمَ الوَسِيطَ.

[258] النَّذَالَةُ: الخِسَّةُ وَالحَقَارَةُ.

[259] أَسْنَدَهُ المُصَنِّفُ مِنْ طَرِيقِ البُخَارِيِّ (٦٠٣٤)، وَأَخْرَجَهُ أَيْضًا مُسْلِمٌ (٢٣١١).

[260] حَدِيثُ أَنَسٍ أَخْرَجَهُ مُسْلِمٌ (٢٣١٢) بِلَفْظِ: «مَا سُئِلَ رَسُولُ اللهِ ﷺ عَلَى الإِسْلَامِ شَيْئًا إِلَّا أَعْطَاهُ....». وَحَدِيثُ سَهْلِ بْنِ سَعْدٍ أَخْرَجَهُ الدَّارِمِيُّ بِرَقْمِ (٧٢) وَغَيْرُهُ بِلَفْظِ: كَانَ رَسُولُ اللهِ ﷺ حَيِيًّا لَا يُسْأَلُ شَيْئًا إِلَّا أَعْطَاهُ. وَإِسْنَادُهُ ضَعِيفٌ.

generous person, and he was the most generous in the month of Ramadan. When he had met with Jibrīl 🕮, he would be more generous than the rushing wind which is sent [with provision]."[262]

Anas narrated about a man who came to ask from the Messenger of Allah 🕮, and was given enough sheep to reach from one mountain to another. He returned to his people and said: "Embrace Islam, for Muhammad gives like a person with no fear of poverty!"[263]

There were a number of accounts of the Prophet 🕮 gifting people one hundred camels. He gave Ṣafwān one hundred, followed by another hundred, and then another hundred,[264] and this was his character even before he was sent as a Messenger. Waraqah ibn Nawfal once said to him: "You will support the vulnerable and provide for the deprived."[265]

The Prophet 🕮 returned six thousand captives to the tribe of Hawāzin.[266] He gave al-ʿAbbās so much gold, he was unable to carry it.[267]

On another occasion, the Prophet 🕮 was given ninety thousand dirhams. He placed all of it on a mat to be divided and distributed. He did not turn away a single person until every dirham had been given away.[268]

Once, a man came to ask from the Prophet 🕮, and he told him:

---

262   Reported by Bukhārī (6) and Muslim (2308).

263   Reported by Muslim (2312).

264   Reported by Muslim (2313).

265   Reported by Bukhārī (3) and Muslim (160) from Khadījah. For other interpretations of this narration see *Fatḥ al-Bārī* (1/24-25).

266   Reported by Bukhārī (2307, 2308) from Marwān ibn al-Ḥakam and al-Miswar ibn al-Makhramah.

267   Reported by Bukhārī (421) from Anas. Ibn Ḥajar said in *Fatḥ al-Bārī* (1/516): "The chain was connected by Abū Nuʿaym in *Al-Mustakhraj* and Ḥākim in *Al-Mustadrak*."

268   Reported by Abū al-Ḥasan ibn al-Ḍaḥḥāk in *Al-Shamāʾil* in a *mursal* narration from al-Ḥasan. See *Al-Manāhil*, p. 192.

مَا كَانَ فِي شَهْرِ رَمَضَانَ، وَكَانَ إِذَا لَقِيَهُ جِبْرِيلُ عليه السلام أَجْوَدَ بِالْخَيْرِ مِنَ الرِّيحِ الْمُرْسَلَةِ[261]. وَعَنْ أَنَسٍ أَنَّ رَجُلًا سَأَلَهُ فَأَعْطَاهُ غَنَمًا بَيْنَ جَبَلَيْنِ، فَرَجَعَ إِلَى قَوْمِهِ فَقَالَ: أَسْلِمُوا فَإِنَّ مُحَمَّدًا يُعْطِي عَطَاءَ مَنْ لَا يَخْشَى فَاقَةً[262]. وَأَعْطَى غَيْرَ وَاحِدٍ مِائَةً مِنَ الْإِبِلِ. وَأَعْطَى صَفْوَانَ مِائَةً، ثُمَّ مِائَةً، ثُمَّ مِائَةً[263]. وَهَذِهِ كَانَتْ خُلُقَهُ ﷺ قَبْلَ أَنْ يُبْعَثَ. وَقَدْ قَالَ لَهُ وَرَقَةُ: إِنَّكَ تَحْمِلُ الْكَلَّ، وَتَكْسِبُ الْمَعْدُومَ[264]. وَرَدَّ عَلَى هَوَازِنَ سَبَايَاهَا، وَكَانُوا سِتَّةَ آلَافٍ[265].

وَأَعْطَى الْعَبَّاسَ مِنَ الذَّهَبِ مَا لَمْ يُطِقْ حَمْلَهُ[266]. وَحُمِلَ إِلَيْهِ تِسْعُونَ أَلْفَ دِرْهَمٍ، فَوُضِعَتْ عَلَى حَصِيرٍ، ثُمَّ قَامَ إِلَيْهَا يَقْسِمُهَا، فَمَا رَدَّ سَائِلًا حَتَّى فَرَغَ مِنْهَا[267]. وَجَاءَهُ رَجُلٌ فَسَأَلَهُ فَقَالَ: «مَا عِنْدِي شَيْءٌ، وَلَكِنِ ابْتَعْ عَلَيَّ، فَإِذَا جَاءَنَا شَيْءٌ قَضَيْنَاهُ». فَقَالَ لَهُ عُمَرُ: مَا كَلَّفَكَ اللهُ مَا لَا تَقْدِرُ عَلَيْهِ، فَكَرِهَ النَّبِيُّ ﷺ ذَلِكَ، فَقَالَ رَجُلٌ مِنَ الْأَنْصَارِ: يَا رَسُولَ اللهِ، أَنْفِقْ وَلَا تَخَفْ

---

٢٦١ أَخْرَجَهُ الْبُخَارِيُّ (٦)، وَمُسْلِمٌ (٢٣٠٨).

٢٦٢ أَخْرَجَهُ مُسْلِمٌ (٢٣١٢). (رَجُلًا): هُوَ صَفْوَانُ ابْنُ أُمَيَّةَ. (غَنَمًا بَيْنَ جَبَلَيْنِ): أَيْ كَثِيرَةً كَأَنَّهَا تَمَلَأُ مَا بَيْنَ جَبَلَيْنِ.

٢٦٣ أَخْرَجَهُ مُسْلِمٌ (٢٣١٣).

٢٦٤ أَخْرَجَهُ - مِنْ قَوْلِ خَدِيجَةَ - الْبُخَارِيُّ (٣)، وَمُسْلِمٌ (١٦٠). (تَحْمِلُ الْكَلَّ) الْكَلُّ: أَصْلُهُ الثِّقْلُ وَيَدْخُلُ فِي حَمْلِ الْكَلِّ: الْإِنْفَاقُ عَلَى الضَّعِيفِ وَالْيَتِيمِ وَالْعِيَالِ، وَغَيْرِ ذَلِكَ. (وَتَكْسِبُ الْمَعْدُومَ): أَيْ تُعْطِي النَّاسَ مَا لَا يَجِدُونَهُ عِنْدَ غَيْرِكَ. وَانْظُرْ مَعَانِيَ أُخْرَى فِي الْفَتْحِ ٢٤/١-٢٥.

٢٦٥ أَخْرَجَهُ الْبُخَارِيُّ (٢٣٠٧، ٢٣٠٨) مِنْ حَدِيثِ مَرْوَانَ بْنِ الْحَكَمِ وَالْمِسْوَرِ بْنِ مَخْرَمَةَ. (هَوَازِنُ): اسْمُ قَبِيلَةٍ. (سَبَايَاهَا): أَسْرَاهَا.

٢٦٦ عَلَّقَهُ الْبُخَارِيُّ (٤٢١) مِنْ حَدِيثِ أَنَسٍ. وَقَالَ الْحَافِظُ فِي الْفَتْحِ ٥١٦/١: «وَصَلَهُ أَبُو نُعَيْمٍ فِي مُسْتَخْرَجِهِ، وَالْحَاكِمُ فِي مُسْتَدْرَكِهِ».

٢٦٧ رَوَاهُ أَبُو الْحَسَنِ بْنُ الضَّحَّاكِ فِي الشَّمَائِلِ عَنِ الْحَسَنِ مُرْسَلًا / الْمَنَاهِلُ (١٩٢).

"I do not have anything, but buy [what you need] in my name, and when we receive something I will pay for it."

'Umar said to the Prophet ﷺ: "O Messenger of Allah! I have given it to him, so Allah has not made you responsible for that which is beyond your ability." The Prophet ﷺ did not like the statement.

Then, a man from the Anṣār said: "O Messenger of Allah! Spend, and do not fear a reduction [of your provision] from the Possessor of the Throne." The face of the Prophet ﷺ lit up with pleasure. He smiled and said: "That is what I was commanded to do."[269]

Muʿawwidh ibn ʿAfrāʾ was reported to have said: "I brought the Prophet ﷺ a plate of cucumber and fresh dates, and he gave me a handful of jewellery and gold."[270]

Anas narrated: "The Prophet ﷺ would never store anything for the next day."[271]

There are so many reports of his generosity and giving. To conclude, we will quote the narration of Abū Hurayrah: "A man who had lent the Messenger of Allah ﷺ half a *wasaq* came to ask for repayment. The Messenger of Allah ﷺ gave him a whole *wasaq* and said: 'Half is to repay the debt and half is a present.'"[272]

---

269 Reported by Tirmidhī in *Al-Shamāʾil* (354), Bazzār (3662), and al-Kharāʾiṭī in *Al-Muntaqā min Makārim al-Akhlāq* (278), from ʿUmar. Haythamī said in *Majmaʿ al-Zawāʾid* (10/242): "The chain contains Isḥāq ibn Ibrāhīm, who was declared a weak narrator by the majority of scholars. Ibn Ḥibbān said that he was trustworthy but made mistakes."

270 I have not found this narration reported from Muʿawwidh ibn ʿAfrāʾ, but it was reported from al-Rubayyiʿ bint Muʿawwidh ibn ʿAfrāʾ by Tirmidhī in *Al-Shamāʾil* (201, 202, 355) and Aḥmad (6/359). The chain was graded *ḥasan* by Haythamī in *Majmaʿ al-Zawāʾid* (9/13) and Suyūṭī in *Al-Manāhil*, p. 194.

271 Reported by Tirmidhī (2362), Baghawī (3690), and others. Authenticated by Ibn Ḥibbān in *Mawārid al-Ẓamʾān* (2139, 2550). Tirmidhī said: "This hadith is *gharīb*."

272 Suyūṭī related this narration in *Al-Manāhil*, p. 196, without mentioning the source.

مِنْ ذِي العَرْشِ إِقْلَالًا، فَتَبَسَّمَ ﷺ وَعُرِفَ البِشْرُ فِي وَجْهِهِ، وَقَالَ: «بِهَذَا أُمِرْتُ»[268] ذَكَرَهُ التِّرْمِذِيُّ. وَذَكَرَ عَنِ الرُّبَيِّعِ بِنْتِ مُعَوِّذِ بْنِ عَفْرَاءَ: أَتَيْتُ النَّبِيَّ ﷺ بِقِنَاعٍ مِنْ رُطَبٍ - تُرِيدُ طَبَقًا - وَأَجْرِ زُغْبٍ - تُرِيدُ قِثَّاءَ - فَأَعْطَانِي مِلْءَ كَفِّهِ حُلِيًّا وَذَهَبًا[269]. وَقَالَ أَنَسٌ: كَانَ النَّبِيُّ ﷺ لَا يَدَّخِرُ شَيْئًا لِغَدٍ[270].

وَالخَبَرُ بِجُودِهِ وَكَرَمِهِ كَثِيرٌ. وَعَنْ أَبِي هُرَيْرَةَ رَضِيَ اللهُ عَنْهُ: أَتَى رَجُلٌ النَّبِيَّ ﷺ يَسْأَلُهُ، فَاسْتَسْلَفَ لَهُ رَسُولُ اللهِ ﷺ نِصْفَ وَسْقٍ، فَجَاءَ الرَّجُلُ يَتَقَاضَاهُ، فَأَعْطَاهُ وَسْقًا، وَقَالَ: «نِصْفُهُ قَضَاءٌ، وَنِصْفُهُ نَائِلٌ»[271].

وَقَدْ قَالَ أَبُو عَلِيٍّ الدَّقَّاقُ مِنْ شُيُوخِ المُتَصَوِّفَةِ المَشَاهِيرِ النَّحَارِيرِ، وَتَكَلَّمَ فِي الفُتُوَّةِ عَلَى رَأْيِهِمْ وَاصْطِلَاحِهِمْ فِي أَلْفَاظِهِمْ، وَهُوَ غَايَةُ الكَرَمِ وَالإِيثَارِ: إِنَّ هَذَا الخُلُقَ لَا يَكُونُ بِكَمَالِهِ إِلَّا لِرَسُولِ اللهِ ﷺ؛ فَإِنَّ كُلَّ وَاحِدٍ فِي القِيَامَةِ يَقُولُ: نَفْسِي نَفْسِي، وَيَقُولُ هُوَ: «أُمَّتِي أُمَّتِي».

---

[268] أَخْرَجَهُ التِّرْمِذِيُّ فِي الشَّمَائِلِ (٣٤٨)، وَالبَزَّارُ (٣٦٦٢)، وَالخَرَائِطِيُّ فِي المُنْتَقَى مِنْ مَكَارِمِ الأَخْلَاقِ (٢٧٨) مِنْ حَدِيثِ عُمَرَ. وَقَالَ الهَيْثَمِيُّ فِي المَجْمَعِ ٢٤٢/١٠: «فِيهِ إِسْحَاقُ بْنُ إِبْرَاهِيمَ الحُنَيْنِيِّ، وَقَدْ ضَعَّفَهُ الجُمْهُورُ، وَوَثَّقَهُ ابْنُ حِبَّانَ، وَقَالَ: يُخْطِئُ».

[269] لَمْ أَجِدْهُ مِنْ حَدِيثِ مُعَوِّذِ بْنِ عَفْرَاءَ. وَأَخْرَجَهُ - مِنْ حَدِيثِ الرُّبَيِّعِ بِنْتِ مُعَوِّذِ بْنِ عَفْرَاءَ -: أَحْمَدُ ٣٥٩/٦، وَالتِّرْمِذِيُّ فِي الشَّمَائِلِ (٢٠٣، ٢٠٤، ٣٤٩) وَحَسَّنَ إِسْنَادَهُ الهَيْثَمِيُّ فِي المَجْمَعِ ١٣/٩، وَالسُّيُوطِيُّ فِي المَنَاهِلِ (١٩٤).

[270] أَخْرَجَهُ التِّرْمِذِيُّ (٢٣٦٢)، وَالبَغَوِيُّ (٣٦٩٠) وَغَيْرُهُ. وَصَحَّحَهُ ابْنُ حِبَّانَ (٢١٣٩، ٢٥٥٠) مَوَارِدُ. وَقَالَ التِّرْمِذِيُّ: هَذَا حَدِيثٌ غَرِيبٌ.

[271] ذَكَرَهُ السُّيُوطِيُّ فِي المَنَاهِلِ (١٩٦) وَلَمْ يَذْكُرْ مَنْ خَرَّجَهُ. (وَسْقٌ) الوَسْقُ: سِتُّونَ صَاعًا. وَالصَّاعُ أَرْبَعَةُ أَمْدَادٍ. وَالمُدُّ: مِلْءُ الكَفَّيْنِ مُجْتَمِعَيْنِ لَا مَبْسُوطَيْنِ وَلَا مَقْبُوضَيْنِ وَيُقَدَّرُ بِـ (٦٠٠) غِرَامٍ. (اسْتَسْلَفَ): اسْتَقْرَضَ. (نَائِلٌ): أَيْ عَطَاءٌ وَهِبَةٌ.

HIS BRAVERY AND COURAGE

Courage (*shajāʿah*) refers to utilizing one's strength with virtue and reason, and "bravery" (*najdah*) refers to fortitude and fearlessness in the face of death. The Prophet ﷺ often entered difficult situations, places from which valiant and heroic men fled, but he was firm and did not budge. Instead, he advanced and did not falter or retreat. No matter how brave the fighter, all courageous men would turn and run at the sight of the Prophet ﷺ.

The following hadith was written for me by Abū ʿAlī al-Jayyānī, who narrated from al-Qāḍī Sirāj, from Abū Muhammad al-Aṣīlī, from Abū Zayd al-Faqīh, from Muhammad ibn Yūsuf, from Muhammad ibn Ismāʿīl, from Ibn Bashshār, from Ghundar, from Shuʿbah, from Abū Isḥāq, who said: "I heard someone asking al-Barāʾ: 'Did you flee from the Messenger of Allah ﷺ during the Battle of Ḥunayn?' He replied: 'But the Messenger of Allah ﷺ did not flee.'

Then, the man said: 'I saw the Messenger of Allah ﷺ on his white mule, with Abū Sufyān holding on to the reins. He was saying: "I am the Prophet, and that is no lie."'"[273] In another wording of the hadith, he added: "I am the son of ʿAbd al-Muṭṭalib."[274] There was nobody more intense than the Prophet ﷺ on that day, and two narrators said: "The Prophet ﷺ dismounted from his mule."[275]

---

273   Reported by Bukhārī (4317).

274   As reported by Muslim (1776/80).

275   The two narrators were Isrāʾīl ibn Yūnus and Zuhayr ibn Muʿāwiyah, who both related the hadith from Abū Isḥāq, from al-Barāʾ (as found with Bukhārī), and included this phrase at the end of the narration.

فصل

وَأَمَّا الشَّجَاعَةُ وَالنَّجْدَةُ: فَالشَّجَاعَةُ: فَضِيلَةُ قُوَّةِ الغَضَبِ وَانْقِيَادِهَا لِلْعَقْلِ. وَالنَّجْدَةُ: ثِقَةُ النَّفْسِ عِنْدَ اسْتِرْسَالِهَا إِلَى المَوْتِ - حَيْثُ يُحْمَدُ فِعْلُهَا - دُونَ خَوْفٍ.

فَكَانَ النَّبِيُّ ﷺ مِنْهَا بِالمَكَانِ الَّذِي لَا يُجْهَلُ، قَدْ حَضَرَ المَوَاقِفَ الصَّعْبَةَ، وَفَرَّ الكُمَاةُ[٢٧٢] وَالأَبْطَالُ عَنْهُ غَيْرَ مَرَّةٍ وَهُوَ ثَابِتٌ لَا يَبْرَحُ، وَمُقْبِلٌ لَا يُدْبِرُ وَلَا يَتَزَحْزَحُ، وَمَا شُجَاعٌ إِلَّا وَقَدْ أُحْصِيَتْ لَهُ فَرَّةٌ، وَحُفِظَتْ عَنْهُ جَوْلَةٌ سِوَاهُ ﷺ.

حَدَّثَنَا أَبُو عَلِيٍّ الجَيَّانِيُّ فِي مَا كَتَبَ إِلَيَّ، حَدَّثَنَا القَاضِي سِرَاجٌ، حَدَّثَنَا أَبُو مُحَمَّدٍ الأَصِيلِيُّ، حَدَّثَنَا أَبُو زَيْدٍ الفَقِيهُ، حَدَّثَنَا مُحَمَّدُ بْنُ يُوسُفَ، حَدَّثَنَا مُحَمَّدُ ابْنُ إِسْمَاعِيلَ، حَدَّثَنَا ابْنُ بَشَّارٍ، حَدَّثَنَا غُنْدَرٌ، حَدَّثَنَا شُعْبَةُ، عَنْ أَبِي إِسْحَاقَ: سَمِعَ البَرَاءَ وَسَأَلَهُ رَجُلٌ: أَفَرَرْتُمْ يَوْمَ حُنَيْنٍ عَنْ رَسُولِ اللهِ ﷺ؟ قَالَ: لَكِنَّ رَسُولَ اللهِ ﷺ لَمْ يَفِرَّ.

ثُمَّ قَالَ: لَقَدْ رَأَيْتُهُ[٢٧٣] عَلَى بَغْلَتِهِ البَيْضَاءِ، وَأَبُو سُفْيَانَ[٢٧٤] آخِذٌ بِلِجَامِهَا، وَالنَّبِيُّ ﷺ يَقُولُ: «أَنَا النَّبِيُّ لَا كَذِبْ». وَزَادَ غَيْرُهُ: «أَنَا ابْنُ عَبْدِ

---

[٢٧٢] الكُمَاةُ: الشُّجْعَانُ.

[٢٧٣] وَفِي البُخَارِيِّ: «رَأَيْتُ رَسُولَ اللهِ ﷺ». وَالمُثْبَتُ مِنَ المَطْبُوعِ.

[٢٧٤] أَبُو سُفْيَانَ هُوَ ابْنُ الحَارِثِ، ابْنُ عَمِّ النَّبِيِّ ﷺ.

Al-ʿAbbās narrated: "When the Muslims confronted the disbelievers, the Muslims turned on their heels, but the Messenger of Allah ﷺ began to spur his mule towards the disbelievers. I was holding on to the reins of his mule to stop it from bolting away, and Abū Sufyān was holding the stirrups. The Messenger ﷺ said: 'O ʿAbbās! Call out to the people of al-Samurah!'"[276]

It was said that when the Messenger of Allah ﷺ became angry – and he only did so for the sake of Allah – then no-one could stand in his way.[277] Ibn ʿUmar related: "I never saw a person more courageous, more heroic, more generous, more supportive to others, or more virtuous than the Messenger of Allah ﷺ."[278]

ʿAlī ﷺ narrated: "When the heat of battle intensified and we were penned in from all sides, the Messenger of Allah ﷺ acted as a protective shield between us and the enemy. Likewise, he was shielding us from the enemy during the Battle of Badr, and he was the fiercest fighter that day."[279] They used to say that whoever stayed close to the Prophet ﷺ was the most courageous, because he was always on the front line.[280]

Anas said: "The Prophet ﷺ was the best person, the most generous, and the most courageous. One night, the people of Madinah were frightened [by a noise they had heard], so they set off in the direction of the sound. They met the Prophet ﷺ on his way back, because he had already gone to investigate the disturbance.

---

276 Reported by Muslim (1775). Also cited in footnote 116.

277 A portion of the hadith of Hind ibn Abī Hālah, which was reported by Tirmidhī in *Al-Shamā'il* (8, 335, 350) and Baghawī in *Sharḥ al-Sunnah* (3705, 3706).

278 Reported by Dārimī (60) with a chain of trustworthy narrators.

279 A *ṣaḥīḥ* hadith. Reported by Aḥmad (1/86), Abū Yaʿlā (302, 412), Abū al-Shaykh, p. 57, Baghawī (3698, 3699), and others. Also reported by Muslim (1776) from al-Barā', who said: "I swear by Allah, when the battle grew fierce, we would seek protection by his side, and the bravest among us was the one at our side; i.e., the Prophet ﷺ."

280 See the references in the previous footnote.

الْمُطَّلِبِ»^{٢٧٥}. قِيلَ: فَمَا رُئِيَ يَوْمَئِذٍ أَحَدٌ كَانَ أَشَدَّ مِنْهُ.

وَقَالَ غَيْرُهُ^{٢٧٦}: نَزَلَ النَّبِيُّ ﷺ عَنْ بَغْلَتِهِ.

وَذَكَرَ مُسْلِمٌ عَنِ الْعَبَّاسِ قَالَ: فَلَمَّا الْتَقَى الْمُسْلِمُونَ وَالْكُفَّارُ وَلَّى الْمُسْلِمُونَ مُدْبِرِينَ، فَطَفِقَ رَسُولُ اللهِ ﷺ يَرْكُضُ بَغْلَتَهُ نَحْوَ الْكُفَّارِ، وَأَنَا آخِذٌ بِلِجَامِهَا أَكُفُّهَا إِرَادَةَ أَنْ لَا تُسْرِعَ، وَأَبُو سُفْيَانَ آخِذٌ بِرِكَابِهِ، ثُمَّ نَادَى: يَا لَلْمُسْلِمِينَ. الْحَدِيثَ^{٢٧٧}. وَقِيلَ: وَكَانَ رَسُولُ اللهِ ﷺ إِذَا غَضِبَ - وَلَا يَغْضَبُ إِلَّا لِلهِ - لَمْ يَقُمْ لِغَضَبِهِ شَيْءٌ. وَقَالَ ابْنُ عُمَرَ: مَا رَأَيْتُ أَشْجَعَ، وَلَا أَنْجَدَ، وَلَا أَجْوَدَ، وَلَا أَرْضَى، وَلَا أَفْضَلَ مِنْ رَسُولِ اللهِ ﷺ^{٢٧٨}.

وَقَالَ عَلِيٌّ رضي الله عنه: إِنَّا كُنَّا إِذَا حَمِيَ الْبَأْسُ - وَيُرْوَى: اشْتَدَّ الْبَأْسُ - وَاحْمَرَّتِ الْحَدَقُ اتَّقَيْنَا بِرَسُولِ اللهِ ﷺ، فَمَا يَكُونُ أَحَدٌ أَقْرَبَ إِلَى الْعَدُوِّ مِنْهُ ﷺ، وَلَقَدْ رَأَيْتُنِي يَوْمَ بَدْرٍ وَنَحْنُ نَلُوذُ بِالنَّبِيِّ ﷺ، وَلَهُوَ أَقْرَبُنَا إِلَى الْعَدُوِّ، وَكَانَ مِنْ أَشَدِّ النَّاسِ يَوْمَئِذٍ بَأْسًا^{٢٧٩}.

---

٢٧٥ أَسْنَدَهُ الْمُصَنِّفُ مِنْ طَرِيقِ الْبُخَارِيِّ (٤٣١٧). وَأَخْرَجَهُ أَيْضًا مُسْلِمٌ (١٧٧٦/٨٠).

٢٧٦ قَالَ غَيْرُهُ: هُمَا إِسْرَائِيلُ بْنُ يُونُسَ وَزُهَيْرُ بْنُ مُعَاوِيَةَ فَقَدْ رَوَيَا هَذَا الْحَدِيثَ - كَمَا فِي الْبُخَارِيِّ (٤٣١٧) - عَنْ أَبِي إِسْحَاقَ عَنِ الْبَرَاءِ فَقَالَا فِي آخِرِهِ: «نَزَلَ النَّبِيُّ ﷺ عَنْ بَغْلَتِهِ».

٢٧٧ أَخْرَجَهُ مُسْلِمٌ (١٧٧٥).

٢٧٨ أَخْرَجَهُ الدَّارِمِيُّ بِرَقْمِ (٦٠) وَرِجَالُهُ ثِقَاتٌ.

٢٧٩ حَدِيثٌ صَحِيحٌ. أَخْرَجَهُ أَحْمَدُ ١/٨٦، وَأَبُو يَعْلَى (٣٠٢، ٤١٢)، وَأَبُو الشَّيْخِ ص: (٥٧)، وَالْبَغَوِيُّ (٣٦٩٨، ٣٦٩٩) وَغَيْرُهُ. وَأَخْرَجَ مُسْلِمٌ (١٧٧٦) مِنْ حَدِيثِ الْبَرَاءِ قَالَ: «كُنَّا وَاللهِ! إِذَا احْمَرَّ الْبَأْسُ، نَتَّقِي بِهِ، وَإِنَّ الشُّجَاعَ مِنَّا لَلَّذِي يُحَاذِي بِهِ، يَعْنِي النَّبِيَّ ﷺ». (احْمَرَّتِ الْحَدَقُ): كِنَايَةٌ عَنِ اشْتِدَادِ الْقِتَالِ. (اتَّقَيْنَا بِرَسُولِ اللهِ ﷺ): أَيْ جَعَلْنَاهُ وَاقِيَةً لَنَا مِنَ الْعَدُوِّ.

He was riding an unsaddled horse belonging to Abū Ṭalḥah and had a sword hanging from his neck, and he was saying: 'Do not be afraid!'"[281]

'Imrān ibn Ḥuṣayn commented: "Any time the Messenger of Allah ﷺ confronted [enemy] troops, he would be the first to strike."[282]

Ubayy ibn Khalaf caught sight of the Prophet ﷺ during the Battle of Ḥunayn and called out: "Where is Muhammad? May I not survive if he survives!" Previously, when he was ransomed after the Battle of Badr, Ubayy had said to the Prophet ﷺ: "I have a horse that I feed corn every day, and I will kill you riding upon it." To which the Prophet ﷺ replied: "I will kill you if Allah wills."

So, when Ubayy saw the Prophet ﷺ at the Battle of Uḥud, he galloped towards him. Some of the Muslims blocked his way, but the Prophet ﷺ told them to let him pass. He took a spear from al-Ḥārith ibn al-Ṣimmah. He shook the spear and the people flew away from him like flies from a camel's back.

Then, the Prophet ﷺ came to face him and pierced him in the neck, causing him to sway and fall from his horse. The people said: "He broke one of his ribs." He went back to the Quraysh saying: "Muhammad has killed me!" They said to him: "There is nothing wrong with you."

But al-Ḥārith insisted: "Any person would have been killed by what happened to me. Did he not say: 'I will kill you'? I swear by Allah, if he spat on me it would have killed me." And al-Ḥārith died at Sarif during their return journey to Makkah.[283]

---

281 Reported by Bukhārī (2908) and Muslim (2307).

282 Reported by Abū al-Shaykh in *Akhlāq al-Nabī* ﷺ *wa Ādābuh*. See *Al-Manāhil*, p. 203.

283 Suyūṭī said in *Al-Manāhil*, p. 204: "[Reported as] a *mursal* narration by Ibn Saʿd and Bayhaqī from ʿUrwah ibn al-Zubayr and Saʿīd ibn al-Musayyib; as a *mursal* narration by ʿAbd al-Razzāq in *Al-Muṣannaf* (9731) from Muqassim, the servant of Ibn ʿAbbās; and as a *mawṣūl*

وَقِيلَ: كَانَ الشُّجَاعُ هُوَ الَّذِي يَقْرُبُ مِنْهُ ﷺ إِذَا دَنَا العَدُوُّ لِقُرْبِهِ مِنْهُ[280].

وَعَنْ أَنَسٍ: كَانَ النَّبِيُّ ﷺ أَحْسَنَ النَّاسِ، وَأَجْوَدَ النَّاسِ، وَأَشْجَعَ النَّاسِ، وَلَقَدْ فَزِعَ أَهْلُ المَدِينَةِ لَيْلَةً، فَانْطَلَقَ نَاسٌ قِبَلَ الصَّوْتِ، فَتَلَقَّاهُمْ رَسُولُ اللهِ ﷺ رَاجِعًا، قَدْ سَبَقَهُمْ إِلَى الصَّوْتِ، وَقَدِ اسْتَبْرَأَ الخَبَرَ عَلَى فَرَسٍ لِأَبِي طَلْحَةَ عُرْيٍ، وَالسَّيْفُ فِي عُنُقِهِ، وَهُوَ يَقُولُ: «لَنْ تُرَاعُوا»[281]. وَقَالَ عِمْرَانُ بْنُ حُصَيْنٍ: مَا لَقِيَ ﷺ كَتِيبَةً إِلَّا كَانَ أَوَّلَ مَنْ يَضْرِبُ. وَلَمَّا رَآهُ أُبَيُّ بْنُ خَلَفٍ يَوْمَ أُحُدٍ، وَهُوَ يَقُولُ: أَيْنَ مُحَمَّدٌ؟ لَا نَجَوْتُ إِنْ نَجَا. وَقَدْ كَانَ يَقُولُ لِلنَّبِيِّ ﷺ حِينَ افْتَدَى يَوْمَ بَدْرٍ: عِنْدِي فَرَسٌ أَعْلِفُهَا كُلَّ يَوْمٍ فَرَقًا مِنْ ذُرَةٍ أَقْتُلُكَ عَلَيْهَا. فَقَالَ لَهُ النَّبِيُّ ﷺ: «أَنَا أَقْتُلُكَ إِنْ شَاءَ اللهُ». فَلَمَّا رَآهُ يَوْمَ أُحُدٍ شَدَّ أُبَيٌّ عَلَى فَرَسِهِ عَلَى رَسُولِ اللهِ ﷺ، فَاعْتَرَضَهُ رِجَالٌ مِنَ المُسْلِمِينَ، فَقَالَ النَّبِيُّ ﷺ: هَكَذَا، أَيْ: خَلُّوا طَرِيقَهُ، وَتَنَاوَلَ الحَرْبَةَ مِنَ الحَارِثِ بْنِ الصِّمَّةِ، فَانْتَفَضَ بِهَا انْتِفَاضَةً تَطَايَرُوا عَنْهُ تَطَايُرَ الشَّعْرَاءِ عَنْ ظَهْرِ البَعِيرِ إِذَا انْتَفَضَ، ثُمَّ اسْتَقْبَلَهُ النَّبِيُّ ﷺ، فَطَعَنَهُ فِي عُنُقِهِ طَعْنَةً تَدَأْدَأَ مِنْهَا عَنْ فَرَسِهِ مِرَارًا. وَقِيلَ: بَلْ كَسَرَ ضِلَعًا مِنْ أَضْلَاعِهِ، فَرَجَعَ إِلَى قُرَيْشٍ يَقُولُ: قَتَلَنِي مُحَمَّدٌ! وَهُمْ يَقُولُونَ لَا بَأْسَ بِكَ. فَقَالَ: لَوْ كَانَ مَا بِي بِجَمِيعِ النَّاسِ لَقَتَلَهُمْ، أَلَيْسَ قَدْ قَالَ: «أَنَا أَقْتُلُكَ»؟!، وَاللهِ لَوْ بَصَقَ عَلَيَّ لَقَتَلَنِي. فَمَاتَ بِـ «سَرِفَ» فِي قُفُولِهِمْ إِلَى مَكَّةَ.

---

280 انْظُرْ تَخْرِيجَ الحَدِيثِ السَّابِقِ.

281 أَخْرَجَهُ البُخَارِيُّ (٢٩٠٨)، وَمُسْلِمٌ (٢٣٠٧). (اسْتَبْرَأَ): اسْتَكْشَفَ. (عُرْيٍ): لَا سَرْجَ عَلَيْهِ. (لَنْ تُرَاعُوا): أَيْ لَا خَوْفٌ وَلَا فَزَعَ، فَاسْكُنُوا.

HIS MODESTY AND LOWERING OF THE SIGHT

The Prophet ﷺ was the most modest person and the most conscientious in lowering his sight. Allah ﷻ said: "Such behaviour is truly annoying to the Prophet, yet he is too shy to ask you to leave. But Allah is never shy of the truth."[284]

I read the following hadith to Abū Muhammad ibn ʿAttāb ﷺ, who narrated from Abū al-Qāsim (Ḥātim ibn Muhammad), from Abū al-Ḥasan al-Qābisī, from Abū Zayd al-Marwazī, from Muhammad ibn Yūsuf, from Muhammad ibn Ismāʿīl, from ʿAbdān, from ʿAbdullāh, from Shuʿbah, from Qatādah, from ʿAbdullāh (the servant of Anas), from Abū Saʿīd al-Khudrī ﷺ, who said: "The Messenger of Allah ﷺ was shyer than a virgin behind her curtains, and if he disliked something we would tell from [the expression of] his face."[285]

The Prophet ﷺ had a sensitive character and a gentle soul. From his modesty and generosity, he would never address someone directly about something he disliked. ʿĀʾishah ﷺ narrated: "If the Prophet ﷺ heard about someone doing something he disliked, he would not say: 'What is wrong with so-and-so who does that?' Rather, he would say: 'What is wrong with the people who do or say that?'"[286] In this way, he would denounce the action without

---

narration by al-Wāqidī in *Al-Maghāzī* (p. 251) from Kaʿb ibn Mālik."

284 *al-Aḥzāb*, 53.

285 Reported here from the chain of Bukhārī (6102). Also reported by Muslim (2320).

286 Reported by Abū Dāwūd (4788) and al-Kharāʾiṭī in *Al-Muntaqā min Makārim al-Akhlāq* (6102). The chain is *ḥasan*.

فَصْل

وَأَمَّا الْحَيَاءُ وَالْإِغْضَاءُ: وَالْحَيَاءُ: رِقَّةٌ تَعْتَرِي وَجْهَ الْإِنْسَانِ عِنْدَ فِعْلِ مَا تَتَوَقَّعُ كَرَاهَتُهُ، أَوْ مَا يَكُونُ تَرْكُهُ خَيْرًا مِنْ فِعْلِهِ.

وَالْإِغْضَاءُ: التَّغَافُلُ عَمَّا يَكْرَهُهُ الْإِنْسَانُ بِطَبِيعَتِهِ.

فَكَانَ النَّبِيُّ ﷺ، أَشَدَّ النَّاسِ حَيَاءً، وَأَكْثَرَهُمْ عَنِ الْعَوْرَاتِ إِغْضَاءً؛ قَالَ اللّٰهُ سُبْحَانَهُ: ﴿إِنَّ ذَٰلِكُمْ كَانَ يُؤْذِى ٱلنَّبِيَّ فَيَسْتَحْيِۦ مِنكُمْ﴾ [الأحزاب: ٥٣] الْآيَةَ.

وَحَدَّثَنِي أَبُو مُحَمَّدِ بْنُ عَتَّابٍ رَحِمَهُ اللّٰهُ بِقِرَاءَتِي عَلَيْهِ، حَدَّثَنَا أَبُو الْقَاسِمِ حَاتِمُ ابْنُ مُحَمَّدٍ، حَدَّثَنَا أَبُو الْحَسَنِ الْقَابِسِيُّ، حَدَّثَنَا أَبُو زَيْدٍ الْمَرْوَزِيُّ، حَدَّثَنَا مُحَمَّدُ بْنُ يُوسُفَ، حَدَّثَنَا مُحَمَّدُ بْنُ إِسْمَاعِيلَ، حَدَّثَنَا عَبْدَانُ، أَخْبَرَنَا عَبْدُ اللّٰهِ، أَخْبَرَنَا شُعْبَةُ، عَنْ قَتَادَةَ سَمِعْتُ عَبْدَ اللّٰهِ مَوْلَى أَنَسٍ، عَنْ أَبِي سَعِيدٍ الْخُدْرِيِّ قَالَ: كَانَ رَسُولُ اللّٰهِ ﷺ أَشَدَّ حَيَاءً مِنَ الْعَذْرَاءِ فِي خِدْرِهَا، وَكَانَ إِذَا كَرِهَ شَيْئًا عَرَفْنَاهُ فِي وَجْهِهِ[٢٨٢].

وَكَانَ ﷺ لَطِيفَ الْبَشَرَةِ، رَقِيقَ الظَّاهِرِ، لَا يُشَافِهُ أَحَدًا بِمَا يَكْرَهُهُ؛ حَيَاءً وَكَرَمَ نَفْسٍ.

وَعَنْ عَائِشَةَ رَضِيَ اللّٰهُ عَنْهَا: كَانَ النَّبِيُّ ﷺ إِذَا بَلَغَهُ عَنْ أَحَدٍ مَا يَكْرَهُهُ لَمْ يَقُلْ: مَا بَالُ فُلَانٍ يَقُولُ كَذَا؟ وَلَكِنْ يَقُولُ: «مَا بَالُ أَقْوَامٍ يَصْنَعُونَ؟ أَوْ يَقُولُونَ

---

٢٨٢ أَسْنَدَهُ الْمُصَنِّفُ مِنْ طَرِيقِ مُحَمَّدِ بْنِ إِسْمَاعِيلَ الْبُخَارِيِّ (٦١٠٢). وَأَخْرَجَهُ أَيْضًا مُسْلِمٌ (٢٣٢٠).

naming the person who did it.

Anas relates that a man came to the Prophet ﷺ with traces of yellow[287] on him. The Prophet ﷺ did not say anything, and in general it was not his custom to confront people about things he disliked. However, when the man left, he said to the people with him: "Could you tell him to wash that." Or, in another transmission: "… to remove that."[288]

'Ā'ishah ﷺ also narrated: "The Prophet ﷺ was not rude or offensive, neither did he shout in the markets. He did not respond to wrongdoing with wrongdoing. Rather, he would pardon and forgive."[289] A narration transmitted from 'Abdullāh ibn Salām[290] and 'Abdullāh ibn 'Amr ibn al-'Āṣ[291] mentions a similar description of the Prophet ﷺ being found in the Torah.

It was related that the Prophet ﷺ was so modest, he would lower his gaze from others.[292] When someone forced a conversation about a topic he disliked, the Prophet ﷺ would address them with a nickname.[293] And 'Ā'ishah ﷺ said: "I never saw the private parts of the Messenger of Allah ﷺ."[294]

---

287   From saffron.

288   Reported by Abū Dāwūd (4182, 4789), Tirmidhī in *Al-Shamā'il* (345), Abū Ya'lā (4277), and others. The chain contains Salam al-'Alawī, who was cited in *Al-Taqrīb* as a weak narrator.

289   Reported by Tirmidhī in *Al-Sunan* (2016) and *Al-Shamā'il* (346), and by Aḥmad (6/174). Tirmidhī said: "This hadith is *ḥasan ṣaḥīḥ*."

290   Ibn Ḥajar said in *Fatḥ al-Bārī* (4/343): "This chain was connected by Dārimī in his *Musnad* (6), Ya'qūb ibn Sufyān in his *Tārīkh*, and Ṭabarānī."

291   Reported by Bukhārī (2125).

292   Mentioned by Ghazālī in *Al-Iḥyā'*. 'Irāqī said he did not find the narration. See *Al-Manāhil*, p. 209.

293   As evidenced in many well-known narrations. See *Al-Manāhil*, p. 210.

294   Reported by Tirmidhī in *Al-Shamā'il* (358), Ibn Mājah (1922), and Aḥmad (6/63) with one of the narrators unnamed.

كَذَا؟»²⁸³ يَنْهَى عَنْهُ، وَلَا يُسَمِّي فَاعِلَهُ.

وَرَوَى أَنَسٌ رَضِيَ اللهُ عَنْهُ أَنَّهُ دَخَلَ عَلَيْهِ رَجُلٌ بِهِ أَثَرُ صُفْرَةٍ، فَلَمْ يَقُلْ لَهُ شَيْئًا - وَكَانَ لَا يُوَاجِهُ أَحَدًا بِمَا يَكْرَهُ - فَلَمَّا خَرَجَ قَالَ: «لَوْ قُلْتُمْ لَهُ يَغْسِلُ هَذَا؟».

وَيُرْوَى: «يَنْزِعُهَا»²⁸⁴.

قَالَتْ عَائِشَةُ فِي الصَّحِيحِ: لَمْ يَكُنِ النَّبِيُّ ﷺ فَاحِشًا، وَلَا مُتَفَحِّشًا، وَلَا سَخَّابًا فِي الْأَسْوَاقِ، وَلَا يَجْزِي بِالسَّيِّئَةِ السَّيِّئَةَ، وَلَكِنْ يَعْفُو وَيَصْفَحُ²⁸⁵.

وَقَدْ حُكِيَ مِثْلُ هَذَا الْكَلَامِ عَنِ التَّوْرَاةِ، مِنْ رِوَايَةِ عَبْدِ اللهِ بْنِ سَلَامٍ، وَعَبْدِ اللهِ بْنِ عَمْرِو بْنِ الْعَاصِ²⁸⁶.

وَرُوِيَ عَنْهُ أَنَّهُ كَانَ مِنْ حَيَائِهِ لَا يُثْبِتُ بَصَرَهُ فِي وَجْهِ أَحَدٍ²⁸⁷، وَأَنَّهُ كَانَ يَكْنِي عَمَّا اضْطَرَّهُ الْكَلَامُ إِلَيْهِ مِمَّا يُكْرَهُ²⁸⁸.

وَعَنْ عَائِشَةَ رَضِيَ اللهُ عَنْهَا: مَا رَأَيْتُ فَرْجَ رَسُولِ اللهِ ﷺ قَطُّ.

---

٢٨٣ أَخْرَجَهُ أَبُو دَاوُدَ (٤٧٨٨)، وَالْخَرَائِطِيُّ فِي الْمُنْتَقَى مِنْ مَكَارِمِ الْأَخْلَاقِ (٣٧٥)، وَإِسْنَادُهُ حَسَنٌ.

٢٨٤ أَخْرَجَهُ أَبُو دَاوُدَ (٤١٨٢، ٤٧٨٩)، وَالتِّرْمِذِيُّ فِي الشَّمَائِلِ (٣٣٩)، وَأَبُو يَعْلَى (٤٢٧٧) وَغَيْرُهُ، وَفِي إِسْنَادِهِ سَلْمٌ الْعَلَوِيُّ. قَالَ فِي التَّقْرِيبِ: «ضَعِيفٌ». (أَثَرُ صُفْرَةٍ): أَيْ طِيبٌ مِنْ زَعْفَرَانَ، وَتَعَمُّدُ التَّزَعْفُرِ مَنْهِيٌّ عَنْهُ.

٢٨٥ أَخْرَجَهُ التِّرْمِذِيُّ فِي السُّنَنِ (٢٠١٦)، وَفِي الشَّمَائِلِ (٣٤٠)، وَأَحْمَدُ ١٧٤/٦. قَالَ التِّرْمِذِيُّ: هَذَا حَدِيثٌ حَسَنٌ صَحِيحٌ.

٢٨٦ مُتَّفَقٌ عَلَيْهِ.

٢٨٧ ذَكَرَهُ صَاحِبُ الْإِحْيَاءِ، وَلَمْ يَجِدْهُ الْعِرَاقِيُّ/ الْمَنَاهِلُ (٢٠٩).

٢٨٨ هُوَ مَعْلُومٌ مِنْ أَحْوَالِهِ، وَأَقْوَالِهِ فِي الْأَحَادِيثِ الْمَشْهُورَةِ/ الْمَنَاهِلُ (٢١٠).

HIS FRIENDLY AND WELL-MANNERED NATURE

The friendly and well-mannered nature of the Prophet ﷺ and his cheerful interactions with all types of people are described in a number of authentic narrations. When ʿAlī described the Prophet ﷺ, he said: "He was the most generous[295] of the people, the most truthful in speech, the softest in nature, and the most generous in companionship."[296]

I read the following hadith to several scholars, and was given permission to narrate by Abū al-Ḥasan (ʿAlī ibn Musharraf al-Anamāṭī), who narrated from Abū Isḥāq al-Ḥabbāl, from Abū Muḥammad ibn al-Naḥḥās, from Ibn al-Aʿrābī, from Abū Dāwūd, from Hishām (Abū Marwān) and Muḥammad ibn al-Muthannā, from al-Walīd ibn Muslim, from al-Awzāʿī, from Yaḥyā ibn Abī Kathīr, from Muḥammad ibn ʿAbd al-Raḥmān ibn Asʿad ibn Zurārah, from Qays ibn Saʿd, who said: "The Messenger of Allah ﷺ visited us". He went on to narrate the story of the visit, and at the end he said: "When he intended to leave, Saʿd brought him a donkey covered with a blanket and the Messenger of Allah ﷺ climbed on. Then, Saʿd said: 'Qays, accompany the Messenger of Allah ﷺ!' The Messenger of Allah ﷺ told me to climb on, but I refused. So, he said: 'Either climb on, or leave.' So I left."[297] In another transmis-

---

295　lit., "he had the most expansive chest".

296　Reported by Tirmidhī in *Al-Sunan* (3638) and *Al-Shamā'il* (7).

297　Reported here from the chain of Abū Dāwūd (5185). Also reported by Aḥmad (3/421), Nasā'ī in ʿAmal al-*Yawm wa al-Laylah* (324, 325), Ibn al-Sunnī (663), and Ibn Mājah (466). Ibn Ḥajar said in *Al-Talkhīṣ al-Ḥabīr* (1/99): "There was a difference of opinion regarding the

فَصْل

وَأَمَّا حُسْنُ عِشْرَتِهِ، وَأَدَبُهُ، وَبَسْطُ خُلُقِهِ ﷺ مَعَ أَصْنَافِ الْخَلْقِ فَبِحَيْثُ انْتَشَرَتْ بِهِ الْأَخْبَارُ الصَّحِيحَةُ.

قَالَ عَلِيٌّ ﵁ فِي وَصْفِهِ عليه الصلاة والسلام: كَانَ أَوْسَعَ النَّاسِ صَدْرًا، وَأَصْدَقَ النَّاسِ لَهْجَةً، وَأَلْيَنَهُمْ عَرِيكَةً، وَأَكْرَمَهُمْ عِشْرَةً[289].

حَدَّثَنَا أَبُو الْحَسَنِ عَلِيُّ بْنُ مُشْرِفٍ الْأَنْمَاطِيُّ فِيمَا أَجَازَنِيهِ، وَقَرَأْتُهُ عَلَى غَيْرِهِ، حَدَّثَنَا أَبُو إِسْحَاقَ الْحَبَّالُ، حَدَّثَنَا أَبُو مُحَمَّدِ بْنُ النَّحَّاسِ، حَدَّثَنَا ابْنُ الْأَعْرَابِيِّ، حَدَّثَنَا أَبُو دَاوُدَ، حَدَّثَنَا هِشَامٌ أَبُو مَرْوَانَ، وَمُحَمَّدُ بْنُ الْمُثَنَّى، قَالَا: حَدَّثَنَا الْوَلِيدُ ابْنُ مُسْلِمٍ، حَدَّثَنَا الْأَوْزَاعِيُّ، سَمِعْتُ يَحْيَى ابْنَ أَبِي كَثِيرٍ يَقُولُ: حَدَّثَنِي مُحَمَّدُ بْنُ عَبْدِ الرَّحْمَنِ بْنِ أَسْعَدَ بْنِ زُرَارَةَ، عَنْ قَيْسِ بْنِ سَعْدٍ، قَالَ: زَارَنَا رَسُولُ اللهِ ﷺ، وَذَكَرَ قِصَّةً فِي آخِرِهَا: فَلَمَّا أَرَادَ الْإِنْصِرَافَ قَرَّبَ لَهُ سَعْدٌ حِمَارًا، وَطَأَ عَلَيْهِ بِقَطِيفَةٍ، فَرَكِبَ رَسُولُ اللهِ ﷺ، ثُمَّ قَالَ سَعْدٌ: يَا قَيْسُ، اصْحَبْ رَسُولَ اللهِ ﷺ، قَالَ قَيْسٌ: فَقَالَ لِي رَسُولُ اللهِ ﷺ: «ارْكَبْ» فَأَبَيْتُ، فَقَالَ: «إِمَّا أَنْ تَرْكَبَ، وَإِمَّا أَنْ تَنْصَرِفَ»، فَانْصَرَفْتُ[290].

---

289 (أَلْيَنَهُمْ عَرِيكَةً) يُقَالُ: فُلَانٌ لَيِّنُ الْعَرِيكَةِ، إِذَا كَانَ سَلِسًا مُطَاوِعًا مُنْقَادًا قَلِيلَ الْخِلَافِ وَالنُّفُورِ/ النِّهَايَة.

290 أَسْنَدَهُ الْمُصَنِّفُ مِنْ طَرِيقِ أَبِي دَاوُدَ (٥١٨٥). وَأَخْرَجَهُ أَيْضًا أَحْمَدُ ٤٢١/٣، وَالنَّسَائِيُّ فِي عَمَلِ الْيَوْمِ وَاللَّيْلَةِ (٣٢٤، ٣٢٥)، وَابْنُ السُّنِّيِّ (٦٦٣)، وَابْنُ مَاجَه (٤٦٦). قَالَ الْحَافِظُ فِي تَلْخِيصِ الْحَبِيرِ ٩٩/١: «اخْتُلِفَ فِي وَصْلِهِ

sion, the Messenger of Allah ﷺ said: "Ride in front of me, for an owner of an animal has more right to the front."

'Alī related from Ibn Abī Hālah: "He (i.e., the Messenger of Allah ﷺ) used to bring people together and would never alienate them. He would honour the leaders of each community and put them in charge of their people. He would caution people and be wary of them, but without abandoning his cheerful manner and exemplary character, and he would check in on his Companions… He would give every person who sat with him their share [of his time and attention], to the extent that each person felt that they had been more looked after than anyone else. If someone sat with him or came to him with a need, he would be patient [and deal with their enquiry] until they were the first to leave, and no-one left without receiving what they asked for, or at least some comforting words. His cheerfulness and wonderful character encompassed people to such an extent that he became a father to them, and they were all equal in respect of their rights."[298]

'Alī said: "The Prophet ﷺ was always cheerful, and he was easy-going, gentle and sympathetic. He was never harsh or rough, nor rude or obscene. Neither would he praise to excess. He would disregard things that were not to his liking, and he would never leave anyone who put their hope in him despairing or disappointed."[299]

Allah Exalted said: "It is out of Allah's Mercy that you [O Prophet] have been lenient with them. Had you been cruel or hard-heart-

---

connection [of the chain] and the transmission [of the narration]. The narrators in the chain of Abū Dāwūd are *ṣaḥīḥ*, although Nawawī mentioned the narration in *Al-Khulāṣah* as *ḍaʿīf*, and Allah knows best."

298 See *Al-Shamāʾil* (335).

299 See *Al-Shamāʾil* (8, 335, 350).

وَفِي رِوَايَةٍ أُخْرَى: «ارْكَبْ أَمَامِي، فَصَاحِبُ الدَّابَّةِ أَوْلَى بِمُقَدَّمِهَا».

وَكَانَ رَسُولُ اللهِ ﷺ يُؤَلِّفُهُمْ، وَلَا يُنَفِّرُهُمْ، وَيُكْرِمُ كَرِيمَ كُلِّ قَوْمٍ، وَيُوَلِّيهِ عَلَيْهِمْ، وَيُحَذِّرُ النَّاسَ، وَيَحْتَرِسُ مِنْهُمْ، مِنْ غَيْرِ أَنْ يَطْوِيَ عَنْ أَحَدٍ مِنْهُمْ بِشْرَهُ وَلَا خُلُقَهُ، يَتَفَقَّدُ أَصْحَابَهُ، وَيُعْطِي كُلَّ جُلَسَائِهِ نَصِيبَهُ، لَا يَحْسَبُ جَلِيسُهُ أَنَّ أَحَدًا أَكْرَمُ عَلَيْهِ مِنْهُ، مَنْ جَالَسَهُ أَوْ قَارَبَهُ²⁹¹ لِحَاجَةٍ صَابَرَهُ حَتَّى يَكُونَ هُوَ الْمُنْصَرِفُ عَنْهُ، وَمَنْ سَأَلَهُ حَاجَةً لَمْ يَرُدَّهُ إِلَّا بِهَا، أَوْ بِمَيْسُورٍ مِنَ الْقَوْلِ، قَدْ وَسِعَ النَّاسَ بَسْطُهُ وَخُلُقُهُ، فَصَارَ لَهُمْ أَبًا، وَصَارُوا عِنْدَهُ فِي الْحَقِّ سَوَاءً.

بِهَذَا وَصَفَهُ ابْنُ أَبِي هَالَةَ²⁹²، قَالَ²⁹³: وَكَانَ دَائِمَ الْبِشْرِ، سَهْلَ الْخُلُقِ، لَيِّنَ الْجَانِبِ، لَيْسَ بِفَظٍّ، وَلَا غَلِيظٍ، وَلَا سَخَّابٍ، وَلَا فَحَّاشٍ، وَلَا عَيَّابٍ، وَلَا مَدَّاحٍ، يَتَغَافَلُ عَمَّا لَا يَشْتَهِي، وَلَا يُويِسُ مِنْهُ.

وَقَالَ اللهُ عَزَّوَجَلَّ: ﴿فَبِمَا رَحْمَةٍ مِّنَ ٱللَّهِ لِنتَ لَهُمْ وَلَوْ كُنتَ فَظًّا غَلِيظَ ٱلْقَلْبِ لَٱنفَضُّواْ مِنْ حَوْلِكَ﴾ [آل عمران: ١٥٩]. وَقَالَ: ﴿ٱدْفَعْ بِٱلَّتِي هِيَ أَحْسَنُ﴾ [المؤمنون: ٩٦] الْآيَةَ.

وَإِرْسَالِهِ، وَرِجَالِ إِسْنَادِ أَبِي دَاوُدَ رِجَالُ الصَّحِيحِ... وَمَعَ ذَلِكَ فَذَكَرَهُ النَّوَوِيُّ فِي الْخُلَاصَةِ فِي فَصْلِ الضَّعِيفِ، وَاللهُ أَعْلَمُ». (القَطِيفَةُ): الدِّثَارُ ذُو الْخَمْلِ.

٢٩١ فِي شَرْحِ السُّنَّةِ (٣٧٠٦): «قَاوَمَهُ». وَقَالَ فِي النِّهَايَةِ: «قَاوَمَهُ: فَاعَلَهُ، مِنَ الْقِيَامِ: أَيْ إِذَا قَامَ مَعَهُ لِيَقْضِيَ حَاجَتَهُ صَبَرَ عَلَيْهِ إِلَى أَنْ يَقْضِيَهَا».

٢٩٢ بَلِ الَّذِي وَصَفَهُ بِذَلِكَ هُوَ عَلِيُّ بْنُ أَبِي طَالِبٍ ﵁.

٢٩٣ الْقَائِلُ هُوَ عَلِيُّ بْنُ أَبِي طَالِبٍ.

ed, they would have certainly abandoned you."[300] And: "Respond to evil with what is best. We know well what they claim."[301]

The Prophet ﷺ would never turn down invitations.[302] He would always accept presents, even if it was only a sheep's trotter, and he would reciprocate.[303] Anas said: "I served the Messenger of Allah ﷺ for ten years and he never said 'Uff!'[304] to me. When I did something, he never asked me why I had done it, and when I left something, he never asked me why I had left it."[305]

'Ā'ishah ﷺ related: "No-one had better manners than the Messenger of Allah ﷺ. Any time one of his Companions or family members called him, he would say: 'At your service.'"[306] And Jarīr ibn 'Abdullāh narrated: "Since I embraced Islam, the Messenger of Allah ﷺ never refused me permission to see him[307], and any time I saw him he was smiling."[308]

The Prophet ﷺ would mix freely with his Companions, joking and chatting with them and playing with the children. He would respond to anyone's invitation, whether they were free, a slave, or poor. He would visit the sick, even if they were at the furthest part of the city from him, and would always accept excuses from others.

---

300   Āl ʿImrān, 159.

301   al-Muʾminūn, 96.

302   Reported by the author of *Jāmiʿ al-Uṣūl* (11/250) from Anas, and attributed to Bukhārī.

303   Reported by Bukhārī (2585) from ʿĀ'ishah: "The Messenger of Allah used to accept gifts and used to give something in return." Also reported by Bukhārī (2568) from Abū Hurayrah: "The Prophet ﷺ said: 'If I was gifted a shank or a trotter, I would accept.'" "Trotter" here can refer to the feet of a sheep or a cow.

304   An expression of frustration or exasperation.

305   Reported by Tirmidhī in *Al-Shamā'il* (350) with this wording. Also reported by Bukhārī (2768) and Muslim (2309).

306   Suyūṭī said in *Al-Manāhil*, p. 218: "[Reported by] Abū Nuʿaym in *Al-Dalā'il* with a weak chain." See also Ibn al-Sunnī (290) and *Majmaʿ al-Zawā'id* (9/20-21).

307   lit., "never screened himself from me".

308   Reported by Bukhārī (3035) and Muslim (2475).

وَكَانَ ﷺ يُجِيبُ مَنْ دَعَاهُ²⁹⁴، وَيَقْبَلُ الْهَدِيَّةَ وَلَوْ كَانَتْ كُرَاعًا، وَيُكَافِئُ عَلَيْهَا²⁹⁵.

قَالَ أَنَسٌ: خَدَمْتُ رَسُولَ اللهِ ﷺ عَشْرَ سِنِينَ، فَمَا قَالَ لِي: أُفٍّ، قَطُّ، وَمَا قَالَ لِي لِشَيْءٍ صَنَعْتُهُ: لِمَ صَنَعْتَهُ؟! وَلَا لِشَيْءٍ تَرَكْتُهُ: لِمَ تَرَكْتَهُ؟!²⁹⁶.

وَعَنْ عَائِشَةَ رَضِيَ اللهُ عَنْهَا قَالَتْ: مَا كَانَ أَحَدٌ أَحْسَنَ خُلُقًا مِنْ رَسُولِ اللهِ ﷺ، مَا دَعَاهُ أَحَدٌ مِنْ أَصْحَابِهِ وَلَا أَهْلِ بَيْتِهِ إِلَّا قَالَ: «لَبَّيْكَ»²⁹⁷.

وَقَالَ جَرِيرُ بْنُ عَبْدِ اللهِ: مَا حَجَبَنِي رَسُولُ اللهِ ﷺ مُنْذُ أَسْلَمْتُ، وَلَا رَآنِي إِلَّا تَبَسَّمَ²⁹⁸.

وَكَانَ يُمَازِحُ أَصْحَابَهُ، وَيُخَالِطُهُمْ، وَيُحَادِثُهُمْ، وَيُدَاعِبُ صِبْيَانَهُمْ، وَيُجْلِسُهُمْ فِي حَجْرِهِ، وَيُجِيبُ دَعْوَةَ الْحُرِّ وَالْعَبْدِ وَالْأَمَةِ وَالْمِسْكِينِ، وَيَعُودُ الْمَرْضَى فِي أَقْصَى الْمَدِينَةِ، وَيَقْبَلُ عُذْرَ الْمُعْتَذِرِ.

قَالَ أَنَسٌ: مَا الْتَقَمَ أَحَدٌ أُذُنَ رَسُولِ اللهِ ﷺ فَيُنَحِّي رَأْسَهُ حَتَّى يَكُونَ

---

٢٩٤ أَوْرَدَهُ صَاحِبُ جَامِعِ الْأُصُولِ (٢٥٠/١١) مِنْ حَدِيثِ أَنَسٍ وَنَسَبَهُ لِلْبُخَارِيِّ.

٢٩٥ أَخْرَجَ الْبُخَارِيُّ (٢٥٨٥) مِنْ حَدِيثِ عَائِشَةَ: «كَانَ رَسُولُ اللهِ ﷺ يَقْبَلُ الْهَدِيَّةَ وَيُثِيبُ عَلَيْهَا». وَأَخْرَجَ الْبُخَارِيُّ أَيْضًا (٢٥٦٨) مِنْ حَدِيثِ أَبِي هُرَيْرَةَ: «وَلَوْ أُهْدِيَ إِلَيَّ ذِرَاعٌ أَوْ كُرَاعٌ لَقَبِلْتُ». (كُرَاعًا): الْكُرَاعُ مِنَ الْبَقَرِ وَالْغَنَمِ: مُسْتَدَقُّ السَّاقِ الْعَارِي مِنَ اللَّحْمِ. وَفِي الْمَثَلِ: «لَا تُطْعِمِ الْعَبْدَ الْكُرَاعَ فَيَطْمَعَ فِي الذِّرَاعِ».

٢٩٦ أَخْرَجَهُ الْبُخَارِيُّ (٢٧٦٨)، وَمُسْلِمٌ (٢٣٠٩)، وَالتِّرْمِذِيُّ فِي الشَّمَائِلِ (٣٣٨) وَاللَّفْظُ لَهُ.

٢٩٧ قَالَ السُّيُوطِيُّ فِي الْمَنَاهِلِ (٢١٨): «أَبُو نُعَيْمٍ فِي دَلَائِلِ النُّبُوَّةِ بِسَنَدٍ وَاهٍ». وَانْظُرِ ابْنَ السُّنِّيِّ (٢٩٠) وَمَجْمَعَ الزَّوَائِدِ ٢١-٢٠/٩.

٢٩٨ أَخْرَجَهُ الْبُخَارِيُّ (٣٠٣٥)، وَمُسْلِمٌ (٢٤٧٥).

Anas recalled: "Any time a person leant towards the ear of the Prophet ﷺ [to speak to him], he would leave his head until the other person drew away, and when a person took his hand, he would never be the first to withdraw. He was never seen with his knees in front of the person sitting next to him."[309]

He was always first to extend the greeting of *salām* when he met someone, and first to shake hands with any of his Companions. He was never seen stretching out his legs whilst with his Companions or constricting their space, and he honoured every person who came to him. Sometimes he would lay out his cloak and offer them the cushion he was sitting on, and would insist even if they refused. He would give his Companions nicknames and address them with the names they loved the most. He never interrupted a conversation until the other person finished or stood up to leave.

It was said that if the Prophet ﷺ was praying and someone was waiting for him, he would shorten his prayer, ask about their needs, and then once their concerns were dealt with, he would return to pray.[310]

He was the most joyful person and was always smiling, unless the Qur'an was being revealed, he was admonishing someone, or he was giving a public address. 'Abdullāh ibn al-Ḥārith[311] narrated: "I did not see anyone smile more often than the Prophet ﷺ."[312]

---

309 Reported, without the last sentence, by Abū Dāwūd (4794) and Abū Yaʿlā (3471). Authenticated by Ibn Ḥibbān in *Mawārid al-Ẓamʾān* (2132), and he reported it in another context. The last sentence of the narration was reported by Tirmidhī (2490), Ibn Mājah (3716), Baghawī (3680), and others. Tirmidhī said: "This hadith is *gharīb*." Ibn Athīr said, in the notes to *Jāmiʿ al-Uṣūl* (11/250): "This hadith is *hasan*."

310 ʿIrāqī said in *Takhrīj Aḥādīth al-Iḥyāʾ*: "I did not find a source for this narration." See *Al-Manāhil*, p. 225.

311 A Companion who settled in Egypt and, according to some opinions, was the last Companion to die in that land, in 86 AH (approx.).

312 Reported by Tirmidhī in *Al-Sunan* (3641) and *Al-Shamāʾil* (226), Aḥmad (4/190), and others. Tirmidhī said: "This hadith is *hasan gharīb*." Suyūṭī cited the narration as *hasan* in

الرَّجُلُ هُوَ الَّذِي يُنْحِي رَأْسَهُ، وَمَا أَخَذَ أَحَدٌ بِيَدِهِ فَيُرْسِلُ يَدَهُ حَتَّى يُرْسِلَهَا الآخِذُ، وَلَمْ يُرَ مُقَدِّمًا رُكْبَتَيْهِ بَيْنَ يَدَيْ جَلِيسٍ لَهُ[299].

وَكَانَ يَبْدَأُ مَنْ لَقِيَهُ بِالسَّلَامِ، وَيَبْدَأُ أَصْحَابَهُ بِالْمُصَافَحَةِ، وَلَمْ يُرَ قَطُّ مَادًّا رِجْلَيْهِ بَيْنَ أَصْحَابِهِ حَتَّى يُضَيِّقَ بِهِمَا عَلَى أَحَدٍ، يُكْرِمُ مَنْ يَدْخُلُ عَلَيْهِ، وَرُبَّمَا بَسَطَ لَهُ ثَوْبَهُ، وَيُؤْثِرُهُ بِالْوِسَادَةِ الَّتِي تَحْتَهُ، وَيَعْزِمُ عَلَيْهِ فِي الْجُلُوسِ عَلَيْهَا إِنْ أَبَى، وَيَكْنِي أَصْحَابَهُ، وَيَدْعُوهُمْ بِأَحَبِّ أَسْمَائِهِمْ تَكْرِمَةً لَهُمْ، وَلَا يَقْطَعُ عَلَى أَحَدٍ حَدِيثَهُ حَتَّى يَتَجَوَّزَ[300] فَيَقْطَعُهُ بِنَهْيٍ أَوْ قِيَامٍ، وَيُرْوَى: بِانْتِهَاءٍ أَوْ قِيَامٍ.

وَرُوِيَ أَنَّهُ كَانَ لَا يَجْلِسُ إِلَيْهِ أَحَدٌ - وَهُوَ يُصَلِّي - إِلَّا خَفَّفَ صَلَاتَهُ وَسَأَلَهُ عَنْ حَاجَتِهِ، فَإِذَا فَرَغَ عَادَ إِلَى صَلَاتِهِ[301]. وَكَانَ أَكْثَرَ النَّاسِ تَبَسُّمًا، وَأَطْيَبَهُمْ نَفْسًا، مَا لَمْ يَنْزِلْ عَلَيْهِ قُرْآنٌ، أَوْ يَعِظْ، أَوْ يَخْطُبْ.

وَقَالَ عَبْدُ اللهِ بْنُ الْحَارِثِ[302]: مَا رَأَيْتُ أَحَدًا أَكْثَرَ تَبَسُّمًا مِنْ رَسُولِ اللهِ ﷺ[303].

---

[299] أَخْرَجَهُ بِدُونِ الْفِقْرَةِ الأَخِيرَةِ: أَبُو دَاوُدَ (٤٧٩٤)، وَأَبُو يَعْلَى (٣٤٧١)، وَصَحَّحَهُ ابْنُ حِبَّانَ (٢١٣٢) مَوَارِدُ، وَأَخْرَجَهُ بِسِيَاقٍ آخَرَ، وَذَكَرَ فِيهِ الْفِقْرَةَ الأَخِيرَةَ مِنَ الْحَدِيثِ: التِّرْمِذِيُّ (٢٤٩٠)، وَابْنُ مَاجَه (٣٧١٦)، وَالْبَغَوِيُّ (٣٦٨٠)، وَغَيْرُهُ. قَالَ التِّرْمِذِيُّ: «هَذَا حَدِيثٌ غَرِيبٌ». وَفِي حَاشِيَةِ جَامِعِ الأُصُولِ ٢٥٠/١١: «حَدِيثٌ حَسَنٌ» (الْتَقَمَ أُذُنَهُ): أَيْ سَارَّهُ.

[300] يَتَجَوَّزُ: يَتَعَدَّى.

[301] قَالَ الْعِرَاقِيُّ فِي تَخْرِيجِ الإِحْيَاءِ: لَمْ أَجِدْهُ أَصْلًا/ الْمَنَاهِلُ (٢٢٥).

[302] صَحَابِيٌّ، سَكَنَ مِصْرَ، وَهُوَ آخِرُ مَنْ مَاتَ بِهَا مِنَ الصَّحَابَةِ مَاتَ سَنَةَ (٨٦) هـ عَلَى خِلَافٍ فِي ذَلِكَ/ التَّقْرِيبُ.

[303] أَخْرَجَهُ التِّرْمِذِيُّ فِي السُّنَنِ (٣٦٤١)، وَفِي الشَّمَائِلِ (٢٢٧)، وَأَحْمَدُ (١٩٠/٤) وَغَيْرُهُ. قَالَ التِّرْمِذِيُّ: «حَدِيثٌ حَسَنٌ غَرِيبٌ»، وَحَسَّنَهُ السُّيُوطِيُّ فِي الْمَنَاهِلِ (٢٢٦).

Anas said: "The servants of Madinah used to bring the Messenger of Allah ﷺ their water containers after the early morning prayer, and he would dip his hand into every container that was brought, even when it was a cold morning. They were seeking blessings from that."[313]

Al-Manāhil, p. 226.

313   Reported by Muslim (2324).

وَعَنْ أَنَسٍ: «كَانَ خَدَمُ المَدِينَةِ يَأْتُونَ رَسُولَ اللهِ ﷺ إِذَا صَلَّى الغَدَاةَ بِآنِيَتِهِمْ فِيهَا المَاءُ، فَمَا يُؤْتَى بِآنِيَةٍ إِلَّا غَمَسَ يَدَهُ فِيهَا، وَرُبَّمَا كَانَ ذَلِكَ فِي الغَدَاةِ البَارِدَةِ»٣٠٤، يُرِيدُونَ بِهِ التَّبَرُّكَ.

صَلَّى اللهُ عَلَيْهِ وَسَلَّمَ كُلَّمَا ذَكَرَهُ الذَّاكِرُونَ وَغَفَلَ عَنْ ذِكْرِهِ الغَافِلُونَ.

----

٣٠٤ أَخْرَجَهُ مُسْلِمٌ (٢٣٢٤).

HIS COMPASSION AND MERCY

The Prophet ﷺ was compassionate, merciful and caring towards all creation. As Allah Exalted said: "He is concerned by your suffering, anxious for your well-being, and gracious and merciful to the believers."[314] And: "We have sent you [O Prophet] only as a mercy for the whole world."[315]

Some commentators noted that Allah Exalted highlights the virtue of the Prophet ﷺ by blessing him with two of His Names, when He describes him as: "gracious and merciful to the believers."[316] Abū Bakr ibn Fūrak made a similar observation.

I read the following hadith to the great jurist Abū Muhammad ('Abdullāh ibn Muhammad al-Khushanī), who narrated from the imam of the Ḥaramayn[317] Abū 'Alī al-Ṭabarī, from 'Abd al-Ghāfir al-Fārisī, from Abū Aḥmad al-Julūdī, from Ibrāhīm ibn Sufyān, from Muslim ibn al-Ḥajjāj, from Abū al-Ṭāhir, from Ibn Wahb, from Yūnus, from Ibn Shihāb, who said: "The Messenger ﷺ gave Ṣafwān ibn Umayyah one hundred camels, then another hundred, and then another." Ibn Shihāb also narrated from Sa'īd ibn al-Musayyib that Ṣafwān said: "I swear by Allah, he kept giving and giving until he changed from the person I hated the most to the person I loved the most."[318]

In another narration, a Bedouin man came to the Prophet ﷺ

---

314 *al-Tawbah*, 128.

315 *al-Anbiyā'*, 107.

316 *al-Tawbah*, 128.

317 The "two sacred sites"; i.e., Makkah and Madinah.

318 Reported here from the chain of Muslim (2313/59). Also cited in footnote 248.

فَصْل

وَأَمَّا الشَّفَقَةُ وَالرَّأْفَةُ وَالرَّحْمَةُ لِجَمِيعِ الخَلْقِ: فَقَدْ قَالَ اللهُ تَعَالَى فِيهِ: ﴿عَزِيزٌ عَلَيْهِ مَا عَنِتُّمْ حَرِيصٌ عَلَيْكُمْ بِالْمُؤْمِنِينَ رَءُوفٌ رَّحِيمٌ﴾ [التوبة: ١٢٨]. وَقَالَ سُبْحَانَهُ: ﴿وَمَا أَرْسَلْنَاكَ إِلَّا رَحْمَةً لِّلْعَالَمِينَ﴾ [الأنبياء: ١٠٧].

قَالَ بَعْضُهُمْ: مِنْ فَضْلِهِ عَلَيْهِ الصَّلَاةُ وَالسَّلَامُ أَنَّ اللهَ تَبَارَكَ وَتَعَالَى أَعْطَاهُ اسْمَيْنِ مِنْ أَسْمَائِهِ، فَقَالَ: ﴿بِالْمُؤْمِنِينَ رَءُوفٌ رَّحِيمٌ﴾ [التوبة: ١٢٨].

وَحَكَى نَحْوَهُ الإِمَامُ أَبُو بَكْرِ بْنُ فُورَكَ.

حَدَّثَنَا الفَقِيهُ أَبُو مُحَمَّدٍ عَبْدُ اللهِ بْنُ مُحَمَّدٍ الخُشَنِيُّ بِقِرَاءَتِي عَلَيْهِ، حَدَّثَنَا إِمَامُ الحَرَمَيْنِ أَبُو عَلِيٍّ الطَّبَرِيُّ، حَدَّثَنَا عَبْدُ الغَافِرِ الفَارِسِيُّ، حَدَّثَنَا أَبُو أَحْمَدَ الجُلُودِيُّ، حَدَّثَنَا إِبْرَاهِيمُ بْنُ سُفْيَانَ، حَدَّثَنَا مُسْلِمُ بْنُ الحَجَّاجِ، حَدَّثَنَا أَبُو الطَّاهِرِ، أَخْبَرَنَا ابْنُ وَهْبٍ[٣٠٥]، أَخْبَرَنَا يُونُسُ، عَنِ ابْنِ شِهَابٍ، قَالَ: غَزَا رَسُولُ اللهِ ﷺ غَزْوَةً، وَذَكَرَ حُنَيْنًا، قَالَ: فَأَعْطَى رَسُولُ اللهِ ﷺ صَفْوَانَ بْنَ أُمَيَّةَ مِائَةً مِنَ النَّعَمِ، ثُمَّ مِائَةً، ثُمَّ مِائَةً.

قَالَ ابْنُ شِهَابٍ: حَدَّثَنَا سَعِيدُ بْنُ المُسَيِّبِ أَنَّ صَفْوَانَ قَالَ: وَاللهِ لَقَدْ أَعْطَانِي مَا أَعْطَانِي وَإِنَّهُ لَأَبْغَضُ الخَلْقِ إِلَيَّ، فَمَا زَالَ يُعْطِينِي حَتَّى إِنَّهُ لَأَحَبُّ

---

[٣٠٥] قَوْلُهُ: «أَخْبَرَنَا ابْنُ وَهْبٍ»، سَاقِطٌ مِنَ المَطْبُوعِ.

and asked for something. The Prophet ﷺ gave it to him and asked: "Have I been good to you?" But the Bedouin man replied: "No, and neither have you been great." The Muslims became angry and went to surround the man, but the Prophet ﷺ gestured for them to restrain themselves. Then he got up and entered his house. He sent for the man [to enter] and added to what he had given him. He asked again: "Have I been good to you?" And this time, the Bedouin man replied: "Yes, and may Allah reward you well in your family and tribe."

The Prophet ﷺ said to him: "You said what you said, and my Companions feel some way about it. If you like, say to them what you have just said to me, so that they can let go of any ill-feeling towards you." The man agreed. So, when he arrived the next day (or evening), the Prophet ﷺ said: "This Bedouin said what he said, so we gave him more. But now he claims to be content. Is that the case?" The Bedouin man replied: "Yes, and may Allah reward you well in your family and tribe."

The Prophet ﷺ said: "The example of me and this man is like a person whose camel goes on the loose. The people try to catch the camel but they just make her run away even more. So, the owner calls to them: 'Leave me with my camel! I am more friendly to her and I know her better than you.' Then, he comes in front of her and takes some earth from the ground. He keeps pushing her back until she comes and kneels. Finally, he fastens the saddlebags and mounts the camel. If I had left you when this man said what he said, you would have killed him, and entered the Hellfire [as a result]."[319]

---

319 Suyūṭī said in *Al-Manāhil*, p. 228: "[Reported by] Bazzār (2476) and Abū al-Shaykh with a weak chain from Abū Hurayrah." Haythamī said in *Majmaʿ al-Zawāʾid* (9/16): "The chain contains Ibrāhīm ibn al-Ḥakam ibn Abān, and we do not take from him."

الْخَلْقِ إِلَيَّ[٣٠٦].

وَرُوِيَ أَنَّ أَعْرَابِيًّا جَاءَهُ يَطْلُبُ مِنْهُ شَيْئًا، فَأَعْطَاهُ، ثُمَّ قَالَ: «آحْسَنْتُ إِلَيْكَ؟» قَالَ الْأَعْرَابِيُّ: لَا! وَلَا أَجْمَلْتَ. فَغَضِبَ الْمُسْلِمُونَ وَقَامُوا إِلَيْهِ، فَأَشَارَ إِلَيْهِمْ: أَنْ كُفُّوا، ثُمَّ قَامَ، وَدَخَلَ مَنْزِلَهُ، وَأَرْسَلَ إِلَيْهِ، وَزَادَهُ شَيْئًا، ثُمَّ قَالَ: «هَلْ أَحْسَنْتُ إِلَيْكَ؟» قَالَ: نَعَمْ، فَجَزَاكَ اللهُ مِنْ أَهْلٍ وَعَشِيرَةٍ خَيْرًا. فَقَالَ لَهُ النَّبِيُّ ﷺ: «إِنَّكَ قُلْتَ مَا قُلْتَ، وَفِي أَنْفُسِ أَصْحَابِي مِنْ ذَلِكَ شَيْءٌ، فَإِنْ أَحْبَبْتَ فَقُلْ بَيْنَ أَيْدِيهِمْ مَا قُلْتَ بَيْنَ يَدَيَّ حَتَّى يَذْهَبَ مَا فِي صُدُورِهِمْ عَلَيْكَ». قَالَ: نَعَمْ. فَلَمَّا كَانَ الْغَدُ أَوِ الْعَشِيُّ جَاءَ، فَقَالَ ﷺ: «إِنَّ هَذَا الْأَعْرَابِيَّ قَالَ مَا قَالَ، فَزِدْنَاهُ فَزَعَمَ أَنَّهُ رَضِيَ، أَكَذَلِكَ؟» قَالَ: نَعَمْ، فَجَزَاكَ اللهُ مِنْ أَهْلٍ وَعَشِيرَةٍ خَيْرًا.

فَقَالَ ﷺ: «مَثَلِي وَمَثَلُ هَذَا مَثَلُ رَجُلٍ لَهُ نَاقَةٌ شَرَدَتْ عَلَيْهِ، فَاتَّبَعَهَا النَّاسُ فَلَمْ يَزِيدُوهَا إِلَّا نُفُورًا، فَنَادَاهُمْ صَاحِبُهَا: خَلُّوا بَيْنِي وَبَيْنَ نَاقَتِي، فَإِنِّي أَرْفَقُ بِهَا مِنْكُمْ وَأَعْلَمُ، فَتَوَجَّهَ لَهَا بَيْنَ يَدَيْهَا، فَأَخَذَ لَهَا مِنْ قُمَامِ الْأَرْضِ، فَرَدَّهَا حَتَّى جَاءَتْ وَاسْتَنَاخَتْ، وَشَدَّ عَلَيْهَا رَحْلَهَا، وَاسْتَوَى عَلَيْهَا، وَإِنِّي لَوْ تَرَكْتُكُمْ حَيْثُ قَالَ الرَّجُلُ مَا قَالَ فَقَتَلْتُمُوهُ دَخَلَ النَّارَ»[٣٠٧].

وَرُوِيَ عَنْهُ أَنَّهُ ﷺ قَالَ: «لَا يُبَلِّغْنِي أَحَدٌ مِنْكُمْ عَنْ أَحَدٍ مِنْ أَصْحَابِي

---

[٣٠٦] أَسْنَدَهُ الْمُصَنِّفُ مِنْ طَرِيقِ مُسْلِمٍ (٥٩/٢٣١٣).

[٣٠٧] قَالَ السُّيُوطِيُّ فِي الْمَنَاهِلِ (٢٢٨): «الْبَزَّارُ (٢٤٧٦)، وَأَبُو الشَّيْخِ بِسَنَدٍ ضَعِيفٍ عَنْ أَبِي هُرَيْرَةَ». قَالَ الْهَيْثَمِيُّ فِي الْمَجْمَعِ ٩/١٦: «فِيهِ إِبْرَاهِيمُ بْنُ الْحَكَمِ بْنِ أَبَانَ وَهُوَ مَتْرُوكٌ». (شَرَدَتْ عَلَيْهِ): نَفَرَتْ وَاسْتَعْصَتْ. (قُمَام): جَمْعُ قُمَامَةٍ وَهِيَ الْكُنَاسَةُ تُجْمَعُ مِنَ الْبُيُوتِ وَالطُّرُقِ (الْمُعْجَمُ الْوَسِيطُ).

The Prophet ﷺ once said: "None of you should convey anything to me about my Companions, for I love to come out to you whilst my heart is clean."[320] He was always trying to make things easy for his nation, and that was a sign of his compassion towards them. For example, he said: "If it was not for making things difficult for my nation, I would have ordered them to use the *miswāk* (toothbrush) with every *wuḍū*."[321] Other examples of the Messenger of Allah ﷺ lightening affairs for his nation include the story of the supererogatory night prayer,[322] the prohibition of fasting continuously,[323] his regret at entering the Kaʿbah when he thought it would bring his community hardship and stress[324], his wish for his Lord to record any negative he said about a believer as a mercy for them,[325] and his shortening of the prayer whenever he heard an infant crying.[326] The Prophet ﷺ supplicated: "O Allah! For any person I have reviled or cursed, make that a source of mercy and

---

320   Reported by Abū Dāwūd (4860), Tirmidhī (3896, 3997), Abū Yaʿlā (5388), and others, from Ibn Masʿūd. Tirmidhī said: "This hadith is *gharīb* in this form."

321   Reported by Nasāʾī in *Al-Kubrā*, Aḥmad (2/250), ʿAbd al-Razzāq (2106), and others, from Abū Hurayrah. Authenticated by Ibn Khuzaymah (140). Also authenticated by Ḥākim (1/146) and Dhahabī concurred. Also reported by Bukhārī and Muslim, but with the phrase "with every prayer" instead of "with every *wuḍū*".

322   Reported by Bukhārī (1129) and Muslim (761) from ʿĀishah, who said: "The Messenger of Allah ﷺ prayed at the mosque one night and the people prayed with him. The next night, he prayed at the mosque again and this time more people joined him. On the third or fourth night the people had gathered, but the Messenger of Allah ﷺ did not come out to them. When morning came, he said: 'I saw what you were doing, and nothing stopped me from coming out to join you except my fear that [this night prayer] would become compulsory for you.'" The wording here is from Muslim.

323   i.e., for two days or more without breaking the fast in between. Reported by Bukhārī and Muslim from Ibn ʿUmar, Anas, ʿĀishah, and Abū Hurayrah. Also reported by Bukhārī from al-Khudrī. See *Jāmiʿ al-Uṣūl* (6/379-382).

324   Reported by Abū Dāwūd (2029), Tirmidhī (873), and Ibn Mājah (3064), from ʿĀishah. Tirmidhī said: "This hadith is *ḥasan ṣaḥīḥ*."

325   Reported by Bukhārī (6361) and Muslim (2601) from Abū Hurayrah, and by Muslim (2602) from Jābir, (2600) from ʿĀishah, and (2603) from Anas.

326   Reported by Bukhārī (709) and Muslim (470) from Anas, and by Bukhārī (707) from Abū Qatādah.

شَيْئًا، فَإِنِّي أُحِبُّ أَنْ أَخْرُجَ إِلَيْكُمْ، وَأَنَا سَلِيمُ الصَّدْرِ»[308].

وَمِنْ شَفَقَتِهِ عَلَى أُمَّتِهِ ﷺ: تَخْفِيفُهُ عَنْهُمْ وَتَسْهِيلُهُ عَلَيْهِمْ، وَكَرَاهَتُهُ أَشْيَاءَ مَخَافَةَ أَنْ تُفْرَضَ عَلَيْهِمْ:

❂ كَقَوْلِهِ ﷺ: «لَوْلَا أَنْ أَشُقَّ عَلَى أُمَّتِي لَأَمَرْتُهُمْ بِالسِّوَاكِ مَعَ كُلِّ وُضُوءٍ عَلَيْهِمْ»[309].

❂ وَخَبَرِ صَلَاةِ اللَّيْلِ[310].

❂ وَنَهْيِهِمْ عَنِ الوِصَالِ[311].

❂ وَكَرَاهَتِهِ دُخُولَ الكَعْبَةِ لِئَلَّا يُعَنِّتَ أُمَّتَهُ[312].

❂ وَرَغْبَتِهِ لِرَبِّهِ أَنْ يَجْعَلَ سَبَّهُ وَلَعْنَهُ لَهُمْ رَحْمَةً بِهِمْ[313].

---

308 أَخْرَجَهُ أَبُو دَاوُدَ (٤٨٦٠)، وَالتِّرْمِذِيُّ (٣٨٩٦، ٣٩٩٧)، وَأَبُو يَعْلَى (٥٣٨٨) وَغَيْرُهُ مِنْ حَدِيثِ ابْنِ مَسْعُودٍ. وَقَالَ التِّرْمِذِيُّ: «هَذَا حَدِيثٌ غَرِيبٌ مِنْ هَذِهِ الوَجْهِ».

309 أَخْرَجَهُ النَّسَائِيُّ فِي الكُبْرَى، وَأَحْمَدُ (٢٥٠/٢)، وَعَبْدُ الرَّزَّاقِ (٢١٠٦)، وَغَيْرُهُ مِنْ حَدِيثِ أَبِي هُرَيْرَةَ، وَصَحَّحَهُ ابْنُ خُزَيْمَةَ (١٤٠)، وَالحَاكِمُ (١٤٦/١)، وَوَافَقَهُ الذَّهَبِيُّ، وَعَلَّقَهُ البُخَارِيُّ بِصِيغَةِ الجَزْمِ (١٥٨/٤ فتح). وَهُوَ فِي الصَّحِيحَيْنِ بِلَفْظِ «مَعَ كُلِّ صَلَاةٍ» بَدَلَ «مَعَ كُلِّ وُضُوءٍ».

310 أَخْرَجَ البُخَارِيُّ (١١٢٩)، وَمُسْلِمٌ (٧٦١) عَنْ عَائِشَةَ: أَنَّ رَسُولَ اللهِ ﷺ صَلَّى فِي المَسْجِدِ ذَاتَ لَيْلَةٍ، فَصَلَّى بِصَلَاتِهِ نَاسٌ، ثُمَّ صَلَّى مِنَ القَابِلَةِ. فَكَثُرَ النَّاسُ. ثُمَّ اجْتَمَعُوا مِنَ اللَّيْلَةِ الثَّالِثَةِ أَوِ الرَّابِعَةِ. فَلَمْ يَخْرُجْ إِلَيْهِمْ رَسُولُ اللهِ ﷺ. فَلَمَّا أَصْبَحَ قَالَ: «قَدْ رَأَيْتُ الَّذِي صَنَعْتُمْ. فَلَمْ يَمْنَعْنِي مِنَ الخُرُوجِ إِلَيْكُمْ إِلَّا أَنِّي خَشِيتُ أَنْ تُفْرَضَ عَلَيْكُمْ». وَاللَّفْظُ لِمُسْلِمٍ.

311 نَهْيُهُ ﷺ عَنِ الوِصَالِ فِي الصَّوْمِ، رَوَاهُ الشَّيْخَانِ مِنْ حَدِيثِ ابْنِ عُمَرَ، وَأَنَسٍ، وَعَائِشَةَ، وَأَبِي هُرَيْرَةَ، وَرَوَاهُ البُخَارِيُّ مِنْ حَدِيثِ الخُدْرِيِّ: انْظُرْ جَامِعَ الأُصُولِ ٣٧٩-٣٨٢/٦. (الوِصَالُ): أَنْ يَصُومَ يَوْمَيْنِ أَوْ أَكْثَرَ بِدُونِ إِفْطَارٍ.

312 أَخْرَجَهُ أَبُو دَاوُدَ (٢٠٢٩)، وَالتِّرْمِذِيُّ (٨٧٣)، وَابْنُ مَاجَه (٣٠٦٤) مِنْ حَدِيثِ عَائِشَةَ. قَالَ التِّرْمِذِيُّ: «هَذَا حَدِيثٌ حَسَنٌ صَحِيحٌ». (يُعَنِّتَ): عَنَّتَهُ: شَدَّدَ عَلَيْهِ وَأَلْزَمَهُ مَا يَصْعُبُ عَلَيْهِ أَدَاؤُهُ (المُعْجَمُ الوَسِيطُ).

313 أَخْرَجَهُ البُخَارِيُّ (٦٣٦١)، وَمُسْلِمٌ (٢٦٠١) مِنْ حَدِيثِ أَبِي هُرَيْرَةَ، وَأَخْرَجَهُ مُسْلِمٌ (٢٦٠٢) مِنْ حَدِيثِ جَابِرٍ،

charity for them, and prayer and purification, and a means of coming closer to You on the Day of Judgement."[327]

When the Prophet ﷺ was rejected by his people, Jibrīl ﷺ came to him and said: "Certainly, Allah Exalted has heard what your people have said and how they rebuffed you. He has sent the Angel of the Mountains so that you can instruct him to do whatever you like with these people." The Angel of the Mountains called and greeted the Prophet ﷺ, and said to him: "Instruct me as you wish. If you like, I will bring these two mountains down on top of them." The Prophet ﷺ replied: "Rather, I hope that Allah will bring from their offspring those who worship Him alone and do not associate anything with Him."[328]

Ibn al-Munkadir related that Jibrīl ﷺ said to the Prophet ﷺ: "Allah Exalted has commanded the sky, the Earth, and the mountains to obey you." So, the Prophet ﷺ said: "Delay [any punishment] from my nation, for perhaps Allah will forgive them."[329]

'Ā'ishah ﷺ narrated: "Whenever the Messenger of Allah ﷺ had to choose between two things, he would choose the easier of the two."[330] And Ibn Mas'ūd ﷺ related: "The Messenger of Allah ﷺ would leave his reminders on certain days, fearing that we would become bored."[331] 'Ā'ishah also said that she was once riding a camel with challenging behaviour, so she started to get frustrated, and hesitated about what to do. The Messenger of Allah ﷺ said to her: "You have to be kind."[332]

---

327 Reported by Bukhārī (6361) and Muslim (2601) from Abū Hurayrah, and by Muslim (2602) from Jābir, (2600) from 'Ā'ishah, and (2603) from Anas.

328 Reported by Bukhārī (3231) and Muslim (1795) from 'Ā'ishah.

329 A *mursal* narration. Muhammad ibn al-Munkadir was a trustworthy narrator from the Followers.

330 Reported by Mālik (2/903), Bukhārī (3560), and Muslim (2327).

331 Reported by Bukhārī (68) and Muslim (2821).

332 Reported by Muslim (2594/79).

۞ وَأَنَّهُ كَانَ يَسْمَعُ بُكَاءَ الصَّبِيِّ فَيَتَجَوَّزُ فِي صَلَاتِهِ³¹⁴. وَمِنْ شَفَقَتِهِ ﷺ أَنْ دَعَا رَبَّهُ وَعَاهَدَهُ، فَقَالَ: «أَيُّمَا رَجُلٍ سَبَبْتُهُ - أَوْ لَعَنْتُهُ - فَاجْعَلْ ذَلِكَ لَهُ زَكَاةً، وَرَحْمَةً، وَصَلَاةً، وَطَهُورًا، وَقُرْبَةً تُقَرِّبُهُ بِهَا إِلَيْكَ يَوْمَ الْقِيَامَةِ». وَلَمَّا كَذَّبَهُ قَوْمُهُ أَتَاهُ جِبْرِيلُ عَلَيْهِمَا الصَّلَاةُ وَالسَّلَامُ فَقَالَ لَهُ: إِنَّ اللهَ قَدْ سَمِعَ قَوْلَ قَوْمِكَ لَكَ، وَمَا رَدُّوا عَلَيْكَ، وَقَدْ أَمَرَ مَلَكَ الْجِبَالِ لِتَأْمُرَهُ بِمَا شِئْتَ فِيهِمْ، فَنَادَاهُ مَلَكُ الْجِبَالِ، وَسَلَّمَ عَلَيْهِ، وَقَالَ: مُرْنِي بِمَا شِئْتَ، إِنْ شِئْتَ أَنْ أُطْبِقَ عَلَيْهِمُ الْأَخْشَبَيْنِ. قَالَ النَّبِيُّ ﷺ: «بَلْ أَرْجُو أَنْ يُخْرِجَ اللهُ تَعَالَى مِنْ أَصْلَابِهِمْ مَنْ يَعْبُدُ اللهَ وَحْدَهُ، لَا يُشْرِكُ بِهِ شَيْئًا»³¹⁵. وَرَوَى ابْنُ الْمُنْكَدِرِ أَنَّ جِبْرِيلَ قَالَ لِلنَّبِيِّ عَلَيْهِمَا الصَّلَاةُ وَالسَّلَامُ: إِنَّ اللهَ أَمَرَ السَّمَاءَ وَالْأَرْضَ وَالْجِبَالَ أَنْ تُطِيعَكَ. فَقَالَ: «أُؤَخِّرُ عَنْ أُمَّتِي لَعَلَّ اللهَ أَنْ يَتُوبَ عَلَيْهِمْ»³¹⁶. قَالَتْ عَائِشَةُ: مَا خُيِّرَ رَسُولُ اللهِ ﷺ بَيْنَ أَمْرَيْنِ إِلَّا اخْتَارَ أَيْسَرَهُمَا.

وَقَالَ ابْنُ مَسْعُودٍ: كَانَ رَسُولُ اللهِ ﷺ يَتَخَوَّلُنَا بِالْمَوْعِظَةِ مَخَافَةَ السَّآمَةِ عَلَيْنَا³¹⁷. وَعَنْ عَائِشَةَ رَضِيَ اللهُ عَنْهَا أَنَّهَا رَكِبَتْ بَعِيرًا، وَفِيهِ صُعُوبَةٌ، فَجَعَلَتْ تُرَدِّدُهُ، فَقَالَ رَسُولُ اللهِ ﷺ: «عَلَيْكِ بِالرِّفْقِ».

وَ(٢٦٠٠) مِنْ حَدِيثِ عَائِشَةَ، وَ(٢٦٠٣) مِنْ حَدِيثِ أَنَسٍ.

٣١٤ أَخْرَجَهُ الْبُخَارِيُّ (٧٠٩)، وَمُسْلِمٌ (٤٧٠) مِنْ حَدِيثِ أَنَسٍ، وَالْبُخَارِيُّ (٧٠٧) مِنْ حَدِيثِ أَبِي قَتَادَةَ. (فَأَتَجَوَّزُ) التَّجَوُّزُ فِي الْأَمْرِ: التَّخْفِيفُ وَالتَّسْهِيلُ.

٣١٥ أَخْرَجَهُ الْبُخَارِيُّ (٣٢٣١)، وَمُسْلِمٌ (١٧٩٥) مِنْ حَدِيثِ عَائِشَةَ. (الْأَخْشَبَانِ): جَبَلُ أَبِي قُبَيْسٍ، وَالَّذِي يُقَابِلُهُ، وَكَأَنَّهُ جَبَلُ قُعَيْقِعَانَ/ الْفَتْحُ.

٣١٦ حَدِيثٌ مُرْسَلٌ. ابْنُ الْمُنْكَدِرِ هُوَ مُحَمَّدٌ، تَابِعِيٌّ ثِقَةٌ. وَيَشْهَدُ لَهُ سَابِقُهُ.

٣١٧ أَخْرَجَهُ الْبُخَارِيُّ (٦٨)، وَمُسْلِمٌ (٢٨٢١). (يَتَخَوَّلُنَا): يَتَعَاهَدُنَا. (السَّآمَةُ): الضَّجَرُ وَالْمَلَلُ.

HIS LOYALTY, TRUSTWORTHINESS IN FULFILLING AGREEMENTS, AND EXCELLENT MANNER IN MAINTAINING THE TIES OF KINSHIP

I read the following hadith to Abū ʿĀmir Muhammad ibn Ismāʿīl, who narrated from Abū Bakr Muhammad ibn Muhammad, from Abū Isḥāq al-Ḥabbāl, from Abū Muhammad ibn al-Naḥḥās, from Ibn al-Aʿrābī, from Abū Dāwūd, from Muhammad ibn Yaḥyā, from Muhammad ibn Sinān, from Ibrāhīm ibn Ṭahmān, from Budayl, from ʿAbd al-Karīm ibn ʿAbdullāh ibn Shaqīq, from his father, from ʿAbdullāh ibn Abī al-Ḥamsāʾ, who said: "I bought something from the Prophet ﷺ before he was blessed with the mission of Prophethood, and I still owed him a portion [of the price]. I had promised to bring him what I owed at his place, but subsequently forgot. I remembered after three [days] and went, finding him still there. He said: 'Young man, you have caused me trouble! I have been waiting here for three [days]!'"[333]

Anas narrated: "Whenever the Prophet ﷺ was presented with a gift, he would say: 'Take this to so-and-so, for she was a friend of Khadījah and Khadījah loved her.'"[334]

ʿĀʾishah said: "I never felt jealous of any woman like I did of

---

333   Reported here from the chain of Abū Dāwūd (4996). ʿIrāqī said in *Takhrīj Aḥādīth al-Iḥyāʾ* (3/132): "It was related by Abū Dāwūd, and there was some difference of opinion regarding the chain of transmission." Shaykh ʿAbd al-Qādir al-Arnāʾūṭ said in his notes to *Jāmiʿ al-Uṣūl* (11/642): "The chain contains weakness and confusion."

334   Reported by Bukhārī in *Al-Adab al-Mufrad* (232), Bazzār (1904), and others. Authenticated by Ibn Ḥibbān (7007). Also authenticated by Ḥākim (4/175) and Dhahabī concurred.

فَصْل

وَأَمَّا خُلُقُهُ ﷺ فِي الْوَفَاءِ، وَحُسْنِ الْعَهْدِ، وَصِلَةِ الرَّحِمِ

فَحَدَّثَنَا الْقَاضِي أَبُو عَامِرٍ مُحَمَّدُ بْنُ إِسْمَاعِيلَ بِقِرَاءَتِي عَلَيْهِ، قَالَ: حَدَّثَنَا أَبُو بَكْرٍ مُحَمَّدُ بْنُ مُحَمَّدٍ، حَدَّثَنَا أَبُو إِسْحَاقَ الْحَبَّالُ، حَدَّثَنَا أَبُو مُحَمَّدٍ ابْنُ النَّحَّاسِ، حَدَّثَنَا ابْنُ الْأَعْرَابِيِّ، حَدَّثَنَا أَبُو دَاوُدَ، حَدَّثَنَا مُحَمَّدُ بْنُ يَحْيَى، حَدَّثَنَا مُحَمَّدُ بْنُ سِنَانٍ، حَدَّثَنَا إِبْرَاهِيمُ بْنُ طَهْمَانَ، عَنْ بُدَيْلٍ، عَنْ عَبْدِ الْكَرِيمِ بْنِ عَبْدِ اللهِ بْنِ شَقِيقٍ، عَنْ أَبِيهِ، عَنْ عَبْدِ اللهِ بْنِ أَبِي الْحَمْسَاءِ: بَايَعْتُ النَّبِيَّ ﷺ بِبَيْعٍ قَبْلَ أَنْ يُبْعَثَ، وَبَقِيَتْ لَهُ بَقِيَّةٌ، فَوَعَدْتُهُ أَنْ آتِيَهُ بِهَا فِي مَكَانِهِ، فَنَسِيتُ، ثُمَّ ذَكَرْتُ بَعْدَ ثَلَاثٍ، فَجِئْتُ فَإِذَا هُوَ فِي مَكَانِهِ، فَقَالَ: «يَا فَتَى، لَقَدْ شَقَقْتَ عَلَيَّ، أَنَا هَاهُنَا مُنْذُ ثَلَاثٍ أَنْتَظِرُكَ»[318].

وَعَنْ أَنَسٍ: كَانَ النَّبِيُّ ﷺ إِذَا أُتِيَ بِهَدِيَّةٍ قَالَ: «اذْهَبُوا بِهَا إِلَى بَيْتِ فُلَانَةَ، فَإِنَّهَا كَانَتْ صَدِيقَةً لِخَدِيجَةَ، إِنَّهَا كَانَتْ تُحِبُّ خَدِيجَةَ»[319].

وَعَنْ عَائِشَةَ رَضِيَ اللهُ عَنْهَا قَالَتْ: مَا غِرْتُ عَلَى امْرَأَةٍ مَا غِرْتُ عَلَى خَدِيجَةَ؛ لِمَا

---

318 أَسْنَدَهُ الْمُصَنِّفُ مِنْ طَرِيقِ أَبِي دَاوُدَ (4996). وَقَالَ الْعِرَاقِيُّ فِي تَخْرِيجِ أَحَادِيثِ الْإِحْيَاءِ (132/3): «رَوَاهُ أَبُو دَاوُدَ، وَاخْتُلِفَ فِي إِسْنَادِهِ، وَقَالَ ابْنُ مَهْدِيٍّ: مَا أَظُنُّ إِبْرَاهِيمَ بْنَ طَهْمَانَ إِلَّا أَخْطَأَ فِيهِ». وَقَالَ الشَّيْخُ عَبْدُ الْقَادِرِ الْأَرْنَاؤُوطُ فِي هَامِشِ جَامِعِ الْأُصُولِ 642/11: فِي إِسْنَادِهِ ضُعْفٌ وَاضْطِرَابٌ.

319 أَخْرَجَهُ الْبُخَارِيُّ فِي الْأَدَبِ الْمُفْرَدِ (232)، وَالْبَزَّارُ (1904) وَغَيْرُهُ. وَصَحَّحَهُ ابْنُ حِبَّانَ (7007) الْإِحْسَانُ، وَالْحَاكِمُ 175/4 وَوَافَقَهُ الذَّهَبِيُّ.

Khadījah, for how often I heard [the Prophet ﷺ] mention her. When he slaughtered a sheep, he would gift [its meat] to her friends."[335] On one occasion, when he heard Khadījah's sister seeking permission to enter, the Prophet ﷺ was reminded of her and felt relaxed.[336]

A woman came to the Prophet ﷺ and he greeted her cheerfully, asking about her affairs with kindness and consideration. When she left, the Prophet ﷺ said: "She used to come when Khadījah was here, and maintaining ties is a part of *īmān* (faith)."[337]

Some scholars mentioned the Prophet ﷺ would ensure he maintained ties of kinship, but without preferring those relations to people who were better than them. He once said: "The family of so-and-so are not my friends or protectors, but they are my kin, so I will fulfil the rights of their kinship."[338]

The Prophet ﷺ used to pray with his granddaughter Umāmah (the daughter of Zaynab ﷺ) on his shoulders. When he went into *sujūd* (prostration) he would put her down, and then when he stood up he would pick her up again.[339]

Abū Qatādah related: "A delegation arrived from al-Najāshī and the Prophet ﷺ stood up to serve them. His Companions said: 'Allow us [to serve them instead].' But the Prophet ﷺ replied: 'They looked after my Companions, and I wish to do the same for

---

335   Reported by Bukhārī (6004) and Muslim (2435/75).

336   Reported by Bukhārī (3821) and Muslim (2437) from 'Ā'ishah, who said: "Once, Hālah bint Khuwaylid, the sister of Khadījah, sought permission from the Messenger of Allah ﷺ [to enter]. It made him remember the way Khadījah used to seek permission, and that relaxed him." This was the wording reported by Muslim. The wording reported by Bukhārī said: "... and that surprised him." Ibn al-Athīr said in *Jāmi' al-Uṣūl* (9/124): "It was as if his heart flew when he heard the sound of her voice."

337   Reported by al-Qudā'ī in *Musnad al-Shihāb* (971), Ibn 'Abd al-Barr in *Al-Istī'āb* (4/269), and others, from 'Ā'ishah. Authenticated by Ḥākim (1/15-16) and Dhahabī concurred.

338   Reported by Bukhārī (5990), and Muslim (215) in a condensed form, from 'Amr ibn al-'Āṣ.

339   Reported by Bukhārī (516) and Muslim (543) from Abū Qatādah.

كُنْتُ أَسْمَعُهُ يَذْكُرُهَا، وَإِنْ كَانَ لَيَذْبَحُ الشَّاةَ فَيُهْدِيهَا إِلَى خَلَائِلِهَا³²⁰.

وَاسْتَأْذَنَتْ عَلَيْهِ أُخْتُهَا فَارْتَاحَ إِلَيْهَا³²¹.

وَدَخَلَتْ عَلَيْهِ امْرَأَةٌ فَهَشَّ لَهَا وَأَحْسَنَ السُّؤَالَ عَنْهَا، فَلَمَّا خَرَجَتْ قَالَ: «إِنَّهَا كَانَتْ تَأْتِينَا أَيَّامَ خَدِيجَةَ، وَإِنَّ حُسْنَ العَهْدِ مِنَ الإِيمَانِ»³²².

وَوَصَفَهُ بَعْضُهُمْ فَقَالَ: كَانَ يَصِلُ ذَوِي رَحِمِهِ، مِنْ غَيْرِ أَنْ يُؤْثِرَهُمْ عَلَى مَنْ هُوَ أَفْضَلُ مِنْهُمْ.

وَقَالَ ﷺ: «إِنَّ آلَ أَبِي فُلَانٍ لَيْسُوا لِي بِأَوْلِيَاءَ، غَيْرَ أَنَّ لَهُمْ رَحِمًا سَأَبُلُّهَا بِبَلَالِهَا»³²³.

وَقَدْ صَلَّى عَلَيْهِ الصَّلَاةُ وَالسَّلَامُ بِأُمَامَةَ ابْنَةِ بِنْتِهِ زَيْنَبَ يَحْمِلُهَا عَلَى عَاتِقِهِ، فَإِذَا سَجَدَ وَضَعَهَا، وَإِذَا قَامَ حَمَلَهَا³²⁴.

وَعَنْ أَبِي قَتَادَةَ: وَفَدَ وَفْدٌ لِلنَّجَاشِيِّ فَقَامَ النَّبِيُّ ﷺ يَخْدُمُهُمْ، فَقَالَ لَهُ أَصْحَابُهُ: نَكْفِيكَ. فَقَالَ: «إِنَّهُمْ كَانُوا لِأَصْحَابِنَا مُكْرِمِينَ، وَإِنِّي أُحِبُّ أَنْ أُكَافِئَهُمْ»³²⁵.

---

³²⁰ أَخْرَجَهُ البُخَارِيُّ (٦٠٠٤)، وَمُسْلِمٌ (٧٥/٢٤٣٥). (خَلَائِلُهَا) صَدِيقَاتُهَا.

³²¹ أَخْرَجَ البُخَارِيُّ (٣٨٢١)، وَمُسْلِمٌ (٢٤٣٧)، عَنْ عَائِشَةَ قَالَتْ: اسْتَأْذَنَتْ هَالَةُ بِنْتُ خُوَيْلِدٍ أُخْتُ خَدِيجَةَ عَلَى رَسُولِ اللهِ ﷺ، فَعَرَفَ اسْتِئْذَانَ خَدِيجَةَ، فَارْتَاحَ لِذَلِكَ... وَالنَّصُّ لِمُسْلِمٍ. وَفِي رِوَايَةِ البُخَارِيِّ: «فَارْتَاعَ لِذَلِكَ». قَالَ ابْنُ الأَثِيرِ فِي جَامِعِ الأُصُولِ ١٢٤/٩: كَأَنَّهُ طَارَ لُبُّهُ لَمَّا سَمِعَ صَوْتَ أُخْتِ خَدِيجَةَ.

³²² أَخْرَجَهُ القُضَاعِيُّ فِي مُسْنَدِ الشِّهَابِ (٩٧١)، وَابْنُ عَبْدِ البَرِّ فِي الاسْتِيعَابِ ٢٦٩/٤ وَغَيْرُهُ، مِنْ حَدِيثِ عَائِشَةَ، وَصَحَّحَهُ الحَاكِمُ ١٦-١٥/١ وَوَافَقَهُ الذَّهَبِيُّ. (هَشَّ لَهَا): أَيْ فَرِحَ بِهَا وَارْتَاحَ لَهَا.

³²³ أَخْرَجَهُ البُخَارِيُّ (٥٩٩٠)، وَمُسْلِمٌ مُخْتَصَرًا (٢١٥) مِنْ حَدِيثِ عَمْرِو بْنِ العَاصِ. (أَبُلُّهَا بِبَلَالِهَا): أَصِلُهَا بِصِلَتِهَا.

³²⁴ أَخْرَجَهُ البُخَارِيُّ (٥١٦)، وَمُسْلِمٌ (٥٤٣) مِنْ حَدِيثِ أَبِي قَتَادَةَ.

³²⁵ أَخْرَجَهُ البَيْهَقِيُّ فِي دَلَائِلِ النُّبُوَّةِ/ المَنَاهِلِ (٢٤٥).

them.'"[340]

One of the prisoners of war from the Hawāzin tribe was a lady named al-Shaymā', the sister of the Prophet ﷺ through breastfeeding,[341] and she made herself known to him. He spread out a mat and said to her: "If you like, you can stay with me and we will treat you with honour and love. Or, if you prefer, I will supply you with provisions and you can return to your people." She chose to return to her people.[342]

Abū al-Ṭufayl[343] said: "When I was a young boy, I saw a woman approaching the Prophet ﷺ. When she got close to him, he spread out a mat for her and she sat down. I asked the people who she was and they told me: 'His mother through breastfeeding.'"[344]

'Umar ibn al-Sā'ib related that the Prophet ﷺ was sitting one day when his father through breastfeeding[345] came to him, so the Prophet ﷺ spread out part of his cloak and he sat. Then, his mother through breastfeeding arrived, so he spread the other side of his cloak and she sat. Finally, his brother through breastfeeding[346] arrived, so the Prophet ﷺ stood and let him sit between the two of them.[347] He used to send clothes and other gifts to his wet-nurse Thuwaybah, a servant of Abū Lahab. When she died, the Messen-

---

340 Reported by Bayhaqī in *Al-Dalā'il*. See *Al-Manāhil*, p. 245.

341 i.e., they had the same wet-nurse.

342 Reported by Ibn Isḥāq and Bayhaqī from Qatādah. See *Al-Manāhil*, p. 246.

343 ʿĀmir ibn Wāthilah. He was born in 1 AH, and he saw the Prophet ﷺ. He died in 110 AH and was the last Companion to pass away.

344 Reported by Abū Dāwūd (5144) without commenting on its authenticity, and Abū Yaʿlā (900). Haythamī said in *Majmaʿ al-Zawā'id* (10/259): "It was related by Ṭabarānī and the narrators are *ṣaḥīḥ*." Suyūṭī graded the chain of Abū Dāwūd as *ḥasan* in *Al-Manāhil*, p. 247. Ibn Kathīr said in *Al-Bidāyah wa al-Nihāyah* (4/317): "This hadith is *gharīb*."

345 i.e., the husband of his wet-nurse.

346 i.e., the son of his wet-nurse.

347 Reported by Abū Dāwūd (5145) and the narrators are trustworthy, although the hadith is *mursal*. Ibn Kathīr said in *Al-Bidāyah wa al-Nihāyah* (4/317): "Allah knows best about its authenticity."

وَلَمَّا جِيءَ بِأُخْتِهِ مِنَ الرَّضَاعَةِ الشَّيْمَاءِ فِي سَبَايَا هَوَازِنَ، وَتَعَرَّفَتْ لَهُ، بَسَطَ لَهَا رِدَاءَهُ، وَقَالَ لَهَا: «إِنْ أَحْبَبْتِ أَقَمْتِ عِنْدِي مُكْرَمَةً مُحَبَّةً[٣٢٦]، أَوْ مَتَّعْتُكِ وَرَجَعْتِ إِلَى قَوْمِكِ»، فَاخْتَارَتْ قَوْمَهَا فَمَتَّعَهَا[٣٢٧].

وَقَالَ أَبُو الطُّفَيْلِ[٣٢٨]: رَأَيْتُ النَّبِيَّ ﷺ - وَأَنَا غُلَامٌ - إِذْ أَقْبَلَتِ امْرَأَةٌ حَتَّى دَنَتْ مِنْهُ، فَبَسَطَ لَهَا رِدَاءَهُ، فَجَلَسَتْ عَلَيْهِ، فَقُلْتُ: مَنْ هَذِهِ؟ قَالُوا: أُمُّهُ الَّتِي أَرْضَعَتْهُ[٣٢٩].

وَعَنْ عُمَرَ بْنِ السَّائِبِ أَنَّ رَسُولَ اللهِ ﷺ كَانَ جَالِسًا يَوْمًا، فَأَقْبَلَ أَبُوهُ مِنَ الرَّضَاعَةِ، فَوَضَعَ لَهُ بَعْضَ ثَوْبِهِ فَقَعَدَ عَلَيْهِ، ثُمَّ أَقْبَلَتْ أُمُّهُ فَوَضَعَ لَهَا شِقَّ ثَوْبِهِ مِنَ الْجَانِبِ الْآخَرِ فَجَلَسَتْ عَلَيْهِ، ثُمَّ أَقْبَلَ أَخُوهُ مِنَ الرَّضَاعَةِ، فَقَامَ رَسُولُ اللهِ ﷺ فَأَجْلَسَهُ بَيْنَ يَدَيْهِ[٣٣٠].

وَكَانَ يَبْعَثُ إِلَى ثُوَيْبَةَ - مَوْلَاةِ أَبِي لَهَبٍ - مُرْضِعَتِهِ بِصِلَةٍ وَكِسْوَةٍ، فَلَمَّا مَاتَتْ سَأَلَ: «مَنْ بَقِيَ مِنْ قَرَابَتِهَا؟» فَقِيلَ: لَا أَحَدٌ[٣٣١].

---

٣٢٦ عَلَى هَامِشِ الْأَصْلِ: «مُحَبَّةً».

٣٢٧ أَخْرَجَهُ ابْنُ إِسْحَاقَ وَالْبَيْهَقِيُّ عَنْ قَتَادَةَ/ الْمَنَاهِلُ (٢٤٦). (مَتَّعَهَا). أَعْطَاهَا شَيْئًا تَنْتَفِعُ بِهِ مِنْ مَالٍ وَنَحْوِهِ.

٣٢٨ أَبُو الطُّفَيْلِ هُوَ عَامِرُ بْنُ وَاثِلَةَ، وُلِدَ عَامَ أُحُدٍ، وَرَأَى النَّبِيَّ ﷺ. مَاتَ سَنَةَ (١١٠) هـ وَهُوَ آخِرُ مَنْ مَاتَ مِنَ الصَّحَابَةِ/ التَّقْرِيبُ.

٣٢٩ أَخْرَجَهُ أَبُو دَاوُدَ (٥١٤٤) وَسَكَتَ عَنْهُ، وَأَبُو يَعْلَى (٩٠٠)، وَقَالَ الْهَيْثَمِيُّ فِي الْمَجْمَعِ ٢٥٩/١٠: «رَوَاهُ الطَّبَرَانِيُّ، وَرِجَالُهُ وُثِّقُوا». وَحَسَّنَ السُّيُوطِيُّ إِسْنَادَ أَبِي دَاوُدَ فِي الْمَنَاهِلِ (٢٤٧). وَقَالَ ابْنُ كَثِيرٍ فِي الْبِدَايَةِ وَالنِّهَايَةِ ٣١٧/٤: «هَذَا حَدِيثٌ غَرِيبٌ...».

٣٣٠ أَخْرَجَهُ أَبُو دَاوُدَ (٥١٤٥)، وَرِجَالُهُ ثِقَاتٌ لَكِنَّهُ مُرْسَلٌ. قَالَ ابْنُ كَثِيرٍ فِي الْبِدَايَةِ وَالنِّهَايَةِ ٣١٧/٤: «اللهُ أَعْلَمُ بِصِحَّتِهِ».

٣٣١ أَخْرَجَهُ ابْنُ سَعْدٍ؛ أَخْبَرَنَا الْوَاقِدِيُّ، عَنْ غَيْرِ وَاحِدٍ مِنْ أَهْلِ الْعِلْمِ، وَمِنْ طَرِيقٍ آخَرَ عَنِ الْقَاسِمِ بْنِ عَبَّاسٍ

ger of Allah ﷺ asked about her relatives, but he was told that none remained.[348]

To conclude, we will cite the famous narration of Khadījah ﴾. She recalled saying to the Prophet ﷺ: "Rejoice, for I swear by Allah that He will never humiliate you. You maintain the ties of kinship, support the vulnerable, provide for the deprived, look after guests, and ensure people's rights are fulfilled."[349]

---

348   Ibn Sa'd reported: "Al-Wāqidī narrated [this hadith] from several people of knowledge, and from a *mursal* chain from al-Qāsim ibn 'Abbās al-Lahabī." See *Al-Manāhil*, p. 249.

349   Reported by Bukhārī (3) and Muslim (160) from 'Ā'ishah.

وَفِي حَدِيثِ خَدِيجَةَ رَضِيَ اللهُ عَنْهَا أَنَّهَا قَالَتْ لَهُ ﷺ: أَبْشِرْ، فَوَاللهِ لَا يُخْزِيكَ اللهُ أَبَدًا، إِنَّكَ لَتَصِلُ الرَّحِمَ، وَتَحْمِلُ الْكَلَّ، وَتَكْسِبُ الْمَعْدُومَ، وَتَقْرِي الضَّيْفَ، وَتُعِينُ عَلَى نَوَائِبِ الْحَقِّ.٣٣٢

اللَّهِي مُرْسَلًا/ الْمَنَاهِلُ (٢٤٩).

٣٣٢ أَخْرَجَهُ الْبُخَارِيُّ (٣)، وَمُسْلِمٌ (١٦٠) مِنْ حَدِيثِ عَائِشَةَ. وَتَقَدَّمَ شَرْحُ غَرِيبِهِ.

HIS HUMILITY

Despite his noble status and lofty rank, the Prophet ﷺ was the humblest person, and the least arrogant. When he was given the choice of being a Prophet and a king or a Prophet and a slave, he chose the latter.[350] Upon that, the Angel Isrāfīl said to him: "On account of your humility to Him, Allah has given you the honour of being the leader of the Children of Adam on the Day of Judgement, the first for whom the Earth will split, and the first to intercede."

I read the following hadith to Abū al-Walīd ibn al-ʿAwwād al-Faqīh at his home in Cordoba in 507 AH, and he narrated from Abū ʿAlī al-Ḥāfiẓ, from Abū ʿUmar, from Ibn ʿAbd al-Muʾmin, from Ibn Dāsah, from Abū Dāwūd, from Abū Bakr ibn Abī Shaybah, from ʿAbdullāh ibn Numayr, from Misʿar, from Abū al-ʿAnbas, from Abū al-ʿAdabbas, from Abū Marzūq, from Abū Ghālib, from Abū Umāmah, who said: "The Prophet ﷺ came out to us leaning on a stick, so we stood for him. He said: 'Do not stand like the Persians do, elevating one another.'"[351]

The Prophet ﷺ also said: "I am a slave. I eat as a slave eats, and I sit as a slave sits."[352] He would ride a donkey and let someone

---

350 Reported by Bazzār (2462), Aḥmad (2/231), and Abū Yaʿlā (6105), from Abū Hurayrah. Authenticated by Ibn Ḥibbān in *Mawārid al-Ẓamʾān* (2137). Haythamī said in *Majmaʿ al-Zawāʾid* (9/18): "It was related by Aḥmad, Bazzār, and Abū Yaʿlā, and the narrators of the first two (i.e., Aḥmad and Bazzār) are *ṣaḥīḥ*." See *Musnad Abū Yaʿlā* (4920) and *Majmaʿ al-Zawāʾid* (9/18-20).

351 Reported here from the chain of Abū Dāwūd (5230). Also reported by Ibn Mājah (3836) with a weak chain. The same meaning was reported by Muslim (413) from Jābir ibn ʿAbdullāh.

352 Reported by Abū Yaʿlā (4920) and others from ʿĀʾishah. The chain was graded as *ḥasan*

فَصْل

وَأَمَّا تَوَاضُعُهُ ﷺ عَلَى عُلُوِّ مَنْصِبِهِ وَرِفْعَةِ رُتْبَتِهِ: فَكَانَ أَشَدَّ النَّاسِ تَوَاضُعًا، وَأَقَلَّهُمْ كِبْرًا.

وَحَسْبُكَ أَنَّهُ خُيِّرَ بَيْنَ أَنْ يَكُونَ نَبِيًّا مَلِكًا أَوْ نَبِيًّا عَبْدًا، فَاخْتَارَ أَنْ يَكُونَ نَبِيًّا عَبْدًا[333]، فَقَالَ لَهُ إِسْرَافِيلُ[334] عِنْدَ ذَلِكَ: فَإِنَّ اللَّهَ قَدْ أَعْطَاكَ بِمَا تَوَاضَعْتَ لَهُ أَنَّكَ سَيِّدُ وَلَدِ آدَمَ يَوْمَ الْقِيَامَةِ، وَأَوَّلُ مَنْ تَنْشَقُّ الْأَرْضُ عَنْهُ، وَأَوَّلُ شَافِعٍ.

حَدَّثَنَا أَبُو الْوَلِيدِ بْنُ الْعَوَّادِ الْفَقِيهُ رَحِمَهُ اللَّهُ بِقِرَاءَتِي عَلَيْهِ فِي مَنْزِلِهِ بِقُرْطُبَةَ سَنَةَ سَبْعٍ وَخَمْسِمِائَةٍ، قَالَ: حَدَّثَنَا أَبُو عَلِيٍّ الْحَافِظُ، حَدَّثَنَا أَبُو عُمَرَ، حَدَّثَنَا ابْنُ عَبْدِ الْمُؤْمِنِ، حَدَّثَنَا ابْنُ دَاسَةَ، حَدَّثَنَا أَبُو دَاوُدَ، حَدَّثَنَا أَبُو بَكْرِ بْنُ أَبِي شَيْبَةَ، حَدَّثَنَا عَبْدُ اللَّهِ بْنُ نُمَيْرٍ، عَنْ مِسْعَرٍ، عَنْ أَبِي الْعَنْبَسِ، عَنْ أَبِي الْعَدَبَّسِ، عَنْ أَبِي مَرْزُوقٍ، عَنْ أَبِي غَالِبٍ، عَنْ أَبِي أُمَامَةَ، قَالَ: خَرَجَ عَلَيْنَا رَسُولُ اللَّهِ ﷺ مُتَوَكِّئًا عَلَى عَصًا، فَقُمْنَا لَهُ، فَقَالَ: «لَا تَقُومُوا كَمَا تَقُومُ الْأَعَاجِمُ، يُعَظِّمُ بَعْضُهَا بَعْضًا»[335].

---

333 أَخْرَجَهُ الْبَزَّارُ (٢٤٦٢)، وَأَحْمَدُ (٢٣١/٢)، وَأَبُو يَعْلَى (٦١٠٥) مِنْ حَدِيثِ أَبِي هُرَيْرَةَ، وَصَحَّحَهُ ابْنُ حِبَّانَ (٢١٣٧) مَوَارِدُ الظَّمْآنِ، وَقَالَ الْهَيْثَمِيُّ فِي الْمَجْمَعِ ١٨/٩: «رَوَاهُ أَحْمَدُ وَالْبَزَّارُ، وَأَبُو يَعْلَى، وَرِجَالُ الْأَوَّلِينَ رِجَالُ الصَّحِيحِ». وَفِي الْبَابِ عَنْ عَدَدٍ مِنَ الصَّحَابَةِ. انْظُرْ مُسْنَدَ أَبِي يَعْلَى (٤٩٢٠)، وَمَجْمَعَ الزَّوَائِدِ ١٨/٩-٢٠.

334 أَثْبَتَ النَّاسِخُ فَوْقَ هَذِهِ الْكَلِمَةِ: «وَجِبْرِيلُ»، وَرَمَزَ بِعَلَامَةِ الصِّحَّةِ.

335 أَسْنَدَهُ الْمُصَنِّفُ مِنْ طَرِيقِ أَبِي دَاوُدَ (٥٢٣٠). وَأَخْرَجَهُ أَيْضًا ابْنُ مَاجَه (٣٨٣٦) وَإِسْنَادُهُ ضَعِيفٌ. وَرَوَى مُسْلِمٌ (٤١٣) مَعْنَاهُ عَنْ جَابِرِ بْنِ عَبْدِ اللَّهِ.

ride behind him, and visit the destitute and sit with the poor. The Prophet ﷺ accepted invitations from anyone, and would mix freely with his Companions.

As 'Umar narrated, the Prophet ﷺ said: "Do not praise me with falsehood as the Christians did with the Son of Maryam. Certainly, I am a slave, so say [about me]: 'The slave of Allah and His Messenger.'"[353]

Anas related: "There was a woman with some learning difficulties who came to the Prophet ﷺ saying that she had something to ask him about. He said: 'Sit in any path of the city you like, O mother of so-and-so, and I will help you.' She sat, and the Prophet of Allah ﷺ sat with her until she got what she needed."[354]

In another narration, Anas said: "The Prophet ﷺ used to ride on a donkey, and would accept the invitation of a servant. On the day [we overcame] the Banū Qurayẓah[355], he was riding a donkey with a saddle made from palm fibres and a rope of fibre as its muzzle."[356]

Anas narrated: "The Prophet ﷺ would be invited to a meal of barley bread and rancid butter (or oil), and he would accept the invitation."[357] He also narrated: "The Prophet ﷺ performed hajj upon a threadbare saddle, covered by a velvet cloth worth four dir-

---

by Haythamī in *Majma' al-Zawā'id* (9/19), and Suyūṭī in *Al-Manāhil*, p. 135, where he records chains from a number of Companions.

353   Reported by Bukhārī (3445).

354   Reported by Muslim (2326).

355   A Jewish tribe who betrayed the Muslims during the Battle of the Trench.

356   Reported by Tirmidhī in *Al-Sunan* (1017) and *Al-Shamā'il* (331), Ibn Mājah (4178), Baghawī (3673), Abū Ya'lā (4243), and others, from the chain of Muslim al-A'war from Anas. Tirmidhī said: "We do not know this narration except from [the chain of] Muslim from Anas. Muslim al-A'war, also known as Muslim ibn Kīsān, is a weak narrator."

357   Reported with this wording by Tirmidhī in *Al-Shamā'il* (332). Also reported by Bukhārī (2069) from Anas, who said that he went to the Prophet ﷺ with some barley bread and rancid butter.

وَقَالَ ﷺ: «إِنَّمَا أَنَا عَبْدٌ، آكُلُ كَمَا يَأْكُلُ العَبْدُ، وَأَجْلِسُ كَمَا يَجْلِسُ العَبْدُ».

وَكَانَ ﷺ يَرْكَبُ الحِمَارَ، وَيُرْدِفُ خَلْفَهُ، وَيَعُودُ المَسَاكِينَ، وَيُجَالِسُ الفُقَرَاءَ، وَيُجِيبُ دَعْوَةَ العَبْدِ، وَيَجْلِسُ بَيْنَ أَصْحَابِهِ مُخْتَلِطًا بِهِمْ حَيْثُمَا انْتَهَى بِهِ المَجْلِسُ جَلَسَ.

وَفِي حَدِيثِ عُمَرَ ﵁ عَنْهُ: «لَا تُطْرُونِي كَمَا أَطْرَتِ النَّصَارَى ابْنَ مَرْيَمَ، إِنَّمَا أَنَا عَبْدٌ، فَقُولُوا: عَبْدُ اللهِ وَرَسُولُهُ»[336].

وَعَنْ أَنَسٍ أَنَّ امْرَأَةً كَانَ فِي عَقْلِهَا شَيْءٌ جَاءَتْهُ فَقَالَتْ: إِنَّ لِي إِلَيْكَ حَاجَةً، قَالَ: «اجْلِسِي يَا أُمَّ فُلَانٍ فِي أَيِّ طُرُقِ المَدِينَةِ شِئْتِ أَجْلِسُ إِلَيْكِ حَتَّى أَقْضِيَ حَاجَتَكِ». قَالَ: فَجَلَسَتْ، فَجَلَسَ النَّبِيُّ ﷺ إِلَيْهَا حَتَّى فَرَغَتْ مِنْ حَاجَتِهَا[337].

قَالَ أَنَسٌ: كَانَ رَسُولُ اللهِ ﷺ يَرْكَبُ الحِمَارَ، وَيُجِيبُ دَعْوَةَ العَبْدِ، وَكَانَ يَوْمَ بَنِي قُرَيْظَةَ عَلَى حِمَارٍ مَخْطُومٍ بِحَبْلٍ مِنْ لِيفٍ عَلَيْهِ إِكَافٌ[338].

قَالَ: وَكَانَ يُدْعَى إِلَى خُبْزِ الشَّعِيرِ وَالإِهَالَةِ السَّنِخَةِ فَيُجِيبُ ﷺ[339].

---

336 أَخْرَجَهُ البُخَارِيُّ (٣٤٤٥). (لَا تُطْرُونِي) الإِطْرَاءُ: المَدْحُ بِالبَاطِلِ/ قَالَهُ فِي الفَتْحِ ٦/٤٩٠.

337 أَخْرَجَهُ مُسْلِمٌ (٢٣٢٦).

338 أَخْرَجَهُ التِّرْمِذِيُّ فِي السُّنَنِ (١٠١٧)، وَفِي الشَّمَائِلِ (٣٢٥)، وَابْنُ مَاجَه (٤١٧٨)، وَالبَغَوِيُّ (٣٦٧٣)، وَأَبُو يَعْلَى (٤٢٤٣) وَغَيْرُهُ مِنْ طَرِيقِ مُسْلِمٍ الأَعْوَرِ عَنْ أَنَسٍ. قَالَ التِّرْمِذِيُّ: «هَذَا حَدِيثٌ لَا نَعْرِفُهُ إِلَّا مِنْ حَدِيثِ مُسْلِمٍ عَنْ أَنَسٍ، وَمُسْلِمٌ الأَعْوَرُ يُضَعَّفُ، وَهُوَ مُسْلِمُ بْنُ كَيْسَانَ». (مَخْطُومٌ): لَهُ خِطَامٌ، وَهُوَ حَبْلٌ يَكُونُ فِي أَنْفِ الدَّابَّةِ تُقَادُ بِهِ. (إِكَافٌ): مَا يُوضَعُ عَلَى الحِمَارِ أَوِ البَغْلِ لِيُرْكَبَ عَلَيْهِ، كَالسَّرْجِ لِلْفَرَسِ.

339 أَخْرَجَهُ - بِهَذَا اللَّفْظِ - التِّرْمِذِيُّ فِي الشَّمَائِلِ (٣٢٦) وَأَخْرَجَهُ البُخَارِيُّ (٢٠٦٩): عَنْ أَنَسٍ أَنَّهُ مَشَى إِلَى النَّبِيِّ ﷺ بِخُبْزِ شَعِيرٍ، وَإِهَالَةٍ سَنِخَةٍ». (الإِهَالَةُ): كُلُّ شَيْءٍ مِمَّا يُؤْتَدَمُ بِهِ. وَقِيلَ: هُوَ مَا أُذِيبَ مِنَ الأَلْيَةِ وَالشَّحْمِ. وَقِيلَ:

hams at most. He said: 'O Allah! Make this a hajj free from showing off and [seeking] renown.'"358 The Prophet ﷺ offered one hundred sacrificial animals during this hajj,359 and this was after the land had been liberated.

When Makkah had been liberated and he entered with the Muslim army, the Prophet ﷺ bowed so far forward that he almost touched the front of the saddle, out of his humbleness towards his Creator.360

There are many further examples of the humility of the Prophet of Allah ﷺ. He said: "Do not elevate me above Yūnus ibn Mattā",361 "Do not distinguish between the Prophets",362 and "Do not give me preference over Mūsā".363

He also said: "We are more liable to doubt than Ibrāhīm, and if I spent the time Yūsuf spent in prison I would have accepted the caller's invitation."364

When someone said to the Prophet ﷺ: "O best of creation!"

---

358   Reported by Tirmidhī in *Al-Shamā'il* (333) and Ibn Mājah (2890) from Anas ibn Mālik. Authenticated by Ḍiyā' in *Al-Mukhtārah*.

359   Reported by Muslim (1218) from Jābir ibn 'Abdullāh.

360   Reported by Abū Ya'lā (3393) from Anas. Authenticated by Ḥākim (3/47) and Dhahabī concurred. Haythamī said in *Majma' al-Zawā'id* (6/169): "The chain contains 'Abdullāh ibn Abī Bakr al-Muqaddamī, who was a weak narrator." Suyūṭī attributed the narration, in *Al-Manāhil*, p. 260, to Ibn Isḥāq and Bayhaqī from 'Ā'ishah.

361   Suyūṭī said in *Al-Manāhil*, p. 261: "I did not come across the narration with this wording."

362   Reported by Bukhārī (3414), and Muslim (2373/159) with this wording, from Abū Hurayrah. Also reported by Bukhārī (2412), and Muslim (2374) from al-Khudrī.

363   Reported by Bukhārī (2411) and Muslim (2373/160) from Abū Hurayrah.

364   Reported by Bukhārī (3372) and Muslim (151) from Abū Hurayrah. Nawawī interprets the first part of the hadith in his *Sharḥ Ṣaḥīḥ Muslim*: "It is totally implausible that Ibrāhīm harboured doubts [in his Lord]. If one of the Prophets was to doubt the resurrection of the dead, then I [i.e., the Prophet g] would be closer to that than Ibrāhīm. Just as you know that I have no such doubts, know that Ibrāhīm had no such doubts." See *al-Baqarah*, 260. The "caller" in the second part of the hadith refers to the King's messenger sent to Yūsuf; i.e., "I would have left prison without insisting my innocence was proven first." See *Yūsuf*, 50.

قَالَ: وَحَجَّ رَسُولُ اللهِ ﷺ عَلَى رَحْلِ رَثٍّ، وَعَلَيْهِ قَطِيفَةٌ مَا تُسَاوِي أَرْبَعَةَ دَرَاهِمَ، فَقَالَ: «اللَّهُمَّ اجْعَلْهُ حَجًّا لَا رِيَاءَ فِيهِ وَلَا سُمْعَةً»[340].

هَذَا، وَقَدْ فُتِحَتْ عَلَيْهِ الْأَرْضُ، وَأَهْدَى فِي حَجِّهِ ذَلِكَ مِائَةَ بَدَنَةٍ[341].

وَلَمَّا فُتِحَتْ عَلَيْهِ مَكَّةُ، وَدَخَلَهَا بِجُيُوشِ الْمُسْلِمِينَ، طَأْطَأَ عَلَى رَحْلِهِ رَأْسَهُ حَتَّى كَادَ يَمَسُّ قَادِمَتَهُ تَوَاضُعًا لِلّهِ تَعَالَى[342].

وَمِنْ تَوَاضُعِهِ ﷺ قَوْلُهُ: «لَا تُفَضِّلُونِي عَلَى يُونُسَ بْنِ مَتَّى»[343].

وَ«لَا تُفَضِّلُوا بَيْنَ الْأَنْبِيَاءِ»[344].

وَ«لَا تُخَيِّرُونِي عَلَى مُوسَى»[345].

وَ«نَحْنُ أَحَقُّ بِالشَّكِّ مِنْ إِبْرَاهِيمَ، وَلَوْ لَبِثْتُ مَا لَبِثَ يُوسُفُ فِي السِّجْنِ

الدَّسَمُ الجَامِدُ. (السَّنِخَةُ): المُتَغَيِّرَةُ الرِّيحِ.

٣٤٠   أَخْرَجَهُ ابْنُ مَاجَه (٢٨٩٠)، وَالتِّرْمِذِيُّ فِي الشَّمَائِلِ (٣٢٧) مِنْ حَدِيثِ أَنَسِ بْنِ مَالِكٍ. وَصَحَّحَهُ الضِّيَاءُ فِي «الْمُخْتَارَةِ». (رَحْلٌ رَثٌّ): الرَّحْلُ لِلْبَعِيرِ كَالسَّرْجِ لِلْفَرَسِ. (رَثٌّ) أَيْ خَلَقٌ بَالٍ.

٣٤١   أَخْرَجَهُ مُسْلِمٌ (١٢١٨) مِنْ حَدِيثِ جَابِرِ بْنِ عَبْدِ اللهِ. (بَدَنَةً): البَدَنَةُ تَقَعُ عَلَى الجَمَلِ وَالنَّاقَةِ وَالبَقَرَةِ، وَهِيَ بِالإِبِلِ أَشْبَهُ. وَسُمِّيَتْ بَدَنَةً لِعِظَمِهَا وَسِمَنِهَا/ النِّهَايَةُ.

٣٤٢   أَخْرَجَهُ أَبُو يَعْلَى (٣٣٩٣) مِنْ حَدِيثِ أَنَسٍ، وَصَحَّحَهُ الحَاكِمُ (٣/٤٧) وَوَافَقَهُ الذَّهَبِيُّ. وَقَالَ الهَيْثَمِيُّ فِي المَجْمَعِ ١٦٩/٦: «فِيهِ عَبْدُ اللهِ بْنُ أَبِي بَكْرٍ الْمَقْدَمِيُّ وَهُوَ ضَعِيفٌ». وَزَادَ نِسْبَتَهُ السُّيُوطِيُّ فِي المَنَاهِلِ (٢٦٠) إِلَى ابْنِ إِسْحَاقَ وَالبَيْهَقِيِّ عَنْ عَائِشَةَ. (قَادِمَتُهُ): قَادِمَةُ الرَّحْلِ: هِيَ الخَشَبَةُ الَّتِي فِي مُقَدِّمَةِ كُورِ البَعِيرِ بِمَنْزِلَةِ قَرَبُوسِ السَّرْجِ/ النِّهَايَةُ.

٣٤٣   قَالَ السُّيُوطِيُّ فِي المَنَاهِلِ (٢٦١): «لَمْ أَقِفْ عَلَيْهِ بِهَذَا اللَّفْظِ».

٣٤٤   أَخْرَجَهُ البُخَارِيُّ (٣٤١٤)، وَمُسْلِمٌ (٢٣٧٣/١٥٩) - وَاللَّفْظُ لَهُ - مِنْ حَدِيثِ أَبِي هُرَيْرَةَ. وَأَخْرَجَهُ البُخَارِيُّ (٢٤١٢)، وَمُسْلِمٌ (٢٣٧٤) مِنْ حَدِيثِ الخُدْرِيِّ بِلَفْظِ: لَا تُخَيِّرُوا بَيْنَ الْأَنْبِيَاءِ.

٣٤٥   أَخْرَجَهُ البُخَارِيُّ (٢٤١١)، وَمُسْلِمٌ (٢٣٧٣/١٦٠) مِنْ حَدِيثِ أَبِي هُرَيْرَةَ.

He replied: "That is Ibrāhīm."[365] These hadiths will be discussed in greater detail later in the text, Allah willing.

ʿĀʾishah, al-Ḥasan, Abū Saʿīd, and other witnesses all gave descriptions of the Prophet ﷺ, and some would give more information than others. They said that at home, he attended to the needs of his family.

He would remove any lice from his clothes, milk his sheep, patch his clothes, mend his sandals, serve himself, take the camels to graze, sweep the house, tie up the camels, eat with the servants and knead bread with them, and carry his own goods from the market.[366]

Anas said: "Any female servant in Madinah could take the hand of the Prophet ﷺ and walk with him wherever she wished, until she had taken care of any issue she had."[367]

A man once entered upon the Prophet ﷺ and began to tremble in awe, so he said to the man: "Be calm, for I am not a king. I am the son of a woman from the Quraysh who used to eat dried meat."[368]

Abū Hurayrah narrated: "I went to the market with the Prophet of Allah ﷺ and he bought a pair of trousers. He said to the person weighing the items: 'Weigh it and then add some.' The man rushed to kiss the hand of the Prophet ﷺ but he withdrew it and said: 'This is what the Persians do with their kings, but I am not a king.

---

365   Reported by Muslim (2369) from Anas.

366   The hadith of ʿĀʾishah was reported by Bukhārī (676) with the wording: "He used to serve his family"; by Tirmidhī in *Al-Shamāʾil* (341) with the wording: "He was a normal human being. He would remove any lice from his clothes, milk his sheep, and serve himself"; and by Baghawī (3675) with the wording: "He would mend his sandals and sew his clothes". See also *Majmaʿ al-Zawāʾid* (9/20).

367   Reported by Bukhārī (6072) and Aḥmad (3/98). Also reported in *Musnad Abū Yaʿlā* (3982) with the commentary of Shaykh Ḥusayn Asad.

368   Reported by Ibn Mājah (3312). Authenticated by Ḥākim (3/47-48) and Dhahabī concurred.

لَأَجَبْتُ الدَّاعِي»³⁴⁶.

وَقَالَ لِلَّذِي قَالَ لَهُ: يَا خَيْرَ الْبَرِيَّةِ: «ذَلِكَ إِبْرَاهِيمُ»³⁴⁷.

وَسَيَأْتِي الْكَلَامُ عَلَى هَذِهِ الْأَحَادِيثِ بَعْدَ هَذَا إِنْ شَاءَ اللهُ تَعَالَى.

وَعَنْ عَائِشَةَ، وَالْحَسَنِ، وَأَبِي سَعِيدٍ، وَغَيْرِهِم فِي صِفَتِهِ ﷺ، وَبَعْضُهُم يَزِيدُ عَلَى بَعْضٍ: كَانَ فِي بَيْتِهِ فِي مِهْنَةِ أَهْلِهِ: يَفْلِي ثَوْبَهُ، وَيَحْلُبُ شَاتَهُ، وَيَرْقَعُ ثَوْبَهُ، وَيَخْصِفُ نَعْلَهُ، وَيَخْدُمُ نَفْسَهُ، وَيَقُمُّ الْبَيْتَ، وَيَعْقِلُ الْبَعِيرَ، وَيَعْلِفُ نَاضِحَهُ، وَيَأْكُلُ مَعَ الْخَادِمِ، وَيَطْحَنُ مَعَهَا، وَيَحْمِلُ بِضَاعَتَهُ مِنَ السُّوقِ³⁴⁸.

وَعَنْ أَنَسٍ: إِنْ كَانَتِ الْأَمَةُ مِنْ إِمَاءِ أَهْلِ الْمَدِينَةِ لَتَأْخُذُ بِيَدِ رَسُولِ اللهِ ﷺ فَتَنْطَلِقُ بِهِ حَيْثُ شَاءَتْ حَتَّى تَقْضِيَ حَاجَتَهَا³⁴⁹.

وَدَخَلَ عَلَيْهِ رَجُلٌ فَأَصَابَتْهُ مِنْ هَيْبَتِهِ رِعْدَةٌ فَقَالَ لَهُ: «هَوِّنْ عَلَيْكَ فَإِنِّي لَسْتُ بِمَلِكٍ، إِنَّمَا أَنَا ابْنُ امْرَأَةٍ مِنْ قُرَيْشٍ تَأْكُلُ الْقَدِيدَ»³⁵⁰.

---

٣٤٦ أَخْرَجَهُ الْبُخَارِيُّ (٣٣٧٢)، وَمُسْلِمٌ (١٥١) مِنْ حَدِيثِ أَبِي هُرَيْرَةَ. (نَحْنُ أَحَقُّ بِالشَّكِّ مِنْ إِبْرَاهِيمَ) مَعْنَاهُ: إِنَّ الشَّكَّ مُسْتَحِيلٌ فِي حَقِّ إِبْرَاهِيمَ. فَإِنَّ الشَّكَّ فِي إِحْيَاءِ الْمَوْتَى لَوْ كَانَ مُتَطَرِّقًا إِلَى الْأَنْبِيَاءِ لَكُنْتُ أَنَا أَحَقُّ بِهِ مِنْ إِبْرَاهِيمَ وَقَدْ عَلِمْتُمْ أَنِّي لَمْ أَشُكَّ، فَاعْلَمُوا أَنَّ إِبْرَاهِيمَ ﷺ لَمْ يَشُكَّ/ شَرْحُ مُسْلِمٍ لِلنَّوَوِيِّ. (الدَّاعِي): رَسُولُ الْمَلِكِ.

٣٤٧ أَخْرَجَهُ مُسْلِمٌ (٢٣٦٩) مِنْ حَدِيثِ أَنَسٍ. (الْبَرِيَّةُ): الْخَلْقُ.

٣٤٨ حَدِيثُ عَائِشَةَ أَخْرَجَهُ الْبُخَارِيُّ (٦٧٦) بِلَفْظِ: «كَانَ يَكُونُ فِي مِهْنَةِ أَهْلِهِ...» وَفِي رِوَايَةِ التِّرْمِذِيِّ فِي الشَّمَائِلِ (٣٣٥): وَكَانَ بَشَرًا مِنَ الْبَشَرِ: يَفْلِي ثَوْبَهُ، وَيَحْلِبُ شَاتَهُ، وَيَخْدُمُ نَفْسَهُ».
وَفِي رِوَايَةِ الْبَغَوِيِّ (٣٦٧٥): «كَانَ رَسُولُ اللهِ ﷺ يَخْصِفُ نَعْلَهُ، وَيَخِيطُ ثَوْبَهُ....» وَانْظُرْ مَجْمَعَ الزَّوَائِدِ ٢٠/٩. (مِهْنَةِ أَهْلِهِ): خِدْمَةِ نَفْسِهِ. (يَقُمُّ الْبَيْتَ): يَكْنِسُهُ. (يَخْصِفُ نَعْلَهُ): يَخْرِزُهَا بِالْمِخْصَفِ وَهُوَ الْمِخْرَزُ. (يَعْقِلُ الْبَعِيرَ) عَقَلَ الْبَعِيرَ: ضَمَّ رُسْغَ يَدِهِ إِلَى عَضُدِهِ وَرَبَطَهُمَا مَعًا بِالْعِقَالِ لِيَبْقَى بَارِكًا.

٣٤٩ عَلَّقَهُ الْبُخَارِيُّ (٦٠٧٢)، وَوَصَلَهُ أَحْمَدُ (٩٨/٣). وَتَمَامُ تَخْرِيجِهِ فِي مُسْنَدِ أَبِي يَعْلَى (٣٩٨٢) تَحْقِيقِ أُسْتَاذِنَا الْفَاضِلِ حُسَيْن أَسَد.

٣٥٠ (رِعْدَةٌ): رَجْفَةٌ. (هَوِّنْ): خَفِّفْ. (الْقَدِيدَ): اللَّحْمَ الْمَمْلُوحَ الْمُجَفَّفَ فِي الشَّمْسِ.

I am simply a man from amongst you.'

Then he picked up the trousers and carried them with him, saying: 'The owner of a thing has a greater obligation to carry it.'"369

---

369 Reported by Abū Yaʻlā (6162) and others. Haythamī said in *Majmaʻ al-Zawāʼid* (6/169): "The chain contains Yūsuf ibn Ziyād al-Baṣrī, who was a weak narrator." Ibn al-Jawzī mentioned the hadith in *Al-Mawḍūʻāt*, his collection of fabricated narrations. The saying of the Prophet ﷺ "Weigh it and then add some" was established in the narration of Saʻīd ibn Qays, which was reported in *Mawārid al-Ẓamʼān* (1444).

وَعَنْ أَبِي هُرَيْرَةَ قَالَ: دَخَلْتُ السُّوقَ مَعَ النَّبِيِّ ﷺ فَاشْتَرَى سَرَاوِيلَ، وَقَالَ لِلْوَزَّانِ: «زِنْ وَأَرْجِحْ»، وَذَكَرَ القِصَّةَ قَالَ: فَوَثَبَ إِلَى يَدِ النَّبِيِّ ﷺ يُقَبِّلُهَا، فَجَذَبَ يَدَهُ، وَقَالَ: «هَذَا تَفْعَلُهُ الأَعَاجِمُ بِمُلُوكِهَا، وَلَسْتُ بِمَلِكٍ، إِنَّمَا أَنَا رَجُلٌ مِنْكُمْ». ثُمَّ أَخَذَ السَّرَاوِيلَ، فَذَهَبْتُ لِأَحْمِلَهُ، فَقَالَ: «صَاحِبُ الشَّيْءِ أَحَقُّ بِشَيْئِهِ أَنْ يَحْمِلَهُ»³⁵¹.

---

³⁵¹ أَخْرَجَهُ أَبُو يَعْلَى (٦١٦٢) وَغَيْرُهُ. قَالَ الهَيْثَمِيُّ فِي مَجْمَعِ الزَّوَائِدِ ١٢٢/٥: «فِيهِ يُوسُفُ بْنُ زِيَادٍ البَصْرِيُّ، وَهُوَ ضَعِيفٌ». وَبَالَغَ ابْنُ الجَوْزِيِّ فَذَكَرَهُ فِي المَوْضُوعَاتِ. وَيَشْهَدُ لِقَوْلِهِ ﷺ: «زِنْ وَأَرْجِحْ» حَدِيثُ سُوَيْدِ بْنِ قَيْسٍ. خَرَّجْنَاهُ فِي مَوَارِدِ الظَّمْآنِ (١٤٤٤). (سَرَاوِيلُ): لِبَاسٌ يُغَطِّي السُّرَّةَ وَالرُّكْبَتَيْنِ وَمَا بَيْنَهُمَا. جَمْعُهُ: سَرَاوِيلَاتٌ.

HIS JUSTNESS AND TRUSTWORTHINESS

The Prophet ﷺ was the most trustworthy person and the most just. He was sincere and morally pure. His enemies and opponents would admit to his truthfulness, and even before Prophethood he was given the title al-Amīn (the trustworthy one).

Ibn Isḥāq said: "He was named al-Amīn because of the righteous character Allah bestowed upon him." Allah Exalted says: "obeyed there [in heaven], and trustworthy."[370] The majority of exegetes agree that the verse refers to Muhammad ﷺ.

When the Quraysh disputed about who should place the Black Stone during the reconstruction of the Kaʿbah, they decided that the first person to arrive would be asked to judge between them. When the Prophet ﷺ arrived (and this was before his Prophethood), they said: "This is Muhammad, al-Amīn, and we are happy with him [as a judge between us]."[371] Al-Rabīʿ ibn Khuthaym[372] narrated: "The people used to ask the Messenger of Allah ﷺ to judge between them during the Days of Jāhiliyyah, before Islam."[373] And the Prophet ﷺ said: "I swear by Allah! I am *amīn* (trustworthy) in the Heavens, and *amīn* on Earth."[374]

I read the following hadith to Abū ʿAlī al-Ṣadafī, who narrated

---

370 *al-Takwīr*, 21.

371 Reported by Aḥmad (3/425) from Mujāhid from his servant ʿAbdullāh ibn al-Sāʾib. Authenticated by Ḥākim (1/458) and Dhahabī concurred. Also authenticated by Ḥākim (1/458-459) from the narration of ʿAlī, and Dhahabī again concurred. Haythamī said in *Majmaʿ al-Zawāʾid* (8/229): "It was related by Ṭabarānī in *Al-Awsaṭ* and the narrators are *ṣaḥīḥ*, except for Ḥafṣ ibn ʿUmar al-Ḍarīr and Khālid ibn ʿArʿarah, who were both trustworthy."

372 A veteran from the Followers and devout worshipper; he died in 61 or 63 AH.

373 Reported by Ibn Saʿd in *Al-Ṭabaqāt*. See *Al-Manāhil*, p. 269.

374 Reported by Ibn Abī Shaybah. See *Al-Manāhil*, p. 270.

فَصْل

وَأَمَّا عَدْلُهُ ﷺ وَأَمَانَتُهُ وَعِفَّتُهُ وَصِدْقُ لَهْجَتِهِ: فَكَانَ ﷺ آمَنَ النَّاسِ، وَأَعْدَلَ النَّاسِ، وَأَعَفَّ النَّاسِ، وَأَصْدَقَهُمْ لَهْجَةً مُنْذُ كَانَ، اعْتَرَفَ لَهُ بِذَلِكَ مُحَادُّوهُ وَعِدَاهُ[352]، وَكَانَ يُسَمَّى قَبْلَ نُبُوَّتِهِ الْأَمِينَ.

قَالَ ابْنُ إِسْحَاقَ: كَانَ يُسَمَّى الْأَمِينَ بِمَا جَمَعَ اللهُ فِيهِ مِنَ الْأَخْلَاقِ الصَّالِحَةِ.

وَقَالَ تَعَالَى: ﴿مُطَاعٍ ثَمَّ أَمِينٍ﴾ [التكوير: 21]، أَكْثَرُ الْمُفَسِّرِينَ عَلَى أَنَّهُ مُحَمَّدٌ ﷺ.

وَلَمَّا اخْتَلَفَتْ قُرَيْشٌ، وَتَحَازَبَتْ عِنْدَ بِنَاءِ الْكَعْبَةِ فِيمَنْ يَضَعُ الْحَجَرَ، حَكَّمُوا أَوَّلَ دَاخِلٍ عَلَيْهِمْ، فَإِذَا بِالنَّبِيِّ ﷺ دَاخِلٌ، وَذَلِكَ قَبْلَ نُبُوَّتِهِ، فَقَالُوا: هَذَا[353] مُحَمَّدٌ، هَذَا الْأَمِينُ، قَدْ رَضِينَا بِهِ[354].

وَعَنِ الرَّبِيعِ بْنِ خُثَيْمٍ ﵁[355]: كَانَ يُتَحَاكَمُ إِلَى رَسُولِ اللهِ ﷺ فِي الْجَاهِلِيَّةِ قَبْلَ الْإِسْلَامِ[356].

---

352 أَيْ مُخَالِفُوهُ وَأَعْدَاؤُهُ.

353 كَلِمَةُ: «هَذَا»، لَمْ تَرِدْ فِي الْمَطْبُوعِ.

354 أَخْرَجَهُ أَحْمَدُ 425/3 مِنْ حَدِيثِ مُجَاهِدٍ عَنْ مَوْلَاهُ عَبْدِ اللهِ بْنِ السَّائِبِ. وَصَحَّحَهُ الْحَاكِمُ (458/1) وَوَافَقَهُ الذَّهَبِيُّ. كَمَا صَحَّحَهُ أَيْضًا الْحَاكِمُ 459-458/1 مِنْ حَدِيثِ عَلِيٍّ وَوَافَقَهُ الذَّهَبِيُّ. وَقَالَ الْهَيْثَمِيُّ فِي الْمَجْمَعِ 229/8: «رَوَاهُ الطَّبَرَانِيُّ فِي الْأَوْسَطِ وَرِجَالُهُ رِجَالُ الصَّحِيحِ غَيْرُ حَفْصِ بْنِ عُمَرَ الضَّرِيرِ، وَخَالِدِ بْنِ عَرْعَرَةَ، وَكِلَاهُمَا ثِقَةٌ». (تَحَازَبَتْ): صَارَتْ فِرَقًا وَأَحْزَابًا.

355 تَابِعِيٌّ مُخَضْرَمٌ، ثِقَةٌ عَابِدٌ مَاتَ سَنَةَ (61) أَوْ (63) هـ / التَّقْرِيب.

356 أَخْرَجَهُ ابْنُ سَعْدٍ فِي الطَّبَقَاتِ/ الْمَنَاهِل (269).

from Abū al-Faḍl ibn Khayrūn, from Abū Yaʿlā ibn Zawj al-Ḥur-rah, from Abū ʿAlī al-Sinjī, from Muhammad ibn Maḥbūb al-Mar-wazī, from Abū ʿĪsā al-Ḥāfiẓ, from Abū Kurayb, from Muʿāwiyah ibn Hishām, from Sufyān, from Abū Isḥāq, from Nājiyah ibn Kaʿb, from ʿAlī, that Abū Jahl said to the Prophet ﷺ: "We are not reject-ing you. Rather, we are rejecting that which you have brought."³⁷⁵ So, Allah Exalted revealed: "It is not your honesty they question – it is Allah's signs that the wrongdoers deny."³⁷⁶ Another transmission states that Abū Jahl said: "We are not rejecting you and you are not known as a liar amongst us."

It is related that al-Akhnas ibn Sharīq³⁷⁷ met Abū Jahl on the Day of Badr³⁷⁸ and said to him: "O Abū al-Ḥakam! No-one is here to hear this conversation between us, so tell me about Muham-mad. Is he a truthful person or a liar?" Abū Jahl replied: "I swear by Allah, Muhammad is truthful, and he has never lied."³⁷⁹ When Heraclius asked Abū Sufyān about the Prophet ﷺ, he said: "Did you ever suspect him of lying before he said what he said?"³⁸⁰ Abū Sufyān said they did not.³⁸¹

Al-Naḍr ibn al-Ḥārith³⁸² said to the Quraysh: "When Muham-

---

375   Reported by Tirmidhī (3064). Authenticated by Ḥākim in *Al-Mustadrak* (2/315) and Aḥmad Shākir in
ʿUmda*h al-Tafsīr* (5/25).

376   *al-Anʿā*m, 33.

377   His name is Ubayy ibn Sharīq, and al-Akhnas was a nickname. He witnessed the Battle of Ḥunayn and the Messenger of Allah ﷺ gave him charity as one of those whose hearts were inclining towards Islam. He died at the beginning of the Caliphate led by ʿUmar, and his biography can be found in *Al-Iṣābah, Usd al-Ghābah*, and other works.

378   Badr was the name of a well but is now a large, bustling town located almost 150 km from Madinah.

379   Suyūṭī said in *Al-Manāhil*, p. 271: "Reported by Ibn Isḥāq and Bayhaqī from al-Zuhrī, and by Ibn Jarīr from al-Suddī."

380   i.e., before he began to convey the message of Islam.

381   Taken from the hadith reported by Bukhārī (7) and Muslim (1773).

382   One of the principal warriors of the Quraysh, he carried their way flag on the Day of

وَقَالَ ﷺ: «وَاللهِ إِنِّي لَأَمِينٌ فِي السَّمَاءِ، أَمِينٌ فِي الأَرْضِ»[357].

حَدَّثَنَا أَبُو عَلِيٍّ الصَّدَفِيُّ الحَافِظُ بِقِرَاءَتِي عَلَيْهِ، حَدَّثَنَا أَبُو الفَضْلِ بْنُ خَيْرُونَ، حَدَّثَنَا أَبُو يَعْلَى بْنُ زَوْجِ الحُرَّةِ، حَدَّثَنَا أَبُو عَلِيٍّ السِّنْجِيُّ، حَدَّثَنَا مُحَمَّدُ بْنُ مَحْبُوبٍ المَرْوَزِيُّ، حَدَّثَنَا أَبُو عِيسَى الحَافِظُ، حَدَّثَنَا أَبُو كُرَيْبٍ، حَدَّثَنَا مُعَاوِيَةُ بْنُ هِشَامٍ، عَنْ سُفْيَانَ، عَنْ أَبِي إِسْحَاقَ، عَنْ نَاجِيَةَ بْنِ كَعْبٍ، عَنْ عَلِيٍّ أَنَّ أَبَا جَهْلٍ قَالَ لِلنَّبِيِّ ﷺ: إِنَّا لَا نُكَذِّبُكَ، وَلَكِنْ نُكَذِّبُ بِمَا جِئْتَ بِهِ. فَأَنْزَلَ اللهُ تَعَالَى فِيهِمْ: ﴿فَإِنَّهُمْ لَا يُكَذِّبُونَكَ﴾ [الأنعام: 33] الآيَةَ.

وَرَوَى غَيْرُهُ: لَا نُكَذِّبُكَ، وَمَا أَنْتَ فِينَا بِمُكَذَّبٍ.

وَقِيلَ: إِنَّ الأَخْنَسَ بْنَ شَرِيقٍ[358] لَقِيَ أَبَا جَهْلٍ يَوْمَ بَدْرٍ، فَقَالَ لَهُ: يَا أَبَا الحَكَمِ لَيْسَ هُنَا غَيْرِي وَغَيْرُكَ يَسْمَعُ كَلَامَنَا، فَخَبِّرْنِي عَنْ مُحَمَّدٍ، صَادِقٌ أَمْ كَاذِبٌ؟ فَقَالَ أَبُو جَهْلٍ: وَاللهِ إِنَّ مُحَمَّدًا لَصَادِقٌ، وَمَا كَذَبَ مُحَمَّدٌ قَطُّ[359].

وَسَأَلَ هِرَقْلُ عَنْهُ أَبَا سُفْيَانَ فَقَالَ: هَلْ كُنْتُمْ تَتَّهِمُونَهُ بِالكَذِبِ قَبْلَ أَنْ يَقُولَ مَا قَالَ؟ قَالَ: لَا[360].

وَقَالَ النَّضْرُ بْنُ الحَارِثِ[361] لِقُرَيْشٍ: قَدْ كَانَ مُحَمَّدٌ فِيكُمْ غُلَامًا حَدَثًا،

---

357 أَخْرَجَهُ ابْنُ أَبِي شَيْبَةَ/ المَنَاهِلُ (270).

358 هُوَ أُبَيُّ بْنُ شَرِيقٍ، وَالأَخْنَسُ لَقَبٌ. شَهِدَ حُنَيْنًا وَأَعْطَاهُ رَسُولُ اللهِ ﷺ مَعَ المُؤَلَّفَةِ قُلُوبُهُمْ. تُوُفِّيَ أَوَّلَ خِلَافَةِ عُمَرَ. لَهُ تَرْجَمَةٌ فِي الإِصَابَةِ وَأُسْدِ الغَابَةِ وَغَيْرِ ذَلِكَ.

359 قَالَ فِي المَنَاهِلِ (271): «ابْنُ إِسْحَاقَ وَالبَيْهَقِيِّ، عَنِ الزُّهْرِيِّ قَالَ: حُدِّثْتُ، فَذَكَرَهُ، وَأَخْرَجَهُ ابْنُ جَرِيرٍ، عَنِ السُّدِّي». (بَدْرٌ): اسْمُ بِئْرٍ، وَهُوَ الآنَ بَلْدَةٌ كَبِيرَةٌ عَامِرَةٌ، عَلَى بُعْدِ حَوَالَيْ (150) كِيلًا مِنَ المَدِينَةِ المُنَوَّرَةِ.

360 قِطْعَةٌ مِنْ حَدِيثٍ أَخْرَجَهُ البُخَارِيُّ (7)، وَمُسْلِمٌ (1773).

361 مِنْ شُجْعَانِ قُرَيْشٍ وَوُجُوهِهَا وَشَيَاطِينِهَا، وَصَاحِبُ لِوَاءِ المُشْرِكِينَ يَوْمَ بَدْرٍ، أَسَرَهُ المُسْلِمُونَ يَوْمَهَا، وَقُتِلَ بِالأَثِيلِ، قُرْبَ المَدِينَةِ. انْظُرِ الأَعْلَامَ 8/33.

mad was a young boy he was the most pleasing, truthful, and trust-worthy amongst you. Then, when you saw grey hairs at his temples and he came to you with what he came with, you said: 'He is a magician.' No, I swear by Allah, he is not a magician!"[383]

The Prophet ﷺ said: "Woe to you! If I do not act with justice, then who would? Indeed, you would be disappointed and at a loss if I did not act with justice."[384] In another narration, we find: "His hand never touched the hand of a woman he did not have rights to."[385] And ʿAlī said: "He was the most truthful in speech."[386]

ʿĀʾishah ﷻ recalled: "Whenever the Messenger of Allah ﷺ had to choose between two things he would choose the easier of the two, as long as it was not a sin. If it was a sin, he was the furthest away from it.[387]

Abū al-ʿAbbās al-Mubarrad[388] said: "Khosrow used to allocate his days [for different purposes], saying: 'A windy day is good for sleep, a cloudy day for hunting, a rainy day for drinking and enter-tainment, and a sunny day for [attending to] the needs [of the peo-ple].'" Ibn Khālawayh[389] observed: "They (i.e., the Persians) were not the most knowledgeable about management and organization in this world of theirs. 'They [only] know the worldly affairs of this

---

Badr, during which the Muslims took him captive. He was killed in al-Athīl, close to Madinah. See *Siyar Aʿlām al-Nubalāʾ* (8/33).

383 Suyūṭī said in *Al-Manāhil*, p. 273: "Reported by Ibn Isḥāq and Bayhaqī from Ibn ʿAbbās."

384 Reported by Bukhārī (3138) and Muslim (1063) from Jābir, Bukhārī (3610) and Muslim (1064/148) from al-Khudrī, and Bukhārī (3150) and Muslim (1062) from Ibn Masʿūd.

385 Reported with a similar wording by Bukhārī (7214) and Muslim (1866) from ʿĀʾishah.

386 Reported by Tirmidhī in *Al-Sunan* (3638) and *Al-Shamāʾil* (7).

387 Reported by Mālik (2/903), Bukhārī (3560), and Muslim (2327).

388 Muhammad ibn Yazīd, an imam, scholar, authoritative source, and author of *Al-Kāmil*. He died at the beginning of 286 AH. See *Siyar Aʿlām al-Nubalāʾ* (13/576).

389 Al-Ḥusayn ibn Aḥmad ibn Khālawayh, a renowned linguist and grammarian. He died in Aleppo in 370 AH. See *Siyar Aʿlām al-Nubalāʾ* (2/231).

أَرْضَاكُمْ فِيكُمْ، وَأَصْدَقَكُمْ حَدِيثًا، وَأَعْظَمَكُمْ أَمَانَةً، حَتَّى إِذَا رَأَيْتُمْ فِي صُدْغَيْهِ الشَّيْبَ، وَجَاءَكُمْ بِمَا جَاءَكُمْ بِهِ، قُلْتُمْ سَاحِرٌ؟! لَا، وَاللهِ مَا هُوَ بِسَاحِرٍ[٣٦٢].

وَفِي الْحَدِيثِ عَنْهُ: مَا لَمَسَتْ يَدُهُ يَدَ امْرَأَةٍ قَطُّ لَا يَمْلِكُ رِقَّهَا[٣٦٣].

وَفِي حَدِيثِ عَلِيٍّ رَضِيَ اللهُ عَنْهُ فِي وَصْفِهِ ﷺ: أَصْدَقُ النَّاسِ لَهْجَةً[٣٦٤].

وَقَالَ فِي الصَّحِيحِ: «وَيْحَكَ! فَمَنْ يَعْدِلُ إِنْ لَمْ أَعْدِلْ، خِبْتَ وَخَسِرْتَ إِنْ لَمْ أَعْدِلْ».

قَالَتْ عَائِشَةُ رَضِيَ اللهُ عَنْهَا: مَا خُيِّرَ رَسُولُ اللهِ ﷺ فِي أَمْرَيْنِ إِلَّا اخْتَارَ أَيْسَرَهُمَا مَا لَمْ يَكُنْ إِثْمًا، فَإِنْ كَانَ إِثْمًا كَانَ أَبْعَدَ النَّاسِ مِنْهُ.

قَالَ أَبُو الْعَبَّاسِ الْمُبَرَّدُ[٣٦٥]: قَسَّمَ كِسْرَى أَيَّامَهُ، فَقَالَ: يَصْلُحُ يَوْمُ الرِّيحِ لِلنَّوْمِ، وَيَوْمُ الْغَيْمِ لِلصَّيْدِ، وَيَوْمُ الْمَطَرِ لِلشُّرْبِ وَاللَّهْوِ، وَيَوْمُ الشَّمْسِ لِلْحَوَائِجِ.

قَالَ ابْنُ خَالَوَيْهِ[٣٦٦]: مَا كَانَ أَعْرَفَهُمْ بِسِيَاسَةِ دُنْيَاهُمْ، ﴿يَعْلَمُونَ ظَاهِرًا مِّنَ ٱلْحَيَوٰةِ ٱلدُّنْيَا وَهُمْ عَنِ ٱلْآخِرَةِ هُمْ غَافِلُونَ﴾ [الروم: ٧]. وَلَكِنْ نَبِيُّنَا ﷺ جَزَّأَ نَهَارَهُ ثَلَاثَةَ أَجْزَاءٍ، جُزْءًا لِلَّهِ، وَجُزْءًا لِأَهْلِهِ، وَجُزْءًا لِنَفْسِهِ. ثُمَّ جَزَّأَ جُزْءَهُ بَيْنَهُ وَبَيْنَ النَّاسِ، فَكَانَ يَسْتَعِينُ بِالْخَاصَّةِ عَلَى الْعَامَّةِ، وَيَقُولُ:

---

٣٦٢ قَالَ فِي الْمَنَاهِلِ (٢٧٣): «ابْنُ إِسْحَاقَ وَالْبَيْهَقِيُّ عَنِ ابْنِ عَبَّاسٍ». (صُدْغَيْهِ) الصُّدْغُ: جَانِبُ الْوَجْهِ مِنَ الْعَيْنِ إِلَى الأُذُنِ، وَالشَّعْرُ فَوْقَهُ/ الْمُعْجَمُ الْوَسِيطُ.

٣٦٣ أَخْرَجَهُ الْبُخَارِيُّ (٧٢١٤)، وَمُسْلِمٌ (١٨٦٦) عَنْ عَائِشَةَ قَرِيبًا مِنْ لَفْظِهِ.

٣٦٤ (اللَّهْجَةُ): اللِّسَانُ.

٣٦٥ هُوَ مُحَمَّدُ بْنُ يَزِيدَ صَاحِبُ كِتَابِ «الْكَامِلِ» كَانَ إِمَامًا، عَلَّامَةً، مُوَثَّقًا، صَاحِبَ نَوَادِرَ وَطُرَفٍ. يُقَالُ: إِنَّ الْمَازِنِيَّ أَعْجَبَهُ جَوَابُهُ. فَقَالَ لَهُ: قُمْ فَأَنْتَ الْمُبَرَّدُ، أَيْ: الْمُثْبِتُ لِلْحَقِّ، ثُمَّ غَلَبَ عَلَيْهِ: بِفَتْحِ الرَّاءِ. تُوُفِّيَ الْمُبَرَّدُ فِي أَوَّلِ سَنَةِ (٢٨٦) هـ. انْظُرْ سِيَرَ أَعْلَامِ النُّبَلَاءِ ١٣/٥٧٦.

٣٦٦ هُوَ الْحُسَيْنُ بْنُ أَحْمَدَ بْنِ خَالَوَيْهِ، لُغَوِيٌّ، مِنْ كِبَارِ النُّحَاةِ. تُوُفِّيَ فِي حَلَبَ سَنَةَ (٣٧٠) هـ. (الأَعْلَامُ ٢/٢٣١).

life, but are [totally] oblivious to the Hereafter.'[390]"

The Prophet ☙, on the other hand, would divide each day into three parts; a part of the day for worshipping Allah, a part for his family, and a part for attending to his own needs. Then, he divided the part for his own needs between himself and the people, and he would say: "Tell me the needs of those who cannot tell me themselves, for Allah will safeguard whoever does so on the Day of the Great Terror[391]."[392]

Al-Ḥasan al-Baṣrī related: "The Messenger of Allah ☙ would never hold someone to account for someone else's actions, nor would he believe one person above another."[393]

Abū Jaʿfar al-Ṭabarī mentioned, on the authority of ʿAlī, that the Prophet ☙ said: "I was never tempted to practice the customs of Jāhiliyyah except on two occasions, and both times Allah distanced me from what I had wanted to do. After that, I was never tempted again right up until Allah honoured me with Messengership. One night, I said to a boy who was guarding his flock of sheep with me: 'Can you watch my sheep so that I can go into Makkah and enjoy the evening as the other young men usually do?'

I set off, and when I reached the first house in Makkah, I heard the sound of tambourines and flutes for someone's wedding party. I sat down to watch, but my ears were struck and I fell asleep. I only woke up with the touch of the Sun, so I returned without doing anything. The same thing happened to me on one other occasion, but I never desired harmful pursuits after that."[394]

---

390 *al-Rūm*, 7.

391 i.e., the Day of Judgement.

392 This is taken from a longer narration from ʿAlī ☙. See *Al-Shamāʾil* (335).

393 A *mursal* hadith with trustworthy narrators. Reported by Abū Dāwūd (514) and al-Ḥasan al-Baṣrī.

394 Reported by Bazzār (2403) and others from ʿAlī.

«أَبْلِغُوا حَاجَةَ مَنْ لَا يَسْتَطِيعُ إِبْلَاغِي، فَإِنَّهُ مَنْ أَبْلَغَ حَاجَةَ مَنْ لَا يَسْتَطِيعُ إِبْلَاغَهَا أَمَّنَهُ اللهُ يَوْمَ الفَزَعِ الأَكْبَرِ».

وَعَنِ الحَسَنِ: كَانَ رَسُولُ اللهِ ﷺ لَا يَأْخُذُ أَحَدًا بِقَرْفِ أَحَدٍ، وَلَا يُصَدِّقُ أَحَدًا عَلَى أَحَدٍ٣٦٧. وَذَكَرَ أَبُو جَعْفَرٍ الطَّبَرِيُّ عَنْ عَلِيٍّ عَنْهُ ﷺ: «مَا هَمَمْتُ بِشَيْءٍ مِمَّا كَانَ أَهْلُ الجَاهِلِيَّةِ يَعْمَلُونَ بِهِ غَيْرَ مَرَّتَيْنِ، كُلَّ ذَلِكَ يَحُولُ اللهُ بَيْنِي وَبَيْنَ مَا أُرِيدُ مِنْ ذَلِكَ، ثُمَّ مَا هَمَمْتُ بِسُوءٍ حَتَّى أَكْرَمَنِي اللهُ بِرِسَالَتِهِ، قُلْتُ لَيْلَةً لِغُلَامٍ كَانَ يَرْعَى مَعِي: لَوْ أَبْصَرْتَ لِي غَنَمِي حَتَّى أَدْخُلَ مَكَّةَ فَأَسْمُرَ بِهَا كَمَا يَسْمُرُ الشَّابُّ. فَخَرَجْتُ لِذَلِكَ حَتَّى جِئْتُ أَوَّلَ دَارٍ مِنْ مَكَّةَ سَمِعْتُ عَزْفًا بِالدُّفُوفِ وَالمَزَامِيرِ لِعُرْسٍ بَعْضِهِمْ، فَجَلَسْتُ أَنْظُرُ، فَضُرِبَ عَلَى أُذُنِي فَنِمْتُ، فَمَا أَيْقَظَنِي إِلَّا مَسُّ الشَّمْسِ، فَرَجَعْتُ، وَلَمْ أَقْضِ شَيْئًا، ثُمَّ عَرَانِي مَرَّةً أُخْرَى مِثْلُ ذَلِكَ، ثُمَّ لَمْ أَهُمَّ بَعْدَ ذَلِكَ بِسُوءٍ»٣٦٨.

٣٦٧　حَدِيثٌ رِجَالُهُ ثِقَاتٌ لَكِنَّهُ مُرْسَلٌ. أَخْرَجَهُ أَبُو دَاوُدَ فِي المَرَاسِيلِ (٥١٤)، وَالحَسَنُ هُوَ البَصْرِيُّ. (بِقَرْفِ أَحَدٍ): أَيْ بِذَنْبِهِ وَكَسْبِهِ.

٣٦٨　(فَأَسْمُرَ بِهَا): السَّمَرُ: الحَدِيثُ بِاللَّيْلِ. (عَرَانِي): انْتَابَنِي وَعَشِيَنِي.

HIS COMPOSURE, SILENCE, AND TRANQUILLITY

I was given permission to narrate the following hadith from Abū ʿAlī al-Jayyānī al-Ḥāfiẓ, and he narrated from Abū al-ʿAbbās al-Dilāʾī, from Abū Dharr al-Harawī, from ʿAbdullāh al-Warrāq, from al-Luʾluʾī, from Abū Dāwūd, from ʿAbd al-Raḥmān ibn Salām, from Ḥajjāj ibn Muhammad, from ʿAbd al-Raḥmān ibn Abī al-Zinād, from ʿUmar ibn ʿAbd al-ʿAzīz ibn Wuhayb, that he heard Khārijah ibn Zayd say: "The Prophet ﷺ was the most composed person in an assembly. His limbs would hardly move."[395]

Abū Saʿīd al-Khudrī related: "When the Messenger of Allah ﷺ sat in the mosque, he would draw his knees up with his hands, and that was how he sat most of the time."[396] Jābir ibn Samurah said that he sat with his legs crossed,[397] and Qaylah said that he would sometimes squat on his heels.[398]

The Prophet ﷺ would often remain silent and did not speak without a purpose. He would turn away from those who spoke in an undesirable manner. His speech was comprehensive; neither verbose nor laconic. His laughter was a smile, and his Companions

---

395 A *mursal* hadith. Reported here from the chain of Abū Dāwūd in *Al-Marāsīl* (505). The chain contains ʿUmar ibn ʿAbd al-ʿAzīz ibn Wahīb, who Ibn Ḥajar cited in *Al-Taqrīb* as "unknown".

396 Reported by Tirmidhī in *Al-Shamāʾil* (128) and Abū Dāwūd (4846). The chain contains ʿAbdullāh ibn Ibrāhīm, who Abū Dāwūd described as "the Shaykh of *munkar* narrations". ʿIrāqī cited the chain as weak in *Takhrīj Aḥādīth al-Iḥyāʾ* (2/366). The narration was graded *ḥasan* by Suyūṭī in *Al-Jāmiʿ al-Ṣaghīr* (6637), and *ṣaḥīḥ* by Shaykh al-Albānī in *Mukhtaṣar al-Shamāʾil* (103).

397 Reported by Abū Dāwūd (4850). See also the narration reported by Muslim (670/287).

398 Reported by Tirmidhī in *Al-Shamāʾil* (126) and Bukhārī in *Al-Adab al-Mufrad* (1178).

فصل

وَأَمَّا وَقَارُهُ ﷺ وَصَمْتُهُ، وَتُؤَدَتُهُ وَمُرُوءَتُهُ وَحُسْنُ هَدْيِهِ: فَحَدَّثَنَا أَبُو عَلِيٍّ الجَيَّانِيُّ الحَافِظُ إِجَازَةً، وَعَارَضْتُ بِكِتَابِهِ، قَالَ: حَدَّثَنَا أَبُو العَبَّاسِ الدِّلَائِيُّ، أَخْبَرَنَا أَبُو ذَرٍّ الهَرَوِيُّ، أَخْبَرَنَا أَبُو عَبْدِ اللهِ الوَرَّاقُ، حَدَّثَنَا اللُّؤْلُؤِيُّ، حَدَّثَنَا أَبُو دَاوُدَ، حَدَّثَنَا عَبْدُ الرَّحْمَنِ ابْنُ سَلَامٍ، حَدَّثَنَا حَجَّاجُ بْنُ مُحَمَّدٍ، عَنْ عَبْدِ الرَّحْمَنِ بْنِ أَبِي الزِّنَادِ، عَنْ عُمَرَ بْنِ عَبْدِ العَزِيزِ بْنِ وُهَيْبٍ: سَمِعْتُ خَارِجَةَ بْنَ زَيْدٍ يَقُولُ: كَانَ النَّبِيُّ ﷺ أَوْقَرَ النَّاسِ فِي مَجْلِسِهِ، لَا يَكَادُ يُخْرِجُ شَيْئًا مِنْ أَطْرَافِهِ٣٦٩.

وَرَوَى أَبُو سَعِيدٍ الخُدْرِيُّ رضي الله عنه: كَانَ النَّبِيُّ ﷺ إِذَا جَلَسَ المَجْلِسَ احْتَبَى بِثَوْبِهِ، وَكَذَلِكَ كَانَ أَكْثَرُ جُلُوسِهِ ﷺ مُحْتَبِيًا٣٧٠.

وَعَنْ جَابِرِ بْنِ سَمُرَةَ أَنَّهُ تَرَبَّعَ٣٧١، وَرُبَّمَا جَلَسَ القُرْفُصَاءَ، وَهُوَ فِي حَدِيثِ قَيْلَةَ٣٧٢.

---

٣٦٩ حَدِيثٌ مُرْسَلٌ. أَسْنَدَهُ المُصَنِّفُ مِنْ طَرِيقِ أَبِي دَاوُدَ فِي المَرَاسِيلِ (٥٠٥). وَفِي إِسْنَادِهِ عُمَرُ بْنُ عَبْدِ العَزِيزِ بْنِ وُهَيْبٍ. قَالَ الحَافِظُ فِي التَّقْرِيبِ: «مَجْهُولٌ». (أَوْقَرُ النَّاسِ) مِنَ الوَقَارِ: الحِلْمُ وَالرَّزَانَةُ.

٣٧٠ أَخْرَجَهُ أَبُو دَاوُدَ (٤٨٤٦)، وَالتِّرْمِذِيُّ فِي الشَّمَائِلِ (١٢١)، وَفِي إِسْنَادِهِ عَبْدُ اللهِ بْنُ إِبْرَاهِيمَ. قَالَ أَبُو دَاوُدَ: «شَيْخٌ مُنْكَرُ الحَدِيثِ»؛ وَضَعَّفَ إِسْنَادَهُ العِرَاقِيُّ فِي تَخْرِيجِ أَحَادِيثِ الإِحْيَاءِ (٣٦٦/٢). وَرَمَزَ لِحُسْنِهِ السُّيُوطِيُّ فِي الجَامِعِ الصَّغِيرِ (٦٦٣٧)، وَصَحَّحَهُ الشَّيْخُ الأَلْبَانِيُّ فِي مُخْتَصَرِ الشَّمَائِلِ (١٠٣). (احْتَبَى بِيَدَيْهِ) احْتَبَى الرَّجُلُ: إِذَا جَمَعَ ظَهْرَهُ وَسَاقَيْهِ بِيَدَيْهِ.

٣٧١ أَخْرَجَهُ أَبُو دَاوُدَ (٤٨٥٠) وَانْظُرْ رِوَايَةَ مُسْلِمٍ (٢٨٧/٦٧٠).

٣٧٢ تَقَدَّمَ حَدِيثُ قَيْلَةَ. (القُرْفُصَاءُ): هِيَ جَلْسَةُ المُحْتَبِي بِيَدَيْهِ/ النِّهَايَةُ.

would also smile rather than laugh in his presence, both as a sign of respect and to follow his example. His assemblies were those of forbearance, modesty, benefit, and trust. Voices were never raised and faults were not publicised. When the Prophet ﷺ spoke, the assembly would fall into silence, [sitting perfectly still] as if they had birds sitting on their heads.[399]

The Prophet ﷺ walked with composure and tranquillity, as if descending a gradient.[400] Another narration states that he walked with purpose, and was neither rushed nor lethargic in his gait.[401]

'Abdullāh ibn Mas'ūd said: "The best guidance is the guidance of Muhammad ﷺ."[402] And Jābir ibn 'Abdullāh ؓ observed: "The Messenger of Allah ﷺ spoke in an unhurried manner."[403]

'Alī said: "He would remain silent for one of four reasons: to show forbearance, as a warning, to convey his agreement, and to reflect."[404]

'Ā'ishah said: "The Messenger of Allah ﷺ used to speak [so clearly] that if a person wished to count [the number of words he said], they would be able to do so."[405]

The Prophet ﷺ loved pleasant scents and perfumes; he wore them often and advised others to do the same. He said: "From this worldly life of yours, I have been made to love women and perfume, and the prayer was made the coolness of my eyes (i.e.,

---

399   Taken from the narration of Ibn Abī Hālah. See *Al-Shamā'il* (335, 350).

400   See *Al-Shamā'il* (8).

401   Mentioned by Ibn al-Athīr in *Al-Nihāyah* (3/360).

402   Reported by Bukhārī (6098).

403   Reported by Abū Dāwūd (4839), and the chain contains a narrator who is not named.

404   Reported by Baghawī (3706) from al-Ḥusayn ibn 'Alī, who narrated from his father 'Alī ibn Abī Ṭālib.

405   Reported by Bukhārī (3567), and Muslim in *Al-Zuhd* (2493/71).

وَكَانَ كَثِيرَ السُّكُوتِ، لَا يَتَكَلَّمُ فِي غَيْرِ حَاجَةٍ، يُعْرِضُ عَمَّنْ تَكَلَّمَ بِغَيْرِ جَمِيلٍ، وَكَانَ ضَحِكُهُ تَبَسُّمًا، وَكَلَامُهُ فَصْلًا، لَا فُضُولَ وَلَا تَقْصِيرَ، وَكَانَ ضَحِكُ أَصْحَابِهِ عِنْدَهُ التَّبَسُّمَ، تَوْقِيرًا لَهُ، وَاقْتِدَاءً بِهِ، مَجْلِسُهُ مَجْلِسُ حِلْمٍ وَحَيَاءٍ وَخَيْرٍ وَأَمَانَةٍ، لَا تُرْفَعُ فِيهِ الْأَصْوَاتُ، وَلَا تُؤْبَنُ فِيهِ الْحُرَمُ، إِذَا تَكَلَّمَ أَطْرَقَ جُلَسَاؤُهُ كَأَنَّمَا عَلَى رُؤُوسِهِمُ الطَّيْرُ.

وَفِي صِفَتِهِ ﷺ: يَخْطُو تَكَفُّؤًا، وَيَمْشِي هَوْنًا، كَأَنَّمَا يَنْحَطُّ مِنْ صَبَبٍ.

وَفِي الْحَدِيثِ الْآخَرِ: إِذَا مَشَى مَشَى مُجْتَمِعًا، يُعْرَفُ فِي مِشْيَتِهِ أَنَّهُ غَيْرُ غَرِضٍ، وَلَا وَكِلٍ[373]، أَيْ: غَيْرُ ضَجِرٍ وَلَا كَسْلَانَ.

وَقَالَ عَبْدُ اللهِ بْنُ مَسْعُودٍ: إِنَّ أَحْسَنَ الْهَدْيِ هَدْيُ مُحَمَّدٍ ﷺ[374].

وَعَنْ جَابِرِ بْنِ عَبْدِ اللهِ: كَانَ فِي كَلَامِ رَسُولِ اللهِ ﷺ تَرْتِيلٌ أَوْ تَرْسِيلٌ[375].

قَالَ ابْنُ أَبِي هَالَةَ[376]: كَانَ سُكُوتُهُ عَلَى أَرْبَعٍ: عَلَى الْحِلْمِ، وَالْحَذَرِ، وَالتَّقْدِيرِ، وَالتَّفَكُّرِ.

قَالَتْ عَائِشَةُ ﵂: كَانَ رَسُولُ اللهِ ﷺ يُحَدِّثُ حَدِيثًا لَوْ عَدَّهُ الْعَادُّ أَحْصَاهُ[377].

---

373 أَوْرَدَهُ ابْنُ الْأَثِيرِ فِي النِّهَايَةِ 360/3. (غَرِضٍ) الْغَرِضُ: الْقَلِقُ الضَّجِرُ. (وَكِلٌ): الْوَكَلُ وَالْوَكِلُ: الْبَلِيدُ وَالْجَبَانُ. وَقِيلَ: الْعَاجِزُ الَّذِي يَكِلُ أَمْرَهُ إِلَى غَيْرِهِ/ النِّهَايَةُ.

374 أَخْرَجَهُ الْبُخَارِيُّ (6098). (الْهَدْيُ): الطَّرِيقَةُ وَالسِّيرَةُ.

375 أَخْرَجَهُ أَبُو دَاوُدَ (4838) وَفِي سَنَدِهِ رَاوٍ لَمْ يُسَمَّ. (تَرْتِيلٌ) التَّرْتِيلُ فِي الْقِرَاءَةِ: تَرْتِيبُهَا وَالتَّأَنِّي فِيهَا، وَكَذَلِكَ التَّرْسِيلُ. وَقِيلَ: التَّرْتِيلُ: التَّبْيِينُ. وَالتَّرْسِيلُ: التُّؤَدَةُ.

376 بَلِ الْقَائِلُ عَلِيُّ بْنُ أَبِي طَالِبٍ ﵁. أَخْرَجَهُ الْبَغَوِيُّ (3706).

377 أَخْرَجَهُ الْبُخَارِيُّ (3567)، وَمُسْلِمٌ فِي الزُّهْدِ (2493/71).

my source of comfort).”[406] He forbade blowing into food[407] and drinks[408], and told people to eat from that which was closest to them.[409] And the Prophet ﷺ encouraged use of the *miswāk*,[410] as well as cleaning between the toes and fingers and observing the ten practices of the *fiṭrah*.[411]

---

406   Reported by Nasā'ī (7/61), Aḥmad (3/128), Abū Ya'lā (3482), Bayhaqī (7/87), and others.

407   Reported by Abū Dāwūd (3728), Tirmidhī (1888), and Ibn Mājah (3428), from Ibn 'Abbās. Authenticated by Ḥākim (4/138) and Dhahabī concurred. Tirmidhī said: “This narration is *hasan ṣaḥīḥ*.”

408   Reported by Abū Dāwūd (3722) and Tirmidhī (1887). Tirmidhī said: “This narration is *hasan ṣaḥīḥ*.”

409   Reported by Bukhārī (5376) and Muslim (2022), from 'Umar ibn Abī Salamah.

410   Reported by Bukhārī (888), Muslim (252), Tirmidhī (22), Nasā'ī (7), and others.

411   Reported by Muslim (261) from 'Ā'ishah.

وَكَانَ ﷺ يُحِبُّ الطِّيبَ، وَالرَّائِحَةَ الحَسَنَةَ، وَيَسْتَعْمِلُهَا كَثِيرًا، وَيَحُضُّ عَلَيْهَا، وَيَقُولُ: «حُبِّبَ إِلَيَّ مِنْ دُنْيَاكُمُ النِّسَاءُ وَالطِّيبُ، وَجُعِلَتْ قُرَّةُ عَيْنِي فِي الصَّلَاةِ».

وَمِنْ مُرُوءَتِهِ ﷺ: نَهْيُهُ عَنِ النَّفْخِ فِي الطَّعَامِ وَالشَّرَابِ³⁷⁸، وَالأَمْرُ بِالأَكْلِ مِمَّا يَلِي³⁷⁹، وَالأَمْرُ بِالسِّوَاكِ، وَإِنْقَاءُ البَرَاجِمِ وَالرَّوَاجِبِ، وَاسْتِعْمَالُ خِصَالِ الفِطْرَةِ³⁸⁰.

---

٣٧٨ نَهْيُهُ ﷺ عَنِ النَّفْخِ فِي الإِنَاءِ، أَخْرَجَهُ أَبُو دَاوُدَ (٣٧٢٨)، وَالتِّرْمِذِيُّ (١٨٨٨)، وَابْنُ مَاجَهْ (٣٤٢٨) مِنْ حَدِيثِ ابْنِ عَبَّاسٍ، وَصَحَّحَهُ الحَاكِمُ ٤/١٣٨، وَوَافَقَهُ الذَّهَبِيُّ. وَقَالَ التِّرْمِذِيُّ: «هَذَا حَدِيثٌ حَسَنٌ صَحِيحٌ». وَلِلتِّرْمِذِيِّ (١٨٨٧)، وَأَبِي دَاوُدَ (٣٧٢٢) نَهَى عَنِ النَّفْخِ فِي الشَّرَابِ. قَالَ التِّرْمِذِيُّ: هَذَا حَدِيثٌ حَسَنٌ صَحِيحٌ.

٣٧٩ أَخْرَجَهُ البُخَارِيُّ (٥٣٧٦)، وَمُسْلِمٌ (٢٠٢٢) مِنْ حَدِيثِ عُمَرَ بْنِ أَبِي سَلَمَةَ.

٣٨٠ أَخْرَجَ مُسْلِمٌ (٢٦١) عَنْ عَائِشَةَ مَرْفُوعًا: «عَشْرٌ مِنَ الفِطْرَةِ: قَصُّ الشَّارِبِ، وَإِعْفَاءُ اللِّحْيَةِ، وَالسِّوَاكُ، وَاسْتِنْشَاقُ المَاءِ، وَقَصُّ الأَظْفَارِ، وَغَسْلُ البَرَاجِمِ، وَنَتْفُ الإِبِطِ، وَحَلْقُ العَانَةِ، وَانْتِقَاصُ المَاءِ. قَالَ أَحَدُ رُوَاةِ الحَدِيثِ: وَنَسِيتُ العَاشِرَةَ إِلَّا أَنْ تَكُونَ المَضْمَضَةَ». (البَرَاجِمُ): العُقَدُ المُتَشَنِّجَةُ فِي ظَاهِرِ الأَصَابِعِ. (الرَّوَاجِبُ): هِيَ مَا بَيْنَ عُقَدِ الأَصَابِعِ مِنْ دَاخِلٍ/ النِّهَايَةِ.

HIS ASCETICISM IN WORLDLY AFFAIRS AND SHUNNING OF MATERIAL WEALTH

We have already presented many accounts of the asceticism and frugality of the Prophet ﷺ. He was content with little in terms of material possessions and turned away from the pleasures of this world. As a prime example of the way the Prophet ﷺ lived, consider the fact that despite enormous wealth being presented to him as a result of the conquests and battles fought by the Muslims, he passed away with his body armour pawned to a Jewish man, which he had done to support his family.[412] The Prophet of Allah ﷺ would supplicate: "O Allah! Provide the family of Muhammad with nourishment!"[413]

Sufyān ibn al-ʿĀṣ, al-Ḥusayn ibn Muhammad al-Ḥāfiẓ, and Abū ʿAbdullāh al-Tamīmī all narrated from Aḥmad ibn ʿUmar, from Abū al-ʿAbbās al-Rāzī, from Abū Aḥmad al-Julūdī, from Ibn Sufyān, from Abū al-Ḥusayn (Muslim ibn al-Ḥajjāj)[414], from Abū Bakr ibn Abī Shaybah, from Abū Muʿāwiyah, from al-Aʿmash, from Ibrāhīm, from al-Aswad, from ʿĀʾishah, who said: "Until he went his way,[415] the Messenger of Allah ﷺ never ate his fill of [wheat][416] bread for three consecutive days."[417]

---

412 Reported by Bukhārī (2916) and Muslim (1603) from ʿĀʾishah, and Bukhārī (2069) from Anas.

413 Reported by Bukhārī (6460), and Muslim (1055) with this wording, from Abū Hurayrah.

414 Imam Muslim.

415 i.e., "until he passed away".

416 This word was reported by Muslim only.

417 Reported here from the chain of Muslim (2970/21).

فَصْل

وَأَمَّا زُهْدُهُ فِي الدُّنْيَا

فَقَدْ تَقَدَّمَ مِنَ الأَخْبَارِ أَثْنَاءَ هَذِهِ السِّيَرِ مَا يَكْفِي، وَحَسْبُكَ مِنْ تَقَلُّلِهِ مِنْهَا وَإِعْرَاضِهِ عَنْ زَهْرَتِهَا - وَقَدْ سِيقَتْ إِلَيْهِ بِحَذَافِيرِهَا، وَتَرَادَفَتْ عَلَيْهِ فُتُوحُهَا - إِلَى أَنْ تُوُفِّيَ ﷺ وَدِرْعُهُ مَرْهُونَةٌ عِنْدَ يَهُودِيٍّ فِي نَفَقَةِ عِيَالِهِ³⁸¹، وَهُوَ يَدْعُو وَيَقُولُ: «اللَّهُمَّ اجْعَلْ رِزْقَ آلِ مُحَمَّدٍ قُوتًا»³⁸².

حَدَّثَنَا سُفْيَانُ بْنُ العَاصِي، وَالحُسَيْنُ بْنُ مُحَمَّدٍ الحَافِظُ، وَالقَاضِي أَبُو عَبْدِ اللهِ التَّمِيمِيُّ، قَالُوا: حَدَّثَنَا أَحْمَدُ بْنُ عُمَرَ، قَالَ: حَدَّثَنَا أَبُو العَبَّاسِ الرَّازِيُّ، قَالَ: حَدَّثَنَا أَبُو أَحْمَدَ الجُلُودِيُّ، حَدَّثَنَا ابْنُ سُفْيَانَ، حَدَّثَنَا أَبُو الحُسَيْنِ ابْنُ الحَجَّاجِ، حَدَّثَنَا أَبُو بَكْرِ بْنُ أَبِي شَيْبَةَ، حَدَّثَنَا أَبُو مُعَاوِيَةَ، عَنِ الأَعْمَشِ، عَنْ إِبْرَاهِيمَ، عَنِ الأَسْوَدِ، عَنْ عَائِشَةَ قَالَتْ: مَا شَبِعَ رَسُولُ اللهِ ﷺ ثَلَاثَةَ أَيَّامٍ تِبَاعًا مِنْ خُبْزِ بُرٍّ³⁸³ حَتَّى مَضَى لِسَبِيلِهِ³⁸⁴.

وَفِي رِوَايَةٍ أُخْرَى: مِنْ خُبْزِ شَعِيرٍ يَوْمَيْنِ مُتَوَالِيَيْنِ، وَلَوْ شَاءَ لَأَعْطَاهُ اللهُ مَا

---

٣٨١   مَوْتُهُ ﷺ وَدِرْعُهُ مَرْهُونَةٌ. أَخْرَجَهُ البُخَارِيُّ (٢٩١٦)، وَمُسْلِمٌ (١٦٠٣) مِنْ حَدِيثِ عَائِشَةَ، وَالبُخَارِيُّ (٢٠٦٩) مِنْ حَدِيثِ أَنَسٍ.

٣٨٢   أَخْرَجَهُ البُخَارِيُّ (٦٤٦٠)، وَمُسْلِمٌ (١٠٥٥) وَاللَّفْظُ لَهُ، مِنْ حَدِيثِ أَبِي هُرَيْرَةَ. (قُوتًا) قِيلَ: هُوَ كِفَايَتُهُمْ مِنْ غَيْرِ إِسْرَافٍ. وَقِيلَ: هُوَ مَا يُمْسِكُ الرَّمَقَ.

٣٨٣   زِيَادَةٌ مِنْ صَحِيحِ مُسْلِمٍ.

٣٨٤   أَسْنَدَهُ المُصَنِّفُ مِنْ طَرِيقِ الإِمَامِ مُسْلِمٍ (٢١/٢٩٧٠).

In another transmission, she said: "Until the Messenger ﷺ was taken, the family of Muhammad ﷺ never ate their fill of barley bread for two consecutive days."[418] And in another wording: "The family of Muhammad ﷺ never ate their fill of wheat bread until the Messenger of Allah ﷺ reunited with Allah Exalted."[419]

ʿĀʾishah said: "The Messenger of Allah ﷺ did not leave behind (after his death) a dinar, a dirham, a sheep, or a camel."[420] ʿAmr ibn al-Ḥārith narrated: "The Prophet ﷺ did not leave anything behind except his weapons, his white mule, and some land he had designated as charity."[421]

ʿĀʾishah also said: "When he died, there was nothing in my house for a living being[422] to eat except some barley on one of the shelves."[423] She continued: "The Prophet ﷺ said to me: 'I was shown that the valley of Makkah would be turned into gold, so I supplicated: "No! O Lord! Some days I am hungry and other days I am full. As for the days I am hungry, I supplicate and call upon You, and as for the days I am full, I thank and praise You."'"[424]

Another narration reports that Jibrīl ﷺ came down to the Prophet ﷺ and said to him: "Allah Exalted greets you and says: 'Would you like Me to turn this mountain into gold that will be with you wherever you go?'" The Prophet ﷺ bowed his head for a long period of time, and then he said: "O Jibrīl! This world is a

---

418   Reported by Muslim (2970/22).

419   Reported by Bukhārī (6454) and Muslim (2970/20).

420   Reported by Muslim (1635).

421   Reported by Bukhārī (3098).

422   The term used for "living being" is "*dhū al-kabid*"; lit., "one with a liver".

423   Reported by Bukhārī (3097) and Muslim (2973).

424   Reported by Tirmidhī (2347) and Aḥmad (5/254) from Abū Umāmah. Tirmidhī graded the hadith as *ḥasan*, and Suyūṭī followed his opinion in *Al-Jāmiʿ al-Ṣaghīr* (5417). Al-Ḥūt al-Bayrūtī said in *Asnā al-Maṭālib* (p. 139): "Al-ʿAlāʾī said: 'The chain contains three weak narrators.' And ʿIrāqī said: '[The hadith is] weak.'"

لَا يَخْطُرُ بِبَالٍ^{٣٨٥}.

وَفِي رِوَايَةٍ أُخْرَى: مَا شَبِعَ آلُ رَسُولِ اللهِ ﷺ مِنْ خُبْزِ بُرٍّ حَتَّى لَقِيَ اللهَ تَعَالَى^{٣٨٦}.

وَقَالَتْ عَائِشَةُ رَضِيَ اللهُ عَنْهَا: مَا تَرَكَ رَسُولُ اللهِ ﷺ دِينَارًا، وَلَا دِرْهَمًا، وَلَا شَاةً، وَلَا بَعِيرًا^{٣٨٧}.

وَفِي حَدِيثِ عَمْرِو بْنِ الحَارِثِ: مَا تَرَكَ إِلَّا سِلَاحَهُ، وَبَغْلَتَهُ، وَأَرْضًا جَعَلَهَا صَدَقَةً^{٣٨٨}.

قَالَتْ عَائِشَةُ رَضِيَ اللهُ عَنْهَا: وَلَقَدْ مَاتَ وَمَا فِي بَيْتِي شَيْءٌ يَأْكُلُهُ ذُو كَبِدٍ، إِلَّا شَطْرَ شَعِيرٍ فِي رَفٍّ لِي^{٣٨٩}.

وَقَالَ لِي: «إِنِّي عُرِضَ عَلَيَّ أَنْ تُجْعَلَ لِي بَطْحَاءُ مَكَّةَ ذَهَبًا، فَقُلْتُ: لَا يَا رَبِّ، أَجُوعُ يَوْمًا، وَأَشْبَعُ يَوْمًا، فَأَمَّا اليَوْمُ الَّذِي أَجُوعُ فِيهِ فَأَتَضَرَّعُ إِلَيْكَ وَأَدْعُوكَ، وَأَمَّا اليَوْمُ الَّذِي أَشْبَعُ فِيهِ فَأَحْمَدُكَ وَأُثْنِي عَلَيْكَ»^{٣٩٠}.

---

^{٣٨٥}   هُوَ فِي مُسْلِمٍ (٢٢/٢٩٧٠) بِلَفْظِ: مَا شَبِعَ آلُ مُحَمَّدٍ ﷺ مِنْ خُبْزِ شَعِيرٍ، يَوْمَيْنِ مُتَتَابِعَيْنِ، حَتَّى قُبِضَ رَسُولُ اللهِ ﷺ.

^{٣٨٦}   أَخْرَجَهُ البُخَارِيُّ (٦٤٥٤)، وَمُسْلِمٌ (٢٠/٢٩٧٠).

^{٣٨٧}   أَخْرَجَهُ مُسْلِمٌ (١٦٣٥).

^{٣٨٨}   أَخْرَجَهُ البُخَارِيُّ (٣٠٩٨).

^{٣٨٩}   أَخْرَجَهُ البُخَارِيُّ (٣٠٩٧) وَمُسْلِمٌ (٢٩٧٣). (شَطْرَ شَعِيرٍ): شَيْءٌ مِنْهُ. (رَفٍّ لِي) الرَّفُّ: خَشَبٌ يُرْفَعُ عَنِ الأَرْضِ إِلَى جَنْبِ الجِدَارِ يُوقَّى بِهِ مَا يُوضَعُ عَلَيْهِ/ النِّهَايَةُ.

^{٣٩٠}   أَخْرَجَهُ التِّرْمِذِيُّ (٢٣٤٧)، وَأَحْمَدُ (٢٥٤/٥) مِنْ حَدِيثِ أَبِي أُمَامَةَ. وَحَسَّنَهُ التِّرْمِذِيُّ، وَتَبِعَهُ السُّيُوطِيُّ فِي الجَامِعِ الصَّغِيرِ (٥٤١٧). وَقَالَ الحَوْتُ فِي أَسْنَى المَطَالِبِ ص (١٣٩): «قَالَ العَلَائِيُّ: فِيهِ ثَلَاثَةُ ضُعَفَاءَ. وَقَالَ العِرَاقِيُّ: ضَعِيفٌ».

home for the one with no home, wealth for the one with no wealth, and both for the one with no intellect." Jibrīl replied: "Allah has made you steady with a firm statement,[425] O Muhammad!"[426]

'Ā'ishah narrated: "We, the family of Muhammad, would pass a whole month without lighting a fire [to cook on]. [We would survive on] nothing but dates and water."[427] 'Abd al-Raḥmān ibn 'Awf said: "When the Messenger of Allah ﷺ died, neither he nor his family had ever eaten their fill of barley bread."[428] Narrations of a similar nature were also reported from 'Ā'ishah[429], Abū Umāmah[430], and Ibn 'Abbās[431].

Ibn 'Abbās said: "On many nights, the family of the Messenger of Allah ﷺ would not find anything to eat for dinner."[432] Anas narrated: "The Messenger of Allah ﷺ never ate at dining tables or from platters. Fine breads were never prepared for him and he never set eyes on poached mutton."[433] And 'Ā'ishah recalled: "The

---

425   Translator's note: Reference to *Ibrāhīm*, 27.

426   Suyūṭī said in *Al-Manāhil*, p. 296: "I did not find the hadith in this form." Reported by Abū Yaʿlā (4920) and others in a *marfūʿ* narration from 'Ā'ishah, with the wording: "O 'Ā'ishah! If I had wanted, I would have a mountain of gold with me." Haythamī graded the chain as *ḥasan* in *Majmaʿ al-Zawāʾid* (9/19). The last part of the hadith, relating to "this life", was reported as *marfūʿ* by Aḥmad (6/71) and Bayhaqī. Al-Mundhirī said in *Al-Targhīb wa al-Tarhīb* (4/78): "Both chains are good." 'Irāqī also approved of the chain in *Takhrīj Aḥādīth al-Iḥyāʾ* (3/203). See also *Majmaʿ al-Zawāʾid* (10/315) and *Al-Targhīb wa al-Tarhīb* (4/196).

427   Reported by Bukhārī (6458), and Muslim (2972) with this wording.

428   Reported by Tirmidhī in *Al-Shamāʾil* (378) with this wording, and Bazzār (3684). The chain was graded *ḥasan* by Bazzār, al-Mundhirī in *Al-Targhīb wa al-Tarhīb* (4/189), Haythamī in *Majmaʿ al-Zawāʾid* (10/312), and Suyūṭī in *Al-Manāhil*, p. 298.

429   Reported by Muslim (2970/21).

430   Reported by Tirmidhī in *Al-Sunan* (2359) and *Al-Shamāʾil* (143). Also reported by Aḥmad (5/253) with the wording: "There was nothing the family of the Messenger of Allah loved [to eat] more than barley bread." Tirmidhī said: "This narration is *ṣaḥīḥ gharīb*."

431   Reported by Tirmidhī in *Al-Sunan* (2360) and *Al-Shamāʾil* (144) with the wording: "On many nights, the family of the Messenger of Allah ﷺ would not find anything to eat for dinner. Most of their bread was barley bread." He said: "This narration is *ḥasan ṣaḥīḥ*."

432   See previous footnote.

433   Reported by Bukhārī in two parts: the last part of the hadith (5457) and the rest (5415).

وَفِي حَدِيثٍ آخَرَ أَنَّ جِبْرِيلَ نَزَلَ عَلَيْهِ - صَلَّى اللهُ عَلَيْهِمَا وَسَلَّمَ - فَقَالَ لَهُ: إِنَّ اللهَ يُقْرِئُكَ السَّلَامَ، وَيَقُولُ لَكَ: أَتُحِبُّ أَنْ أَجْعَلَ هَذِهِ الْجِبَالَ ذَهَبًا، وَتَكُونَ مَعَكَ أَيْنَ كُنْتَ؟ فَأَطْرَقَ سَاعَةً، ثُمَّ قَالَ: «يَا جِبْرِيلُ، إِنَّ الدُّنْيَا دَارُ مَنْ لَا دَارَ لَهُ، وَمَالُ مَنْ لَا مَالَ لَهُ، قَدْ يَجْمَعُهَا مَنْ لَا عَقْلَ لَهُ». فَقَالَ لَهُ جِبْرِيلُ: ثَبَّتَكَ اللهُ يَا مُحَمَّدُ بِالْقَوْلِ الثَّابِتِ³⁹¹.

وَعَنْ عَائِشَةَ رَضِيَ اللهُ عَنْهَا قَالَتْ: إِنْ كُنَّا آلَ مُحَمَّدٍ لَنَمْكُثُ شَهْرًا مَا نَسْتَوْقِدُ نَارًا، إِنْ هُوَ إِلَّا التَّمْرُ وَالْمَاءُ³⁹².

وَعَنْ عَبْدِ الرَّحْمَنِ بْنِ عَوْفٍ: هَلَكَ رَسُولُ اللهِ ﷺ، وَلَمْ يَشْبَعْ هُوَ وَأَهْلُ بَيْتِهِ مِنْ خُبْزِ الشَّعِيرِ³⁹³.

وَعَنْ عَائِشَةَ وَأَبِي أُمَامَةَ وَابْنِ عَبَّاسٍ نَحْوُهُ³⁹⁴.

قَالَ ابْنُ عَبَّاسٍ رَضِيَ اللهُ عَنْهُمَا: كَانَ ﷺ يَبِيتُ هُوَ وَأَهْلُهُ اللَّيَالِيَ الْمُتَتَابِعَةَ

---

٣٩١ قَالَ السُّيُوطِيُّ فِي الْمَنَاهِلِ (٢٩٦): «لَمْ أَجِدْهُ هَكَذَا». وَأَخْرَجَ أَبُو يَعْلَى (٤٩٢٠) وَغَيْرُهُ مِنْ حَدِيثِ عَائِشَةَ مَرْفُوعًا: «يَا عَائِشَةُ! لَوْ شِئْتُ لَسَارَتْ مَعِي جِبَالُ الذَّهَبِ» وَحَسَّنَ إِسْنَادَهُ الْهَيْثَمِيُّ فِي الْمَجْمَعِ ٩/١٩. وَمَا يَتَعَلَّقُ بِالدُّنْيَا وَرَدَ عَنْهَا مَرْفُوعًا عِنْدَ أَحْمَدَ ٦/٧١ وَالْبَيْهَقِيِّ. قَالَ الْحَافِظُ الْمُنْذِرِيُّ فِي التَّرْغِيبِ وَالتَّرْهِيبِ ٤/٨٧: «وَإِسْنَادُهُمَا جَيِّدٌ» وَجَوَّدَ إِسْنَادَهُ أَيْضًا الْحَافِظُ الْعِرَاقِيُّ فِي تَخْرِيجِ أَحَادِيثِ الْإِحْيَاءِ (٣/٢٠٣). وَانْظُرْ مَجْمَعَ الزَّوَائِدِ ١٠/٣١٥، وَالتَّرْغِيبَ وَالتَّرْهِيبَ ٤/١٩٦.

٣٩٢ أَخْرَجَهُ الْبُخَارِيُّ (٦٤٥٨)، وَمُسْلِمٌ (٢٩٧٢) وَاللَّفْظُ لَهُ.

٣٩٣ أَخْرَجَهُ التِّرْمِذِيُّ فِي الشَّمَائِلِ (١٣٩)، وَاللَّفْظُ لَهُ. وَالْبَزَّارُ (٣٦٨٤)، وَحَسَّنَ إِسْنَادَ الْبَزَّارِ الْمُنْذِرِيُّ فِي التَّرْغِيبِ وَالتَّرْهِيبِ ٤/١٨٩، وَالْهَيْثَمِيُّ فِي الْمَجْمَعِ ١٠/٣١٢، وَالسُّيُوطِيُّ فِي الْمَنَاهِلِ (٢٩٨).

٣٩٤ حَدِيثُ أَبِي أُمَامَةَ أَخْرَجَهُ التِّرْمِذِيُّ فِي السُّنَنِ (٢٣٥٩)، وَفِي الشَّمَائِلِ (١٤٦)، وَأَحْمَدُ ٥/٢٥٣ وَلَفْظُهُ: مَا كَانَ يَفْضُلُ عَنْ أَهْلِ بَيْتِ رَسُولِ اللهِ خُبْزُ الشَّعِيرِ. قَالَ التِّرْمِذِيُّ: «حَسَنٌ صَحِيحٌ غَرِيبٌ». وَحَدِيثُ ابْنِ عَبَّاسٍ أَخْرَجَهُ التِّرْمِذِيُّ فِي السُّنَنِ (٢٣٦٠)، وَفِي الشَّمَائِلِ (١٤٧) وَلَفْظُهُ: كَانَ رَسُولُ اللهِ ﷺ يَبِيتُ اللَّيَالِيَ الْمُتَتَابِعَةَ طَاوِيًا، وَأَهْلُهُ، لَا يَجِدُونَ عَشَاءً، وَكَانَ أَكْثَرُ خُبْزِهِمْ خُبْزَ الشَّعِيرِ. قَالَ التِّرْمِذِيُّ: حَسَنٌ صَحِيحٌ.

bed of the Messenger of Allah ﷺ was an animal hide covering stuffed with palm fibres."[434] Ḥafṣah said: "In my house, the bed of the Messenger of Allah ﷺ was coarse fabric that we folded into two layers for him to sleep on.

One night, we folded it into four layers. When he woke up, he said: 'What did you lay out for me last night?' We told him what we had done, and he said: 'Return the bedding to its original state, for its softness prevented me from performing my night prayers.'"[435] Sometimes, the Prophet ﷺ would sleep on a bed made from date palm stalks which left marks on his side.[436]

ʿĀʾishah related: "Not once did the Prophet ﷺ fill his stomach, yet he never complained to anyone. Privation was more beloved to him than wealth. Even if he spent the whole night suffering from hunger, it would not prevent him from fasting the following day. If he wished, he could have asked his Lord for all the fruits and treasures of the world, and a life of ease and comfort. I used to cry for him and rub his stomach because of his severe hunger, and I would say: 'May I be your ransom! If only you had enough from this world to sustain you!'

He replied: 'O ʿĀʾishah! What concern do I have with this world? My brothers from amongst the Messengers of Firm Resolve were patient in the face of trials that were more severe than this.[437]

They died as they were and proceeded to their Lord, and how honoured they were! Their reward was immense. I feel shy to enjoy a life of ease if it means that tomorrow I will fall short in compari-

---

434   Reported by Bukhārī (6456), and Muslim (2082) with this wording.

435   Reported by Tirmidhī in *Al-Shamāʾil* (328). Graded as *ḥasan* by Suyūṭī in *Al-Jāmiʿ al-Ṣa-ghīr* (6841). Munāwī said in *Fayḍ al-Qadīr* (5/172): "The chain is not strong, and ʿIrāqī said it is 'disconnected'."

436   Reported by Bukhārī (5191) and Muslim (1479) from ʿUmar, in a lengthy hadith.

437   Translator's note: See *al-Aḥqāf*, 35.

طَاوِيًا، لَا يَجِدُونَ عَشَاءً٣٩٥.

وَعَنْ أَنَسٍ رضي الله عنه: مَا أَكَلَ رَسُولُ اللهِ ﷺ عَلَى خِوَانٍ قَطُّ، وَلَا فِي سُكُرُّجَةٍ، وَلَا خُبِزَ لَهُ مُرَقَّقٌ، وَلَا رَأَى شَاةً سَمِيطًا قَطُّ٣٩٦.

وَعَنْ عَائِشَةَ رضي الله عنها: إِنَّمَا كَانَ فِرَاشُ رَسُولِ اللهِ ﷺ الَّذِي يَنَامُ عَلَيْهِ أَدَمًا حَشْوُهُ لِيفٌ٣٩٧.

وَعَنْ حَفْصَةَ رضي الله عنها: كَانَ فِرَاشُ رَسُولِ اللهِ ﷺ فِي بَيْتِي مِسْحًا نَثْنِيهِ ثِنْيَيْنِ، فَيَنَامُ عَلَيْهِ، فَثَنَيْنَاهُ لَهُ لَيْلَةً بِأَرْبَعَ، فَلَمَّا أَصْبَحَ قَالَ: «مَا فَرَشْتُمُونِي اللَّيْلَةَ؟» فَذَكَرْنَا ذَلِكَ لَهُ، فَقَالَ: «رُدُّوهُ بِحَالِهِ، فَإِنَّ وَطَاءَتَهُ مَنَعَتْنِي اللَّيْلَةَ صَلَاتِي»٣٩٨.

وَكَانَ ﷺ يَنَامُ أَحْيَانًا عَلَى سَرِيرٍ مَرْمُولٍ بِشَرِيطٍ حَتَّى يُؤَثِّرَ فِي جَنْبِهِ٣٩٩.

وَعَنْ عَائِشَةَ قَالَتْ: لَمْ يَمْتَلِئْ جَوْفُ النَّبِيِّ ﷺ شِبَعًا قَطُّ، وَلَمْ يَبُثَّ شَكْوَى إِلَى أَحَدٍ، وَكَانَتِ الفَاقَةُ أَحَبَّ إِلَيْهِ مِنَ الغِنَى، وَإِنْ كَانَ لَيَظَلُّ جَائِعًا يَلْتَوِي

---

٣٩٥ (طَاوِيًا): أَيْ خَالِي البَطْنِ جَائِعًا، لَمْ يَأْكُلْ.

٣٩٦ رَوَاهُ البُخَارِيُّ مُقَطَّعًا: رَوَى الفِقْرَةَ الأَخِيرَةَ بِرَقْمِ (٥٤٥٧)، وَبَاقِيَهُ بِرَقْمِ (٥٤١٥). (الخِوَانُ): مَا يُؤْكَلُ عَلَيْهِ. (سُكُرُّجَةٍ): إِنَاءٌ صَغِيرٌ يُؤْكَلُ فِيهِ الشَّيْءُ القَلِيلُ مِنَ الأُدْمِ. (سَمِيطًا) مَشْوِيَّةً.

٣٩٧ أَخْرَجَهُ البُخَارِيُّ (٦٤٥٦)، وَمُسْلِمٌ (٢٠٨٢) وَاللَّفْظُ لَهُ. (أَدَمًا): جَمْعُ أَدِيمٍ، وَهُوَ الجِلْدُ المَدْبُوغُ. (لِيفٌ): هُوَ لِيفُ النَّخْلِ.

٣٩٨ أَخْرَجَهُ التِّرْمِذِيُّ فِي الشَّمَائِلِ (٣٢٢). وَرَمَزَ لِحُسْنِهِ السُّيُوطِيُّ فِي الجَامِعِ الصَّغِيرِ (٦٨٤١)، قَالَ المُنَاوِي فِي فَيْضِ القَدِيرِ ٥/١٧٢: «وَلَيْسَ بِجَيِّدٍ، فَقَدْ قَالَ الحَافِظُ العِرَاقِيُّ: هُوَ مُنْقَطِعٌ» (المِسْحُ): كِسَاءٌ خَشِنٌ يُعَدُّ لِلْفَرْشِ مِنْ صُوفٍ. (وَطَاءَتَهُ): لِينَهُ.

٣٩٩ أَخْرَجَهُ البُخَارِيُّ (٥١٩١)، وَمُسْلِمٌ (١٤٧٩) عَنْ عُمَرَ فِي حَدِيثٍ طَوِيلٍ. (مَرْمُولٍ): مَنْسُوجٌ بِحَبْلٍ مَفْتُولٍ بِسَعَفٍ.

son to them, and nothing is more beloved to me than being reunited with my brothers and dear friends.' Less than a month later, the Prophet ﷺ had passed away."[438]

---

438   Suyūṭī said in *Al-Manāhil*, p. 307: "I did not come across the narration in this form". It was, however, reported by Ibn Abī Ḥātim in his *Tafsīr*. The first part of this hadith is cited in footnote 142.

طُولَ لَيْلَتِهِ مِنَ الجُوعِ فَلَا يَمْنَعُهُ صِيَامَ يَوْمِهِ، وَلَوْ شَاءَ سَأَلَ رَبَّهُ جَمِيعَ كُنُوزِ الأَرْضِ وَثِمَارَهَا وَرَغَدَ عَيْشِهَا، وَلَقَدْ كُنْتُ أَبْكِي رَحْمَةً لَهُ مِمَّا أَرَى بِهِ، وَأَمْسَحُ بِيَدِي عَلَى بَطْنِهِ مِمَّا بِهِ مِنَ الجُوعِ، وَأَقُولُ: نَفْسِي لَكَ الفِدَاءُ، لَوْ تَبَلَّغْتَ مِنَ الدُّنْيَا بِمَا يَقُوتُكَ؟ فَيَقُولُ: «يَا عَائِشَةُ، مَا لِي وَلِلدُّنْيَا، إِخْوَانِي مِنْ أُولِي العَزْمِ مِنَ الرُّسُلِ صَبَرُوا عَلَى مَا هُوَ أَشَدُّ مِنْ هَذَا، فَمَضَوْا عَلَى حَالِهِمْ، فَقَدِمُوا عَلَى رَبِّهِمْ، فَأَكْرَمَ مَآبَهُمْ، وَأَجْزَلَ ثَوَابَهُمْ، فَأَجِدُنِي أَسْتَحْيِي إِنْ تَرَفَّهْتُ فِي مَعِيشَتِي أَنْ يَقْصُرَ بِي غَدًا دُونَهُمْ، وَمَا مِنْ شَيْءٍ هُوَ أَحَبُّ إِلَيَّ مِنَ اللُّحُوقِ بِإِخْوَانِي وَأَخِلَّائِي». قَالَتْ: فَمَا أَقَامَ بَعْدُ إِلَّا شَهْرًا حَتَّى تُوُفِّيَ[400].

صَلَوَاتُ اللهِ وَسَلَامُهُ وَرَحْمَتُهُ الدَّائِمَةُ عَلَيْهِ.

---

[400] قَالَ السُّيُوطِيُّ فِي المَنَاهِلِ (٣٠٧): «الحَدِيثُ لَمْ أَقِفْ عَلَيْهِ هَكَذَا» وَلَكِنْ أَخْرَجَ ابْنُ أَبِي حَاتِمٍ فِي تَفْسِيرِهِ مِنْ حَدِيثِهَا...».

HIS FEAR OF HIS LORD, OBEDIENCE TO HIM, AND INTENSE WORSHIP

Because of the knowledge of his Lord possessed by the Prophet ﷺ, he was the most fearful of Him, the most obedient, and the most diligent and intense in worship.

I read the following hadith to Abū Muhammad ibn ʿAttāb, who narrated from Abū al-Qāsim al-Ṭarābulsī, from Abū al-Ḥasan al-Qābisī, from Abū Zayd al-Marwazī, from Abū ʿAbdullāh al-Farabrī, from Muhammad ibn Ismāʿīl, from Yaḥyā ibn Bukayr, from al-Layth, from ʿUqayl, from Ibn Shihāb, from Saʿīd ibn al-Musayyib, from Abū Hurayrah ﷺ, that the Messenger of Allah ﷺ said: "If you knew what I knew, you would laugh little and cry often."[439]

In the narration of Abū Dharr, the Prophet ﷺ said: "I see that which you do not see and hear that which you do not hear. I swear by Allah, if you knew what I knew, you would laugh little and cry often. You would not lie down and enjoy women. Instead, you would go out on the paths crying and praying to Allah: 'If only I were a tree standing here!'"[440] Other transmissions suggest that Abū Dharr was the person saying "If only I were a tree standing here!" about himself, and this view is more accurate.

Al-Mughīrah mentioned that the Prophet ﷺ would stand in prayer until his feet were swollen.[441] Another transmission adds: "He was asked: 'Why do you burden yourself in such a way when

---

439   Reported here from the chain of Bukhārī (6485).

440   Reported by Tirmidhī (2312), Ibn Mājah (4190), and Aḥmad (5/173). Tirmidhī said: "This narration is *hasan gharīb*."

441   Reported by Muslim (2819).

فَصْل

وَأَمَّا خَوْفُهُ رَبَّهُ، وَطَاعَتُهُ لَهُ، وَشِدَّةُ عِبَادَتِهِ فَعَلَى قَدْرِ عِلْمِهِ بِرَبِّهِ: وَلِذَلِكَ قَالَ فِيمَا حَدَّثَنَا بِهِ أَبُو مُحَمَّدِ بْنُ عَتَّابٍ قِرَاءَةً مِنِّي عَلَيْهِ، قَالَ: حَدَّثَنَا أَبُو القَاسِمِ الطَّرَابُلُسِيُّ، حَدَّثَنَا أَبُو الحَسَنِ القَابِسِيُّ، حَدَّثَنَا أَبُو زَيْدٍ المَرْوَزِيُّ، حَدَّثَنَا أَبُو عَبْدِ اللهِ الفَرَبْرِيُّ، حَدَّثَنَا مُحَمَّدُ بْنُ إِسْمَاعِيلَ، حَدَّثَنَا يَحْيَى بْنُ بُكَيْرٍ، عَنِ اللَّيْثِ، عَنْ عُقَيْلٍ، عَنِ ابْنِ شِهَابٍ، عَنْ سَعِيدِ بْنِ المُسَيَّبِ، أَنَّ أَبَا هُرَيْرَةَ كَانَ يَقُولُ: قَالَ رَسُولُ اللهِ ﷺ: «لَوْ تَعْلَمُونَ مَا أَعْلَمُ، لَضَحِكْتُمْ قَلِيلًا، وَلَبَكَيْتُمْ كَثِيرًا»[401].

زَادَ فِي رِوَايَتِنَا عَنْ أَبِي عِيسَى التِّرْمِذِيِّ رَفَعَهُ إِلَى أَبِي ذَرٍّ: «إِنِّي أَرَى مَا لَا تَرَوْنَ، وَأَسْمَعُ مَا لَا تَسْمَعُونَ، أَطَّتِ السَّمَاءُ، وَحُقَّ لَهَا أَنْ تَئِطَّ، مَا فِيهَا مَوْضِعُ أَرْبَعِ أَصَابِعَ إِلَّا وَمَلَكٌ وَاضِعٌ جَبْهَتَهُ سَاجِدًا لِلهِ، وَاللهِ لَوْ تَعْلَمُونَ مَا أَعْلَمُ، لَضَحِكْتُمْ قَلِيلًا، وَلَبَكَيْتُمْ كَثِيرًا، وَمَا تَلَذَّذْتُمْ بِالنِّسَاءِ عَلَى الفُرُشِ، وَلَخَرَجْتُمْ إِلَى الصُّعُدَاتِ تَجْأَرُونَ إِلَى اللهِ، لَوَدِدْتُ أَنِّي شَجَرَةٌ تُعْضَدُ»[402].

رُوِيَ هَذَا الكَلَامُ: «وَدِدْتُ أَنِّي شَجَرَةٌ تُعْضَدُ» مِنْ قَوْلِ أَبِي ذَرٍّ نَفْسِهِ، وَهُوَ أَصَحُّ.

---

401 أَسْنَدَهُ المُصَنِّفُ مِنْ طَرِيقِ البُخَارِيِّ (٦٤٨٥).

402 أَخْرَجَهُ التِّرْمِذِيُّ (٢٣١٢)، وَابْنُ مَاجَه (٤١٩٠)، وَأَحْمَدُ ١٧٣/٥. وَقَالَ التِّرْمِذِيُّ: «هَذَا حَدِيثٌ حَسَنٌ غَرِيبٌ» وَقَوْلُهُ: «لَوَدِدْتُ أَنِّي شَجَرَةٌ تُعْضَدُ» مُدْرَجٌ فِي الحَدِيثِ مِنْ قَوْلِ أَبِي ذَرٍّ كَمَا جَاءَ مُصَرَّحًا بِهِ فِي رِوَايَةِ أَحْمَدَ. (أَطَّتْ): صَوَّتَتْ. (الصُّعُدَاتُ): الطُّرُقُ. (تَجْأَرُونَ): تَسْتَغِيثُونَ وَتَدْعُونَ. (تُعْضَدُ) تُقْطَعُ.

you have already been forgiven your past and future mistakes?' He replied: 'Should I not be a grateful slave?'"[442] Similar narrations were reported from Abū Salamah[443] and Abū Hurayrah.[444]

'Ā'ishah observed: "The actions of the Messenger of Allah ﷺ were consistent, and which one of you is capable of doing what he did?"[445]

She also said: "He would fast for so long that we thought that he would never not fast again, and then he would not fast for so long that we thought that he would never fast again."[446] Similar narrations were reported from Ibn 'Abbās,[447] Umm Salamah,[448] and Anas.[449] Anas added: "If you wanted to see him praying at night, you would, and if you wanted to see him sleeping at night, you also would."[450]

'Awf ibn Mālik narrated: "I was with the Messenger of Allah ﷺ one night. He used the *miswāk* and then performed *wuḍū'*. Then, he stood to pray, and I stood with him. He began with Sūrah al-Baqa-

---

442   Reported by Bukhārī (6371) and Muslim (2819/80) from al-Mughīrah, and Bukhārī (4837),
and Muslim (2820) from 'Ā'ishah.

443   I did not come across this narration in the sources available to me.

444   Reported by Tirmidhī in *Al-Shamā'il* (261), Ibn Mājah (1420), and others. Authenticated by Ibn Khuzaymah (1184), and Būṣīrī strengthened the chain in *Miṣbāḥ al-Zujājah*. Haythamī said in *Majma' al-Zawā'id* (2/271): "It was related by Bazzār with a number of chains, one of which consisted of *ṣaḥīḥ* narrators."

445   Reported by Bukhārī (1987) and Muslim (783). Translator's note: The second part of the narration is a rhetorical question; i.e., "none of you are capable of that".

446   Reported by Muslim (1156/175).

447   Reported by Bukhārī (1971) and Muslim (1157/179).

448   Reported by Tirmidhī in *Al-Sunan* (736) and *Al-Shamā'il* (300), Abū Dāwūd (2336), and Nasā'ī (4/200). Tirmidhī graded the hadith as *ḥasan*.

449   Reported by Bukhārī (1972) and Muslim (1158).

450   Reported by Bukhārī (1972) from Anas ibn Mālik. Ibn Ḥajar explained the narration in *Fatḥ al-Bārī* (3/23): "Meaning, his prayer and sleep used to differ from one night to the next. He did not set a specific time for praying at night. Rather, he would stand in prayer according to his ability."

وَفِي حَدِيثِ المُغِيرَةِ: صَلَّى رَسُولُ اللهِ ﷺ حَتَّى انْتَفَخَتْ قَدَمَاهُ[٤٠٣].

وَفِي رِوَايَةٍ أَنَّهُ كَانَ يُصَلِّي حَتَّى تَرِمَ قَدَمَاهُ، فَقِيلَ لَهُ: أَتَكَلَّفُ هَذَا وَقَدْ غُفِرَ لَكَ مَا تَقَدَّمَ مِنْ ذَنْبِكَ وَمَا تَأَخَّرَ؟ قَالَ: «أَفَلَا أَكُونُ عَبْدًا شَكُورًا؟»[٤٠٤].

وَنَحْوُهُ عَنْ أَبِي سَلَمَةَ، وَأَبِي هُرَيْرَةَ[٤٠٥].

وَقَالَتْ عَائِشَةُ: كَانَ عَمَلُ رَسُولِ اللهِ ﷺ دِيمَةً، وَأَيُّكُمْ يُطِيقُ مَا كَانَ يُطِيقُ؟![٤٠٦].

وَقَالَتْ: كَانَ يَصُومُ حَتَّى نَقُولَ: لَا يُفْطِرُ، وَيُفْطِرُ حَتَّى نَقُولَ: لَا يَصُومُ[٤٠٧].

وَنَحْوُهُ عَنِ ابْنِ عَبَّاسٍ وَأُمِّ سَلَمَةَ وَأَنَسٍ[٤٠٨].

وَقَالَتْ: كُنْتَ لَا تَشَاءُ أَنْ تَرَاهُ مِنَ اللَّيْلِ مُصَلِّيًا إِلَّا رَأَيْتَهُ مُصَلِّيًا، وَلَا نَائِمًا إِلَّا رَأَيْتَهُ نَائِمًا[٤٠٩]. وَقَالَ عَوْفُ بْنُ مَالِكٍ: كُنْتُ مَعَ رَسُولِ اللهِ ﷺ لَيْلَةً فَاسْتَاكَ

---

٤٠٣   أَخْرَجَهُ مُسْلِمٌ (٢٨١٩). وَانْظُرِ الرِّوَايَةَ التَّالِيَةَ.

٤٠٤   أَخْرَجَهُ البُخَارِيُّ (٦٣٧١)، وَمُسْلِمٌ (٨٠/٢٨١٩) مِنْ حَدِيثِ المُغِيرَةِ. وَالبُخَارِيُّ (٤٨٣٧)، وَمُسْلِمٌ (٢٨٢٠) مِنْ حَدِيثِ عَائِشَةَ.

٤٠٥   حَدِيثُ أَبِي سَلَمَةَ لَمْ أَجِدْهُ فِيمَا لَدَيَّ مِنْ مَصَادِرَ. وَحَدِيثُ أَبِي هُرَيْرَةَ أَخْرَجَهُ التِّرْمِذِيُّ فِي الشَّمَائِلِ (٢٦٠)، وَابْنُ مَاجَه (١٤٢٠)، وَغَيْرُهُ، وَصَحَّحَهُ ابْنُ خُزَيْمَةَ (١١٨٤)، وَقَوَّى إِسْنَادَهُ البُوصِيرِيُّ فِي مِصْبَاحِ الزُّجَاجَةِ. وَقَالَ الهَيْثَمِيُّ فِي المَجْمَعِ ٢٧١/٢: «رَوَاهُ البَزَّارُ بِأَسَانِيدَ وَرِجَالُ أَحَدِهِمَا رِجَالُ الصَّحِيحِ».

٤٠٦   أَخْرَجَهُ البُخَارِيُّ (١٩٨٧)، وَمُسْلِمٌ (٧٨٣). (دِيمَةً): أَيْ دَائِمًا فِي رِفْقٍ وَاقْتِصَادٍ.

٤٠٧   أَخْرَجَهُ مُسْلِمٌ (١٧٥/١١٥٦).

٤٠٨   حَدِيثُ ابْنِ عَبَّاسٍ أَخْرَجَهُ البُخَارِيُّ (١٩٧١)، وَمُسْلِمٌ (١٧٩/١١٥٧). وَحَدِيثُ أُمِّ سَلَمَةَ أَخْرَجَهُ التِّرْمِذِيُّ فِي السُّنَنِ (٧٣٦)، وَفِي الشَّمَائِلِ (٢٩٤)، وَأَبُو دَاوُدَ (٢٣٣٦)، وَالنَّسَائِيُّ (٢٠٠/٤)، وَحَسَّنَهُ التِّرْمِذِيُّ. وَحَدِيثُ أَنَسٍ أَخْرَجَهُ البُخَارِيُّ (١٩٧٢)، وَمُسْلِمٌ (١١٥٨).

٤٠٩   أَخْرَجَهُ البُخَارِيُّ (١٩٧٢) مِنْ قَوْلِ أَنَسِ بْنِ مَالِكٍ قَالَ الحَافِظُ فِي الفَتْحِ ٢٣/٣: «أَيْ إِنَّ صَلَاتَهُ وَنَوْمَهُ كَانَ يَخْتَلِفُ بِاللَّيْلِ وَلَا يُرَتِّبُ وَقْتًا مُعَيَّنًا بَلْ بِحَسَبِ مَا تَيَسَّرَ لَهُ القِيَامُ».

rah. Any time he reached a verse of mercy, he would pause and ask [for mercy], and any time he reached a verse of punishment, he would pause and seek refuge [from punishment]. Then, he went into *rukūʿ* (bowing), and stayed in that position for as long as he had stood. He was supplicating: 'Glory to the Possessor of Power, Sovereignty, and Might.'[451] Then, he went into *sujūd* (prostration), and made the same supplication. [In the next *rakʿah*], he read Sūrah Āl ʿImrān, and he would continue from *sūrah* to *sūrah*, repeating the process [in every *rakʿah*]."[452]

A similar narration was reported from Ḥudhayfah, who added: "He remained in *sujūd* for as long as he stood, and sat between the two *sujūds* for the same. [In four *rakʿahs* of prayer] he recited Sūrahs al-Baqarah, Āl ʿImrān, al-Nisāʾ, and al-Māʾidah."[453]

ʿĀʾishah said: "One night, the Messenger of Allah ﷺ stood in prayer reciting just one verse from the Qurʾan."[454]

ʿAbdullāh ibn al-Shikhkhīr remembered: "I came to the Messenger of Allah ﷺ whilst he was praying and his chest was throbbing like the sound of a boiling pot (i.e., he was weeping)."[455]

Ibn Abī Hālah related: "The Messenger of Allah ﷺ was always

---

451   *"Subḥāna dhī al-jabarūti wa al-malakūti wa al-ʿaẓamah".*

452   Reported by Abū Dāwūd (873), Tirmidhī in *Al-Shamāʾil* (312) with this wording, and Nasāʾī (2/191). Authenticated by Nawawī in *Al-Adhkār* (146).

453   Reported by Abū Dāwūd (874). The narration reported by Muslim (772) states that the Prophet ﷺ recited Sūrahs *al-Baqarah, al-Nisāʾ,* and *Āl ʿImrān* within one *rakʿah.*

454   Reported by Tirmidhī (448) and graded as *ḥasan.* Aḥmad Shākir mentioned the narration of Abū Dharr, which was reported by Ibn Mājah (1350), as a supporting evidence. Abū Dharr said: "The Prophet ﷺ stood in prayer reciting a single verse, and repeating that verse until morning came: 'If You punish them, they belong to You after all. But if You forgive them, You are surely the Almighty, All-Wise' (*al-Māʾidah*, 118)."

455   Reported by Abū Dāwūd (904), Tirmidhī in *Al-Shamāʾil* (321), Nasāʾī (3/13), and others. Authenticated by Ibn Khuzaymah (900), Ibn Ḥibbān in *Mawārid al-Ẓamʾān* (522), and Nawawī in *Riyāḍ al-Ṣāliḥīn* (480). Also authenticated by Ḥākim (1/264) and Dhahabī concurred. Ibn al-Athīr said in *Jāmiʿ al-Uṣūl* (5/436) that the "throbbing sound" mentioned was due to his fear [of his Lord].

ثُمَّ تَوَضَّأَ، ثُمَّ قَامَ يُصَلِّي، فَقُمْتُ مَعَهُ، فَبَدَأَ فَاسْتَفْتَحَ الْبَقَرَةَ، فَلَا يَمُرُّ بِآيَةِ رَحْمَةٍ إِلَّا وَقَفَ فَسَأَلَ، وَلَا يَمُرُّ بِآيَةِ عَذَابٍ إِلَّا وَقَفَ فَتَعَوَّذَ، ثُمَّ رَكَعَ، فَمَكَثَ بِقَدْرِ قِيَامِهِ، يَقُولُ: «سُبْحَانَ اللهِ ذِي الْجَبَرُوتِ وَالْمَلَكُوتِ وَالْعَظَمَةِ»، ثُمَّ سَجَدَ وَقَالَ مِثْلَ ذَلِكَ، ثُمَّ قَرَأَ آلَ عِمْرَانَ، ثُمَّ سُورَةً سُورَةً، يَفْعَلُ مِثْلَ ذَلِكَ[410].

وَعَنْ حُذَيْفَةَ مِثْلُهُ وَقَالَ: سَجَدَ نَحْوًا مِنْ قِيَامِهِ، وَجَلَسَ بَيْنَ السَّجْدَتَيْنِ نَحْوًا مِنْهُ، وَقَالَ: حَتَّى قَرَأَ الْبَقَرَةَ وَآلَ عِمْرَانَ وَالنِّسَاءَ وَالْمَائِدَةَ[411].

وَعَنْ عَائِشَةَ: قَامَ رَسُولُ اللهِ ﷺ بِآيَةٍ مِنَ الْقُرْآنِ لَيْلَةً[412].

وَعَنْ عَبْدِ اللهِ بْنِ الشِّخِّيرِ: أَتَيْتُ رَسُولَ اللهِ ﷺ وَهُوَ يُصَلِّي، وَلِجَوْفِهِ أَزِيزٌ كَأَزِيزِ الْمِرْجَلِ[413].

قَالَ ابْنُ أَبِي هَالَةَ: كَانَ ﷺ مُتَوَاصِلَ الْأَحْزَانِ، دَائِمَ الْفِكْرَةِ، لَيْسَتْ لَهُ رَاحَةٌ.

وَقَالَ ﷺ: «إِنِّي لَأَسْتَغْفِرُ اللهَ فِي الْيَوْمِ مِائَةَ مَرَّةٍ»[414].

---

410 أَخْرَجَهُ أَبُو دَاوُدَ (٨٧٣)، وَالتِّرْمِذِيُّ فِي الشَّمَائِلِ (٣٠٦) وَاللَّفْظُ لَهُ، وَالنَّسَائِيُّ ٢/١٩١، وَصَحَّحَهُ النَّوَوِيُّ فِي الْأَذْكَارِ رَقْم (١٤٦) بِتَحْقِيقِي.

411 أَخْرَجَهُ أَبُو دَاوُدَ (٨٧٤). وَلَهُ سِيَاقٌ آخَرُ عِنْدَ مُسْلِم (٧٧٢) وَفِيهِ: أَنَّهُ ﷺ قَرَأَ الْبَقَرَةَ وَالنِّسَاءَ وَآلَ عِمْرَانَ.

412 أَخْرَجَهُ التِّرْمِذِيُّ (٤٤٨) وَحَسَّنَهُ. وَقَالَ الْعَلَّامَةُ أَحْمَدُ شَاكِرٌ: «وَلَهُ شَاهِدٌ صَحِيحٌ مِنْ حَدِيثِ أَبِي ذَرٍّ، قَالَ: قَامَ النَّبِيُّ ﷺ بِآيَةٍ حَتَّى أَصْبَحَ يُرَدِّدُهَا، وَالْآيَةُ: ﴿إِن تُعَذِّبْهُمْ فَإِنَّهُمْ عِبَادُكَ وَإِن تَغْفِرْ لَهُمْ فَإِنَّكَ أَنتَ الْعَزِيزُ الْحَكِيمُ﴾ [المائدة: ١١٨].

413 أَخْرَجَهُ أَبُو دَاوُدَ (٩٠٤)، وَالتِّرْمِذِيُّ فِي الشَّمَائِلِ (٣١٥)، وَالنَّسَائِيُّ (٣/١٣) وَغَيْرُهُ، وَصَحَّحَهُ ابْنُ خُزَيْمَةَ (٩٠٠)، وَابْنُ حِبَّانَ (٥٢٢) مَوَارِدُ الظَّمْآنِ، وَالْحَاكِمُ (٢٦٤/١) وَوَافَقَهُ الذَّهَبِيُّ، وَصَحَّحَهُ أَيْضًا النَّوَوِيُّ فِي رِيَاضِ الصَّالِحِينَ بِرَقْم (٤٨٠) بِتَحْقِيقِي. (لِجَوْفِهِ): لِصَدْرِهِ. (أَزِيزٌ كَأَزِيزِ الْمِرْجَلِ) الْأَزِيزُ: صَوْتُ غَلَيَانِ الْقِدْرِ. قَالَ ابْنُ الْأَثِيرِ فِي جَامِعِ الْأُصُولِ ٤٣٦/٥: «وَالْمُرَادُ بِهِ مَا كَانَ يَعْرِضُ لَهُ فِي الصَّلَاةِ مِنَ الْخَوْفِ الَّذِي يُوجِبُ ذَلِكَ الصَّوْتَ».

414 أَخْرَجَهُ مُسْلِمٌ (٢٧٠٢) مِنْ حَدِيثِ الْأَغَرِّ الْمُزَنِيِّ.

sorrowful and reflective. He never had a rest."[456]

The Prophet ﷺ said: "I seek the forgiveness of Allah one hundred times per day."[457] Another narration mentions: "…seventy times".[458]

'Alī said: "I asked the Messenger of Allah ﷺ about his Sunnah, and he said: 'True knowledge is my original capital, intelligence is the basis of my religion, love is my foundation, longing is my riding-animal, the remembrance of Allah is my close companion, dependence is my treasure, sorrow is my friend, knowledge is my weapon, patience is my cloak, pleasure and satisfaction are my war spoils, poverty is my honour, abstaining is my vocation, absolute certainty is my strength, truthfulness is my intercessor, obedience is sufficient for me, struggle (jihad) is my character, and prayer is the coolness of my eyes.'"[459] Another narration adds: "The fruits of my heart lie in the remembrance of Allah, my sorrow is for the sake of my nation, and my longing is for my Lord."

---

456   See *Al-Shamā'il* (335).

457   Reported by Muslim (2702) from al-Agharr al-Muzanī.

458   Reported by Bukhārī from Abū Hurayrah, as it appears in *Jāmi' al-Uṣūl* (4/387). Authenticated by Ibn Ḥibbān from the hadith of Anas in *Mawārid al-Ẓam'ān* (2457). The hadith reported by Bukhārī (6307) from Abū Hurayrah says: "…more than seventy times".

459   Mentioned by Ghazālī in *Al-Iḥyā'* (4/361). 'Irāqī said: "It was mentioned by al-Qāḍī 'Iyāḍ [the author] from 'Alī ibn Abī Ṭālib, but I cannot find a chain for that." Ibn Ḥajar said: "It has no basis." And Suyūṭī said in *Al-Manāhil*, p. 322: "It is fabricated."

وَرُوِيَ: «سَبْعِينَ مَرَّةً»^{٤١٥}.

وَعَنْ عَلِيٍّ ﵁ قَالَ: سَأَلْتُ رَسُولَ اللهِ ﷺ عَنْ سُنَّتِهِ، فَقَالَ: «الْمَعْرِفَةُ رَأْسُ مَالِي، وَالْعَقْلُ أَصْلُ دِينِي، وَالْحُبُّ أَسَاسِي، وَالشَّوْقُ مَرْكَبِي، وَذِكْرُ اللهِ أَنِيسِي، وَالثِّقَةُ كَنْزِي، وَالْحُزْنُ رَفِيقِي، وَالْعِلْمُ سِلَاحِي، وَالصَّبْرُ رِدَائِي، وَالرِّضَى غَنِيمَتِي، وَالْفَقْرُ فَخْرِي، وَالزُّهْدُ حِرْفَتِي، وَالْيَقِينُ قُوَّتِي، وَالصِّدْقُ شَفِيعِي، وَالطَّاعَةُ حَسْبِي، وَالْجِهَادُ خُلُقِي، وَقُرَّةُ عَيْنِي فِي الصَّلَاةِ»^{٤١٦}.

وَفِي حَدِيثٍ آخَرَ: «وَثَمَرَةُ فُؤَادِي فِي ذِكْرِهِ، وَغِنَى لِأَجْلِ أُمَّتِي، وَشَوْقِي إِلَى رَبِّي».

---

٤١٥ أَخْرَجَهُ الْبُخَارِيُّ عَنْ أَبِي هُرَيْرَةَ كَمَا فِي جَامِعِ الْأُصُولِ (٣٨٧/٤). وَصَحَّحَهُ ابْنُ حِبَّانَ (٢٤٥٧) مَوَارِدَ الظَّمْآنِ مِنْ حَدِيثِ أَنَسٍ. وَفِي رِوَايَةِ الْبُخَارِيِّ (٦٣٠٧) عَنْ أَبِي هُرَيْرَةَ: «أَكْثَرَ مِنْ سَبْعِينَ مَرَّةً».

٤١٦ أَوْرَدَهُ الْغَزَالِيُّ فِي الْإِحْيَاءِ (٣٦١/٤). قَالَ الْحَافِظُ الْعِرَاقِيُّ: «ذَكَرَهُ الْقَاضِي عِيَاضٌ مِنْ حَدِيثِ عَلِيِّ بْنِ أَبِي طَالِبٍ وَلَمْ أَجِدْ لَهُ إِسْنَادًا». وَقَالَ الْحَافِظُ ابْنُ حَجَرٍ: «لَا أَصْلَ لَهُ»، وَقَالَ السُّيُوطِيُّ فِي الْمَنَاهِلِ (٣٢٢): «مَوْضُوعٌ».

THE CHARACTERISTICS OF PROPHETS
AND MESSENGERS

Understand – and may Allah help us – that all the Prophets and Messengers ﷺ were blessed with a perfected character, beautiful appearance, noble lineage, excellent manners, and every desirable trait, for they were of the highest standing and loftiest rank of all creation. Nevertheless, Allah gave preference to some above others.

Allah Exalted said: "We have chosen some of those Messengers above others."[460] He also revealed: "And indeed, We chose [the Children of Israel] knowingly above the others."[461]

The Prophet ﷺ said: "The first group of people to enter Paradise will be [shining] like a full moon." At the end of the narration, he added: "All of them will look alike and they will resemble their father Adam ﷺ, sixty cubits tall."[462]

In the narration of Abū Hurayrah, the Prophet ﷺ said: "I saw Mūsā and he was a man of medium build, with curly hair and an aquiline nose, and he looked like the people of Shanū'ah[463]. And I saw 'Īsā and he was a man of medium height. His face had several beauty spots and had a reddish complexion[464], as if he had just

---

460   *al-Baqarah*, 253.

461   *al-Dukhān*, 32.

462   Reported by Bukhārī (3327) and Muslim (2834/15) from Abū Hurayrah.

463   A tribe from Yemen.

464   For the Arabs, "reddish" referred to an extremely bright complexion with red undertones. See *Fatḥ al-Bārī* (6/486).

فصل

اعْلَمْ وَفَّقَنَا اللهُ وَإِيَّاكَ، أَنَّ صِفَاتِ جَمِيعِ الْأَنْبِيَاءِ وَالرُّسُلِ - صَلَوَاتُ اللهِ عَلَيْهِمْ - مِنْ كَمَالِ الْخَلْقِ، وَحُسْنِ الصُّورَةِ، وَشَرَفِ النَّسَبِ، وَحُسْنِ الْخُلُقِ، وَجَمِيعِ الْمَحَاسِنِ: هِيَ هَذِهِ الصِّفَةُ، لِأَنَّهَا صِفَاتُ الْكَمَالِ، وَالْكَمَالُ وَالتَّمَامُ الْبَشَرِيُّ وَالْفَضْلُ الْجَمِيعُ لَهُمْ صَلَوَاتُ اللهِ عَلَيْهِمْ وَسَلَامُهُ؛ إِذْ رُتَبَتُهُمْ أَشْرَفُ الرُّتَبِ، وَدَرَجَاتُهُمْ أَرْفَعُ الدَّرَجَاتِ، وَلَكِنْ فَضَّلَ اللهُ بَعْضَهُمْ عَلَى بَعْضٍ؛ قَالَ اللهُ تَعَالَى: ﴿تِلْكَ ٱلرُّسُلُ فَضَّلْنَا بَعْضَهُمْ عَلَىٰ بَعْضٍ﴾ [البقرة: ٢٥٣]، وَقَالَ تَعَالَى: ﴿وَلَقَدِ ٱخْتَرْنَٰهُمْ عَلَىٰ عِلْمٍ عَلَى ٱلْعَٰلَمِينَ﴾ [الدخان: ٣٢].

وَقَدْ قَالَ ﷺ: «إِنَّ أَوَّلَ زُمْرَةٍ يَدْخُلُونَ الْجَنَّةَ عَلَى صُورَةِ الْقَمَرِ لَيْلَةَ الْبَدْرِ». ثُمَّ قَالَ آخِرَ الْحَدِيثِ: «عَلَى خَلْقِ رَجُلٍ وَاحِدٍ، عَلَى صُورَةِ أَبِيهِمْ آدَمَ عليه السلام، طُولُهُ سِتُّونَ ذِرَاعًا فِي السَّمَاءِ»[417].

وَفِي حَدِيثِ أَبِي هُرَيْرَةَ: «رَأَيْتُ مُوسَى فَإِذَا رَجُلٌ ضَرْبٌ، رَجُلٌ، أَقْنَى، كَأَنَّهُ مِنْ رِجَالِ شَنُوءَةَ، وَرَأَيْتُ عِيسَى فَإِذَا هُوَ رَجُلٌ رَبْعَةٌ، كَثِيرُ خِيلَانِ الْوَجْهِ، أَحْمَرُ كَأَنَّمَا خَرَجَ مِنْ دِيمَاسٍ»[418].

---

417 أَخْرَجَهُ الْبُخَارِيُّ (٣٣٢٧)، وَمُسْلِمٌ (٢٨٣٤/١٥) مِنْ حَدِيثِ أَبِي هُرَيْرَةَ.

418 أَخْرَجَهُ الْبُخَارِيُّ (٣٣٩٤)، وَمُسْلِمٌ (١٦٨). (الضَّرْبُ): هُوَ الرَّجُلُ بَيْنَ الرَّجُلَيْنِ فِي كَثْرَةِ اللَّحْمِ وَقِلَّتِهِ. (رَجُلٌ): أَيْ دَهِينُ الشَّعْرِ، مُسْتَرْسِلُهُ. (أَقْنَى): الْقَنَا فِي الْأَنْفِ: طُولُهُ وَرِقَّةُ أَرْنَبَتِهِ مَعَ حَدَبٍ فِي وَسَطِهِ. (شَنُوءَةَ): حَيٌّ مِنَ الْيَمَنِ، مَعْرُوفُونَ بِالطُّولِ. (رَبْعَةٌ): بَيْنَ الطَّوِيلِ وَالْقَصِيرِ. (خِيلَانٌ): جَمْعُ خَالٍ، وَهُوَ الشَّامَةُ. (أَحْمَرُ) الْأَحْمَرُ عِنْدَ

come out of a bath."[465] In another narration he described ʿĪsā as: "…slender, like a sword".[466] And he described Mūsā as: "…the most handsome brown man you ever saw."[467] The Prophet ﷺ also related seeing Ibrāhīm, and observed: "From the descendants of Ibrāhīm, I resemble him the most."

In another narration of Abū Hurayrah, the Prophet ﷺ said: "Allah Exalted did not send a Prophet after Lūṭ except from the highest rank of his people."[468] Another transmission states: "…from the wealthiest and the most powerful".[469]

Qatādah narrated: "Allah blessed every Prophet with a handsome face and beautiful voice. Your Prophet ﷺ was the most handsome of them and had the most beautiful voice."[470]

In his conversation with Abū Sufyān, Heraclius said, regarding the Prophet ﷺ: "I asked about his lineage and you said he is from a noble family amongst you. Likewise, the Messengers were from noble families amongst their people."[471]

We can cite many verses from the Qurʾan regarding the virtuous characteristics of Messengers and Prophets. Allah Exalted said:

---

465   Reported by Bukhārī (3394) and Muslim (168).

466   Reported by Aḥmad (1/374) and Abū Yaʿlā (2720) from Ibn ʿAbbās, with a slightly different wording. Ibn Kathīr graded the chain as *ṣaḥīḥ* in *Al-Tafsīr* (3/915), and also attributed it to Nasāʾī.

467   Reported by Bukhārī (5902) and Muslim (169) from Ibn ʿUmar, but it was describing Prophet ʿĪsā ﷺ rather than Prophet Mūsā ﷺ. See also *Fatḥ al-Bārī* (6/486).

468   Reported by Tirmidhī (3116) from the chain of the author, and by Aḥmad (2/533) from the chains of Ḥammād ibn Salamah and Abū ʿUmar al-Ḍarīr. All three narrated from Muhammad ibn ʿAmr, from Abū Salamah, from Abū Hurayrah.

469   Reported by Tirmidhī (3116) at the end of the previous narration, and by Aḥmad (2/532) from Ḥammād ibn Salamah with the same chain as before. It was authenticated by Ḥākim (2/561). Tirmidhī said: "This hadith is more authentic than from the chain of the author [i.e., the previous narration], and it is *hasan*."

470   Reported by Tirmidhī in *Al-Shamāʾil* (319) from Qatādah, in a weak *mursal* narration. The present author attributes a similar hadith, narrated by Qatādah on the authority of Anas, to Dāraquṭnī.

471   Taken from the narration of Abū Sufyān reported by Bukhārī (7) and Muslim (1773).

وَفِي حَدِيثٍ آخَرَ: «مُبَطَّنٌ مِثْلُ السَّيْفِ»[419].

قَالَ: «وَأَنَا أَشْبَهُ وَلَدِ إِبْرَاهِيمَ بِهِ».

وَقَالَ فِي حَدِيثٍ آخَرَ فِي صِفَةِ مُوسَى: «كَأَحْسَنِ مَا أَنْتَ رَاءٍ مِنْ أُدْمِ الرِّجَالِ»[420].

وَفِي حَدِيثِ أَبِي هُرَيْرَةَ عَنْهُ ﷺ: «مَا بَعَثَ اللهُ تَعَالَى مِنْ بَعْدِ لُوطٍ نَبِيًّا إِلَّا فِي ذِرْوَةٍ مِنْ قَوْمِهِ»[421].

وَيُرْوَى: «فِي ثَرْوَةٍ مِنْ قَوْمِهِ»[422] أَيْ: كَثْرَةٍ وَمَنَعَةٍ.

وَحَكَى التِّرْمِذِيُّ عَنْ قَتَادَةَ، وَرَوَاهُ الدَّارَقُطْنِيُّ مِنْ حَدِيثِ قَتَادَةَ عَنْ أَنَسٍ: «مَا بَعَثَ اللهُ نَبِيًّا إِلَّا حَسَنَ الوَجْهِ، حَسَنَ الصَّوْتِ، وَكَانَ نَبِيُّكُمْ أَحْسَنَهُمْ وَجْهًا، وَأَحْسَنَهُمْ صَوْتًا»[423]. صَلَّى اللهُ عَلَيْهِ وَسَلَّمَ تَسْلِيمًا.

العَرَبُ الشَّدِيدُ البَيَاضِ مَعَ الحُمْرَةِ (الفَتْحُ: ٤٨٦/٦). (خَرَجَ مِنْ دِيمَاسٍ) يَعْنِي فِي نَضَارَتِهِ، وَكَثْرَةِ مَاءِ وَجْهِهِ، كَأَنَّهُ خَرَجَ مِنْ كِنٍّ.

٤١٩ أَخْرَجَهُ أَحْمَدُ ٣٧٤/١، وَأَبُو يَعْلَى (٢٧٢٠) مِنْ حَدِيثِ ابْنِ عَبَّاسٍ بِلَفْظِ: «مُبَطَّنُ الخَلْقِ». وَصَحَّحَ إِسْنَادَهُ ابْنُ كَثِيرٍ فِي التَّفْسِيرِ (٩١٥/٣) وَزَادَ نِسْبَتَهُ إِلَى النَّسَائِيِّ. (المُبَطَّنُ): الضَّامِرُ البَطْنِ.

٤٢٠ أَخْرَجَهُ البُخَارِيُّ (٥٩٠٢)، وَمُسْلِمٌ (١٦٩) مِنْ حَدِيثِ ابْنِ عُمَرَ. لَكِنَّهُ فِي حَقِّ عِيسَى لَا مُوسَى، وَانْظُرِ الفَتْحَ ٤٨٦/٦. (أُدْمٌ) جَمْعُ آدَمَ. كَسُمْرٍ وَأَسْمَرَ، وَزْنًا وَمَعْنًى.

٤٢١ أَخْرَجَهُ التِّرْمِذِيُّ (٣١١٦) مِنْ طَرِيقِ الفَضْلِ بْنِ مُوسَى، وَأَخْرَجَهُ أَحْمَدُ ٥٣٣/٢ مِنْ طَرِيقِ حَمَّادِ بْنِ سَلَمَةَ وَأَبِي عُمَرَ الضَّرِيرِ، ثَلَاثَتُهُمْ عَنْ مُحَمَّدِ بْنِ عَمْرٍو، عَنْ أَبِي سَلَمَةَ، عَنْ أَبِي هُرَيْرَةَ بِهِ. وَانْظُرِ الرِّوَايَةَ التَّالِيَةَ. (ذِرْوَةٌ) ذِرْوَةُ كُلِّ شَيْءٍ أَعْلَاهُ/ المُعْجَمُ الوَسِيطُ.

٤٢٢ أَخْرَجَهُ التِّرْمِذِيُّ عَقِبَ الحَدِيثِ (٣١١٦)، وَأَحْمَدُ ٣٣٢/٢ مِنْ طُرُقٍ عَنْ مُحَمَّدِ بْنِ عَمْرٍو بِإِسْنَادِ الحَدِيثِ السَّابِقِ، وَصَحَّحَهُ الحَاكِمُ ٥٦١/٢. قَالَ التِّرْمِذِيُّ: «وَهَذَا أَصَحُّ مِنْ رِوَايَةِ الفَضْلِ بْنِ مُوسَى - أَيِ الرِّوَايَةِ السَّابِقَةِ - وَهَذَا حَدِيثٌ حَسَنٌ».

٤٢٣ حَدِيثُ قَتَادَةَ أَخْرَجَهُ التِّرْمِذِيُّ فِي الشَّمَائِلِ (٣١٣). وَهُوَ مُرْسَلٌ ضَعِيفٌ. وَحَدِيثُ قَتَادَةَ عَنْ أَنَسٍ عَزَاهُ

"We truly found him patient. What an excellent servant [he was]! Indeed, he [constantly] turned [to Allah]."[472] "[It was later said,] 'O Yaḥyā! Hold firmly to the Scriptures.' And We granted him wisdom while [he was still] a child, as well as purity and compassion from Us. And he was God-fearing, and kind to his parents. He was neither arrogant nor disobedient."[473]

And: "Allah gives you good news of [the birth of] Yaḥyā who will confirm the Word of Allah and will be a great leader, chaste, and a Prophet among the righteous."[474] "Indeed, Allah chose Adam, Nūḥ, the family of Ibrāhīm, and the family of 'Imrān above all people [of their time]. They are descendants of one another. And Allah is All-Hearing, All-Knowing."[475]

He said about Nūḥ: "He was indeed a grateful servant."[476]

And about 'Īsā: "Allah gives you good news of a Word from Him, his name will be the Messiah, 'Īsā, son of Maryam; honoured in this world and the Hereafter, and he will be one of those nearest [to Allah]. And he will speak to people in [his] infancy and adulthood and will be one of the righteous."[477] "I am truly a servant of Allah. He has destined me to be given the Scripture and to be a Prophet. He has made me a blessing wherever I go, and bid me to establish prayer and give alms-tax as long as I live."[478]

Allah Exalted also said: "O believers! Do not be like those who slandered Mūsā, but Allah cleared him of what they said. And he

---

472 *Ṣād*, 44.

473 *Maryam*, 12-15.

474 Āl 'Imrān, 39.

475 Āl 'Imrān, 33-34.

476 *al-Isrā'*, 3.

477 Āl 'Imrān, 45-46.

478 *Maryam*, 30-31.

وَفِي حَدِيثِ هِرَقْلَ: وَسَأَلْتُكَ عَنْ نَسَبِهِ، فَذَكَرْتَ أَنَّهُ فِيكُمْ ذُو نَسَبٍ، وَكَذَلِكَ الرُّسُلُ تُبْعَثُ فِي أَنْسَابِ قَوْمِهَا.

وَقَالَ تَعَالَى فِي أَيُّوبَ: ﴿إِنَّا وَجَدْنَاهُ صَابِرًا نِّعْمَ ٱلْعَبْدُ إِنَّهُۥ أَوَّابٌ﴾ [ص: ٤٤].

وَقَالَ تَعَالَى: ﴿يَٰيَحْيَىٰ خُذِ ٱلْكِتَٰبَ بِقُوَّةٍ وَءَاتَيْنَٰهُ ٱلْحُكْمَ صَبِيًّا ⑫ وَحَنَانًا مِّن لَّدُنَّا وَزَكَوٰةً وَكَانَ تَقِيًّا ⑬ وَبَرًّا بِوَٰلِدَيْهِ وَلَمْ يَكُن جَبَّارًا عَصِيًّا ⑭ وَسَلَٰمٌ عَلَيْهِ يَوْمَ وُلِدَ وَيَوْمَ يَمُوتُ وَيَوْمَ يُبْعَثُ حَيًّا ⑮﴾ [مريم: ١٢-١٥].

وَقَالَ: ﴿أَنَّ ٱللَّهَ يُبَشِّرُكَ بِيَحْيَىٰ مُصَدِّقًا بِكَلِمَةٍ مِّنَ ٱللَّهِ وَسَيِّدًا وَحَصُورًا وَنَبِيًّا مِّنَ ٱلصَّٰلِحِينَ﴾ [آل عمران: ٣٩].

وَقَالَ: ﴿إِنَّ ٱللَّهَ ٱصْطَفَىٰٓ ءَادَمَ وَنُوحًا وَءَالَ إِبْرَٰهِيمَ وَءَالَ عِمْرَٰنَ عَلَى ٱلْعَٰلَمِينَ﴾ [آل عمران: ٣٣] الْآيَتَيْنِ.

وَقَالَ فِي نُوحٍ: ﴿إِنَّهُۥ كَانَ عَبْدًا شَكُورًا﴾ [الإسراء: ٣].

وَقَالَ: ﴿إِنَّ ٱللَّهَ يُبَشِّرُكِ بِكَلِمَةٍ مِّنْهُ ٱسْمُهُ ٱلْمَسِيحُ عِيسَى ٱبْنُ مَرْيَمَ وَجِيهًا فِي ٱلدُّنْيَا وَٱلْأَخِرَةِ وَمِنَ ٱلْمُقَرَّبِينَ ⑮ وَيُكَلِّمُ ٱلنَّاسَ فِي ٱلْمَهْدِ وَكَهْلًا وَمِنَ ٱلصَّٰلِحِينَ ⑯﴾ [آل عمران: ⑮- ⑯]. ﴿هُنَالِكَ دَعَا زَكَرِيَّا رَبَّهُۥ قَالَ رَبِّ هَبْ﴾ [آل عمران: ٣٨].

وَقَالَ: ﴿إِنِّي عَبْدُ ٱللَّهِ ءَاتَٰنِيَ ٱلْكِتَٰبَ وَجَعَلَنِي نَبِيًّا ⑳ وَجَعَلَنِي

____

الْمُصَنَّفُ لِلدَّارَقُطْنِيِّ.

was honourable in the sight of Allah."[479] The Prophet ﷺ mentioned [in explaining this verse]: "Mūsā was a shy person and he used to keep his body completely covered up.[480]"[481]

Allah Exalted conveys the words of Mūsā: "Then my Lord granted me wisdom and made me one of the Messengers."[482] And his address to a group from his community: "I am truly a trustworthy Messenger to you."[483] Mūsā was also described by one of the two sisters in Sūrah al-Qaṣaṣ, who says to her father: "The best man for employment is definitely the strong and trustworthy [one]."[484]

Allah Exalted said: "So endure patiently, as did the Messengers of Firm Resolve."[485] He also revealed: "And We blessed him with Isḥāq and Yaʿqūb. We guided them all as We previously guided Nūḥ and those among his descendants: Dāwūd, Sulaymān, Ayyūb, Yūsuf, Mūsā, and Hārūn. This is how We reward the good-doers. Likewise, [We guided] Zakariyyā, Yaḥyā, ʿĪsā, and Ilyās, who were all of the righteous. [We also guided] Ismāʿīl, al-Yasaʿ, Yūnus, and Lūṭ, favouring each over other people [of their time]. And [We favoured] some of their forefathers, their descendants, and their brothers. We chose them and guided them to the Straight Path. This is Allah's guidance with which He guides whoever He wills of His servants. Had they associated others with Him [in worship], their [good] deeds would have been wasted. Those were the ones

---

479 *al-Aḥzāb*, 69.

480 Translator's note: The narration goes on to explain that his people accused him of covering his body to hide a physical defect. So, one day, Allah Exalted caused the stone Mūsā had left his clothes on whilst bathing to flee. As he chased the stone, the people saw that he was the best of creation. In this way, Allah cleared him of their accusations.

481 Reported by Bukhārī (3404) in a *marfūʿ* narration from Abū Hurayrah, and by Muslim (339/156) also from Abū Hurayrah but in a *mawqūf* narration.

482 *al-Shuʿarāʾ*, 21.

483 *al-Shuʿarāʾ*, 107.

484 *al-Qaṣaṣ*, 26.

485 *al-Aḥqāf*, 35.

مُبَارَكًا أَيْنَ مَا كُنتُ وَأَوْصَنِي بِالصَّلَوٰةِ وَالزَّكَوٰةِ مَا دُمْتُ حَيًّا ۝ [مريم: ٣٠-٣١].

وَقَالَ: ﴿يَٰٓأَيُّهَا ٱلَّذِينَ ءَامَنُوا۟ لَا تَكُونُوا۟ كَٱلَّذِينَ ءَاذَوْا۟ مُوسَىٰ فَبَرَّأَهُ ٱللَّهُ مِمَّا قَالُوا۟ وَكَانَ عِندَ ٱللَّهِ وَجِيهًا﴾ [الأحزاب: ٦٩].

قَالَ النَّبِيُّ ﷺ: «كَانَ مُوسَى رَجُلًا حَيِيًّا سِتِّيرًا، مَا يُرَى مِن جَسَدِهِ شَيْءٌ اسْتِحْيَاءً»⁴²⁴ الحَدِيثَ.

وَقَالَ تَعَالَى عَنْهُ: ﴿فَوَهَبَ لِي رَبِّي حُكْمًا وَجَعَلَنِي مِنَ ٱلْمُرْسَلِينَ﴾ [الشعراء: ٢١] الآيَةَ.

وَقَالَ فِي وَصْفِ جَمَاعَةٍ مِنْهُمْ: ﴿إِنِّي لَكُمْ رَسُولٌ أَمِينٌ﴾ [الشعراء: ١٠٧].

وَقَالَ: ﴿إِنَّ خَيْرَ مَنِ ٱسْتَـٔجَرْتَ ٱلْقَوِيُّ ٱلْأَمِينُ﴾ [القصص: ٢٦].

وَقَالَ: ﴿فَٱصْبِرْ كَمَا صَبَرَ أُو۟لُوا۟ ٱلْعَزْمِ مِنَ ٱلرُّسُلِ﴾ [الأحقاف: ٣٥].

وَقَالَ: ﴿وَوَهَبْنَا لَهُۥٓ إِسْحَٰقَ وَيَعْقُوبَ كُلًّا هَدَيْنَا﴾ [الأنعام:٨٤]، إِلَى قَوْلِهِ: ﴿فَبِهُدَىٰهُمُ ٱقْتَدِهْ﴾ [الأنعام: ٩٠].

فَوَصَفَهُمْ بِأَوْصَافٍ جَمَّةٍ مِنَ الصَّلَاحِ، وَالْهُدَى، وَالِاجْتِبَاءِ، وَالْحُكْمِ، وَالنُّبُوَّةِ.

وَقَالَ: ﴿فَبَشَّرْنَٰهُ بِغُلَٰمٍ﴾ [الصافات: ١٠١] ﴿عَلِيمٍ﴾ [الحجر: ٥٣]، وَ﴿حَلِيمٍ﴾ [الصافات: ١٠١].

---

٤٢٤ أَخْرَجَهُ البُخَارِيُّ (٣٤٠٤) عَنْ أَبِي هُرَيْرَةَ مَرْفُوعًا. وَأَخْرَجَهُ مُسْلِمٌ فِي الفَضَائِلِ (١٥٦/٣٣٩) مَوْقُوفًا عَلَيْهِ.

to whom We gave the Scripture, wisdom, and Prophethood. But if these [pagans] disbelieve in this [message], then We have already entrusted it to a people who will never disbelieve in it. These [Prophets] were [rightly] guided by Allah, so follow their guidance."[486]

Allah Exalted characterises the Messengers with the qualities of righteousness, guidance, astute choice, wisdom and Prophethood. Allah Exalted said: "Indeed, before them We tested Pharoah's people: a noble Messenger came to them, [proclaiming,] 'Hand over the servants of Allah to me. I am truly a trustworthy Messenger to you.'"[487]

He revealed about Ibrāhīm: "…We gave him good news of a forbearing son."[488] And his son says to him: "Allah willing, you will find me steadfast."[489]

And he revealed regarding Ismāʿīl: "He was truly a man of his word, and was a Messenger and a Prophet. He used to urge his people to pray and give alms-tax. And his Lord was well pleased with him."[490] Allah Exalted said about Mūsā: "He was truly a chosen man".[491] And about Sulaymān: "…what an excellent servant [he was]! Indeed, he [constantly] turned [to Allah]."[492] Allah Exalted said: "And remember Our servants: Ibrāhīm, Isḥāq, and Yaʿqūb – the men of strength and insight. We truly chose them for the honour of proclaiming the Hereafter. And in Our Sight they are truly among the chosen and the finest. Also remember Ismāʿīl, al-Yasaʿ,

---

486   *al-Anʿām*, 84-90.

487   *al-Dukhān*, 17-18.

488   *al-Ṣāffāt*, 101.

489   *al-Ṣāffāt*, 102.

490   *Maryam*, 54-55.

491   *Maryam*, 51.

492   *Ṣād*, 30.

وَقَالَ: ﴿وَلَقَدْ فَتَنَّا قَبْلَهُمْ قَوْمَ فِرْعَوْنَ وَجَآءَهُمْ رَسُولٌ كَرِيمٌ ۝ أَنْ أَدُّوٓاْ إِلَيَّ عِبَادَ ٱللَّهِ إِنِّى لَكُمْ رَسُولٌ أَمِينٌ ۝﴾ [الدخان: ١٧-١٨].

وَقَالَ: ﴿سَتَجِدُنِىٓ إِن شَآءَ ٱللَّهُ مِنَ ٱلصَّٰبِرِينَ﴾ [الصافات: ١٠٢].

وَقَالَ فِي إِسْمَاعِيلَ: ﴿إِنَّهُۥ كَانَ صَادِقَ ٱلْوَعْدِ﴾ [مريم: ٥٤- ٥٥] الْآيَتَيْنِ.

وَفِي مُوسَى: ﴿إِنَّهُۥ كَانَ مُخْلَصًا﴾ [مريم: ٥١].

وَفِي سُلَيْمَانَ: ﴿نِعْمَ ٱلْعَبْدُ إِنَّهُۥ أَوَّابٌ﴾ [ص: ٣٠].

وَقَالَ: ﴿وَٱذْكُرْ عِبَٰدَنَآ إِبْرَٰهِيمَ وَإِسْحَٰقَ وَيَعْقُوبَ أُوْلِى ٱلْأَيْدِى وَٱلْأَبْصَٰرِ﴾ إِلَى ﴿ٱلْأَخْيَارِ﴾ [ص: ٤٥-٤٧].

وَفِي دَاوُدَ: ﴿إِنَّهُۥ أَوَّابٌ﴾ [ص: ١٧]، ثُمَّ قَالَ: ﴿وَشَدَدْنَا مُلْكَهُۥ وَءَاتَيْنَٰهُ ٱلْحِكْمَةَ وَفَصْلَ ٱلْخِطَابِ﴾ [ص: ٢٠].

وَقَالَ عَنْ يُوسُفَ: ﴿ٱجْعَلْنِى عَلَىٰ خَزَآئِنِ ٱلْأَرْضِ إِنِّى حَفِيظٌ عَلِيمٌ﴾ [يوسف: ٥٥].

وَفِي مُوسَى: ﴿سَتَجِدُنِىٓ إِن شَآءَ ٱللَّهُ صَابِرًا﴾ [الكهف: ٦٩].

وَقَالَ عَنْ شُعَيْبٍ: ﴿سَتَجِدُنِىٓ إِن شَآءَ ٱللَّهُ مِنَ ٱلصَّٰلِحِينَ﴾ [القصص: ٢٧].

وَقَالَ: ﴿وَمَآ أُرِيدُ أَنْ أُخَالِفَكُمْ إِلَىٰ مَآ أَنْهَىٰكُمْ عَنْهُ إِنْ أُرِيدُ إِلَّا ٱلْإِصْلَٰحَ مَا ٱسْتَطَعْتُ وَمَا تَوْفِيقِى إِلَّا بِٱللَّهِ﴾ [هود: ٨٨].

وَقَالَ: ﴿وَلُوطًا ءَاتَيْنَٰهُ حُكْمًا وَعِلْمًا﴾ [الأنبياء: ٧٤].

and Dhū al-Kifl. All are among the best."[493] He praised Dāwūd: "Indeed, he [constantly] turned [to Allah]."[494] "We strengthened his kingship, and gave him wisdom and sound judgment."[495]

He conveyed the speech of Yūsuf: "Put me in charge of the store-houses of the land, for I am truly reliable and adept"[496]; the saying of Mūsā: "You will find me patient, Allah willing"[497]; and the words of Shuʿayb, who said to his people: "Allah willing, you will find me an agreeable man"[498]; and: "I do not want to do what I am forbidding you from. I only intend reform to the best of my ability."[499] Allah Exalted said: "And to Lūṭ We gave wisdom and knowledge".[500] And He said, regarding Zakariyyā and his wife: "Indeed, they used to race in doing good, and call upon Us with hope and fear, totally humbling themselves before Us."[501] Commenting on the verse, Sufyān al-Thawrī said: "['Humbling themselves' through] a persistent sense of sorrow in their hearts." As we have shown, there are many verses conveying the perfection and virtues of the Messengers. Similarly, their qualities are praised in numerous narrations.

For example, the Prophet ﷺ said: "The noble one, son of the noble one, son of the noble one, son of the noble one: Yūsuf, son of Yaʿqūb, son of Isḥāq, son of Ibrāhīm."[502] Anas said: "…that is the example of the Prophets. Their eyes sleep but their hearts do

---

493 *Ṣād*, 45-47.

494 *Ṣād*, 17.

495 *Ṣād*, 20.

496 *Yūsuf*, 55.

497 *al-Kahf*, 69.

498 *al-Qaṣaṣ*, 27.

499 *Hūd*, 88.

500 *al-Anbiyā'*, 74.

501 *al-Anbiyā'*, 90.

502 Reported by Bukhārī (3390) from Ibn ʿUmar, and Tirmidhī (3116) from Abū Hurayrah.

وَقَالَ: ﴿إِنَّهُمْ كَانُوا يُسَرِعُونَ فِي ٱلْخَيْرَتِ﴾ [الأنبياء: ٩٠] الآيَةَ. قال سُفْيَانُ: هُوَ الحُزْنُ الدَّائِمُ.

فِي آيٍ كَثِيرَةٍ، ذَكَرَ فِيهَا مِنْ خِصَالِهِمْ وَمَحَاسِنِ أَخْلاقِهِمِ الدَّالَّةِ عَلَى كَمَالِهِمْ.

وَجَاءَ مِنْ ذَلِكَ فِي الأَحَادِيثِ كَثِيرٌ، كَقَوْلِهِ عليه الصلاة والسلام: «إِنَّمَا الكَرِيمُ ابْنُ الكَرِيمِ ابْنِ الكَرِيمِ ابْنِ الكَرِيمِ، يُوسُفُ بْنُ يَعْقُوبَ بْنِ إِسْحَاقَ بْنِ إِبْرَاهِيمَ، نَبِيٌّ ابْنُ نَبِيٍّ ابْنِ نَبِيٍّ ابْنِ نَبِيٍّ»[425].

وَفِي حَدِيثٍ: «وَكَذَلِكَ الأَنْبِيَاءُ تَنَامُ أَعْيُنُهْمْ، وَلَا تَنَامُ قُلُوبُهُمْ»[426].

وَرُوِيَ أَنَّ سُلَيْمَانَ ﷺ كَانَ مَعَ مَا أُعْطِيَ مِنَ المُلْكِ لَا يَرْفَعُ بَصَرَهُ إِلَى السَّمَاءِ تَخَشُّعًا وَتَوَاضُعًا لِلّهِ تَعَالَى[427]، وَكَانَ يُطْعِمُ النَّاسَ لَذَائِذَ الأَطْعِمَةِ، وَيَأْكُلُ خُبْزَ الشَّعِيرِ[428].

وَأَوْحَى اللهُ تَعَالَى إِلَيْهِ: يَا رَأْسَ العَابِدِينَ، وَابْنَ مَحَجَّةِ الزَّاهِدِينَ.

وَكَانَتِ العَجُوزُ تَعْتَرِضُهُ، وَهُوَ عَلَى الرِّيحِ فِي جُنُودِهِ، فَيَأْمُرُ الرِّيحَ فَتَقِفُ فَيَنْظُرُ فِي حَاجَتِهَا وَيَمْضِي.

وَقِيلَ لِيُوسُفَ: مَا لَكَ تَجُوعُ وَأَنْتَ عَلَى خَزَائِنِ الأَرْضِ؟ قَالَ: أَخَافُ أَنْ أَشْبَعَ فَأَنْسَى الجَائِعَ.

وَرَوَى أَبُو هُرَيْرَةَ عَنْهُ ﷺ: «خُفِّفَ عَلَى دَاوُدَ القُرْآنُ، فَكَانَ يَأْمُرُ بِدَوَابِّه

---

٤٢٥   أَخْرَجَهُ البُخَارِيُّ (٣٣٩٠) مِنْ حَدِيثِ ابْنِ عُمَرَ، وَالتِّرْمِذِيُّ (٣١١٦) مِنْ حَدِيثِ أَبِي هُرَيْرَةَ.

٤٢٦   أَخْرَجَهُ البُخَارِيُّ (٣٥٧٠) وَانْظُرْ صَحِيحَ مُسْلِمٍ (٢٦٢/١٦٢).

٤٢٧   رَوَاهُ الطَّبَرَانِيُّ عَنْ أَبِي هُرَيْرَةَ مَرْفُوعًا/ المَنَاهِلُ (٣٣٠).

٤٢٨   رَوَاهُ أَحْمَدُ فِي الزُّهْدِ عَنْ فَرْقَدِ السَّبَخِيِّ/ المَنَاهِلِ (٣٣١).

not."[503]

It was said that Sulaymān, despite the immense kingdom bestowed upon him, would never look up at the Heavens out of his modesty and fear of Allah Exalted.[504] He would provide his people with the most delicious foods whilst sufficing with barley bread for himself.[505] Allah Exalted revealed to him: "O leader of the worshippers! Objective of the ascetics!" Once, whilst riding the winds with his army, he found an old woman standing in front of him. He ordered the wind to stop so that he could deal with her concerns before proceeding on his way.

Yūsuf was asked: "Why do you go hungry when you are in charge of the store-houses of the land?" He replied: "I am afraid that I will become full and forget what it is like to be hungry."

Abū Hurayrah narrated that the Prophet ﷺ said: "Reciting the Zābūr (Psalms)[506] was made easy for Dāwūd. He used to give instructions for his riding animals to be saddled, and would have finished reciting before they were. He would only consume [wealth] earned from his own labour."[507] And Allah Exalted said: "We made iron mouldable for him, instructing: 'Make full-length armour, [perfectly] balancing the links.'[508] Dāwūd would ask his Lord to provide for him from his own labour so that he would have no need to consume from the funds of the community.

The Prophet ﷺ said: "The most beloved prayer to Allah is the prayer of Dāwūd, and the most beloved fasts to Allah are the fasts of Dāwūd. He would sleep for half of the night, stand in prayer

---

503   Reported by Bukhārī (3570). See also Muslim (162/262).
504   Reported by Ṭabarānī in a *marfūʿ* narration from Abū Hurayrah. See *Al-Manāhil*, p. 330.
505   Reported by Aḥmad in *Al-Zuhd* from Farqad al-Sabkhī. See *Al-Manāhil*, p. 331.
506   The word used in the original narration is "Qur'an".
507   Reported by Bukhārī (3417).
508   *Sabaʾ*, 10-11.

فَتُسْرِجُ، فَيَقْرَأُ الْقُرْآنَ قَبْلَ أَنْ تُسْرَجَ، وَلَا يَأْكُلُ إِلَّا مِنْ عَمَلِ يَدِهِ»^{٤٢٩}.

قَالَ اللهُ تَعَالَى: ﴿وَأَلَنَّا لَهُ الْحَدِيدَ ۝ أَنِ اعْمَلْ سَابِغَاتٍ وَقَدِّرْ فِي السَّرْدِ﴾ [سبأ: ١٠-١١]^{٤٣٠}، وَكَانَ سَأَلَ رَبَّهُ أَنْ يَرْزُقَهُ عَمَلًا بِيَدِهِ يُغْنِيهِ عَنْ بَيْتِ مَالِ اللهِ تَعَالَى.

وَقَالَ ﷺ: «أَحَبُّ الصَّلَاةِ إِلَى اللهِ صَلَاةُ دَاوُدَ، وَأَحَبُّ الصِّيَامِ إِلَى اللهِ صِيَامُ دَاوُدَ، كَانَ يَنَامُ نِصْفَ اللَّيْلِ، وَيَقُومُ ثُلُثَهُ، وَيَنَامُ سُدُسَهُ، وَيَصُومُ يَوْمًا، وَيُفْطِرُ يَوْمًا»^{٤٣١}.

وَكَانَ يَلْبَسُ الصُّوفَ، وَيَفْتَرِشُ الشَّعَرَ، وَيَأْكُلُ خُبْزَ الشَّعِيرِ بِالْمِلْحِ وَالرَّمَادِ، وَيَمْزُجُ شَرَابَهُ بِالدُّمُوعِ، وَلَمْ يُرَ ضَاحِكًا بَعْدَ الْخَطِيئَةِ^{٤٣٢}، وَلَا شَاخِصًا بِبَصَرِهِ إِلَى السَّمَاءِ، حَيَاءً مِنْ رَبِّهِ عَزَّوَجَلَّ^{٤٣٣}، وَلَمْ يَزَلْ بَاكِيًا حَيَاتَهُ كُلَّهَا.

وَقِيلَ: بَكَى حَتَّى نَبَتَ الْعُشْبُ مِنْ دُمُوعِهِ^{٤٣٤}، وَحَتَّى اتَّخَذَتِ الدُّمُوعُ فِي خَدِّهِ أُخْدُودًا.

وَقِيلَ: كَانَ يَخْرُجُ مُتَنَكِّرًا يَتَعَرَّفُ سِيرَتَهُ، فَيَسْتَمِعُ الثَّنَاءَ عَلَيْهِ، فَيَزْدَادُ تَوَاضُعًا.

---

٤٢٩ أَخْرَجَهُ الْبُخَارِيُّ (٣٤١٧).

٤٣٠ (اعْمَلْ سَابِغَاتٍ): دُرُوعًا وَاسِعَةً كَامِلَةً. (قَدِّرْ فِي السَّرْدِ): أَحْكِمْ صَنْعَتَكَ فِي نَسْجِ الدُّرُوعِ.

٤٣١ أَخْرَجَهُ الْبُخَارِيُّ (١١٣١)، وَمُسْلِمٌ (١١٥٩/١٨٩) مِنْ حَدِيثِ عَبْدِ اللهِ بْنِ عَمْرِو بْنِ الْعَاصِ.

٤٣٢ رَوَاهُ ابْنُ أَبِي حَاتِمٍ عَنْ وَهْبِ بْنِ مُنَبِّهٍ، وَمُجَاهِدٍ مَوْقُوفًا/ الْمَنَاهِلُ (٣٣٤).

٤٣٣ رَوَاهُ أَحْمَدُ فِي الزُّهْدِ عَنْ أَبِي عَبْدِ اللهِ الْجَدَلِيِّ مَوْقُوفًا/ الْمَنَاهِلُ (٣٣٦).

٤٣٤ رَوَاهُ ابْنُ أَبِي حَاتِمٍ عَنْ أَنَسٍ مَرْفُوعًا، وَعَنْ مُجَاهِدٍ وَغَيْرِهِ مَوْقُوفًا/ الْمَنَاهِلُ (٣٣٧).

for a third, and then sleep for a sixth, and he would fast on one day and not fast the next[509]."[510] He wore woolly clothes and slept on mats made from [camel's or goat's] hair. He ate barley bread with salt and ashes, mixed his drinks with tears, and would never be seen laughing after a mistake.[511] Dāwūd was shy in front of his Lord, so he would never lift his eyes to the sky,[512] and he continued to weep for the rest of his life. Some said he wept for so long that plants sprouted from the ground[513] and his tears formed grooves in his cheeks. Dāwūd would only go out in disguise, in order to find out the community's opinion of his actions, but hearing their praise only increased his humble attitude.

'Īsā ﷺ was asked: "Why not take a donkey [as a riding-animal]?" He replied: "I am too honoured with Allah to be occupied with [looking after] a donkey."[514] He used to wear clothes made from [camel's or goat's] hair and eat produce from the trees, and he did not have a house of his own. He would rest wherever he found himself when he needed to sleep.[515] The name he preferred to be addressed with was: "Poor one".[516] It was said that when Prophet Mūsā ﷺ came to the well of Madyan, he was so emaciated you

---

509   i.e., he would fast on alternate days.

510   Reported by Bukhārī (1131) and Muslim (1159/189) from 'Abdullāh ibn 'Amr ibn al-'Āṣ.

511   Reported by Ibn Abī Ḥātim in a *mawqūf* narration from Wahb ibn Munabbih and Mujā-hid. See *Al-Manāhil*, p. 334.

512   Reported by Aḥmad in *Al-Zuhd* in a *mawqūf* narration from Abū 'Abdullāh al-Jadalī. See *Al-Manāhil*, p. 336.

513   Reported by Ibn Abī Ḥātim in a *marfū'* narration from Anas, and in a *mawqūf* narration from Mujāhid and others. See *Al-Manāhil*, p. 337.

514   Reported by Aḥmad in *Al-Zuhd* and Ibn Abī Shaybah in *Al-Muṣannaf*. See *Al-Manāhil*, p. 338.

515   Reported by Ibn 'Asākir in his *Tārīkh*, and Aḥmad in *Al-Zuhd* from 'Ubayd ibn 'Umayr, Mujāhid, and al-Sha'bī. See *Al-Manāhil*, p. 339.

516   Reported by Aḥmad in *Al-Zuhd*. See *Al-Manāhil*, p. 340.

وَقِيلَ لِعِيسَى عَلَيْهِ السَّلَام: لَوِ اتَّخَذْتَ حِمَارًا؟ فَقَالَ: أَنَا أَكْرَمُ عَلَى اللهِ مِنْ أَنْ يَشْغَلَنِي بِحِمَارٍ⁴³⁵.

وَكَانَ يَلْبَسُ الشَّعَرَ، وَيَأْكُلُ الشَّجَرَ، وَلَمْ يَكُنْ لَهُ بَيْتٌ، أَيْنَمَا أَدْرَكَهُ النَّوْمُ نَامَ⁴³⁶. وَكَانَ أَحَبَّ الأَسَامِي إِلَيْهِ أَنْ يُقَالَ لَهُ: مِسْكِينٌ⁴³⁷.

وَقِيلَ: إِنَّ مُوسَى عَلَيْهِ السَّلَام لَمَّا وَرَدَ مَاءَ مَدْيَنَ كَانَتْ تُرَى خُضْرَةُ البَقْلِ فِي بَطْنِهِ مِنَ الهُزَالِ⁴³⁸.

وَقَالَ نَبِيُّنَا ﷺ: «لَقَدْ كَانَ الأَنْبِيَاءُ قَبْلِي يُبْتَلَى أَحَدُهُمْ بِالفَقْرِ وَالقَمْلِ، وَكَانَ ذَلِكَ أَحَبَّ إِلَيْهِمْ مِنَ العَطَاءِ إِلَيْكُمْ»⁴³⁹.

وَقَالَ عِيسَى عَلَيْهِ السَّلَام لِخِنْزِيرٍ لَقِيَهُ: اذْهَبْ بِسَلَامٍ. فَقِيلَ لَهُ فِي ذَلِكَ، فَقَالَ: أَكْرَهُ أَنْ أُعَوِّدَ لِسَانِي النُّطْقَ بِسُوءٍ.

وَقَالَ مُجَاهِدٌ: كَانَ طَعَامُ يَحْيَى العُشْبَ⁴⁴⁰، وَكَانَ يَبْكِي مِنْ خَشْيَةِ اللهِ حَتَّى

---

٤٣٥ رَوَاهُ أَحْمَدُ فِي الزُّهْدِ وَابْنُ أَبِي شَيْبَةَ فِي المُصَنَّفِ/ المَنَاهِلُ (٣٣٨).

٤٣٦ رَوَاهُ ابْنُ عَسَاكِرٍ فِي تَارِيخِهِ عَنِ ابْنِ عَبَّاسٍ. وَأَحْمَدُ فِي الزُّهْدِ عَنْ عُبَيْدِ بْنِ عُمَيْرٍ، وَمُجَاهِدٍ وَالشَّعْبِيِّ المَنَاهِلُ (٣٣٩).

٤٣٧ رَوَاهُ أَحْمَدُ فِي الزُّهْدِ/ المَنَاهِلُ (٣٤٠).

٤٣٨ رَوَاهُ أَحْمَدُ فِي الزُّهْدِ وَابْنُ أَبِي حَاتِمٍ عَنِ ابْنِ عَبَّاسٍ مَوْقُوفًا/ المَنَاهِلُ (٣٧٠).

٤٣٩ أَخْرَجَهُ الحَاكِمُ ٣٠٧/٤ مِنْ حَدِيثِ الخُدْرِيِّ، وَصَحَّحَهُ وَوَافَقَهُ الذَّهَبِيُّ. وَصَحَّحَهُ أَيْضًا الحَافِظُ العِرَاقِيُّ فِي تَخْرِيجِهِ لِأَحَادِيثِ الإِحْيَاءِ ٢٢٢/٤، وَلَفْظُهُ:.... أَيُّ النَّاسِ أَشَدُّ بَلَاءً؟ قَالَ: الأَنْبِيَاءُ. قُلْتُ [القَائِلُ أَبُو سَعِيدٍ الخُدْرِيُّ]: ثُمَّ مَنْ؟ قَالَ: ثُمَّ الصَّالِحُونَ، إِنْ كَانَ الرَّجُلُ لَيُبْتَلَى بِالفَقْرِ حَتَّى مَا يَجِدُ إِلَّا العَبَاءَ فَيَحْوِيهَا وَيَلْبَسُهَا، وَإِنْ كَانَ أَحَدُهُمْ لَيُبْتَلَى بِالقَمْلِ حَتَّى يَقْتُلَهُ القَمْلُ، وَكَانَ ذَلِكَ أَحَبَّ إِلَيْهِمْ مِنَ العَطَاءِ إِلَيْكُمْ».

٤٤٠ رَوَاهُ ابْنُ أَبِي حَاتِمٍ وَأَحْمَدُ فِي الزُّهْدِ/ المَنَاهِلُ (٣٤٣).

could see the outline of vegetables in his stomach.[517] The Prophet of Allah ﷺ said: "When Prophets before me were tested with poverty and lice, that was more beloved to them than the blessings you have been given."[518] 'Īsā ﷺ said to a pig he came across: "Go with peace." When he was asked about that, he explained: "I hate to make my tongue accustomed to expressing evil."[519]

Mujāhid related that Yaḥyā used to eat wild plants and herbs.[520] He too would cry from his fear of Allah Exalted, until his tears formed grooves in his cheeks, and he would eat with the wild animals in order to avoid the company of people.

Ṭabarī narrated from Wahb that Mūsā ﷺ used to seek the shade of the trees and would eat and drink from a depression in a rock just as an animal would, so humbled was he by the honour of Allah Exalted having spoken to him directly.

The Prophets were well-known for their righteous personalities and beautiful appearances, and all of these reports have been written down and recorded. We will not protract the discussion in this regard, but be sure to avoid the baseless arguments put forward in the books of some of the more ignorant historians and exegetes.

---

517   Reported by Aḥmad in *Al-Zuhd*, and Ibn Abī Ḥātim in a *mawqūf* narration from Ibn 'Abbās. See *Al-Manāhil*, p. 370.

518   Reported by Ḥākim (4/307) from al-Khudrī. Ḥākim authenticated the narration and Dhahabī concurred. Also authenticated by 'Irāqī in *Takhrīj Aḥādīth al-Iḥyā'* (4/222), where the hadith reads: "I [i.e., Abū Saʿīd al-Khudrī] asked: 'Which people experienced the most intense trials?' He [i.e., the Messenger of Allah g] said: 'The Prophets.' I said: 'Then who?' He replied: 'The righteous ones. Sometimes they would be tested with poverty to the extent that they found nothing but a cloak, and they would simply put it on, and sometimes they would be tested with lice until the lice killed them, and that was more beloved to them than the blessings you have been given.'"

519   Reported by Aḥmad in *Al-Zuhd*, and Ibn Abī Ḥātim. See *Al-Manāhil*, p. 343.

520   Reported by Aḥmad in *Al-Zuhd* from Abū Idrīs al-Khawlānī al-Dārānī. See *Al-Manāhil*, p. 344.

اتَّخَذَ الدَّمْعُ مَجْرًى فِي خَدِّهِ، وَكَانَ يَأْكُلُ مَعَ الوَحْشِ لِئَلَّا يُخَالِطَ النَّاسَ[441].

وَحَكَى الطَّبَرِيُّ عَنْ وَهْبٍ أَنَّ مُوسَى ﷺ كَانَ يَسْتَظِلُّ بِعَرِيشٍ، وَيَأْكُلُ فِي نُقْرَةٍ[442] مِنْ حَجَرٍ، وَيَكْرَعُ[443] فِيهَا إِذَا أَرَادَ أَنْ يَشْرَبَ كَمَا تَكْرَعُ الدَّابَّةُ، تَوَاضُعًا لِلّٰهِ بِمَا أَكْرَمَهُ اللّٰهُ بِهِ مِنْ كَلَامِهِ.

وَأَخْبَارُهُمْ فِي هَذَا كُلِّهِ مَسْطُورَةٌ، وَصِفَاتُهُمْ فِي الكَمَالِ وَجَمِيلِ الأَخْلَاقِ وَحُسْنِ الصُّوَرِ وَالشَّمَائِلِ مَعْرُوفَةٌ مَشْهُورَةٌ، فَلَا نُطَوِّلُ بِهَا.

وَلَا تَلْتَفِتْ إِلَى مَا تَجِدُهُ فِي كُتُبِ بَعْضِ جَهَلَةِ المُؤَرِّخِينَ أَوِ المُفَسِّرِينَ مِمَّا يُخَالِفُ هَذَا.

---

441 رَوَاهُ أَحْمَدُ فِي الزُّهْدِ عَنْ أَبِي إِدْرِيسَ الخَوْلَانِيِّ الدَّارَانِيِّ/ المَنَاهِلُ (٣٤٤).

442 نُقْرَةٌ: حُفْرَةٌ.

443 يَكْرَعُ: أَيْ يَتَنَاوَلُ المَاءَ بِفِيهِ مِنْ مَوْضِعِهِ مِنْ غَيْرِ أَنْ يَشْرَبَ بِكَفَّيْهِ وَلَا بِإِنَاءٍ.

THE HADITH OF HIND IBN ABĪ HĀLAH AND ʿALĪ ABOUT THE QUALITIES AND TRAITS OF THE PROPHET ﷺ

May Allah honour you, beloved readers. We have presented an overview of the praiseworthy characteristics, magnificent virtues, and perfect features of the Prophet ﷺ, and we have provided reliable evidence from numerous narrations, most of which was taken from authentic and well-known sources. But the topic is vast, so although this chapter covers a lot of ground, it does not begin to do justice. Taking buckets of water does not even begin to exhaust an ocean of knowledge.

Nevertheless, it seems appropriate to conclude the chapter with the hadith narrated by al-Ḥasan from Ibn Abī Hālah, as it gives a detailed and comprehensive description of the Prophet ﷺ.

I read the following hadith to Abū ʿAlī al-Ṣadafī in 508 AH, and he narrated from Imam Abū al-Qāsim (ʿAbdullāh ibn Ṭāhir al-Tamīmī), from the jurist and linguist Abū Bakr (Muhammad ibn ʿAbdullāh ibn al-Ḥasan al-Nīsābūrī), the esteemed scholar Abū ʿAbdullāh (Muhammad ibn Aḥmad ibn al-Ḥasan al-Muḥammadī, and the *qāḍī* Abū ʿAlī (al-Ḥasan ibn ʿAlī ibn Jaʿfar al-Wakhshī)[521], from Abū al-Qāsim (ʿAlī ibn Aḥmad ibn Muhammad ibn al-Ḥasan al-Khuzāʿī), from Abū Saʿīd (al-Haytham ibn Kulayb al-Shāshī), from Abū ʿĪsā (Muhammad ibn Sawrah al-Ḥāfiẓ), from Sufyān ibn Wakīʿ, who dictated from Jumayʿ ibn ʿUmayr ibn

---

521   He was named after his hometown, Waksh. Ibn Ḥajar said in *Tabṣīr al-Muntabih*: "It was a town in the Balkh region." See *Siyar Aʿlām al-Nubalāʾ* (18/365-367).

فَصْل

قَدْ أَتَيْنَا أَكْرَمَكَ اللهُ مِنْ ذِكْرِ الأَخْلَاقِ الحَمِيدَةِ وَالفَضَائِلِ المَجِيدَةِ، وَخِصَالِ الكَمَالِ العَدِيدَةِ، وَأَرَيْنَاكَ صِحَّتَهَا لَهُ ﷺ، وَجَلَبْنَا[444] مِنَ الآثَارِ مَا فِيهِ مَقْنَعٌ، وَالأَمْرُ أَوْسَعُ، فَمَجَالُ هَذَا البَابِ فِي حَقِّهِ ﷺ مُمْتَدٌّ، تَنْقَطِعُ دُونَ نَفَادِهِ الأَدِلَّاءُ[445]، وَبَحْرُ عِلْمِ خَصَائِصِهِ زَاخِرٌ لَا تُكَدِّرُهُ الدِّلَاءُ[446]، وَلَكِنَّا أَتَيْنَا فِيهِ بِالمَعْرُوفِ مِمَّا أَكْثَرُهُ فِي الصَّحِيحِ وَالمَشْهُورِ مِنَ المُصَنَّفَاتِ، وَاقْتَصَرْنَا فِي ذَلِكَ بِقُلٍّ[447] مِنْ كُلٍّ، وَغَيْضٍ مِنْ فَيْضٍ[448]، وَرَأَيْنَا أَنْ نَخْتِمَ هَذِهِ الفُصُولَ بِذِكْرِ حَدِيثِ الحَسَنِ عَنِ ابْنِ أَبِي هَالَةَ لِجَمْعِهِ مِنْ شَمَائِلِهِ وَأَوْصَافِهِ كَثِيرًا، وَإِدْمَاجِهِ جُمْلَةً كَافِيَةً مِنْ سِيرِهِ وَفَضَائِلِهِ، وَنَصِلَهُ بِتَنْبِيهٍ لَطِيفٍ عَلَى غَرِيبِهِ وَمُشْكِلِهِ[449].

حَدَّثَنَا القَاضِي أَبُو عَلِيٍّ الحُسَيْنُ بْنُ مُحَمَّدٍ الحَافِظُ رَحِمَهُ اللهُ بِقِرَاءَتِي عَلَيْهِ سَنَةَ ثَمَانٍ وَخَمْسِ مِائَةٍ، قَالَ: حَدَّثَنَا الإِمَامُ أَبُو القَاسِمِ عَبْدُ اللهِ بْنُ طَاهِرٍ التَّمِيمِيُّ، قَرَأْتُ عَلَيْهِ: أَخْبَرَكُمُ الفَقِيهُ الأَدِيبُ أَبُو بَكْرٍ مُحَمَّدُ بْنُ عَبْدِ اللهِ بْنِ الحَسَنِ

---

٤٤٤ (جَلَبْنَا): نَقَلْنَا وَأَوْرَدْنَا.

٤٤٥ نَفَادِهِ الأَدِلَّاءُ: (نَفَادِهِ) فَنَائِهِ. (الأَدِلَّاءُ): جَمْعُ دَلِيلٍ.

٤٤٦ لَا تُكَدِّرُهُ الدِّلَاءُ: جَمْعُ دَلْوٍ، وَهُوَ إِنَاءٌ يُسْتَقَى بِهِ مِنَ البِئْرِ. وَعَدَمُ تَكْدِيرِهِ عِبَارَةٌ عَنْ عَدَمِ بُلُوغِ آخِرِهِ.

٤٤٧ (بِقُلٍّ): القُلُّ: القَلِيلُ.

٤٤٨ غَيْضٌ مِنْ فَيْضٍ: قَلِيلٌ مِنْ كَثِيرٍ.

٤٤٩ الكَلِمَاتُ الغَرِيبَةُ الَّتِي لَمْ يَشْرَحْهَا المُصَنِّفُ شَرَحْتُهَا فِي الحَاشِيَةِ.

'Abd al-Raḥmān al-'Ijlī, who narrated from a man from the Banū Tamīm tribe nicknamed Abū 'Abdullāh, who was from amongst the descendants of Abū Hālah (the first husband of the Mother of the Believers Khadījah ﷺ), and he narrated from one of the sons of Abū Hālah, from al-Ḥasan ibn 'Alī ibn Abī Ṭālib ﷺ, who said: "I asked my maternal uncle Hind ibn Abī Hālah...".[522]

I also read the hadith to Shaykh Abū al-Ṭāhir (Aḥmad ibn al-Ḥasan ibn Aḥmad ibn Khudhādād[523] al-Karajī al-Bāqillānī, who was given permission to narrate from Shaykh Abū al-Faḍl (Aḥmad ibn al-Ḥasan ibn Khayrūn). They both read to Abū 'Alī (al-Ḥasan ibn Aḥmad ibn Ibrāhīm ibn al-Ḥasan ibn Muhammad ibn Shādhān ibn Ḥarb ibn Mihrān al-Fārisī), who narrated from Abū Muhammad (al-Ḥasan ibn Muhammad ibn Yaḥyā ibn al-Ḥasan ibn Ja'far ibn 'Ubaydullāh ibn al-Ḥusayn ibn 'Alī ibn al-Ḥusayn ibn 'Alī ibn Abī Ṭālib, better known as Ibn Akhī Ṭāhir al-'Alawī), from Ismā'īl ibn Muhammad ibn Isḥāq ibn Ja'far ibn Muhammad ibn 'Alī ibn al-Ḥusayn ibn 'Alī ibn Abī Ṭālib, from 'Alī ibn Ja'far ibn Muhammad ibn 'Alī ibn al-Ḥusayn, from his brother Mūsā ibn Ja'far, from Ja'far ibn Muhammad, from his father Muhammad ibn 'Alī, from 'Alī ibn al-Ḥusayn, from al-Ḥasan ibn 'Alī,[524] who said: "I asked my maternal uncle Hind ibn Abī Hālah about

---

522 Reported here from the chain of Tirmidhī in *Al-Shamā'il* (8, 335, 350), the chain of Tirmidhī reported by Baghawī in *Sharḥ al-Sunnah* (3705, 3706), and the chain recorded by Ibn al-Athīr in *Usd al-Ghābah* in his biography of Hind ibn Abī Hālah. Also reported by al-Fasawī, as found in *Shamā'il Ibn Kathīr*, p. 50, from the two chains of Jumay' ibn 'Umayr. Haythamī said in *Majma' al-Zawā'id* (8/273-278): "It was related by Ṭabarānī and there are narrators in the chain who are not named." Graded as *ḥasan* by Suyūṭī in *Al-Jāmi' al-Ṣaghīr* (6493). Al-Albānī said in *Mukhtaṣar Shamā'il al-Tirmidhī* (6): "[The narration is] very weak." See also *Al-Maqāṣid al-Ḥasanah* (11) and *Shamā'il Ibn Kathīr*, pp. 50-56.

523 "Khudhādād" is a Persian name meaning "the gift of Allah".

524 Al-Khafājī said in *Nasīm al-Riyāḍ* (2/167): "A noble chain of transmission, because they all narrated from the family of the Prophet ﷺ (another example of which would be the hadith describing the prayer) and every narrator in the chain is well-known. Al-Tilmisānī said that if this narration was read to a person who was sick, they would recover."

النَّيْسَابُورِيُّ، وَالشَّيْخُ الفَقِيهُ أَبُو عَبْدِ اللهِ مُحَمَّدُ بْنُ أَحْمَدَ بْنِ الحَسَنِ المُحَمَّدِيُّ، وَالقَاضِي أَبُو عَلِيٍّ الحَسَنُ بْنُ عَلِيِّ بْنِ جَعْفَرٍ الوَخْشِيُّ[450]، قَالُوا: حَدَّثَنَا أَبُو القَاسِمِ عَلِيُّ بْنُ أَحْمَدَ ابْنِ مُحَمَّدِ بْنِ الحَسَنِ الخُزَاعِيُّ، أَخْبَرَنَا أَبُو سَعِيدٍ الهَيْثَمُ بْنُ كُلَيْبٍ الشَّاشِيُّ، قَالَ: أَخْبَرَنَا أَبُو عِيسَى مُحَمَّدُ بْنُ عِيسَى بْنِ سَوْرَةَ الحَافِظُ، قَالَ: حَدَّثَنَا سُفْيَانُ بْنُ وَكِيعٍ، حَدَّثَنَا جُمَيْعُ بْنُ عُمَرَ بْنِ عَبْدِ الرَّحْمَنِ العِجْلِيُّ إِمْلَاءً مِنْ كِتَابِهِ، قَالَ: حَدَّثَنِي رَجُلٌ مِنْ بَنِي تَمِيمٍ مِنْ وَلَدِ أَبِي هَالَةَ زَوْجِ خَدِيجَةَ أُمِّ المُؤْمِنِينَ رَضِيَ اللهُ عَنْهَا، يُكْنَى أَبَا عَبْدِ اللهِ، عَنِ ابْنٍ لِأَبِي هَالَةَ، عَنِ الحَسَنِ بْنِ عَلِيِّ بْنِ أَبِي طَالِبٍ رَضِيَ اللهُ عَنْهُ، قَالَ: سَأَلْتُ خَالِي هِنْدَ بْنَ أَبِي هَالَةَ.

قَالَ القَاضِي أَبُو عَلِيٍّ رَحِمَهُ اللهُ: وَقَرَأْتُ عَلَى الشَّيْخِ أَبِي طَاهِرٍ أَحْمَدَ ابْنِ الحَسَنِ ابْنِ أَحْمَدَ بْنِ خُذَادَاذَ[451] الكَرَجِيِّ البَاقِلَّانِي، قَالَ: وَأَجَازَ لَنَا الشَّيْخُ الأَجَلُّ أَبُو الفَضْلِ أَحْمَدُ بْنُ الحُسَيْنِ بْنِ خَيْرُونَ، قَالَا: أَخْبَرَنَا أَبُو عَلِيٍّ الحَسَنُ بْنُ أَحْمَدَ بْنِ إِبْرَاهِيمَ بْنِ الحَسَنِ بْنِ مُحَمَّدِ بْنِ شَاذَانَ بْنِ حَرْبِ بْنِ مِهْرَانَ الفَارِسِيُّ قِرَاءَةً عَلَيْهِ فَأَقَرَّ بِهِ، قَالَ: أَخْبَرَنَا أَبُو مُحَمَّدٍ الحَسَنُ بْنُ مُحَمَّدِ بْنِ الحَسَنِ بْنِ جَعْفَرٍ ابْنِ عُبَيْدِ اللهِ بْنِ الحُسَيْنِ بْنِ عَلِيِّ بْنِ الحُسَيْنِ بْنِ عَلِيِّ بْنِ أَبِي طَالِبٍ، المَعْرُوفُ بِابْنِ أَخِي طَاهِرٍ العَلَوِيِّ، قَالَ: حَدَّثَنَا إِسْمَاعِيلُ بْنُ مُحَمَّدِ بْنِ إِسْحَاقَ بْنِ جَعْفَرِ بْنِ مُحَمَّدِ بْنِ عَلِيِّ بْنِ الحُسَيْنِ بْنِ عَلِيِّ بْنِ أَبِي طَالِبٍ، قَالَ: حَدَّثَنِي عَلِيُّ

---

٤٥٠ وَهُوَ مَنْسُوبٌ إِلَى «وَخْشٍ». قَالَ ابْنُ حَجَرٍ فِي تَبْصِيرِ المُنْتَبِهِ ١٤٧٩/٤: «مَدِينَةٌ مِنْ أَعْمَالِ بَلْخٍ». انْظُرْ تَرْجَمَتَهُ فِي سِيَرِ أَعْلَامِ النُّبَلَاءِ ١٨/٣٦٥-٣٦٧.

٤٥١ خُذَادَاذُ: ضَبَطَهُ ابْنُ حَجَرٍ فِي تَبْصِيرِ المُنْتَبِهِ ص (٥٢٦) بِضَمِّ الخَاءِ وَفَتْحِ الذَّالِ المُعْجَمَةِ ثُمَّ دَالٍ مُهْمَلَةٍ بَيْنَ الأَلِفَيْنِ ثُمَّ ذَالٍ مُعْجَمَةٍ. وَمَعْنَاهُ بِالفَارِسِيَّةِ: عَطِيَّةُ اللهِ.

the beauty of the Messenger of Allah ﷺ. He was well-known for his describing abilities, and I was hoping that he would give me something to hold on to.

He said: 'The Messenger of Allah ﷺ was imposing and majestic. His face shone like a full moon. He was taller than average height, but shorter than someone who was noticeably lanky.[525] He had a large, magnificent head, and his hair was neither completely curly nor straight. If his hair parted by itself, he would leave it parted, but otherwise he would leave his hair long and it would not go past his earlobes. He had a radiant[526] complexion and a broad forehead. His eyebrows were thick – perfected without being conjoined[527] – and there was a vein between them which pulsated when he became angry or vexed. He had an aquiline nose, with light that shone above it; if you did not look carefully, it gave his nose an elevated appearance. His beard was thick and full. He had incredibly black pupils,[528] firm cheeks, a wide mouth, and white teeth, and there was a gap between his two front teeth. A fine line of hair extended from his chest to his navel. His neck was like that of a statue cast from pure silver. His physique was perfectly proportioned;[529] firm and

---

525 Similar to the saying of ʿAlī ibn Abī Ṭālib ﷺ: "He was neither extremely tall or short, but somewhere between the two." See Tirmidhī (3637, 3638).

526 "*Azhar*", which can also be translated as "beautiful". From the same root, we find the following expressions: "…the [fleeting] splendour of this worldly life (*zahrah al-ḥayāh al-dun-yā*)" (*Ṭā Hā*, 131) and "…adornment of this worldly life (*zīnatuhā*)" (al-*Qaṣaṣ*, 60).
As we find in the narration of Anas: "He had a radiant complexion, neither a pure white or a deep brown." See Bukhārī (3547) and Muslim (2347).
ʿAlī mentions "a blended white" colour, meaning it was mixed with reddish tones. See Tirmidhī (3638).

527 Umm Maʿbad described his eyebrows as: "…beautifully arched and connected". See Baghawī (3704).

528 Jābir described the Prophet ﷺ having: "…long slits in the eye". Reported by Muslim (2339). Another narration mentioned the whites of his eyes being "mixed with reddish tones", although the term was also subject to alternative interpretations.
ʿAlī said the Prophet ﷺ had: "…long eyelashes". See Tirmidhī (3638).

529 ʿAlī said: "He was neither plump nor double-chinned". Meaning, "he did not carry excess

بْنُ جَعْفَرِ بْنِ مُحَمَّدِ بْنِ عَلِيِّ بْنِ الْحُسَيْنِ، عَنْ أَخِيهِ مُوسَى بْنِ جَعْفَرٍ، عَنْ جَعْفَرِ بْنِ مُحَمَّدٍ، عَنْ أَبِيهِ مُحَمَّدِ بْنِ عَلِيٍّ، عَنْ عَلِيِّ بْنِ الْحُسَيْنِ، قَالَ: قَالَ الْحَسَنُ بْنُ عَلِيٍّ – وَاللَّفْظُ لِهَذَا السَّنَدِ – سَأَلْتُ خَالِي هِنْدَ بْنَ أَبِي هَالَةَ عَنْ حِلْيَةِ رَسُولِ اللهِ ﷺ، وَكَانَ وَصَّافًا، وَأَنَا أَرْجُو أَنْ يَصِفَ لِي مِنْهَا شَيْئًا أَتَعَلَّقُ بِهِ، قَالَ:

«كَانَ رَسُولُ اللهِ ﷺ فَخْمًا مُفَخَّمًا[452]، يَتَلَأْلَأُ[453] وَجْهُهُ تَلَأْلُؤَ الْقَمَرِ لَيْلَةَ الْبَدْرِ، أَطْوَلَ مِنَ الْمَرْبُوعِ، وَأَقْصَرَ مِنَ الْمُشَذَّبِ، عَظِيمَ الْهَامَةِ، رَجِلَ الشَّعَرِ، إِنِ انْفَرَقَتْ عَقِيقَتُهُ فَرَقَ وَإِلَّا فَلَا. يُجَاوِزُ شَعَرُهُ شَحْمَةَ أُذُنِهِ، إِذَا هُوَ وَفَّرَهُ[454]، أَزْهَرَ اللَّوْنِ، وَاسِعَ الْجَبِينِ، أَزَجَّ الْحَوَاجِبِ، سَوَابِغَ مِنْ غَيْرِ قَرَنٍ، بَيْنَهُمَا عِرْقٌ يُدِرُّهُ الْغَضَبُ[455].

أَقْنَى الْعِرْنِينِ[456]، لَهُ نُورٌ يَعْلُوهُ، وَيَحْسِبُهُ مَنْ لَمْ يَتَأَمَّلْهُ أَشَمَّ، كَثَّ اللِّحْيَةِ، أَدْعَجَ، سَهْلَ الْخَدَّيْنِ، ضَلِيعَ الْفَمِ، أَشْنَبَ، مُفَلَّجَ الْأَسْنَانِ، دَقِيقَ الْمَسْرُبَةِ، كَأَنَّ عُنُقَهُ جِيدُ دُمْيَةٍ[457] فِي صَفَاءِ الْفِضَّةِ، مُعْتَدِلَ الْخَلْقِ، بَادِنًا، مُتَمَاسِكًا، سَوَاءَ الْبَطْنِ وَالصَّدْرِ، مُشِيحَ الصَّدْرِ، بَعِيدَ مَا بَيْنَ الْمَنْكِبَيْنِ، ضَخْمَ الْكَرَادِيسِ.

---

٤٥٢ فَخْمًا مُفَخَّمًا: أَيْ عَظِيمًا مُعَظَّمًا فِي الصُّدُورِ وَالعُيُونِ وَلَمْ تَكُنْ خِلْقَتُهُ فِي جِسْمِهِ الضَّخَامَةَ. وَقِيلَ: الفَخَامَةُ فِي وَجْهِهِ: نُبْلُهُ وَامْتِلَاؤُهُ مَعَ الجَمَالِ وَالمَهَابَةِ/ النِّهَايَةُ.

٤٥٣ يَتَلَأْلَأُ: يُشْرِقُ.

٤٥٤ وَفَّرَهُ: الوَفْرَةُ: الشَّعَرُ إِلَى شَحْمَةِ الأُذُنِ، وَالجُمَّةُ إِلَى المَنْكِبِ، وَاللِّمَّةُ: الَّتِي أَلَمَّتْ بِالمَنْكِبَيْنِ.

٤٥٥ بَيْنَهُمَا عِرْقٌ يُدِرُّهُ الغَضَبُ: يَعْنِي بَيْنَ حَاجِبَيْهِ عِرْقٌ يَمْتَلِئُ دَمًا إِذَا غَضِبَ.

٤٥٦ العِرْنِينُ: الأَنْفُ. وَقِيلَ: رَأْسُهُ (النِّهَايَةُ).

٤٥٧ كَأَنَّ عُنُقَهُ جِيدُ دُمْيَةٍ: (الجِيدُ) العُنُقُ. (الدُّمْيَةُ): الصُّورَةُ الَّتِي بُولِغَ فِي تَحْسِينِهَا.

muscular. His stomach and chest were level. He had a wide chest and broad shoulders. His limbs were solid and his skin seemed to glow. Apart from the line of hair from chest to navel, his torso and stomach were bare, but he did have hair on his forearms, shoulders, and the upper part of his chest. He had long forearms, large palms, strong hands and feet, and long fingers. He had high insteps and his feet were so smooth that water ran off them.[530]

He walked swiftly and with composure, as if he was descending a gradient. When he turned to address somebody, he turned with his entire body. He would lower his gaze, looking towards the ground more often than towards the sky, and his glances were brief. He would lead his Companions by walking behind them and was always first to greet any person he met.'

Then, I asked him to describe how the Prophet ﷺ spoke.

He said: 'The Messenger of Allah ﷺ was always sorrowful and reflective. He never had a rest. The Prophet ﷺ would often remain silent and did not speak without a purpose. When he did, he always began and ended in the proper manner, and his speech was comprehensive; neither verbose nor laconic. He had a mild temperament and was neither rude nor disparaging towards others. He valued gifts and blessings, even if they were small. He never censured, neither would he criticise or praise the taste of foods and drinks. He never became overly insistent on claiming something he was due, nor did he get angry or seek to avenge for his own sake. When he gestured, he did so with a full hand. When he was taken aback by something, he would turn his palms upwards, and as he spoke, he would strike his left palm with his right thumb. When he

---

weight". See *Al-Shamā'il* (7).

530   Jābir described the Prophet ﷺ having: "…thin heels". Reported by Tirmidhī in *Al-Sunan* (3647) and *Al-Shamā'il* (8).

أَنْوَرَ المُتَجَرِّدِ⁴⁵⁸، مَوْصُولَ مَا بَيْنَ اللَّبَّةِ⁴⁵⁹ وَالسُّرَّةِ بِشَعَرٍ يَجْرِي كَالخَطِّ، عَارِيَ الثَّدْيَيْنِ⁴⁶⁰ مِمَّا سِوَى ذَلِكَ، أَشْعَرَ الذِّرَاعَيْنِ وَالمَنْكِبَيْنِ وَأَعَالِي الصَّدْرِ، طَوِيلَ الزَّنْدَيْنِ، رَحْبَ الرَّاحَةِ، شَثْنَ الكَفَّيْنِ وَالقَدَمَيْنِ⁴⁶¹، سَايِلَ الأَطْرَافِ- أَوْ قَالَ: سَايِنَ الأَطْرَافِ، سَبْطَ العَصَبِ⁴⁶²، خُمْصَانَ الأَخْمَصَيْنِ، مَسِيحَ القَدَمَيْنِ، يَنْبُو عَنْهُمَا المَاءُ⁴⁶³.

إِذَا زَالَ زَالَ تَقَلُّعًا، وَيَخْطُو تَكَفُّؤًا، وَيَمْشِي هَوْنًا، ذَرِيعَ المِشْيَةِ، إِذَا مَشَى كَأَنَّمَا يَنْحَطُّ مِنْ صَبَبٍ⁴⁶⁴، وَإِذَا الْتَفَتَ الْتَفَتَ جَمِيعًا⁴⁶⁵، خَافِضَ الطَّرْفِ، نَظَرُهُ إِلَى الأَرْضِ أَطْوَلُ مِنْ نَظَرِهِ إِلَى السَّمَاءِ، جُلُّ نَظَرِهِ المُلَاحَظَةُ⁴⁶⁶، يَسُوقُ أَصْحَابَهُ⁴⁶⁷، وَيَبْدَأُ مَنْ لَقِيَ بِالسَّلَامِ».

قُلْتُ: صِفْ لِي مَنْطِقَهُ.

---

٤٥٨ أَنْوَرَ المُتَجَرِّدِ: أَيْ مُشْرِقَ الجَسَدِ.

٤٥٩ اللَّبَّةُ: مَوْضِعُ الثَّغْرَةِ فَوْقَ الصَّدْرِ.

٤٦٠ عَارِيَ الثَّدْيَيْنِ: يُرِيدُ أَنَّهُ لَمْ يَكُنْ عَلَى ذَلِكَ المَوْضِعِ مِنْهُ شَعْرٌ.

٤٦١ شَثْنَ الكَفَّيْنِ وَالقَدَمَيْنِ: غِلَظَهُمَا.

٤٦٢ «القَصَب» بِالقَافِ. قَالَ فِي النِّهَايَةِ: «السَّبْطُ: المُمْتَدُّ الَّذِي لَيْسَ فِيهِ تَعَقُّدٌ وَلَا نُتُوٌّ، وَالقَصَب يُرِيدُ بِهَا: سَاعِدَيْهِ وَسَاقَيْهِ».

٤٦٣ أَيْ لَا ثَبَاتَ لِلْمَاءِ عَلَيْهِمَا.

٤٦٤ الصَّبَبُ: الأَرْضُ المُنْحَدِرَةُ.

٤٦٥ يُرِيدُ: لَا يَلْوِي عُنُقَهُ يَمْنَةً وَيَسْرَةً نَاظِرًا إِلَى الشَّيْءِ، وَإِنَّمَا يَفْعَلُ ذَلِكَ الطَّائِشُ الخَفِيفُ.

٤٦٦ المُلَاحَظَةُ: هُوَ أَنْ يَنْظُرَ الرَّجُلُ بِلِحَاظِ عَيْنِهِ إِلَى الشَّيْءِ. يُقَالُ: لَحَظَ إِلَيْهِ وَلَحَظَهُ: إِذَا نَظَرَ إِلَيْهِ بِمُؤَخِّرِ عَيْنِهِ.

٤٦٧ أَيْ يُقَدِّمُ أَصْحَابَهُ بَيْنَ يَدَيْهِ وَيَمْشِي خَلْفَهُمْ.

became angry, he would turn away. If he was joyful, he would lower his gaze. His laughter was a broad smile which spread [across his face] until his teeth were visible, [as white] as hailstones.'

I did not tell al-Ḥusayn ibn ʿAlī about what I had heard for a period of time. When I did tell him, I found that he had already beaten me to it by asking his father about how the Prophet ﷺ behaved at home and when he was out, the manner of his assemblies and gatherings, and his appearance. He had not omitted anything.

Al-Ḥusayn said: 'I asked my father about how the Prophet ﷺ entered [the home]. He replied: "The Prophet ﷺ was permitted to enter his home for his own comfort. When he retired to the house, he would divide the day into three parts; a part of the day for worshipping Allah, a part for his family, and a part for attending to his own needs. Then, he divided the part for his own needs between himself and the people. He would prioritize the general public rather than the elite with his time, and he would not prevent others from anything to reserve for himself. In the part of the day allocated to his own needs, his manner was to show preference to the people of virtue, in accordance with their excellence in the religion. Some people needed one thing, some needed two, and some had many needs. He would busy himself with attending to their needs, and would prioritize that which would benefit both the people who came to him and the wider Muslim community. The Prophet ﷺ would say: 'Tell me the needs of those who cannot tell me themselves, for Allah will safeguard whoever does so on the Day of the Great Terror.'"

My father added: "They would enter as seekers, but would not part without having a taste. They would leave as testaments [to the truth]; meaning, they would leave as scholars."[531]

---

531 This statement is taken from the narration of Sufyān ibn Wakīʿ. See *Nasīm al-Riyāḍ*

قَالَ: «كَانَ رَسُولُ اللهِ ﷺ مُتَوَاصِلَ الأَحْزَانِ، دَائِمَ الفِكْرَةِ، لَيْسَت لَهُ رَاحَةٌ، وَلَا يَتَكَلَّمُ فِي غَيرِ حَاجَةٍ، طَوِيلَ السُّكُوتِ، يَفْتَتِحُ الكَلَامَ وَيَخْتِمُهُ بِأَشْدَاقِهِ، وَيَتَكَلَّمُ بِجَوَامِعِ الكَلِمِ فَصْلًا، لَا فُضُولَ فِيهِ وَلَا تَقْصِيرَ، دَمِثًا، لَيسَ بِالجَافِي وَلَا المَهِينِ.

يُعَظِّمُ النِّعْمَةَ وَإِنْ دَقَّتْ، لَا يَذُمُّ شَيئًا، وَلَم يَكُنْ يَذُمُّ ذَوَاقًا[٤٦٨] وَلَا يَمْدَحُهُ، وَلَا يُقَامُ لِغَضَبِهِ إِذَا تُعُرِّضَ لِلْحَقِّ بِشَيءٍ حَتَّى يَنْتَصِرَ لَهُ، وَلَا يَغْضَبُ لِنَفْسِهِ، وَلَا يَنْتَصِرُ لَهَا، إِذَا أَشَارَ أَشَارَ بِكَفِّهِ كُلِّهَا، وَإِذَا تَعَجَّبَ قَلَبَهَا، وَإِذَا تَحَدَّثَ اتَّصَلَ بِهَا، فَضَرَبَ بِإِبْهَامِهِ اليُمْنَى[٤٦٩] رَاحَتَهُ اليُسْرَى، وَإِذَا غَضِبَ أَعْرَضَ وَأَشَاحَ، وَإِذَا فَرِحَ غَضَّ طَرْفَهُ، جُلُّ ضَحِكِهِ التَّبَسُّمُ، وَيَفْتَرُّ[٤٧٠] عَن مِثلِ حَبِّ الغَمَامِ».

قَالَ الحَسَنُ: فَكَتَمْتُهَا الحُسَينَ بْنَ عَلِيٍّ زَمَانًا، ثُمَّ حَدَّثْتُهُ عَن هَذَا فَوَجَدْتُهُ قَدْ سَبَقَنِي إِلَيهِ، فَسَأَلَ أَبَاهُ عَن مَدْخَلِ رَسُولِ اللهِ ﷺ، وَمَخْرَجِهِ، وَمَجْلِسِهِ، وَشَكْلِهِ، فَلَم يَدَعْ مِنْهُ شَيئًا.

قَالَ الحُسَينُ: سَأَلْتُ أَبِي عَن دُخُولِ رَسُولِ اللهِ ﷺ، فَقَالَ: كَانَ دُخُولُهُ لِنَفْسِهِ مَأْذُونًا لَهُ فِي ذَلِكَ، فَكَانَ إِذَا أَوَى إِلَى مَنزِلِهِ جَزَّأَ دُخُولَهُ ثَلَاثَةَ أَجْزَاءٍ: جُزْءًا لِلهِ تَعَالَى، وَجُزْءًا لِأَهْلِهِ، وَجُزْءًا لِنَفْسِهِ، ثُمَّ جَزَّأَ جُزْأَهُ بَينَهُ وَبَينَ النَّاسِ،

---

٤٦٨ أَي شَيئًا مِمَّا يُذَاقُ، وَيَقَعُ عَلَى المَأْكُولِ وَالمَشْرُوبِ، فَعَالٌ بِمَعْنَى مَفْعُولٍ.

٤٦٩ وَيُقَالُ: إِبْهَامُ يَمِينٍ وَيُمْنَى. لِأَنَّ الإِبْهَامَ مُؤَنَّثٌ وَقَدْ تُذَكَّرُ.

٤٧٠ يَفْتَرُّ: أَي يَبْتَسِمُ وَيَكْثِرُ حَتَّى تَبْدُوَ أَسْنَانُهُ مِن غَيرِ قَهْقَهَةٍ/ النِّهَايَةُ.

Then, I asked how the Prophet ﷺ was when he went out. He said: "The Messenger of Allah ﷺ would hold his tongue except regarding that which was relevant to the people. He used to bring people together and would never alienate them. He would honour the leaders of each community and put them in charge of their people. He would caution people and be wary of them, but without abandoning his cheerful manner and exemplary character, and he would check in on his Companions, and would ask people to inform him about others.

He praised anything good and encouraged it, and was repulsed by anything that constituted shameful conduct and discouraged it. He was balanced, without making [unnecessary] changes. He was not negligent, fearing that others would also become negligent or weary. He was prepared for any eventuality. He did not neglect [people's] rights or pass on the responsibility to others. His favourite people were those who gave advice to anyone [who needed it], and the best in his eyes were those who offered comfort and support [to the community]."

Next, I asked about his gatherings, and how he behaved at them. He said: "The Messenger of Allah ﷺ did not sit down or stand up without mentioning Allah. He did not reserve a special place for himself and forbade other people to do so.[532] Rather, when he came to people, he would sit at the edge of the gathering and he instructed others to do the same. He would give every person who sat with him their share [of his time and attention], to the extent that each person felt that they had been more looked after than anyone else.

(2/181).

532   Reported by Abū Dāwūd (862), Nasā'ī (2/214), Ibn Mājah (1429), and others, from 'Abd al-Raḥmān ibn Shibl. Authenticated by Ibn Ḥibbān in *Mawārid al-Ẓam'ān* (476). Also authenticated by Ḥākim (1/229) and Dhahabī concurred. Also reported by Aḥmad (5/447) from Abū Salamah.

فَيَرُدُّ ذَلِكَ عَلَى الْعَامَّةِ بِالْخَاصَّةِ، وَلَا يَدَّخِرُ عَنْهُمْ شَيْئًا.

فَكَانَ مِنْ سِيرَتِهِ فِي جُزْءِ الْأُمَّةِ إِيثَارُ أَهْلِ الْفَضْلِ بِإِذْنِهِ[471]، قِسْمَتُهُ عَلَى قَدْرِ فَضْلِهِمْ فِي الدِّينِ، مِنْهُمْ ذُو الْحَاجَةِ، وَمِنْهُمْ ذُو الْحَاجَتَيْنِ، وَمِنْهُمْ ذُو الْحَوَائِجِ، فَيَتَشَاغَلُ بِهِمْ، وَيَشْغَلُهُمْ فِيمَا أَصْلَحَهُمْ وَالْأُمَّةَ مِنْ مَسْأَلَتِهِ عَنْهُمْ، وَإِخْبَارِهِمْ بِالَّذِي يَنْبَغِي لَهُمْ، وَيَقُولُ: « لِيُبَلِّغِ الشَّاهِدُ مِنْكُمُ الْغَائِبَ، وَأَبْلِغُونِي حَاجَةَ مَنْ لَا يَسْتَطِيعُ إِبْلَاغِي حَاجَتَهُ، فَإِنَّهُ مَنْ أَبْلَغَ سُلْطَانًا حَاجَةَ مَنْ لَا يَسْتَطِيعُ إِبْلَاغَهَا ثَبَّتَ اللهُ قَدَمَيْهِ يَوْمَ الْقِيَامَةِ». لَا يَذْكُرُ عِنْدَهُ إِلَّا ذَلِكَ، وَلَا يَقْبَلُ مِنْ أَحَدٍ غَيْرَهُ.

قَالَ[472] فِي حَدِيثِ سُفْيَانَ بْنِ وَكِيعٍ: يَدْخُلُونَ رُوَّادًا، وَلَا يَفْتَرِقُونَ إِلَّا عَنْ ذَوَاقٍ، وَيَخْرُجُونَ أَدِلَّةً، يَعْنِي: فُقَهَاءَ.

قُلْتُ: فَأَخْبِرْنِي عَنْ مَخْرَجِهِ كَيْفَ كَانَ يَصْنَعُ فِيهِ؟

قَالَ: كَانَ رَسُولُ اللهِ ﷺ يَخْزُنُ لِسَانَهُ إِلَّا مِمَّا يَعْنِيهِمْ، وَيُؤَلِّفُهُمْ وَلَا يُفَرِّقُهُمْ، يُكْرِمُ كَرِيمَ كُلِّ قَوْمٍ، وَيُوَلِّيهِ عَلَيْهِمْ، وَيَحْذَرُ النَّاسَ، وَيَحْتَرِسُ مِنْهُمْ، مِنْ غَيْرِ أَنْ يَطْوِيَ عَنْ أَحَدٍ بِشْرَهُ وَخُلُقَهُ، وَيَتَفَقَّدُ أَصْحَابَهُ، وَيَسْأَلُ النَّاسَ عَمَّا فِي النَّاسِ، وَيُحَسِّنُ الْحَسَنَ وَيُصَوِّبُهُ، وَيُقَبِّحُ الْقَبِيحَ وَيُوَهِّنُهُ، مُعْتَدِلَ الْأَمْرِ غَيْرَ مُخْتَلِفٍ، لَا يَغْفَلُ مَخَافَةَ أَنْ يَغْفَلُوا أَوْ يَمَلُّوا، لِكُلِّ حَالٍ عِنْدَهُ عَتَادٌ، لَا يَقْصُرُ عَنِ الْحَقِّ،

---

471   فِي شَرْحِ السُّنَّةِ لِلْبَغَوِيِّ (٣٧٠٥) وَشَمَائِلِ الرَّسُولِ ص (٥٢): «أَدَبُهُ».

472   (قَالَ): أَيْ عَلِيُّ بْنُ أَبِي طَالِبٍ ﷺ/ نَسِيمِ الرِّيَاضِ ١٨١/٢.

If someone sat with him or came to him with a need, he would be patient [and deal with their enquiry] until they were the first to leave, and no-one left without receiving what they asked for, or at least some comforting words. His cheerfulness and wonderful character encompassed people to such an extent that he became a father to them, and they were all equal in respect of their rights. The people respected righteousness and acted with humility. The elderly were respected and the young were shown mercy. People with a need were provided for and newcomers were treated leniently.'"

Another narration reports: "His assemblies were those of forbearance, modesty, benefit, and trust. Voices were never raised, faults were never publicised, and lapses were never broadcast."[533]

The narration of al-Ḥusayn continues: "Then, I asked [my father] about the manner of the Prophet ﷺ with those he sat with (i.e., the Companions). He said: 'The Prophet ﷺ was always cheerful, and he was easy-going, gentle and sympathetic. He was never harsh or rough, nor rude or obscene. Neither would he praise to excess. He would disregard things that were not to his liking, and he would never leave anyone who put their hope in him despairing or disappointed.

With regard to himself, the Prophet ﷺ abandoned three things: showing off, hoarding, and [getting involved in] anything that did not concern him. With regard to other people, he also abandoned three things: he would never castigate people, berate them, or seek out their faults.

He only spoke about things for which he expected a reward from Allah. When he spoke, the people sitting with him were as

---

533 This is actually from the narration of Sufyān ibn Wakīʿ, as reported in *Al-Shamāʾil*, *Sharḥ al-Sunnah*, and other texts.

وَلَا يُجَاوِزُهُ إِلَى غَيْرِهِ، الَّذِينَ يَلُونَهُ مِنَ النَّاسِ خِيَارُهُمْ، وَأَفْضَلُهُمْ عِنْدَهُ أَحْسَنُهُمْ نَصِيحَةً، وَأَعْظَمُهُمْ عِنْدَهُ مَنْزِلَةً أَحْسَنُهُمْ مُوَاسَاةً وَمُوَازَرَةً.

فَسَأَلْتُهُ عَنْ مَجْلِسِهِ عَمَّا كَانَ يَصْنَعُ فِيهِ؟

فَقَالَ: كَانَ رَسُولُ اللهِ ﷺ لَا يَجْلِسُ وَلَا يَقُومُ إِلَّا عَلَى ذِكْرٍ، وَلَا يُوطِنُ الْأَمَاكِنَ، وَيَنْهَى عَنْ إِيطَانِهَا، وَإِذَا انْتَهَى إِلَى الْقَوْمِ جَلَسَ حَيْثُ يَنْتَهِي بِهِ الْمَجْلِسُ، وَيَأْمُرُ بِذَلِكَ، وَيُعْطِي كُلَّ جُلَسَائِهِ نَصِيبَهُ حَتَّى لَا يَحْسِبَ جَلِيسُهُ أَنَّ أَحَدًا أَكْرَمُ عَلَيْهِ مِنْهُ.

مَنْ جَالَسَهُ أَوْ قَاوَمَهُ[473] لِحَاجَةٍ صَابَرَهُ حَتَّى يَكُونَ هُوَ الْمُنْصَرِفَ عَنْهُ، مَنْ سَأَلَهُ حَاجَةً لَمْ يَرُدَّهُ إِلَّا بِهَا أَوْ بِمَيْسُورٍ مِنَ الْقَوْلِ، قَدْ وَسِعَ النَّاسَ بَسْطُهُ وَخُلُقُهُ فَصَارَ لَهُمْ أَبًا، وَصَارُوا عِنْدَهُ فِي الْحَقِّ مُتَقَارِبِينَ مُتَفَاضِلِينَ فِيهِ بِالتَّقْوَى. وَفِي الرِّوَايَةِ الْأُخْرَى: وَصَارُوا عِنْدَهُ فِي الْحَقِّ سَوَاءً.

مَجْلِسُهُ مَجْلِسُ حِلْمٍ، وَحَيَاءٍ، وَصَبْرٍ، وَأَمَانَةٍ، لَا تُرْفَعُ فِيهِ الْأَصْوَاتُ، وَلَا تُؤْبَنُ فِيهِ الْحُرَمُ، وَلَا تُنْثَى فَلَتَاتُهُ. وَهَذِهِ الْكَلِمَةُ مِنْ غَيْرِ الرِّوَايَتَيْنِ[474].

يَتَعَاطَفُونَ بِالتَّقْوَى، مُتَوَاضِعِينَ، يُوَقِّرُونَ الْكَبِيرَ، وَيَرْحَمُونَ الصَّغِيرَ، وَيَرْفِدُونَ ذَا الْحَاجَةِ، وَيَحْفَظُونَ الْغَرِيبَ.

فَسَأَلْتُهُ عَنْ سِيرَتِهِ ﷺ فِي جُلَسَائِهِ؟

---

[473] قَاوَمَهُ: فَاعَلَهُ مِنَ الْقِيَامِ: أَيْ إِذَا قَامَ مَعَهُ لِيَقْضِيَ حَاجَتَهُ صَبَرَ عَلَيْهِ إِلَى أَنْ يَقْضِيَهَا/ النِّهَايَةُ.

[474] بَلْ هِيَ فِي رِوَايَةِ سُفْيَانَ بْنِ وَكِيعٍ فِي الشَّمَائِلِ وَشَرْحِ السُّنَّةِ وَغَيْرِهِ.

still as if there were birds on their heads. When the Prophet ﷺ was silent, they chatted, but without arguing. They would allow whoever spoke to finish without interruption. They would discuss whatever subject was mentioned first. The Prophet ﷺ laughed at what they laughed at, was surprised at what surprised them, and would show patience with a newcomer who used coarse language.

The Prophet ﷺ said: "If you see someone requesting something he needs, then provide it to him." He never sought praise, except as a counterbalance[534]. He never interrupted a conversation until the other person finished or stood up to leave.'"

And here, the narration of Sufyān ibn Wakīʿ comes to an end.

In other transmissions, al-Ḥusayn added: "I asked about his [periods of] silence. He (i.e., ʿAlī ﷺ) replied: 'He would remain silent for one of four reasons: forbearance, caution, appraisal, and reflection. As for his appraisal, he would observe and listen to others, and he would reflect on the things that remain and perish. He displayed patience in his forbearance, and nothing provocative would anger him. He was cautious about four things: adopting something good that would then be followed, leaving something reprehensible which would then be abandoned, working to decide what would be beneficial for his nation, and establishing for them that which would combine [the blessings of] this life and the Hereafter.'"

With the Help of Allah, and all Praise and Gratitude due to Him, here ends their descriptions of the Prophet ﷺ.

---

534   This phrase has also been interpreted as "except in moderation" or "except from a Muslim".

فَقَالَ: كَانَ رَسُولُ اللهِ ﷺ دَائِمَ البِشْرِ، سَهْلَ الْخُلُقِ، لَيِّنَ الجَانِبِ، لَيْسَ بِفَظٍّ، وَلَا غَلِيظٍ، وَلَا سَخَّابٍ، وَلَا فَحَّاشٍ، وَلَا عَيَّابٍ، وَلَا مَدَّاحٍ، يَتَغَافَلُ عَمَّا لَا يَشْتَهِي، وَلَا يُوئِسُ مِنْهُ، قَدْ تَرَكَ نَفْسَهُ مِنْ ثَلَاثٍ: الرِّيَاءِ، وَالإِكْثَارِ، وَمَا لَا يَعْنِيهِ، وَتَرَكَ النَّاسَ مِنْ ثَلَاثٍ: كَانَ لَا يَذُمُّ أَحَدًا وَلَا يُعَيِّرُهُ، وَلَا يَطْلُبُ عَوْرَتَهُ، وَلَا يَتَكَلَّمُ إِلَّا فِيمَا يَرْجُو ثَوَابَهُ.

إِذَا تَكَلَّمَ أَطْرَقَ جُلَسَاؤُهُ كَأَنَّمَا عَلَى رُؤُوسِهِمُ الطَّيْرُ، وَإِذَا سَكَتَ تَكَلَّمُوا، لَا يَتَنَازَعُونَ عِنْدَهُ الحَدِيثَ، مَنْ تَكَلَّمَ عِنْدَهُ أَنْصَتُوا لَهُ حَتَّى يَفْرُغَ، حَدِيثُهُمْ حَدِيثُ أَوَّلِيَّتِهِمْ، يَضْحَكُ مِمَّا يَضْحَكُونَ مِنْهُ، وَيَعْجَبُ مِمَّا يَعْجَبُونَ مِنْهُ، وَيَصْبِرُ لِلْغَرِيبِ عَلَى الجَفْوَةِ فِي المَنْطِقِ، وَيَقُولُ: «إِذَا رَأَيْتُمْ صَاحِبَ الحَاجَةِ يَطْلُبُهَا فَأَرْفِدُوهُ»، وَلَا يَقْبَلُ الثَّنَاءَ إِلَّا مِنْ مُكَافِئٍ، وَلَا يَقْطَعُ عَلَى أَحَدٍ حَدِيثَهُ حَتَّى يَتَجَوَّزَهُ فَيَقْطَعُهُ بِانْتِهَاءٍ أَوْ قِيَامٍ.

هُنَا انْتَهَى حَدِيثُ سُفْيَانَ بْنِ وَكِيعٍ. وَزَادَ الآخَرُ: قُلْتُ: كَيْفَ كَانَ سُكُوتُهُ ﷺ؟ قَالَ: كَانَ سُكُوتُهُ عَلَى أَرْبَعٍ: عَلَى الحِلْمِ، وَالحَذَرِ، وَالتَّقْدِيرِ، وَالتَّفَكُّرِ. فَأَمَّا تَقْدِيرُهُ فَفِي تَسْوِيَةِ النَّظَرِ والاسْتِمَاعِ مِنَ النَّاسِ، وَأَمَّا تَفَكُّرُهُ فَفِيمَا يَبْقَى وَيَفْنَى. وَجُمِعَ لَهُ الحِلْمُ ﷺ فِي الصَّبْرِ، فَكَانَ لَا يُغْضِبُهُ شَيْءٌ يَسْتَفِزُّهُ، وَجُمِعَ لَهُ فِي الحَذَرِ أَرْبَعٌ: أَخْذُهُ بِالحَسَنِ لِيُقْتَدَى بِهِ، وَتَرْكُهُ القَبِيحَ لِيُنْتَهَى عَنْهُ، وَاجْتِهَادُ الرَّأْيِ بِمَا أَصْلَحَ أُمَّتَهُ، وَالقِيَامُ لَهُمْ بِمَا جَمَعَ لَهُمْ أَمْرَ الدُّنْيَا والآخِرَةِ.

انْتَهَى الوَصْفُ بِحَمْدِ اللهِ تَعَالَى.

9 798349 217340